Practical and Professional Ethics

Also available from Bloomsbury

An Ethical Guidebook to the Zombie Apocalypse, by Bryan Hall
Environmental Ethics, by Marion Hourdequin
Ethics Within Engineering, by Wade L. Robison
Euthanasia and the Ethics of a Doctor's Decisions, by Ole Hartling
Introduction to Applied Ethics, by Robert L. Holmes
Morality and Ethics at War, by Deane-Peter Baker

Practical and Professional Ethics

Key Concepts

Wade L. Robison

BLOOMSBURY ACADEMIC
LONDON • NEW YORK • OXFORD • NEW DELHI • SYDNEY

BLOOMSBURY ACADEMIC
Bloomsbury Publishing Plc
50 Bedford Square, London, WC1B 3DP, UK
1385 Broadway, New York, NY 10018, USA
29 Earlsfort Terrace, Dublin 2, Ireland

BLOOMSBURY, BLOOMSBURY ACADEMIC and the Diana logo are
trademarks of Bloomsbury Publishing Plc

First published in Great Britain 2021

Cover design by Louise Dugdale

A catalogue record for this book is available from the British Library.

Library of Congress Cataloging-in-Publication Data
Names: Robison, Wade L., author.
Title: Practical and professional ethics : key concepts / Wade L. Robison.
Description: London ; New York : Bloomsbury Academic, 2021. |
Includes bibliographical references and index. |
Identifiers: LCCN 2021000341 (print) | LCCN 2021000342 (ebook) |
ISBN 9781350226081 (pb) | ISBN 9781350226074 (hb) |
ISBN 9781350226098 (epdf) | ISBN 9781350226104 (ebook)
Subjects: LCSH: Professional ethics.
Classification: LCC BJ1725 .R63 2021 (print) |
LCC BJ1725 (ebook) | DDC 174—dc23
LC record available at https://lccn.loc.gov/2021000341
LC ebook record available at https://lccn.loc.gov/2021000342

ISBN: HB: 978-1-3502-2607-4
PB: 978-1-3502-2608-1
ePDF: 978-1-3502-2609-8
eBook: 978-1-3502-2610-4

Typeset by Newgen KnowledgeWorks Pvt. Ltd., Chennai, India
Printed and bound in Great Britain

To find out more about our authors and books visit www.bloomsbury.com
and sign up for our newsletters.

Contents

Figures

Preface

I began this book without realizing it. Students in my ethics classes are required to write a significant paper on some ethical issue, preferably within their major, but I soon discovered I needed to do more than I had been doing to give them the conceptual background to recognize and assess ethical problems. I found the standard ways of thinking about ethical problems too spare and appealing to ethical theories unnecessary for students to make reasoned ethical judgments. They came to such judgments using fairly commonsensical principles we would be hard-pressed to deny.

I also found it helpful to introduce ethical problems by appealing to cases that arise for professionals. These are real cases culled from the news, my students, colleagues, and my own experience. They are topical, but typical of recurring problems. They can be rich in detail and difficulties, occasioning significant research and commentary as to what went wrong and so providing a great deal of background information to allow anyone not conversant with the professions involved to get a good grip on the ethical issues involved. Think of the Challenger or the Boeing 737 MAX. Some cases can also be bizarrely intriguing—as with the lawyer who slept through a good part of his client's trial, or the surgeon who amputated the wrong leg. It is easy, that is, to find cases where we must ask, "How on earth did that happen?"—leading us to try to figure that out.

The aim of this book is to present a method for identifying and assessing ethical problems, laying out what is needed for an understanding of the kinds of ethical problems we face every day and the method we are to pursue to resolve them when that is possible. That is why it is a book on practical and professional ethics, but there is no checklist to use. Instead we must get inside an ethical problem, as it were, to understand why there is a problem and so see how to resolve it if we can. This understanding of what we are required to do to identify and assess ethical problems is why we do not approach these cases with ethical tools already in hand. The point of using cases is to let them tell us what we need to understand and assess them. We will discover that we cannot understand some cases if we think all ethical problems are dilemmas, for example, or if we fail to take into account the points of view of all those involved.

What we gain from considering such cases is that the ethical problems professionals face are no different in kind from those we face in our ordinary lives and that the method we are to use to understand and assess them is exactly what we generally do as we go about our daily lives. Professionals do not face exotic kinds of ethical problems, and we have no need for special ethical theories to understand the ethical problems they face. In coming to understand and assess those problems, we gain the understanding we need to recognize and assess the ethical problems we face in our everyday lives.

I have come to see two common misunderstandings about ethics. One is that a person's intentions are all that matter. "But the engineer didn't intend to cause harm" does not get the engineer off the ethical hook. The engineer may have been negligent, for instance, or careless in calculating stresses. Even though the engineer had no intent to cause harm, we would still properly hold the engineer ethically at fault. The other common misunderstanding is that a person's moral beliefs have ethical weight, that we are to determine what we ought to do by consulting what we happen to believe is morally right rather than determining what is ethical. This particular contrast between the moral and the ethical has its place when we are examining whether the mores of a society are ethical, for instance, but it is a mistake to suppose that what we happen to believe is moral needs to be taken into account when deciding what is ethical. Otherwise we risk tainting our ethical judgments with false beliefs.

The book proceeds step-by-step, with each chapter introducing, in sequence, what we are to do, and not do, to recognize and resolve ethical problems. Some chapters may be read independently of what precedes them, but their point in helping the overall aim will be missed. The aim is to show how we are to recognize and, when we can, resolve ethical problems, and so the most useful exercise for readers is to find cases on their own and analyze and assess them. The method is straightforward: we begin by constructing arguments we can plausibly attribute to each of those involved in the case, and we then examine the premises for their plausibility and for their truth or falsity. We then back off and make the kind of judgment a judge makes after hearing the prosecution and the defense present their positions on an issue. The method is straightforward, but not necessarily easy, especially when we are a party to a case.

Acknowledgments

I owe much to many, but since I did not begin my work in practical and professional ethics with any idea that I would end up writing a book, I failed to keep complete track of where I picked up ideas along the way.

I first got interested in professional ethics when Michael Bayles started running ideas past me for his book on it, and I have since spoken with countless colleagues and read numerous articles and books. The material on the Challenger comes from a class I taught on the subject and a paper I authored on the matter with Rodger Boisjoly and two of my students, David Hoeker and Stefan Young, all of whom contributed enormously to my take on the Challenger.[1] It is a measure of my problems giving proper credit that the students presented versions of this paper at conferences at Case Western University and Duke and that we all learned a lot from the various questions from the audience. I have no idea who asked some of the crucial questions that forced us to go back and rework the paper.

The idea for moral powers comes from Michael Pritchard. He broached the question in a class in graduate school. He did not pursue the matter, and I can only hope I have done justice to his original idea.

Beyond that, not having in mind a book as I chatted and read, I cannot give proper credit to those colleagues and authors whose ideas I absorbed without quite realizing that I was taking them in and turning them into my own. For that I apologize to all those from whom I have learned and whom I have failed to credit. I should credit several anonymous reviewers for some very helpful suggestions, and I especially thank my students who pressed me to provide better explanations and provided me with intriguing examples of ethical problems that encouraged me to look for more.

I do owe thanks to my wife, Christina, both for her help with advice on my writing and for her willingness to give me the time away from her and our companions to work on this. I also owe thanks to our companions—the three kitties, Peaches, Pepper, and Pixie, each of whom adopted us, the first two after living in our barn awhile, and the two pups, Laddie and the newest, Charlie, both rescues of indeterminate breeding, but sweet and cheerful. They all brighten the day as did our two other rescues, Sunny, who looked like an American fox hound, and Gage as well, part American bulldog, both gone, but both here for a good portion of the work on this book and always ready with tail wags. Gage's was so vigorous he looked like a contortionist with his body bent in half. Sunny was the sweetest and most gentle of them all. They both brought a sense of life and joy into the house that is sorely missed.

Some chapters and some parts of some chapters have appeared in somewhat different form before. Each has been revised, some somewhat extensively. I thank the publishers for permission to use the articles, in whole or in part.

"Ethical Judgments" is a significant revision of "Professional Norms," *Teaching Ethics*, vol. 16, no. 2, December 2016, pp. 185–94.

"Internecine Strife" appeared in a slightly different form in *Ethics Across the Curriculum: Pedagogical Perspectives*, ed. Michael Pritchard and Elaine Englehardt (Heidelberg: Springer, 2018), pp. 179–90.

"Understanding Cases" is a revision of "Understanding Cases Within Professions," *Teaching Ethics*, vol. 18, no. 2, March 2018, pp. 127–47.

"Rules of Skill: Ethics in Engineering" has changed only slightly from its publication in *Philosophy and Engineering: Reflections, Practice, Principles and Process*, ed. David Goldberg, Natasha McCarthy, and Diane Michelfelder (Dordrecht: Springer, 2014), pp. 15–26.

"A Floating Conjecture: Identification through Facial Recognition," in *Paradigm Shifts in ICT Ethics*, ed. Jorge Pelegrin Boronto et al. (La Rioja, Spain: University of La Rioja, 2020), pp. 127–30 makes use of material and some passages from $3. Floaters, in Chapter 12, Rules of Skill, Yet Again.

1

Objects of Ethical Concern

We have been making ethical judgments since our earliest days. "It's not fair!" comes early in our childhood, and it is only one in a long list of judgments we make throughout our lives. We may find ourselves making such critical judgments, or hear or read about others making them, all too often, unfortunately, since the world is never wholly as it ought to be.

There is much that would need to change to make it an ethically better place, but we will focus on individuals, on the personal conduct of other human beings. We shall find it is a nice question, sometimes very difficult to answer, if at all, which ethical judgments are justified. A first step in answering that question is to get clarity about the proper objects of ethical concern. When we make a critical ethical judgment, what is the focus of our criticism?

Identifying the objects of ethical concern when we examine an ethical problem allows us to see what exactly went wrong so that we can avoid that difficulty in the future and have an understanding of what we ought to do if we are to make things right.

§1 What We Judge

Go to any playground, and you will hear parents and children making ethical judgments that span the range of possibilities, from assessments of character—"Yes, that kid's a bully"—to reminders that consequences matter—"I warned you your friend's toy would break if you did that." You will hear appeals to intentions—"I'm sure that kid didn't mean to hit you." You will hear remarks about the ethical implications of knowledge and ignorance—"That kid has no idea how dangerous that can be." And, all too frequently, you will hear parents chastising children for what they do and fail to do—"Don't hit people!" and "Don't just stand there. You knocked 'em down. Help 'em up."

As we mature, we play on different grounds, as it were, but the objects of ethical concern are no different than those we find on a children's playground. We judge

1. a person's character,
2. knowledge,

3. intentions,
4. acts (or failures to act), and
5. the consequences of acting or failing to act.

In our daily lives we judge what other drivers do as they weave in and out of traffic or let their attention lapse as they text. We wonder about our neighbor ignoring our morning greeting. We judge the fellow employee who clearly begrudges holding the elevator door for us. Ethical considerations permeate our interactions with others. We may not think that we are being ethical when we respond politely to an enquiry into how we are doing, but just imagine the contrast with a snarling response, "It's none of your business!" We do not give ourselves ethical credit for being nice, but whether we realize it or not, we are being ethical in treating others with respect rather than disdain.

Unfortunately, we often fail to see that something is unethical, and that creates a problem: we cannot avoid a problem we do not see. Sometimes we can cause great harm by failing to see a problem in the making and so failing to figure out how to avoid it.

The introduction of airbags is a classic example of how engineers solved a problem, but, in failing to see that they were making an ethical choice, created a new problem they did not foresee.

The physics are simple. When an accident occurs, the driver moves toward the steering wheel, and the exploding airbag expands toward the driver. The sweet spot occurs when the airbag fully deploys just as the driver reaches it. The driver is then cradled by the airbag. Since the first-generation airbags deployed at about 180 miles per hour (mph), they could seriously injure or kill drivers whose heads were in their path as they were still deploying, and if a driver was still some distance from the airbag after it fully deployed, the driver's head would hit a relatively solid object with the risk of causing serious injury or death.

The engineers' aim was an airbag that would meet drivers at that sweet spot, but they were working with an airbag they could not vary: one size had to work for all drivers. But drivers vary. They are tall and short, weighty and light, and their size makes a difference. If the driver is short and has to sit close to the steering wheel, the airbag will hit the driver in the face at high speed. If the driver is tall and has to sit farther away, the airbag will fully deploy while the driver is still some distance away, moving toward the now inflated airbag at speed.

To solve the problem posed by variable drivers meeting up with an invariable airbag, the engineers chose "the norm," the middle point in the bell curves of height and weight. This meant that a driver at the norm would be at the sweet spot in an accident, fully protected, while those on either side of the norm would be at diminishing degrees of protection, with the ones at the far ends the least protected, the most at risk of injury from the airbag in an accident.

A line had to be drawn somewhere, and no matter where it was drawn, the engineers would put some drivers at greater risk than others. There was only one sweet spot. They could have drawn it at the 50th percentile for all drivers, or the 50th percentile of those involved in the most accidents, for instance. An obvious choice would be the height and weight of those individuals who had fatal accidents. Men had almost five times as many deaths as women in 1976 (15,706 and 3,642, respectively). They were almost 60 percent of those driving, they drove more miles, and the fatality rate per miles of driving was 62 percent higher for men.[1] So that sweet spot would, as it were, favor men.

The spot they chose did favor men. They chose the 50th percentile for men in 1976, a 170 pound five-foot-nine-inch tall male. Since the 50th percentile for men was the 95th percentile for women, that choice put most women at much greater risk of injury from the airbag than most men. That choice may have been exactly the right choice, the one providing protection for those most likely to be killed in an accident. But if so, that would be a lucky accident.

There is no evidence that the engineers did any research to ensure that the 50th percentile for men would in fact be the sweet spot for those most likely to have fatal accidents. They would need to find the 50th percentile in height and weight for the 19,348 men and women who died. Given that they picked the 95th for women, it is highly unlikely the sweet spot they chose was the one that best protected all drivers, men and women. The data necessary to make that decision might not have been easily available, and so the engineers may have decided not to bother. But there is no evidence the engineers considered any other option than the one they chose. They seemed absolutely clueless that their choice could be biased and so ethically at fault.[2]

We have no trouble recognizing that what the engineers did may have been biased against women. We have no trouble making that judgment because the harm would be obvious, and that gives us a clue about how we determine that we have an ethical issue. In each case in the children's playground that gave rise to an admonition, harm was involved—a toy being broken, a child being hit, another being knocked down. And the harms were unnecessary. That is what the parents were chastising the children for, and that is what we are chastising the engineers for, making a choice that may well have caused unnecessary harm.

We have an ethical problem when we have an unnecessary harm, and hunting for them in what we do is one way to see if we have an ethical problem. It is not possible to do anything without causing at least a ripple in the causal stream of the world, and so anything we do will produce effects, some beneficial and, no doubt, some not. In creating an airbag, the engineers were benefitting a great many drivers by making it less likely they would be injured in accidents, but by picking the 50th percentile for men rather than, say, the 50th percentile of those most likely to have accidents, they may unnecessarily have discriminated against women. That is why we judge them ethically at fault—for not taking the care to ensure their choice was unbiased.

We are not judging their character or what they intended to do, but what they did and the consequences of what they did. We may judge them for failing to realize how discriminatory their choice could be, a failure of knowledge, but part of the fault for that lies with the engineering profession and its failure until recently to emphasize the ethical aspects of engineering decisions. However that may be, what they did and its consequences are the primary objects of ethical concern in this situation.

All the ethical problems we examine will have at least one object of ethical concern. Some may involve all of them, as we will find with a case involving a patient and her physicians.

§2 Professional Failure

When I was a medical humanities fellow at the University of Tennessee Medical Center in Memphis, I was witness to a number of situations that raised ethical concerns. One of the most striking involved a 47-year-old woman who was brought to the hospital after suffering a massive stroke. This was on a Wednesday afternoon, and the medical team gave her an electroencephalogram (EEG) that showed she had no brain function.

The standard procedure or protocol in such a case is to wait forty-eight hours and administer the test again along with a set of other tests such as yelling in the patient's ear and sticking a pin in an arm. The second test would be performed two days later, on Friday afternoon. I was with the group that administered the second test, a physician and a set of three or four interns. The test was negative again, showing no brain waves, and rather obviously, she did not respond in any way to the other tests.

Tennessee had passed a brain death law just prior to this, and the legal criteria for determining brain death was the standard protocol the physicians had followed for this patient. The result was that the woman was legally dead. She did not look dead since she was hooked up to a respirator and appeared to be asleep, breathing in and out, but that is one of the disconcerting features of brain death: a body can be kept alive, as it were, without a functioning brain.

When we left her and went into the waiting room to her family, we found about fifteen older women, all dressed in Sunday finery, and one younger woman, more casually dressed. The dead woman was the matriarch of a large family. The younger woman was her daughter and a college student. She asked the questions. When she asked, "How is she?," the physician said, "I don't want to give you false hope. She's in a bad way, but we'll do the best we can to help her." The daughter then asked whether her mother was in pain and whether they could see her. The physician told her that she was not in pain, but that they should not disturb the patient. "She should rest quietly."

I was still trying to digest what I had just heard when we went out of the waiting room and were getting ready to disband to go our separate ways. As an observer, I rarely said anything as we went on our rounds, spending my time looking and learning as much as I could about how the medical staff interacted with their patients and each other. I dressed the way the physicians dressed—khaki pants, dress shirt and tie, and a white hospital coat. I even had my own special identification pin, identical to what the physicians and interns wore except mine was black and said "PhD" rather than "MD." My look brought others to speak to me, mistaking me for a physician, but I did not usually get involved in any case. This one was different.

"I may have misunderstood something," I said, "but weren't the two EEG's both flat?" The physician responded that they were. "Then isn't she dead?" "No," he responded. "But," I said, "Tennessee has a brain death law. It was discussed at the 8 o'clock meeting two weeks ago." The "8 o'clock meeting" was on Tuesday mornings and covered important information that medical staff should know. Not everyone attended, but I did because I was trying to bury myself as deeply as possible into the regular hospital routine. And, I continued, "If I understand the law properly, she's not 'in a bad way'. She's dead."

The physician and the interns looked surprised. They had clearly never heard that Tennessee had enacted a brain death law and obviously had not attended the 8 o'clock meeting I had attended. I then said, "Don't take my word for it. Check with the hospital lawyer. But if she's dead, you've got to let the family know."

My concern was obvious, I thought. The family should not be living with false hope. There were such other issues as keeping the deceased in one of the emergency rooms of the hospital rather than a morgue and charging the family accordingly.

I assumed the physician would check with the hospital lawyers, find out if I was correct or not, and if I was, go back to tell the family that the woman had died. They need not say that they had made a mistake. All they had to do, I thought, was to say that she had died without regaining consciousness.

I ran into one of the interns late that afternoon and asked him what had happened, but he brushed me off, saying he had to go deliver a baby. I was off that weekend and so did not know what had happened with the woman, but when I went on rounds on Monday morning, I found myself in her room with the physician, the interns, and the head nurse. The woman looked unchanged. She was on a respirator, laying peacefully, as though asleep.

I intervened yet again, saying, "You really need to pull the plug." The head nurse responded, "We can't do that." "Why not?" "Because I would have to ask a nurse to come hold her hand, and I can't ask anyone to do that."

It took me a second to understand her point. On the one hand, a nurse would need to hold the woman's hand to comfort her as the plug was pulled, but, on the other hand, the head nurse could not ask anyone to hold the woman's hand. She was somehow holding in her head the two conflicting thoughts:

- "The woman is dead, and I can't ask anyone to hold the hand of a corpse."
- "If we pull the plug, the woman will die, and someone needs to hold her hand to comfort her."

We have here a lesson in how difficult it can be to come to grips with brain death. If the woman was dead, pulling the cord would not make her any more dead and would certainly not require anyone holding her hand to "comfort" her. But since she looked to be lying on the bed asleep, as though she were alive, the head nurse's first reaction was to ensure that she be comforted as the plug was pulled. In short, the head nurse treated the woman as alive, and so needing a comforting hand, and also as dead, a corpse not to be touched.

Needless to say, the plug was not pulled. We all left the room with nothing having been settled, I thought, about what to do with a corpse in a room in the emergency ward. As it turned out, the physician and the interns were having the same problem the head nurse had. They could not get their heads around the idea that the woman was dead. So the physician did what he could to ensure that she "really" died, that her heart stopped, that is.

The woman had been getting digitalis the previous week, and the physician cut that off Friday afternoon after I told him about the brain death law. His hope, I presume, was that without a stimulant for her heart, it would stop and she would "die." When that did not work, the physician ordered on Monday that the respirator be turned down so that the woman was no longer getting ten breathes every minute. It was to be adjusted by lowering it two points every 12 or 24 hours until she eventually "died." We bypassed her room on Tuesday when we did rounds, her "condition" not having changed, I was informed. On Wednesday morning she "died" after the respirator had been adjusted down to two breaths per minute. A full week after she came in after a massive stroke, the physician felt he could tell her extended family that she had died.

One obvious consequence of his failure to inform the family the previous Friday was that they were left with the false hope that the woman could recover. That consequence is one object of ethical concern. It would be one thing if telling them on Friday would cause them harm they need not have suffered, but the delay only put off the inevitable harm they experienced on Wednesday while leaving them hanging in suspense about the woman's condition until then and coming to the hospital every day to try to see the woman. I am not sure how the physician could have responded honestly to the inevitable "Is she doing any better?"

Another consequence is that a hospital room in the emergency ward was being used as a morgue. It was unavailable for other patients, obviously, and someone had to be paying for it. I do not know if the family was charged for the Saturday, Sunday, Monday, Tuesday, and Wednesday the dead matriarch was there, but if so, that would add insult to injury, as it were, and they could hardly challenge the hospital bill since they had no idea the woman had been dead the whole time.

A third consequence is that the hospital staff, including the head nurse and those cleaning the room, had to deal with a "patient" who was not a patient, but a corpse, treating the corpse as though she were alive by checking the respirator, for instance, to be sure it was still working and cleaning up whatever bodily fluids were still leaking from the body.

We may or may not hold the physician and interns responsible for not knowing that Tennessee had passed a brain death law. They are busy, and it is easy enough to miss even information important to one's practice. But once I informed them and suggested they check with the hospital lawyer, they had no excuse to act as though they did not know.

Worse, they broke the law through their failure to acknowledge that the woman was dead. What they did was illegal. It is not always ethically wrong to break the law. Those who are being civilly disobedient break it on purpose to try to change it, but the physician and interns were not breaking the law for some higher purpose. They just refused to face the conclusion the law required them to draw.

That refusal brings in another object of ethical concern—the physician's intentions. When he first told the family that the woman was "in a bad way," he was not being honest with the family, but he was then operating on the assumption she was not dead. It would be hard to fault his intentions however much we might disagree with how he gave them false hope. But once he knew, or should have known, that the woman was brain dead, it is hard not to fault his intention to continue to give them false hope in not telling them that she was dead.

His refusal is a good example of how a failure to act, inaction, can be an object of ethical concern. It caused all sorts of harms that could have been easily avoided had he simply gone back into the waiting room that Friday and told the family that the woman had passed away.

What he did do can be faulted as well. He ordered that she should no longer get digitalis and then that the respirator should be slowly turned down from ten breaths a minute to two. He clearly knew what the result would be: her heart would stop. And so he clearly intended to ensure that it stop. We cannot accuse him of intentionally killing her since she was already dead, but we can certainly accuse him of attempting to cover up his unwillingness, for whatever reason, to accept that she was dead because her brain was dead.

That may well lead us to question his character. It may well be that he just could not get it into his head that brain death is death. We may well sympathize with that, understanding the problems such a conceptual switch in our understanding of something we thought we knew—"If the heart beats, the person's alive"—creates for us. But if he was reluctant to tell the family that despite her condition not having changed, she was dead, that forces us to ask about his character. He could easily have told them at any time, as I suggested, that she had died without regaining consciousness.

We have succeeded in checking off all the objects of ethical concern with this case. We have raised questions about

1. the physician's character,
2. his failure to know about the brain death law,
3. his purposeful intent, upon learning about it, not to let the family know and so knowingly break the law,
4. his actions in cutting her digitalis and instructing the respirator to be lowered slowly, and
5. the consequences of his actions and inaction, leaving the family with false hope and using a hospital room as a morgue.

We would not properly capture what went wrong were we not to include all these judgments. Any one of the faults in this case would be enough to cause ethical concern, but, as with any case, we can only fully understand and properly assess it by examining all the possible objects of ethical concern. The set of ethical objects provides us with a checklist, as it were, for any situation we are trying to understand. We may discover only one object of concern or, as with this case, all five, but checking out all five gives us assurance that we have covered everything that could be right or wrong ethically.

But our judgments would not properly map onto what can be a case's complex ethical terrain were we not to make clear the details of each fault. It matters that the physician's failure to come to grips with the woman's being brain dead was not a one-off, but persisted. We cannot pass it off as a simple mistake. We have no evidence that he set about to cause all the harm he caused to the family and the hospital and, ultimately, to himself. He intended to deceive, but not maliciously, it seems. It rather appears that he got caught up in his initial mistake and let it play out in the way he was used to dealing with such cases rather than figure out how to navigate in unfamiliar territory.

Unlike the engineers who simply failed to see an ethical issue in biassing airbags against females, the physician could not have failed to understand that he had made a mistake in treating the brain dead woman as though she were alive and not informing the family that she was dead. We fault the engineers for failing to see the ethical issue and the consequences of that failure, but not for intending to cause such harms. They were not guilty of that particular ethical fault.

If they had intentionally chosen to put women and children at greater risk, we would fault them all the more and wonder about their character, but one advantage of sorting through the five objects of ethical concern when we examine a particular ethical problem is that we can get a more accurate assessment of what went wrong. We can thus get a better understanding of how to make things right and, we may hope, avoid the harms next time.

The ideal would be for them to be immune from ethical criticism, not to be faulted for anything—their character, their knowledge, their intentions, what they do or do not do, or the consequences. They would then be, as it were, in the ethical zone.

§3 In the Ethical Zone

For an athlete in the zone, everything goes right: the ball always goes in the hoop, or out of the park, or in the pocket, or whatever else required by the game to score. The player does everything right, with no miscues and with an admirable and easy grace. Being in the zone is rare, but frequent enough that we have a phrase for it.

We are in the ethical zone if we know what is right, intend to do what is right, and do it without ethically unacceptable consequences while being of good character. Being in the zone is an ideal, something to strive for. We cannot expect to live the ideal because, for one thing, we all presumably have character flaws of some sort or other. For another, we often do not have time to think through what we are doing, or the possible consequences, let alone consider alternative courses of action, and even our past experience may not help where we are surprised by an awkward event for which we have no ready response. This is not news. We all know from our own experience how easy it is to be wrong. There are so many different ways we can fail to achieve the ideal that we would be skilled indeed, and lucky, to be in the zone ethically.

We can get a grip on just how difficult it would be if we ask what it would be like in the ideal case, where we are in the zone ethically. We can determine clearly what count as deviations from the ideal and see how they affect what is in question. Understanding how the flow of traffic down a street would occur in ideal conditions allows us to see how various features of the street affect that flow and thus what might be done to mitigate the problems those features create for achieving the ideal. Just so, it is helpful to consider what it would be like for someone to be in that ideal state in ethics, doing everything right and precluding any foothold for ethical criticism of any sort. We can then better understand how things can go wrong, providing an opening for ethical criticism, of course, but also allowing us to understand more fully what must happen for things to go right. If we take these five characteristics sequentially, we can see how essential each is to being in the ethical zone and get a sense of their extent and ethical weight.

We might imagine someone, like Adam, created with "his rational faculties ... entirely perfect," awakening in the world without any knowledge of what is right and what is wrong or any intention, obviously, to do anything right, or wrong—an observer capable of being ethical because he is a human being, but not capable of choosing to do what is ethical because he lacks knowledge of what he ought to do.[3] We would think him an ethical innocent. If he then suddenly came to know what is right and what is wrong, by some mysterious inner light, but formed no intentions regarding what he knew, we would begin to think his innocence greatly diminished. How could he not proceed to do more than simply observe the world given his ethical knowledge? If we add to that knowledge the intention to do what is right, we would think him on the right path, but if that were all he did, intend to do what is right, we would soon chastise him for apparently having no capacity or willingness to act on his good intentions. If we then add his doing what is right to these characteristics of having knowledge of what is right, and an intention to do what is right, we would begin to applaud. Our only ethical hesitation would come if his understanding of what is right did not include at least the obviously predictable consequences of his action. Only if he took all those into consideration, a possibility he could only have with fairly extensive experience, would we think him capable of being in the ethical zone, and it is only with a fair amount of experience that we could determine the nature of his character, a sterling character cementing his being in the ethical zone.

For everything to be right and for us to be in the ethical zone, we must

1. be of good character,
2. know what is right,
3. intend to do what is right,
4. do what is right, and
5. do what is right without ethically unacceptable consequences.

If anything is wrong regarding any of these, we subject ourselves to ethical criticism.

1. Character—We regularly judge individuals on the basis of their character. A Mother Theresa is an ethical marvel, an Adolf Hitler evil personified. Character matters in and of itself, and though we will come to have a set of characteristics as we mature, whether or not we pay attention to our patterns of behavior, we can build our character through controlling our behavior. We can choose what we say, for instance, and how we say it. We can control our temper—or not. We are responsible, that is, for our failings as well as our successes. So it is appropriate to praise someone for being honest, for instance, and to chastise someone who characteristically lies. We are assessing character traits when we do that and in that way making an ethical judgment about someone's character.

Our character traits mark us out—thoughtful and deliberate, foolhardy and irresponsible, kind and caring, and on and on. How we manifest each of these traits matters to our character as much as the traits themselves. We can be quietly thoughtful, or make a show of it. We may be witty, but cutting. We may persevere, but about something not particularly praiseworthy. How a person displays character traits is part of what we assess when we judge the person's character.

Character matters enough ethically that we take it into consideration even if we are assessing what someone has done or failed to do. Indeed, we wonder when someone with a bad character does something right. "Why he did he do that? He must have some ulterior motive." Any good act of a person with a bad character is subject to skepticism just because it is the act of a bad character. It does not matter that the act is exactly the right thing and that a person of good character would have done just that. Judgments of character are ethically so weighty that they force us to question what someone with a bad character has done even if what was done would be ethically pristine behavior by someone with a good character.

A character is built upon patterns of behavior that we presume display the underlying character, and we think persons good who, say, help others, are polite, correct their mistakes, are honest and forthright, and on and on. We tend to presume a good character in our dealings with others and do not automatically recalibrate our judgment of someone's character when the person does something wrong, depending, of course, on what the wrong is. Even the best can make mistakes, and so we tend to give the person the benefit of the doubt and try to determine what went wrong. A single problematic act or failure to act is generally not enough to change a well-founded judgment of character.

That is not to say that we do not have second thoughts sometimes. It can take only one incident to force us to reassess someone. Clark Clifford was the consummate Washington insider, for instance, an advisor to many presidents and Secretary of Defense under Lyndon Johnson, among other things. In his later years, he became chairman of First American Bankshares, secretly controlled by the Bank of Credit and Commerce International (BCCI) that was accused of a variety of crimes from money laundering and bribery to arms trafficking and tax evasion. Clifford claimed not to know that First American Bankshares was controlled by BCCI, but reaped $6 million in profits from bank stock he had purchased with an unsecured BCCI loan. As he put it to a *New York Times* reporter, "I have a choice of seeming either stupid or venal"—a lifetime of good character put to question by a single circumstance.[4] What was worse for him was that although he was a wealthy man, "his true capital," as a reporter put it at the time, "is in the name Clark Clifford, and what it stands for."[5]

It is difficult to make a properly nuanced judgment here. We would presumably not judge him as having a bad character because of that one incident, but, at the least, of neglecting to find out something he ought to have known and thus of having made a bad judgment. That would be a mark against him, but not fundamentally alter our judgment of his character. In fact, his realization that he will seem "stupid or venal" displays the good character we have been attributing to him. He recognized the problem and saw its implications. But, still, as he put it, he seems to have been either stupid or venal.

Our judgment of Clifford is nuanced just because we take into account a person's character in assessing what the person did. Clifford's behavior seems out of character. This is not what we would expect from him. That is why a judgment of someone's character affects our judgments of what the person does and does not do.

Just as we admire an athlete in the zone because all the person does seems seamlessly to flow from the person's athleticism, we admire someone whose behavior reflects an ethical character. What the person does seems to flow from the person's character, and that is why we tend to give a pass to someone of good character who, we think, just made a mistake. A sterling character is a capital asset for all of us—as it was for Clark Clifford.

2. Knowledge—Even if we have the best of characters, we must know what is right if ethical criticism is to find no foothold. It is not enough to walk around with a good character, ignorant of what is right and wrong, any more than it would be enough just to do what is right. We might do that by accident or inadvertently while trying to do something else for which we would be ethically blameworthy. Just as we gain no credit for clairvoyance if we guess the winner of a horse race, we must know that what we are doing is right if we are not to be subject to ethical criticism. "You lucked into that!" would not be praise, but ethical criticism if the act in question was what the person ought to have done though the person did not know that.

Clark Clifford is subject to ethical criticism, for instance, because he failed to know something that, as chairman of a bank, he ought to have known, as he admitted. It was his lack of knowledge that was questioned and led to questions about his character.

It is not the capacity to know that is at issue here. That is assumed. If someone is judged "not to know the nature and quality of the act he was doing; or if he did know it, ... did not know he was doing what was wrong," an ethical version of the M'Naghten rule for legal insanity kicks in: we judge the person incapable of ethical behavior.[6] What is at issue here is a failure to know what ought to be known, and could be known, to make a proper judgment. This is a requirement for any judgment, not just those that are ethical.

So a surgeon who mistakes a kidney for a liver because of a failure to know the difference is as subject to ethical criticism as Clark Clifford if he failed to know the banking details that put a footnote on his reputation. We would, of course, need to explore the reasons for their ignorance. The reasons matter ethically. Ensuring plausible deniability by not attempting to discover the facts in a situation is far different from having the facts withheld so one would not make the right decision.

3. Intention—We must also intend to do what is right. Just as we may do what is right without knowing that it is right, we may do what is right without intending to do so. We may think we know what we ought to do, do something that we think we are not supposed to do, and yet have it turn out that what we did was what we ought to have done. "But you didn't intend to do that!" is a serious ethical criticism when directed at someone who unintentionally does the right thing, especially when the intent was to do something different. "You were lucky!" is also, again, a perfectly appropriate ethical criticism when directed at someone who did what they ought to do without intending to do so. Lucking into doing the right thing whatever our intentions does not make us immune from ethical criticism. We may praise an athlete who somehow makes an

impossible play, attributing it in part to the training and experience which makes it possible for someone sometimes to do what seems impossible, but we do not praise a person who does the right thing without intending to do it. We hold back our full approval if the act or omission was unintended.

Indeed, intentions are important enough for ethical judgments that we learn early on to use our not having had an intent to cause harm as an excuse when we do cause harm. Children quickly become adept at understanding how it helps fend off responsibility to say, "Sorry, I didn't mean to hit you." An unintended harm is not as ethically blameworthy generally as one driven by intent. "Be more careful!" works as an admonition for an unintended harm on a playground, but cannot replace "Don't hit people!"

Intention is clearly an object of ethical concern. Along with our character and our knowledge, or lack of it, we fault or praise the intentions we have. We are in the ethical zone if we intend to do what we know is the right thing and the intention flows from our character.

That is not to suggest that intentions are necessary for ethical fault or blame. It is all too common an assumption, I think, that we cannot hold people ethically responsible for harms they cause if they did not intend to cause harm. But that is false. We can be ethically at fault for doing something we did not intend to do—if we were negligent, for instance.[7] It does not seem likely that anyone at Boeing intended to produce an airplane that would so readily crash as the 737 MAX, but Boeing ended up with an airplane with only one air sensor whose failure would give pilots forty seconds to realize what the problem was and then push three buttons and levers to override the software pushing the plane's nose down.[8] Assessing the intentions of those involved in the design and manufacture of the plane is not likely to provide us with anything helpful in figuring out what went wrong. It is likely to be far more promising to look for negligence, a failure to check on what would happen if the single sensor went awry after being hit by a bird, for instance.

So intentions are not necessary for ethical blame, but we do hold people ethically accountable for not having the relevant intent. While I was a medical humanities fellow, I witnessed a surgeon first tear into a nurse for not having called him at three in the morning to get permission to increase the dose he had prescribed for a patient he was to operate on that morning. The nurse had increased it because the surgeon had prescribed the dose as though the patient weighed 140 pounds or so, and the patient weighed over 300 pounds. I then saw him enter the room and return with a look of absolute disgust on his face. He said, "I'm not going to operate on her. She's too fat." I assume he had the relevant knowledge and skills to operate, but had no intention of performing the appendectomy he had been scheduled to perform. We should fault him for that just as we should fault him for faulting the nurse and failing to read the woman's medical records, which listed her weight, or to meet with her ahead of time. He successfully caused real harm through his intention. Some other surgeon would have to get involved, and the patient's operation would be put on hold while other arrangements were made. All the while, the patient risked a burst appendix.

The surgeon presumably did not intend to cause such harms, but those were the effects of his fulfilling his intention not to operate. He took himself out of the ethical zone by not operating. In fact, he took himself out of the ethical zone as soon as he decided not to operate. Not having the proper intent is enough in itself to justify ethical criticism.

4. Doing what is right—But even if we intend to do what is right, our intention is moot unless we act on it. We can hardly claim to be in the ethical zone if we intend to do what we know is the right thing, the intention flows from our character, and we fail to act. That would be like a soccer player having gotten into position for a clear shot, being posed to shoot, and then not shooting. Teammates and spectators would wonder whether it was something physical or mental that caused the problem, for surely, they would think, something went wrong. To be in the ethical zone, we must not only intend to do what is right, but do it.

We are all familiar with the saying, "The road to hell is paved with good intentions," and we have all either ourselves had good intentions which went for naught or know of others who had good intentions which were never realized. We do not give ourselves, or them, much ethical credit, if any, for the good intentions if they are not followed with what we intended to do.

Doing what is right is admittedly not easy. We can, no doubt, all recall some situation that we did not handle as well as we should. If we need reminders of how easy it is to go wrong, think of children: the child who thanks the grandparents for last year's gift only just before the next birthday; the young child who answers his aunt about why he is not eating the crust of his mother's less-than-wonderful homemade pie, "I don't eat cardboard." These are not unethical, but they do counter norms of what constitutes good behavior and so are subject to criticism. "That's not polite."

We can also no doubt recall situations we thought we handled as well as possible, but went wrong because of something not wholly within our control. I had an aunt with a bluish skin, caused by mercury poisoning when she was young. She always looked frail, but when I saw her at an anniversary party for my parents, she looked radiant. I said, "You look wonderful!" She smiled in appreciation just as another aunt of mine said, to my astonishment, "How dare you lie to her like that!" My blue aunt looked at me with doubt on her face, but there was nothing I could do to erase my blue aunt's doubt. A well-meant compliment had gone awry, to be replaced with doubt about its sincerity. The problem arose not because of anything I did or intended to do, but because of circumstances beyond my control. I had no idea my other aunt could be so catty.

5. Consequences—Anything we do or fail to do has consequences. We do not act in a vacuum, but in a world of causes and effects where our action or inaction will have effects, whatever they may be. We often have a pretty good sense of what will result from what we do or fail to do. We do not just act, but initiate a course of action, with the understanding that a particular act, in that circumstance, will cause a series of effects, a particular course of events, that is.

Generally, for short runs of events at least, we can pretty well predict what will occur. We cannot always do that, and the ways in which we can fail constitute a laundry list of the various ways in which we can go wrong in this world. We may fail to understand that one action generally has such and such consequences. "What did you think was going to happen?" is a question with a decided snap to it. It tells the person to whom the question is addressed that they obviously did not think at all before acting.

We may fail to consider that a particular course of events will initiate other events. A person pulls their car in front of another to slip into the next lane and roar merrily on their way, ignoring the effects of that sudden movement on those behind who must slow down because there was a car where they would have been and because caution seems called for given that they have first-hand evidence of yet another driver on the road capable of doing damage.

We may also fail to consider that any complex course of action that involves others may be changed by the actions of others. A reckless speedster switching lanes can succeed only if other drivers nearby are not being reckless and switching lanes as well. A timid or irritated driver may cause havoc as well by slowing up suddenly or speeding up to block the speedster.

We are not ethically responsible for everything that flows from our action, but we are responsible for what occurs that is within our control. We ought to consider what anyone could predict would happen, what anyone should have foreseen, what anyone who did not neglect the circumstances in which they were acting would have been able to foresee, and so on.

2

Making Ethical Judgments

Ethical judgments are not descriptive, but normative. They do not tell us how things are, but how they ought to be. We may thus applaud individuals for doing what they ought to do or critique them for doing what they do, not what they ought to do. In either case, we must do more than simply respond. A response may simply reflect our personal beliefs, but however deeply we may hold them, they have no ethical weight unless they are backed by ethical principle.

Making ethical judgments about individuals thus requires more than knowing that the objects of ethical concern are a person's character, knowledge, intent, and action (or failure to act) and the consequences. We need, in addition, at least the following:

1. We need to be able to recognize when an ethical judgment is appropriate. What about a situation occasions an ethical concern?
2. We need to understand the situation from the point of view of everyone involved and, like a judge trying a case, back off to view the situation objectively.
3. We need to justify any judgment we make. Do the facts support it? Do we have good reasons that justify it? Is our judgment backed by an ethical principle?

Our aim is to recognize ethical problems and understand how they arose and are playing out, as it were. The ultimate end is to mitigate them, if we can, and understand how to avoid them later, but we first need to understand what kind of judgment we are making when we make an ethical judgment.

§1 Normative Judgments

When I described what the engineers did who chose the 50th percentile of men as the sweet spot for airbags, I was using statements that are true or false. We can check them out to determine whether the description I gave is accurate. The same is true for the physician who told the grieving family of the woman who had a stroke that she was "in a bad way." He did say that, and what he said was false, implying that she was still alive but not doing well.

I then went on to criticize the engineers and the physician and others in the hospital, tracking what went wrong ethically by using the five objects of ethical concern I marked out—character, knowledge, intention, action or inaction, and the consequences. But when we go from saying something is the case to saying something ought or ought not to be the case, we are going from what can be supported by factual evidence to what requires a different form of support. It may be that the way things are is the way they ought to be, but it is all too obvious that they need not be. In any event, we must appeal to something other than the way things are to justify our claim.

This distinction between descriptive and normative claims is central to our understanding of ethics. When a parent tells a child, "You should always tell the truth!," that is a statement about what the child ought to do, not, unfortunately, a description of what everyone does. The distinction is one we are all familiar with and make use of all the time. We use it when we tell someone how to do something in contrast to how individuals usually do it. We use it when we criticize someone, even under our breath, for driving erratically, or texting while driving, or skateboarding on a sidewalk through pedestrians, or talking loudly on a cellphone in an elevator.

The contrast between normative and descriptive judgments may not seem as sharp when people generally do what they ought to do. Then a statement of what they ought to do is effectively a description of what they in fact do. Indeed, from an observer's point of view, for an alien in a spacecraft unfamiliar with stop signs, for instance, it will be difficult, if not impossible, to tell the difference between people stopping at stop signs and people stopping at stop signs because they ought to. The behavior is the same. But when they ought to stop, we can properly criticize them for not stopping. When stopping at a stop sign is a norm, we have a standard for how we ought to behave, and a failure to meet that standard licenses a critical response.[1]

We can fail to make the distinction at our own peril. At one time, in response to a report that most pedestrian accidents occurred in its crosswalks, the City of Santa Barbara completely solved the problem, reducing the accident rate in crosswalks to zero, by painting over the crosswalks. No pedestrians were ever again going to be hit by a vehicle in a crosswalk!

This solution seems right out of Monty Python—a weird out-of-kilter take on how to solve a serious problem. But the city had a reason for that solution. California law requires that drivers stop for pedestrians in crosswalks, and quite to the surprise of someone from, say, New York, they generally do. But too many pedestrians in Santa Barbara were assuming that drivers always did what they ought to do, and so they were not looking before walking. The crosswalks gave pedestrians a false sense of security, and painting them over nudged them into taking more care to look before walking.

What seemed more than a little silly, that is, depended upon a failure on the part of too many pedestrians to distinguish between what drivers ought to do and what they do. They confused the norm with reality, as it were.

That sort of mistake is easy to make in part at least because the way people behave can readily become the norm. Think about how fast people drive in a 55 mph zone. It is a rare individual, at least in my neck of the woods, who drives 55 mph or slower on the dual-lane highway nearby. The standard speed is at least 62–64 mph. That is prudent since the police are more likely to ticket a driver who goes faster, but it does not set the upper limit, obviously. Those willing to risk a ticket drive much faster. But it does effectively set the lower limit. Those who drive the speed limit are an impediment to traffic. They force other drivers to go around, impeding the flow of traffic just like a boulder in a stream. So just as it is more dangerous to drive faster than the standard speed, it is more dangerous to drive at less than the standard speed. The standard speed has become the norm, what drivers ought to do to ensure safe driving conditions for all.

How a practice becomes a norm is an intriguing question we do not need to pursue here, but we should note what happens when it happens. What changes? I was once charged with drawing up a set of rules for a departmental library. The practice had been that members of the department could take any book or journal out at any time and keep it as long as they wished. There was no procedure for checking them out, and so a second part of the practice was that members of the department who needed a missing book or journal were permitted to go into any other member's office and take what they needed if they found it there. That is a description of the practice, and my charge was to figure out a procedure that would resolve the difficulties that practice created, the most obvious being able to find out where a particular book or journal was without searching through the offices of other members of the department, who, in turn, would be unable to find a book or journal they thought they had and have no idea where to look.

I developed a set of rules that included what I thought was obvious and simple: those taking a book or journal from the library were to write down in a notebook what they took, with their name, the date, and appropriate identifying information of what they were taking out. In proposing such a rule, I was proposing a norm—"this is the way we ought to do things"—that, were it adopted and followed, would change the practice and allow members to criticize other members who took a book or journal without letting the rest know they took it. That is one feature of a norm: it tells us what we ought to do and provides grounds for a judgment that someone has failed to do what ought to be done.

As it turned out, the proposed set of rules was not adopted, too many members of the department being unwilling to subject themselves to the "burden" of letting others know whether and when they had a book or journal. So what had been the practice remained the practice and effectively became the norm. We would tell anyone new, "This is how we do things here" with the implicit message, "You ought to do what everyone else does." We could then criticize someone who complained about not finding a book, but had failed to rifle through the offices of other members trying to find it or, finding it, had for some reason failed to take it. The process of voting to reject a set of rules made the current practice the norm.

What changed? Before my attempt to fashion a set of rules, no one criticized anyone in the department for not doing what everyone else did. A member who failed to scour the bookshelves and desks of fellow members for a needed book was thought eccentric, to say the least, since the likelihood of the book being returned to the library approached nil. But no one would tell anyone they ought to scour the offices of others. What changed was that the department's voting to reject my proposal effectively made the current practice the rule, converting the practice into the norm and thus licensing a critical response to those who failed to do what the norm licensed them to do.

It is the switch from "this is what people do" to "this is what people ought to do," with the subsequent licensing of censure for a failure to do what ought to be done, that marks the switch from what is purely descriptive to what is normative. What is different is not what we do when looking for a book or stopping at a stop sign, but how we behave regarding someone who fails to abide by what has become the norm. The difference is in how we treat the practice. It is no longer just what we do, but what we ought to do.

But that "ought" covers different admonitions. It can certainly be prudential. Many of our judgments about what people ought to do are prudential. In Edinburgh once, as I was about to step off the curb and cross when the crossing light was red, I was caught up by a slight elderly woman who touched my sleeve and said, in a wonderful Scottish brogue, "'Tis best to wait for the wee green man"—the "wee" image on the crosswalk signal of a man walking. That was a prudent admonition as a bus just then went barreling around our corner.

It is the law that pedestrians are not to cross when the no-crossing light is on, and so she could have said, "You ought to wait for the wee green man"—appealing in that "ought" to what the law requires. Or she could have said, "It's wrong to cross when the light is red," appealing to an ethical principle that we ought to obey the law or perhaps to the unfortunate consequences of my setting a precedent that others might follow, reducing the orderly flow of pedestrians and traffic in Edinburgh to the likes of, say, New York.

These different judgments—the prudential, the legal, the ethical—do not necessarily compete with each other. The same act may be imprudent, illegal, and unethical, and in each case we can appropriately criticize those who fail to follow the norm. That is why we cannot get too upset at drivers honking at someone going 55 mph in a 55 mph zone when everyone else is driving in the sixties. The norm then is not what is legal, but what has become standard practice, and it is imprudent to impede the flow of traffic.

It should thus be no surprise that the norms that mark out professions like engineering and medical practice may be backed by different reasons—prudential, legal, and ethical. A dental surgeon ought to use Novocain when extracting a tooth for prudential as well as ethical and legal reasons: it is wrong to cause unnecessary harm, prudent not to put your fingers in the mouth of someone who may chomp down because in intense pain, and risky to open oneself to a lawsuit.

But these reasons are not wedded, none implying the others. A veterinarian may be prudent in muzzling an unruly dog before an examination, but there is no legal or ethical requirement to do that. A dentist would be ethical to explain to a patient exactly how a procedure will go, but no law requires that, and it may be imprudent if it makes the patient nervous.

In short, these reasons operate independently of one another. What is prudent may not be unethical or unlawful. What is unethical may not be unlawful or imprudent. What is unlawful may not be unethical or imprudent. Our concern is with the ethical reasons, and so we can examine how they are to be grounded without concerning ourselves with questions of prudence or law. We would like to find a ground for our ethical judgments at least as firm as our ground for empirical statements.

§2 Morality and Ethics

Some distinguish morality from ethics and claim that morally we can believe whatever we wish. The conversation goes like this:

"I believe it's O.K. to cheat."
"But that's wrong."
"You believe it's wrong. I believe it's right."
"But what you believe is false."
"No, it's true."
"How do you know it's true?"

The person with whom I was having this conversation looked utterly astonished that I could ask such a question. What he was saying must have seemed as obviously true to him as that, say, historians are to write the truth about the past. "It could not be false," he claimed in surprise, because, after all, he said, "I believe it."—in a tone of voice that said, "I just told you. I believe it. What else could you possibly want?" That odd answer betrays the mistake he was making.

Grammatically, a belief requires an object, a noun clause. "I believe that something is the case." So whenever someone claims to have a belief, we have two different matters at issue: does the person have a belief, and is what the person believes true or false? These are separate enquiries. A person can believe what is the case or is not the case. Merely having a belief that something is the case does not make it the case—unless we have the odd case of people believing that they have beliefs. Except for that oddity, we need an independent investigation to determine whether what the person believes is true, independent, that is, of the person having a belief that it is so.

It should not be a surprise to discover that something we believed turns out to be false. This happens all the time in science when a new discovery upends our previous beliefs. We once believed that chimpanzees could not speak, but have since discovered that they are quite capable of a relatively sophisticated vocabulary in sign language. They communicate with each other in the wild through hand gestures, for instance,[2] and are capable of learning signs in human sign language.

If believing made it so, we could create for ourselves wonderful worlds. "I believe that I am a billionaire." "I believe that I have written a book that surpasses any other book that ever can be written." If believing made it true, I would be famous and rich. We can pretend that believing makes it so and so create all sorts of imaginary worlds for ourselves, but, alas, the real world tends to intervene and force us to come to our senses.

But I suspect the person with whom I was having this discussion was somewhat confusedly making a different point. He was claiming that there are no truths in ethical matters, just what people want to believe is right or wrong, good or bad. Yet if the only support he can provide for this claim is that he believes it, he has no support for it at all.

We all know that engineers ought not to make mistakes in calculation when determining how to support a building. Whatever they may happen to believe, that is, engineers are committed, because they are engineers, to certain truths about what they need to do in their jobs. These are not just any truths, but are normative: it is what they ought to do—for prudential, legal, and ethical reasons. Just so, a physician ought not to cause unnecessary pain. A teacher ought to grade exams and essays fairly, without any bias.

The real world intervenes whenever it is at odds with our beliefs. Whatever the physician may have believed about the woman who was brain dead, she was dead. That was made true by a law that declared that someone who is brain dead is dead. So it did not matter what the physician believed. What he believed was false unless he believed that the woman was dead.

Some seem to think that although there are truths in ethical matters, what a person believes is moral ought to be taken into consideration in deciding what to do. They think, that is, that a person's morals have ethical weight. This confusion is all too common. One of the engineering departments at my university has its students read an essay on how they ought to act as engineers that claims the first step in determining what they ought to do is to see if it accords with their morals. If it fails that test, the essay claims, there is no need to go on to see if it is ethical. Their believing it wrong suffices, it is claimed, to outweigh any ethical considerations.

In determining what we ought to do, however, we are to be concerned only with what has ethical weight. What one believes is moral has no ethical weight unless it is in fact ethical. Our beliefs about what we ought to do can certainly differ, and some individuals have reprehensible moral beliefs which cannot be justified by any ethical principles. They have no ethical weight and so ought not count against what is ethical. As Isaac Asimov has Salvor Hardin say in *Foundation*, "Never let your sense of morals get in the way of doing what's right."[3]

I will use "moral" and "ethical" interchangeably, always with the implication that for something to be moral it must be ethical. One reason is to discourage the use of morals as a counterweight to ethics. To distinguish between the two gives license to compare the two as though one's morals had some ethical weight, perhaps even enough to outweigh what is ethical. The distinction serves no ethical, or moral, purpose and can obviously mislead us, as it does an engineering department at my university. I will use the two interchangeably because I will call something "moral" only if it is also ethical and not just what someone happens to believe.

§3 Making Ethical Judgments

The judgments we made about the engineers making a biased decision and the physician in Memphis being wrong in not informing the family were relatively easy. The wrongs are obvious, for one thing, and we do not need to know much about engineering or medical practice to understand that they failed to fulfill the obligations they took on when they entered into those professions. Engineers are not to privilege men over women while trying to make driving safer, and physicians are to be honest with their patients and their families.

So we did not have to work at figuring out what was wrong any more than we have to stop and think about how to open a door before opening it or "refrain from understanding simple sentences in [our] own language or from orienting to a loud unexpected noise."[4] As with much of what we do, Daniel Kahneman has made clear, we react quickly and do not consciously go through any elaborate process to arrive at such judgments. We do this

> many times each day. Most of us are pitch-perfect in detecting anger in the first word of a telephone call, recognize as we enter a room that we were the subject of the conversation, and react quickly to subtle signs that the driver of the car in the next lane is dangerous.[5]

Life is too short, as it were, for critical reflection on what to do when a child darts into the street in front of us or a driver wanders into our lane as we are about to pass or someone stumbles toward us. We stop our car, we slow down, we steady ourselves. Indeed, as Kahneman says, "You will find that you have responded to the threat before you became fully conscious of it."[6]

The same is true for ethical judgments. We make them without necessarily being fully conscious that we need to respond. A parent is quick to pull back a child who is about to step off the curb against the light or who is yet again about to hit a sibling. All this is done without reflection, and that is how our false beliefs and subconscious biases enter into our judgments.

We repeat what we picked up on the playground, as it were, without really thinking through whether what we do is the right thing to do. It may be, or it may not, but however that may be, the lesson to learn from our coming to judgment without taking the time, or effort, to work out beforehand whether our judgment is correct is that we cannot be assured that what we believe is right is right. As we know, merely believing something does not make it true, and, as Kahneman emphasizes, there is "a puzzling limitation of our mind: our excessive confidence in what we believe, and our apparent inability to acknowledge the full extent of our ignorance and the uncertainty of the world we live in."[7]

We can be in for a shock when our confidence is shattered. One of my students believed that Hollywood had somehow figured out how to make movies that could not be seen by those 13 and under. As a child, he had been told by his parents when he ran into the TV room to see what they were laughing at that he could not see it because it was PG-13. He took that literally and did not realize it was false until he explained to some friends at a cinema that there was no sense going into a particular movie because it was PG-13 and they could not see it. He was ten years old and said he never lived it down.

More problematic are the biases we have that we are completely unaware of, that do not lead to anything quite so dramatic. We all share a spatial bias, for example.[8] When we eyeball a line—a garden edge, a putt, where to cut a board—we may think we have done it exactly right or close enough, to the right or left, not to matter. But the line our eyeball makes is skewed slightly to the left. The phenomenon is called pseudo-neglect. It is well-documented, and the result is that we pay more attention to the left side of our visual field than our right side so that when we eyeball a line we tend to steer to the left.[9]

Other biases may skew our judgments without our realizing it. That is one reason why we must distinguish between what we believe and what we ought to believe, between what some call morality and what is ethical. It is the reason that it is always appropriate to ask someone to justify their judgment.

It is not anywhere near as easy to do that as it is to make a judgment—or turn a doorknob. We must back off from our beliefs and become as best as we can an objective observer of our judgment, asking, as it turns out, a number of different questions about our judgment. It is only by going back over our judgments, that is, and examining the steps we would have followed had we carefully evaluated what we ought to do that we can be sure that we have acted ethically and not just responded.

We can illustrate some of what we must do, and begin to see how challenging it is to evaluate our ethical judgments, by examining a case involving the five-year-old daughter of a friend who said, as I was driving her home from nursery school, "It must be terrible to be ugly."

My first thought—after my "Uh, oh, where is this going?"—was that she was talking about herself, but I quickly realized she was talking about someone else. So I asked in response, "Why do you say that?"

"Well, they don't have any friends. They sit in the corner by themselves. They are always the last person chosen for a game."

"That's certainly true."

"It's not fair."

"You're right, Katie," I agreed, letting her continue the conversation if she wished.

We drove for a few more minutes, and I thought the conversation was over. Then she said, "And besides, it's not their fault."

"Why is that?"

"They were just born that way, and it's not their fault they were born that way."

I was trying not to smile, afraid that she would misinterpret my smile of recognition of a very basic principle of justice that tells us that we should discount accidents of birth in distributing the goods of society, including, she was saying, getting picked for games by other children. I said, yet again, "You're right."

We then drove on some distance to her house, and as we drove into the driveway, she said, "You know what else?"

"No, what?"

"They're still ugly."

We might take this to mean that she thought they were, well, ugly, but I think she was struggling with something deeper. Even though we know it is wrong to treat people differently because of a contingent feature they have for which they are not responsible, Katie was saying, we still see them as ugly. Our social norms are so powerful we cannot help ourselves. We continue to make such judgments despite now knowing they are false.

Her remarks mapped three essential capacities for being ethical. Unlike the engineers who failed to see that they had made a biased decision, she recognized an ethical problem—in that the norms of our lives are unfair to some, at least, who are penalized for being who they are; she laid out a variety of ways in which that unfairness plays itself out and so recognized the generality of the problem; and she began to articulate a principle about how we ought to treat others. Each of these three capacities is essential to doing what is ethical.

(1) She recognized an ethical problem. That capacity is fundamental. We can hardly begin to respond ethically if we are blind to an ethical issue. It is unfortunately commonplace for individuals to fail to see that anything is wrong. We are so accustomed to the world as we live it—how we walk, how we talk, how we see ourselves, how we see others—that it takes no small effort to wrench ourselves out of ourselves, as it were, to see the world anew and thus see what is wrong with the world we are accustomed to.

This is especially so when we have so mastered a practice that we no longer have to think through any of its details. Chess masters are masters at making just the right move. The same is true for any skills we learn. As with the engineers who failed to see the ethical problem they created, we just do what we have learned and honed over the years, going blithely on, without thinking much, if at all, about how we are going on. Being blind to ethical problems is obviously a major difficulty as we wend our way through the world. Katie's seeing as problematic behavior that is all too common, too "normal," is a testament to her ethical intuitions.

(2) She saw the child's treatment as a kind of problem. Understanding the nature of an ethical issue depends in part upon our capacity to generalize from a single situation to other situations, all equally problematic. We are then seeing the problem as a kind of problem, one calling for a principled response, rather than as a single isolated instance of something that is wrong.

Someone may point out that you are frowning when asked a question, and you then realize, as you pay attention to how you react when others ask questions, that far from being a singular event, perhaps occasioned by what was being asked, you do this all the time—generally sending the visual signal that you are not at all happy being asked questions, whatever their content.

Just so, ethical problems are kinds of problems, ones that may display themselves in a variety of situations, from where one sits to when one gets picked for a game. It does not constitute a problem, let alone an ethical problem, for someone to be picked last. Someone has to be last. A problem occurs when that sort of treatment happens generally, most or all of the time, in that and other contexts, and for no good reason. Someone with two left feet is not going to be a top choice for any soccer game, but it is hardly discriminatory to be last or close to last for such a reason. But if no one will sit or play with that person and the person is generally treated differently from others for no good reason, then we have an ethical problem.

(3) She appealed to an ethical principle. What ties together all the instances of poor treatment of Katie's classmate is that they are all examples of injustice, and so Katie implicitly appealed to the ethical principle that is unfair to treat individuals differently

just because of accidental features for which they are not responsible. It is that principle which makes the judgment an ethical judgment.

We may wonder in particular cases what counts as fair and unfair. We are all too familiar with such problems in sports. A referee, seeing something problematic, must decide whether it is a foul. That means deciding whether it is an accidental bumping, for instance, or something prohibited. An umpire calls balls and strikes and must make a judgment when either call seems problematic because of the swerve of the throw, for instance. Because the situation is problematic, whatever the umpire or referee decides will be open to question: fair or unfair?

But however problematic particular judgments may be, we have no problem at all with the principle that it is unfair to treat individuals differently for no good reason. No one can reasonably fault Katie for appealing to that principle given the treatment she saw her classmate suffer.

The capacity to see a moral problem, the capacity to see the problem as part of a pattern, one of a kind, as it were, and the capacity to generate a principled response to that problem—none of these is easy. They evince a moral sophistication we should encourage and cultivate as much as we can in ourselves and in others. Katie took things to a higher level of sophistication with her recognition that however powerful the principle, the norms of our lives can still have their way.

We made use of the capacities Katie displayed when we assessed the engineers and the physician. We have seen plenty of examples of discrimination and, in particular, plenty of examples where men are favored over women. So what the engineers did was readily recognizable as discriminatory. I appealed there not to justice, but to the principle that we should not cause unnecessary harm, and I did that because the engineers were supposed to be making it safer for those in accidents. The discrimination against women drivers was particularly egregious because they put the women at greater risk of harm.

In the case of the physician, I again appealed to the principle that we should not cause unnecessary harms. Not being fully honest with a patient or a patient's family might be appropriate in some cases, but implying that the woman with the stroke was still a patient and so might become better causes harms for no good reason.

The three characteristics Katie made explicit are necessary for anyone making a proper moral judgment, but we will need more to prepare ourselves for a full understanding of the ethical problems we meet and to become capable of making a reasonable ethical judgment. Katie displayed a fourth characteristic that we will need to examine in more detail, the capacity to see the world from another's point of view, the child who was being treated so badly.

To tease out that capacity and the rest of what we need, we will be looking at real cases, in situ—as we find them, that is. They will embody sometimes very complex and complicated ethical issues along with a variety of extraneous matters of no ethical import. We are not going to look at cases that have been dissected ahead of time for easy observation. We are going to be doing the dissecting, and so we will need to be sure we know how to identify what is of ethical concern from what is extraneous. We will need to identify the ethical principles we appeal to. We will need to learn how to distinguish different kinds of ethical problems so that we are not misled into trying to understand and resolve one kind through a procedure appropriate for another.

We will find that the very best cases for our purposes are found in professions, and so we will need to spend some time discussing the nature of professions and explaining why cases within professions serve our purposes so well. We shall use that discussion to tease out, among other things, some ethical principles we use in assessing ethical issues both in professions and in our ordinary lives.

3

Professions

We go to physicians, not lawyers, to check on our health. We go to lawyers, not engineers, to write a will. We all generally know, that is, what professionals are to do in their various professions, and that gives us grounds for ethical judgments about what they do, or fail to do, as professionals.

These professional roles are imposed by society and serve ends for society as a whole as well as for its members. A healthy society is more likely to be wealthy than one with its members racked with illness and unrelieved suffering. A society with well-trained police and well-educated lawyers and judges is more likely to be safer for its citizens than one racked by gang warfare and rogue police officers. Professions exist for social ends, that is, both for the benefit of society as a whole and for the benefit of its citizens.

That is why professional roles are laid out in some detail. Only by knowing what a professional is licensed to do can citizens know whom to see about their health or wealth or any other matter of importance that requires someone with the appropriate skills and knowledge.

§1 Professions

An additional reason our judgments about the engineers and the physician were so easy is thus that we were implicitly appealing to what we know engineers and physicians ought to do. They are in professions defined by the roles they play in society. We generally have no problems making judgments about professionals who fail to satisfy the requirements of their profession—lawyers who sleep while their client is on trial[1] or physicians who profit from unnecessary tests they order for their patients[2] or veterinarians who mistreat the animals they are supposed to help.[3]

We shall be examining cases throughout as we come to grips with what we still need to do to make ethical judgments, and, as it turns out, we can find a rich supply of cases in professional practices. Focusing on them has advantages over casting about randomly for cases.

First, we have some clarity about what a professional ought to do. Lawyers are to defend their clients, physicians are to care for and try to cure their patients, historians are to tell what happened in the past. Each of them takes on a role as a professional of a certain kind, and we can find some ground for any ethical judgments we make by appealing to a professional's role.

In addition, cases in professions are often rich in commentary from the public and from others within the same profession. Engineers harm the reputation of engineering and other engineers by discriminating against women in making decisions about airbags. It is no surprise that others in their profession will be critical, and, in disasters, there will be major investigations to discover what went wrong so they are not repeated. This happens all the time with plane crashes.

A third reason for concentrating upon cases within professions is that they are rich in complications and so provide a good testing ground for determining how to recognize, understand, and assess ethical problems.

We will discover that although professionals specialize, there is nothing special about how we assess them ethically. The terms of moral criticism are the same that we use in our ordinary lives, and the objects of ethical concern are the same. We gain some ethical leverage because we can appeal to the roles they have as professionals, but we also have leverage for the roles we have in life—as a child, a sibling, a parent, an employee or employer, driver, and so on. The leverage is the same. Parents are to care for their children, employees are to do their jobs, drivers are to follow the rules of the road. They are at fault if they fail to do what their role requires of them.

But if we are to take advantage of the ethical leverage we get by looking at cases in the professions, we need to examine the nature of a profession and what follows just from being a professional.

1. A professional has special knowledge. A historian should know enough about how to track down and cite sources so that future historians, among others, can double check the sources and see if they support the historian's understanding of them. A surgeon should know enough anatomy so as not to mistake a kidney for a liver. A surgeon does not need to cite sources for that knowledge any more than a historian needs to know what distinguishes them.

2. A professional has special skills. A historian needs to learn how to assess evidence. For example, the members of the Constitutional Convention discussed briefly whether the original thirteen states should have a special status vis-à-vis any new states that might be formed. We have one source for what was discussed in Madison's notes on the Convention.[4] Is some independent source required? And if that source tells a different story?[5] A historian needs to learn how to respond to such concerns and adjudicate between competing accounts. A surgeon needs to learn how to handle tools requiring intricate hand-eye coordination and great care. There are rules for what to use to perform one kind of surgery and what to use for another. So in learning the relevant rules of skill, a surgeon is learning what rule to use when as well as the capacity to tie those rules together into the coherent whole that defines the profession.

3. A professional learns to think in a certain way. Learning to be a professional means learning to see the world in a certain way. I may see an apple tree in full bloom and admire its beauty, and an arborist may see a diseased tree spending

what little energy it has left on producing seed. An arborist may see a blemish on my skin where an oncologist sees skin cancer. Professionals in one discipline are distinguished from non-professionals and other professionals by the ways they have learned how to look at the world. An engineer may see a bridge in need of repair while a lawyer sees a pending lawsuit. A lawyer may see a couple needing a divorce lawyer while a therapist may see a couple in need of counseling. There is, of course, a great deal more to this than just learning to see things in different ways. Those differences carry with them different ways of thinking about the world which have their own distinct implications, including distinct character traits. Surgeons who slice and dice will not last much longer than their first patient. A highflyer of an engineer will not find work in that risk-averse field. The traits that mark out one professional from another are as different as the differing rules of skill and the different ways of thinking.

4. A professional takes on a special set of moral relations. A professional is empowered, legally and morally, in ways that others are not and in ways distinct from other professions. Physicians are empowered to examine their patients in a way in which, say, professors are not. Were I, a professor, to try to examine one of my students as my physician examines me, I would be morally, and legally, in the wrong—and not last long in my job. My students have a right that I examine them, and examine them fairly, but through tests and papers, not by disrobing for a physical. My physician is obligated to give me a thorough and careful physical, among other things, just as a lawyer takes on obligations to a client and responsibilities to the court and other relevant legal parties. There are a variety of moral relations that make up the set for any one profession, and sorting them out, even roughly, will provide us with an understanding of how a professional can get it right, as it were, and go wrong.

5. A profession has a social purpose. We want those who teach history to be historians because we think our history helped make us who we are and because we think we can better understand ourselves and how to respond to the challenges we face as a society if we see how those before us fared because of their solutions to similar problems. Because we want our citizens to be healthy, we license individuals to provide health-care services—nurses, physicians, physician assistants, surgeons. They are licensed for a personal and social end, our health. Because we want people to live and work in structures that will withstand the stresses of storms and heavy use, we have structural engineers, trained professionals who are to sign off, or not, on whether a structure passes an inspection to ensure it is safe to use.

These five features are not distinct and separable features that one can pick up, one by one, on one's way to becoming a professional. They are different aspects, integral parts, of what it is to be a professional. In becoming a professional, one takes on a role, and that role is defined by at least these features. Other features may distinguish professionals as well, but these five will give us access to all we need to demarcate a person's professional identity and allow us to understand how ethical considerations enter into the professions.[6]

§2 Terms of Criticism

When we examined objects of ethical concern, we used different terms of criticism as our object of ethical concern differed. What we are criticizing determines the terms of criticism. We assess statements as true or false, meaningful or meaningless, clear or ambiguous, coherent or incoherent, lies or truths, and so on. We assess individuals as intelligent or stupid, knowledgeable or ignorant, agreeable or stubborn, circumspect or foolhardy, and on and on. A statement requires different terms of criticism than a person, and a person different terms of criticisms than action or inaction, and intentions a different set of terms than consequences.

This is not to suggest that the same term of criticism cannot be appropriate for all the objects of ethical concern. A person can be malicious, with malicious thoughts and intentions, and act maliciously with malicious consequences. But the terms of criticism can differ, and we can best understand how by examining a situation that puts all five objects of ethical concern in play. The example will also set us up for understanding the social and ethical ends of professions since one object of concern in the example is a historian not just failing to further those ends, but impeding them.

Stephan Ambrose was a professor of history who became famous for his book *Band of Brothers*, among others, and what had become the standard biography of President Eisenhower. It is a historian's dream when a former president asks you to write a biography and makes himself available, one-on-one, for "hundreds and hundreds of hours." With such access, gaps in the public record can be filled by more than a historian's conjectures and the president's motivations and goals can be checked just by asking. So when the historian writes that the president thought so-and-so, for such-and-such a reason, we have good evidence that he did—almost straight from the horse's mouth, as it were. Such a biography would be as close to an autobiography as we could expect. Ambrose said he lived that dream.

He said that Eisenhower had approached him about writing the biography. "I thought I had flown to the moon," Ambrose said. "I'd walk in to interview him, and his eyes would lock on mine and I would be there for three hours and they never left my eyes." Ambrose told C-SPAN, "I was teaching at Johns Hopkins and going up two days a week to Gettysburg to work with him in his office."[7]

We now know that Eisenhower did not approach him, that the two never met alone, and that the meticulous records of Eisenhower's meetings "contradict the notion that the pair had any lengthy face-to-face contact," showing instead that

> Eisenhower saw Ambrose only three times, for a total of less than five hours. The two men were never alone together. The footnotes to Ambrose's first big Eisenhower book, "The Supreme Commander," published in 1970, cite nine interview dates; seven of these conflict with the record. On October 7, 1965, when Ambrose claimed that he was interviewing Eisenhower at Gettysburg, Ike was traveling from Abilene to Kansas City.[8]

These revelations transformed what was taken to be a historically invaluable biography into a historical fiction. Indeed, as I discovered, Ambrose was sloppy in giving references, and some simply cannot be checked out.[9] So we cannot even be sure that he got it right when he appealed to the records. The consequence is that we cannot believe what he wrote, and history is the big loser. Historians have used Ambrose's biography as a reference source for what Eisenhower thought about various events in his life, but the records of their meetings put into doubt everything in his biography and everything written by other historians who used the biography as a source. His deception had ramifications far beyond giving us a picture of Eisenhower we must now view with credulity. Lies have lives.

Ambrose had ample time and opportunities before he died to correct himself, but never did, and the lie was not a trivial matter, but had significant consequences—for our understanding of Eisenhower, for historians specializing in that period of our history, for Ambrose's reputation, and for our trust of historians.

Here is what we are entitled to say:

1. Professor Ambrose lied.
2. We cannot trust what he wrote or said.

The first judgment is about something he did that was wrong. Lying is wrong unless there is some compelling ethical reason to justify it, but Ambrose had no compelling ethical reason to lie.

We might also be tempted to say that he was a liar, but that judgment is about his overall character, about what he characteristically would do. We have no evidence that he lied about other matters, but he did embellish his lie with his description of Eisenhower locking eyes with him for three hours, not the sign of a casual mistake. Lying about something so momentous and not correcting oneself is a character flaw in anyone and certainly runs counter to the character we would expect of a historian, someone professionally committed to finding and telling the truth.

The second judgment is about the consequences of his actions. We cannot trust what he wrote about Eisenhower, but if he lied about that, what are we to make of his other works? He wrote twenty-five books, co-authored another five, and edited five more—each now subject to doubt. They cannot be relied upon by anyone, let alone other historians—without serious reservations and a great deal of research to verify the claims made.

If we have to verify each of his claims, why bother reading him? The worry any other historian has to have is that citing Ambrose pollutes the text. In reading *No Ordinary Time* by Doris Kearns Goodwin, I found myself brought up short when she quotes Ambrose about how the American people responded to the Normandy invasion.[10] I decided the quotation did not matter for the point she wanted to make, but the example makes the point of how citing Ambrose will cause problems for other historians—and their readers.

He was able to claim an intimate relation with Eisenhower without serious questions being raised because he had a historian's credentials and was already a much-published author of presumptively historical works. Becoming a professor requires vetting by others within one's chosen discipline, including an assessment of one's PhD dissertation and other scholarly writings. Ambrose's having succeeded in becoming a professor of history testifies to the judgment of historians that he was entitled to call himself a historian. Unfortunately, after what we have discovered, we cannot agree. His lie about Eisenhower and his failure ever to correct himself might not be thought enough to justify that judgment: people often end up living the life of their lies, psychologically unable or unwilling to correct the record. So we may sympathize. But it was not a one-off failure of judgment on his part, and his failure to provide proper citations ought to tip the point given, as Gordon Wood notes regarding another historian gone astray, "that we historians are telling the truth is what distinguishes us from fiction writers."[11]

It is not an easy task laying out what any professional's role is, but Wood has marked out one crucial component for historians when he says of a fellow historian's remark that there are many variants of each historical event, "It is the historian's responsibility to analyze and evaluate all these different views and narrations and then arrive at as fully and as objective an explanation and narration of the events as possible."[12]

Historians must use their imagination, he adds, but it is an imagination "sensitive to the differentness of the past and constrained and constricted by the documentary record" because the historian must "believe intelligently and not naively in an objective truth about the past that can be observed and empirically verified."[13]

Someone who creates a documentary record, out of whole cloth, is not writing as a historian, but passing off fiction as history. That is what Ambrose did with his supposed interviews with President Eisenhower, and so, at least for that portion of his life's work, we must say,

3.   he was not writing as a historian.

He was able to pass off his work as history because

4.   he was a historian and presented his work as history.

The third judgment relies on our understanding of what it is to be a historian, and the fourth concerns the way he presented himself—as a historian, certainly, but also as a historian with special access to a famous person and so especially positioned to tell us the truth about that person. He thus harmed other historians by making us wonder whether others with the credentials of a historian are masquerading as well.

There is no denying that Ambrose wrote well, telling a good story. There is no denying that it takes some genius to write good historical fiction, a story with enough connection to reality to be mistaken for truth. There is no denying as well that his writings were well received and that he deserves credit for exciting many about the study of history.

Yet good historical fiction is still fiction. It is not history. Ambrose did not measure up as a historian when he wrote about Eisenhower. He failed to meet even the minimal standards for being a historian, trying to find and tell the truth. Those standards are norms—what someone ought to do or refrain from doing to be a historian—and so in saying he failed to measure up, we are making a normative judgment.

We must presume that he knew better. He was a professor of history, after all, and would supposedly have taught his students about how to do historical research, the sort of research we would expect him to model in his own work. That makes his failures all the more reprehensible.

We can fault his character as a historian, his knowledge since he knew he was wrong to lie, his intentions because he meant to deceive us, his actions in doing so and his failure to correct the record, and then the consequences to history, to our understanding of Eisenhower and of the other historical events Ambrose wrote about. The terms of criticism we marshal for each of these objects of ethical concern differ, but the overriding result is that he frustrated the ends of his profession, to determine and present the truth about the past as objectively as possible.

In calling Ambrose out as unprofessional, I am effectively appealing to the Statement on Standards of Professional Conduct of the American Historical Association:

> All historians believe in honoring the integrity of the historical record. They do not fabricate evidence ... An undetected counterfeit undermines not just the historical arguments of the forger, but all subsequent scholarship that relies on the forger's work. Those who invent, alter, ignore, remove, or destroy evidence of any kind make it difficult for any serious historian ever wholly to trust their work again.[14]

That standard clearly puts the lie, as it were, to any claim Ambrose might have had to being a historian, but it is only a first step in assessing what Ambrose did because we need to understand why historians are to value "the integrity of the historical record." The history profession, like other professions, is recognized and given special status, by us and by the state, because it is to serve social purposes, backed by ethical principles with implications for its practitioners.

§3 A Profession Has a Social Purpose

There are formal qualifications that must be satisfied for someone to be a practitioner in certain professions. These criteria are either set by or approved by the state, and it is in those criteria that we find the raison d'être for a profession's existence. Not anyone with a scalpel and a surgical needle has a license to operate even if the results are as good or better than those achieved by someone accredited as a surgeon. The state wants to ensure that those practicing medicine are fully competent.

A surgeon's mistakes can be harmful in the extreme, causing death or serious injury. So the state has good reasons for ensuring that surgeons have in fact obtained the special knowledge and skills necessary to be a surgeon and the special training they need if they specialize. Not just any surgeon can be a brain surgeon.

We find this same care to ensure competency for lawyers. Graduating from law school does not entitle someone to practice law. A bar exam must be passed in each state in which a graduate is to practice in order to ensure that the graduate knows that state's laws as well as the general knowledge and skills to be a lawyer.

What is required for these professions is a history that includes significant training in the special knowledge and skills of the profession, in a state-certified university or institute, and even with that history, an individual needs to satisfy additional criteria set by the state to practice in that profession. A lawyer, for instance, will have earned a bachelor degree, taken the Law School Admission Test (LSAT), applied for and been admitted into an accredited law school, earned a Juris Doctor degree, and passed a state bar exam to practice in that state. A lawyer is barred from practicing in any other state until its bar exam is passed.

Note especially the hurdles the state puts in front of those who wish to enter these professions. The first is that the skills and knowledge a person needs are to be gained through state-certified institutions, universities, and schools of law or medicine, say, that have satisfied those responsible for ensuring that those institutions are capable of teaching at that level. For some professions at least, there are two hurdles in this first step—getting a BA or BS from an accredited university and then going on and completing studies in an accredited law school or medical school.[15] Getting a degree at either hurdle from a university that lacks accreditation is a waste of time and money in any case, but especially for anyone who wants to go on to become a professional.

The second hurdle is for the state to ensure that a person does indeed have the knowledge and skills. Medical students must be interns for what must seem to them to be a very long time, and lawyers must pass bar exams.[16] They may generally retake them if they fail to pass, but unless they pass, they cannot practice law.

The state does not set up such a string of hurdles for some professions. A historian usually has an advanced degree in history and so has completed a dissertation that a group of historians has examined and approved as worthy of a historian. Recognition as a historian does not depend upon jumping an additional hurdle.

Indeed, for history at least, individuals may be recognized as historians even without a degree, but only if their work is acceptable to historians, only if, that is, those already certified as historians find that the work meets the standards historians require. We do not call those without credentials historians, or even amateur historians, that is, unless their work satisfies the criteria adopted by those who have the credentials to make such judgments, historians, that is, who have come into the profession by getting a PhD in history with all that entails about their competencies as historians. The distinction between those who have met the criteria for being a historian through the rigorous training individuals undergo in obtaining a PhD in history and those who are good enough to have their work accepted by those individuals with PhDs becomes meaningless in such a situation. History is history: individuals are there judged to be professionals by what they are capable of doing, not by their history, as it were.

This distinction between amateur and professional does not readily map onto all professions. A student may graduate from an accredited school of engineering and be hired as an engineer, for instance, but to become what the engineering profession calls a professional engineer, a graduate must "work under a Professional Engineer for at least four years, pass two intensive competency exams and earn a license from their state's licensure board. Then, to retain their licenses, [they] must continually maintain and improve their skills throughout their careers."[17] Individuals who want to start an engineering consulting business would want to become professional engineers. But we are using the term "professional" in a looser sense than the engineering profession. We are going to consider as a professional engineer someone who has graduated with an engineering degree from an accredited college or university—knowing that there is an additional step they would need to take to be recognized as professionals by their engineering colleagues. It is this broader sense of "professional" that allows an amateur to be a professional historian if their work is found worthy by those educated into the profession, by those who have been judged by their future peers to have written a dissertation worthy of a historian. The aim in opting for a looser sense of who can be a professional is to ensure that we not exclude someone who becomes an expert in that field, and is recognized as an expert by other experts, from being a professional— provided only that the discipline allows for that possibility. Lawyers cannot be amateurs. Neither can physicians. Nor police officers. And so on.

So why does a state impose conditions upon those who would be in a profession? Why are there conditions, that is, for being a health-care practitioner, or a lawyer, or a police officer? The reason lies in the basic needs of the members of a society.

Any society will try to ensure that no member harms another and that there is a civil way to settle disputes just as any society will come to have some way of caring for those who are ill or otherwise incapacitated. These features of a society are what I call natural social artifacts.[18] Like language, they are a natural outgrowth of individuals living together in a society because they satisfy basic needs they all have—for protection from others and for health, for instance. The state imposes conditions upon those who wish to enter into the professions which are charged with satisfying those needs in order to ensure that they are satisfied satisfactorily.

Society has an interest in its members being healthy. Benjamin Franklin might well have said, "A healthy society is a wealthy society." Healthy citizens contribute to the society's well-being. Just so, the society has an interest in minimizing conflict between its members just as each member has an interest in not being subject to assault, robbery, or other infractions. A society thus imposes conditions for entry into the professions that satisfy such basic societal and individual needs.

Professions exist for a purpose, that is, and it is in the interest of the state and of its members to ensure that those purposes are realized by ensuring that the members of professions are competent to realize the ends for which the professions exist. Just as a society cannot function without some health-care system with experts, it cannot function without a set of laws to try to ensure the civility which is essential to the safety of its members. It cannot function without a way of educating its members, without a way of keeping track of its wealth, without a way of defending itself from outsiders, and so on. Each social goal requires experts, those having the special knowledge and skills to achieve those goals. Professionals thus serve social goals which a society has recognized as essential—for the health of its members, for their safety, for a fair resolution of the inevitable disputes that arise when people live together, and on and on.

§4 The Moral Ends of Professions

Professions serve moral ends—the well-being of the members of the society and their safety, for example. The professions are themselves artifacts, the contingent creation of a variety of actors—from practitioners to the state, and they are thus as subject to change as any artifact. Just as language is always gaining new words and phrases while others languish and disappear from common usage, a profession is in constant change. Medical advances require different skills from those a practitioner learned in medical school. New legislation and court decisions require that lawyers come to grips with them and their reverberations through the legal system. But what stays constant are the purposes for which we have professions, and those are underwritten by ethical principle.

For instance, we have accountants, and requirements for those who are to practice as accountants, because we all need information about our financial situation as well as the financial situation of companies and organizations so that we can make proper decisions about how to spend and invest our money. We have investment advisors so that we can get advice, we presume, about how best to invest our funds to maximize our return. We have actuaries to predict how much an insurance company will need to pay out to cover damages from, say, future floods so it will know how much to charge us when we purchase insurance.

Autonomy is an ethical value. It is the right of individuals to make their own choices.[19] It is one of the ethical values that underlays our having professions. The end of accountants and investment advisors is to provide us with information so we can make reasonable decisions about our finances. When that information is faulty, but is represented as accurate, it prevents us from being the autonomous individuals we have a right to be. We have lost one feature that makes it possible for us to be ethical beings, the right to choose to do one thing rather than another. For that right is barren if we are faced with false choices. I call the right sterile in such a case, but its exercise has effects, and we end up thinking that we have exercised our autonomy when we have not.

We find in the ethical value of autonomy one of the ethical principles that explains why we have professions and why we demand of our practitioners that they have the knowledge and skills their professional practice demands. We cannot be fully autonomous if our options are limited by being constantly on guard, in fear of being attacked, mugged or killed, or even just concerned that others will not obey the traffic laws. One of my options has been curtailed if I am trying to decide whether to go to the grocery store or make do at home and I do not know that, generally at least, other drivers will keep to their lanes, stop at stop signs and stop lights when red, keep within reasonable reach of the posted speed limit, and so on. We have professionals to enforce these matters and to adjudicate infractions, and we have them, in part at least, to ensure that we can all make autonomous decisions.

Just so, we cannot be fully autonomous if our options are limited by disease or some physical handicap or mental fault. So one reason for having health-care professionals is to ensure our autonomy, to allow us to realize our life's goals through our own choices and, as much as possible, not be limited in what we can choose by disease or bodily faults. We cannot, indeed, make fully autonomous decisions without having a raft of professionals competent do their jobs—by providing information about the past to inform our current decisions to being healthy enough to act on them. We have a system of qualified professionals who are to provide us with the autonomy we need to fashion for ourselves the kind of life we wish to lead.

That is not to imply that they always succeed or even, in some cases, that they are able to give us what we need to exercise our autonomy. The information some professionals provide us is faulty. Investment advisors are not obligated to follow the fiduciary rule, for instance. That requires them to act in the best interest of their clients. They instead advise on what is "suitable" for their clients. That is a license to advise clients to purchase stock, say, that will do for the client, but is in the best interests of the investment advisor, not the client's best interests.[20] If you are an investor who does not know that investment advisors are not obligated to give you the best advice, you may well not be getting the best advice from your advisor. It is rather like walking into a store to purchase a vacuum cleaner, say, having done all the research you need so you know exactly what make and model you want, only to be persuaded by a salesperson to buy "a better machine," one on which the store makes much more profit. At least you can know in that situation that you made a mistake, but unless you know that investment advisors are not obligated to follow the fiduciary rule, you will likely think the recommended investment is in your best interests.

We have the right to make our own decisions, but we cannot make an autonomous choice when our options are not what they are represented to be. It is no more autonomous than it is when we are coerced into doing what someone else wants us to do. So the failure of investment advisors to provide us with accurate information is an ethical failure, undercutting one reason for having such professions—providing for our autonomy.

That is not the only reason, of course. Another ethical principle that justifies our having professions and qualified professions is perhaps even more obvious. It is that those we call upon to help us with our health and our wealth, for instance, do nothing that is unnecessarily harmful. This is the principle of non-maleficence, which I parse as the admonition that we are to do no unnecessary harm.

It is often parsed as the principle that, above all, we should do no harm. But that cannot be the proper way of understanding the principle. It is not that physicians are to do no harm, for instance. We would hardly hold a physician morally accountable for causing a patient pain while trying to stanch a serious wound. We would hold the physician accountable for causing unnecessary pain, and that is the point of the principle of non-maleficence. Minimize the harms that must occur to provide treatment. As the teacher of an old country doctor put it, "think first always what harm the treatment may do."[21]

We expect all professionals to act in accordance with the principle of non-maleficence. When engineers solve design problems, they should take care to choose a design solution that will not cause unnecessary harm. The General Motors engineer who approved an ignition switch that failed to meet specifications made a choice that ended up causing a number of deaths. While the vehicle was in motion, the ignition switch would turn off unexpectedly, giving the driver no way to control the vehicle as it took on a life of its own and generally crashed, often at high speed.[22]

The engineers at Takata who decided to use ammonium nitrate as the explosive material in airbags and then manipulated test data made choices that turned a safety feature into a deadly device responsible for a large number of deaths and injuries when the airbags exploded and sent shrapnel into drivers and passengers.[23] Perhaps those engineers failed to think first of what harm their decisions might do or, worse, thought about it and went ahead anyway.

In any event, we can understand why we have professions and why the state requires that professionals have the knowledge and skills essential to their profession. Ensuring autonomy and ensuring that professionals do not cause unnecessary harms are goods for society as a whole as well as for its individual members. The goods are both public and private.

This is not to suggest that there are no other reasons for having professions. It is in the self-interest of practitioners to band together into a profession since they can increase the value of what they offer with that branding and can minimize their competition. Nor is it to suggest that there are only two ethical principles underlying our having professions and demanding that their members be, as it were, real professionals.

These two principles of autonomy and of causing no unnecessary harm are enough to explain how professions and professional requirements are grounded ultimately in ethical outcomes, but we would be remiss not to mention justice and the principle of beneficence. The latter is the principle that we are to act for the good of others, "helping them to further their important and legitimate interests, often by preventing or removing possible harms."[24] Physicians are not only not to cause unnecessary harm, but are also, and more importantly, to act for the good of their patients. Accountants and financial advisors are to do the same. And so when we critique them for failing to provide accurate information that is important to their clients, we are not only faulting them for causing unnecessary harm by preventing the clients from acting autonomously but also for failing to further the interests of their clients. The terms of criticism apply not only to individual professionals, but also to the professions themselves. The professions have failed to fulfill their obligation to act for the public good.

The other principle concerns justice. When the engineers designing the first airbags chose the 50th percentile of men as the mean, the best weight and height to be cushioned and not harmed by an exploding airbag, they unjustly put more women than need be at risk. A physician who refuses to take on patients because of their ethnic background or the color of their skin is acting unjustly, and when a profession limits access by excluding classes of individuals because of their ethnic backgrounds, skin color, sex, or any other feature that is irrelevant to being that sort of professional, the profession is acting unjustly. The most telling examples are those in which a profession skews the entrance requirements so that only "its own kind" can become members.

It should come as no surprise that the values expressed by these principles—autonomy, beneficence, justice, and unnecessary harm—are just the ones we find at playgrounds. Autonomy? "You threw it. You go get it." Beneficence? "You should share your toy with your friend." Justice? "That's not fair. Let your friend have a turn."

Unnecessary harm? "There's no reason for you to hit that kid!" That these values become the matter for professionals simply means that society has recognized their importance for the well-being of society as a whole, and we find them, in fact, in any social group—from families to unions. These are principles that guide our interactions with others, and it does not matter what setting we are in, the principles apply—in our ordinary lives as well as in professions.[25]

§5 Monopolies

Having professions is not an unalloyed good, and the difficulties could well fill a book in itself. We will look at two kinds of ethical issues and those only lightly. The first concerns the monopolistic character of professions. Once an entry gate is in place, those within the gated area have a great deal of power to set the conditions for those who want in. After all, if they are in, that must mean that they have been judged competent practitioners of the profession in question, by themselves at least, but presumably by those reliant on their profession and by the state recognizing their profession and licensing them. And who else but those who are already taken to be professionals are best placed to judge who else might be accepted as a professional?

One effect of having a gated community is that those within can stifle competition. Adam Smith argued that one effect of tariffs on a product or commodity is to create a monopoly for those in the home market who are now protected from competition.[26] They can thus raise their prices for their product or commodity without fear of being undercut by those who are denied entry into the market or can enter only if importers pay the tariff, thus raising their price. An imposition of tariffs on steel from outside the United States permitted those producing steel within the United States to raise their prices at least as high as the imported material. That is why the price of steel in the United States rose almost 100 percent from May 2017 to December 2017.[27] Tariffs are gates, and as with all gates, keeping people out has advantages for those within.

For professions, entry conditions allow those within to raise their rates in the same way steel companies raised theirs because of the gift to them of tariffs on foreign steel. The tensions between midwives and obstetricians give us a sense of professional turf wars. The midwives at New York-Presbyterian Hospital were informed that the hospital was moving "to a model that would have our deliveries being performed by obstetricians," with the midwives at the hospital playing little or no part. As a representative of the American College of Nurse-Midwives put it, "Our concern is that this is a physician land grab, and they want to be able to bill physician rates for all the patients."[28]

We have, in that comment and the accusation of a land grab, exactly the combination Adam Smith warned about in regard to tariffs. The conflict concerns turf, who can do what and where, and the hospital has shut the gate against midwives. Keeping them out of the delivery room means that only obstetricians can perform deliveries, charging their higher rates and providing more business for the hospital.

The comparison with other developed countries is striking:

> One factor that has helped keep costs down in other developed countries is the
> extensive use of midwives, who perform the bulk of prenatal examinations and
> even simple deliveries; obstetricians are regarded as specialists who step in only
> when there is risk or need. Sixty-eight percent of births are attended by a midwife
> in Britain and 45 percent in the Netherlands, compared with 8 percent in the
> United States. In Germany, midwives were paid less than $325 for an 11-hour
> delivery and about $30 for an office visit in 2011.[29]

Not only is the cost considerably less than in the United States, but also the mortality
rate in the United States is considerably higher. It "has one of the highest rates of infant
and maternal deaths in industrialized countries."[30] The mortality rate for mothers in
the United States rose 26.6 percent from 2000 to 2014 "while the international trend
was in the opposite direction,"[31] and there are thirty-one countries with lower mortality
rates for infants than the United States.[32] We are spending significantly more money
than other countries and not serving mothers and newborns as well as they are.

It would certainly seem that turf wars between midwives and obstetricians have
not made birth safer for mothers or their infants. To come to a judgment one way or
the other, we would need far more detail about the conditions under which midwives
work in Europe, their training versus those in the United States, what kinds of issues
arise for midwives that may call for special knowledge and skills, how frequent such
issues are, the conditions under which midwives work in the United States, and so
on. But the only point I am making here is that there is tension between professions,
each claiming it is best positioned to deliver babies. Midwives are claiming that they
can deliver babies safely and at less expense. Obstetricians are claiming that with their
special credentials, only they can safely deliver babies. The effect will be that midwives
will cease to be competitors.

The most effective way to stifle competition is to create the professional equivalent
of a high tariff. A profession can make the entry conditions so onerous, or so expensive,
or so time-consuming that few can make it through. Ethical issues arise when those
conditions seem unnecessary to the end in question or when they are themselves
biased—against women, for instance, or minorities. I hesitate to begin a list of those
discriminated against for fear of discriminating against some by leaving them out, but
we all know that the history of exclusion of Blacks and Jews and women and others
because of their color, religion, or sex is long and sad.

Recent controversies about transgender individuals serving in the military or earlier
ones about women serving in combat positions are instances of the ethical issues that
almost inevitably will arise about the entry conditions into professions. Those who
argue for exclusion must claim either that for some reason transgender individuals and
women cannot achieve the ends of the profession or that opening the gate to let them
in somehow taints the profession and so harms it and its other members. These reasons
do not obviously provide good grounds for exclusion.

But even conditions for entry that seem to have been set for good reasons can be discriminatory and unfair. Going to medical school is expensive, for instance, and so those who are perfectly competent but poor may be unable to attend because that barrier for entry is too high if it is not offset by grants or loans or discounts. Or the procedure that must be followed to gain entry may have consequences that turn out to be discriminatory. Law schools require that applicants take the LSAT, and one result is that those unable to take courses on the LSAT, because of the expense, for instance, are disadvantaged by the requirement. A friend of mine who had just received his PhD in philosophy from Harvard was denied entry into Harvard Law School. When he went to the dean to find out why, he discovered that the law school used a formula for calculating a potential student's expected first-year average and excluded from consideration those who failed to meet the acceptable bar. The formula took an applicant's average grade for college and multiplied it by a number that indicated the quality of the college. My friend had gone to a small religious college that had a rank of zero, and so his projected first-year average obviously fell well below the acceptable bar. He got in when the dean intervened and used his graduate school grades with Harvard's ranking, but the point is that procedures, however well-intended, are not value-neutral and may have discriminatory implications.[33]

Such problems are endemic to any gated community. The forms of discrimination illustrate all too well the rich imagination insiders have for figuring out how to protect what they have got against even the most reasonable claims of others. We will not pursue the ethical problems that arise from professions having a monopoly over the ends for which they were created. The underlying ethical problem is clear: professions create barriers that preclude certain classes of individuals from gaining entry. That is unjust. That is the proper term of criticism. It is unjust for a society to permit such exclusion just as it is unjust for the individual professionals within the society to permit it.

It is equally unjust for those who gain entry into a profession to be treated differentially once they are in because of their sex or their race or any other feature that is irrelevant to being a professional. The principle is so obvious, and the harms so great of failing to abide by it, that it is shocking that we still have such discrimination. It is a shock to discover, for instance, that the principal flutist for the Boston Symphony was being paid on the average $70,000 less than the principal oboist—because she is a woman. We know that in 2017 women only earned 82 cents for every dollar a man earned for doing the same job.[34] So women may not be shocked at such a disparity in the musical world, but it is certainly disheartening to realize how widespread such disparities are and how deeply entrenched they seem to be in professions.

And, we should add, in our ordinary lives as well. We have gated communities. We have swimming pools that restrict who can swim and "public" beaches that prohibit some from entering. We have clubs that exclude "those kind." Name your "kind," and there is no doubt some club that excludes them. In short, the difficulties with entry conditions that we find regarding professions are the same sorts of difficulties we find in a playground where some are excluded because they are not "acceptable."

§6 Self-Regulation

Professions not only have significant control over entry conditions, but also over policing the practices of its members and, in the worst case scenario, ousting them. When I was a humanities fellow in Memphis, rotating through various hospitals to investigate whether, and how, medical practice impacts patients' privacy, I was party to a discussion about a surgeon there who routinely cut too much off when doing circumcisions. Somewhere in the neighborhood of 90 percent of his patients had to return within a couple of years for a skin graft. It appears that he did not do this to ensure future patients, but was simply incompetent. Perhaps he failed to learn how to do circumcisions or, having learned how, was unable, or unwilling, to follow the relevant rules of skill. In any event, we should hold him at fault for the pain, the suffering, and the expense he caused. Such a pattern of harm is sufficient to justify an ethical judgment.

But it did not suffice to prevent him from continuing to do circumcisions. I was in an elevator while one physician complained to the head of the department, and the head asked, "Are you willing to testify?" "Well, no, I haven't witnessed any of his operations." "That's the problem. We all know it's a problem, but no one is willing to come forward and testify against him." I did not ask, and do not know, the reasons for other physicians holding back from testifying. I suspected that it had something to do with ratting out a colleague, hardly enough of a problem to justify letting him continue to maim little boys. But what is most important is what was implied about the procedure for self-regulation. The physicians had in place a procedure that necessitated other physicians testifying against a fellow physician. One can understand a reason for that. We may think that only other professionals are in a position to make a judgment that someone is not doing a professional job. But it is not obvious why anyone has to testify against the surgeon. Having roughly 90 percent of his patients return for a skin graft is so out of the ordinary that the numbers themselves should suffice. Surely no parents would choose that surgeon if they knew that in nine out of ten cases boys had to return for another operation. It does not take a professional to make that judgment. All it takes is someone concerned about the well-being of infants.

The physicians in that hospital in Memphis had apparently trapped themselves in a decision procedure that made it impossible even to criticize a fellow physician without physicians testifying against one another. Having such a decision procedure put them in a position where the hard evidence of great harm to a great many children did not count for anything.

Decision procedures are not value neutral. Flipping a coin to settle some matter only makes sense under certain conditions. If my buddy and I steal a car and then flip for it, I can tell an arresting police officer that it is mine because I won a coin toss, but the officer is not going to say, "Oh well, on your way then." If I steal your cellphone and you catch me out, I cannot properly offer to settle the matter by flipping a coin for it. It is yours, after all. Just so, a decision procedure that excludes hard evidence of harm is ethically wrong. It permits the harms to continue by requiring testimony that is not needed for any judgment.

We can glean from this example at least some of the features a system of self-regulation ought to have and some of the ethical issues that can arise because of self-regulation. One issue concerns the ways in which the decision procedure a profession uses is not value-neutral. Does it exclude objective evidence the way the one in Memphis did, apparently presuming that the judgment of fellow professionals is more trustworthy than assessing the harm a professional does?

A second issue concerns how effective the decision procedure is in coming to the correct judgment. We know that any decision procedure is going to be imperfect.[35] We cannot design a procedure that will ensure that all and only those who have acted unprofessionally will be found to have acted unprofessionally. Any procedure of self-regulation amounts to a trial, and we have yet to devise a system whereby all and only those who have committed a crime are found guilty. We cannot expect to do any better for any procedure adopted by a profession. So the ethical question concerns how imperfect the decision procedure is and whether its results are random or whether they generally err on the side of finding the guilty innocent or finding the innocent guilty. The trust we can have in the decision procedure is a function of how effective it is in calling to account those who have acted unprofessionally.

A third set of ethical issues arises because bias can enter into any procedure of professional self-regulation. A judge who has a stake of any sort in the outcome of a case has recusal as an option, and some other judge without a conflict of interest takes the case. Individual professionals may opt out of judging their peers, but it is likely that some fellow professional has to make a judgment. Opting out is not an option for every professional if there is to be self-regulation relying on the judgment of experts, other professionals in the field, that is, and yet professionals judging other professionals necessarily have a stake in the outcome.

One reason is that they have a commitment to their profession, and putting into question what one of its members has done carries the risk of tainting the profession. We need only consider how hard the Catholic Church has worked to hide child sex abuse by priests and bishops to understand the concern about tainting. Of course, the sheer number of priests and abused children would suffice to explain the Church's concerns about how the issue reflects on it. The grand jury that issued a report in Pennsylvania found over "three hundred predator-priests" and "one thousand child victims." It was able to identify thousands more who did not come forward.[36] But even one well-publicized case can put a profession into question. That single case tells the public at large that someone who made it through the gate into the profession should not have made it through, and that implies that the criteria for admission are not strict enough to prevent others who are unqualified from entering. If one made it through, the one you were going to see may have as well. That is why historians ought to be upset about Ambrose's lying.

We thus have to question whether professionals judging their own are biased because of the damage that may be done to the profession, and to them, by saying one of its own acted unprofessionally. A second reason for concern about the objectivity of professionals judging their own is that they are judging fellow professionals. These are individuals with whom they may have gone to school, may work and socialize with, may see and work with after any judgment is made. It may not be as bad as a friend judging a friend, but it is surely cause for skepticism about how objective a professional can be in judging a fellow professional.

As soon as we have professionals judging other professionals, in other words, we risk skewing the procedure. Those within a profession may decide that the profession itself will be called into question if one of its members is found to have acted unprofessionally, and they may, independent of that, hesitate to question what they are likely to presume is the professional judgment of a colleague—especially since they know they may later find themselves working beside that colleague.

For all these reasons, we ought to be chary of putting too much faith in professions regulating themselves, and our skepticism will no doubt be enhanced by the ways in which some professionals have treated miscreants. It is not just the procedure itself and the objectivity of the judges that causes skepticism, but the outcomes of the procedures. The Catholic Church again serves as an example of what not to do. It simply transferred many priests accused of child sexual abuse to other parishes without warning those whose children were now at risk.[37] In addition, few abusers were subject to whatever procedures the Catholic Church had in place, if any. Only 2 percent of those priests and bishops accused of child sexual abuse were incarcerated, leaving 98 percent free to abuse again.[38] We need no more evidence that self-policing does not work—certainly in regard to the Catholic Church. It is so ineffective that the Attorney General of Michigan "warned Michigan's seven Catholic dioceses to 'stop self-policing, … and comply with the state investigation.'"[39]

Other organizations seem equally adept at ridding themselves of their unwanted by passing them onto others without any particular concern to explain why they are unwanted. In at least four cases, the city of New York has "agreed to conceal the behavior [of substantiated sexual harassment] from future employers who might inquire as part of a reference check." With the city's agreement, the employees agreed to resign and not challenge their firing.[40]

Self-regulation in professions seems as ineffective as it is unethical. One problem in determining how ineffective is that disciplinary hearings are treated like suits settled out of court with clauses prohibiting any discussion of the terms of the settlement or the causes of the suit. The hearings are generally not public, and the records are, so to speak, off the record. Two journalists filed a public records request in California for a list of police officers convicted of a crime. They were "inadvertently" sent a list of over twelve thousand individuals. Not all of those individuals had committed a crime, but some had been convicted of "domestic abuse, child molestation—even murder." As one journalist put it,

> We're talking about a police officer who was arrested, accused of a crime by another law enforcement agency, formally in a court of law, went through adjudication and, at the end of it, either took a plea to a crime or was found guilty and convicted.

The journalists complained of "an impenetrable wall of secrecy" that "surrounds police officer records or misconduct."[41] That information is not available to other law enforcement officials, and so officials in other jurisdictions would have no way of knowing they were hiring any of those individuals. The records are kept private.

Professionals can also ensure that there are no records that could be revealed. When faced with the threat of a disciplinary hearing, professionals can just surrender their licenses, ensuring that there is no hearing. With no hearing, there is no public record for the professionals to worry about.

A surgeon in California misdiagnosed a patient as having appendicitis. He operated, but removed a fallopian tube instead. The patient did not have an appendix. The patient later returned, complaining again of intestinal pain. She was diagnosed as having a hernia in two difference places, but in repairing them by using mesh to strengthen the area that overlapped the hernia, the surgeon used mesh a half-inch wide and so failed to ensure that the mesh overlapped the hernia by at least 1.2 inches on each side. The patient returned shortly thereafter complaining again of intestinal pain. This time a hernia was found on her small intestine. The surgeon removed part of the intestine, but left a portion unconnected. We do not need further details to get the point.

We have a case "of overwhelming evidence of unprofessional conduct," but the surgeon simply surrendered his license in California rather than face disciplinary action. He saved himself

the time, expense, and reputational harm that might come with formal charges and a hearing before a state medical board. Typically, it comes with no restriction on practicing elsewhere.

So the surgeon went to practice in Cincinnati.

States can take action against physicians based on license surrenders in other places. But, as with other matters in the broken world of physician discipline, such a step is spotty. Some states don't even search a national database of troubled physicians.

An investigation by the *Milwaukee Journal Sentinel*, *USA Today*, and MedPage Today found that "more than 250 physicians who surrendered a medical license were able to practice in another state"—like the surgeon from California.[42]

Illinois, for instance, "was one of 13 states in the country that didn't use the database to query a physicians' background a single time" in 2017.[43] Perhaps no physician who surrendered a license elsewhere went on to practice in Illinois that year, but there is no way to know, and if they did, the citizens of Illinois are at risk when they do not need to be. And that is the public health problem with the secretive way in which self-regulation works in the medical profession: "voluntary license surrenders can mean the public gets no access to information about what happened, putting future patients at risk."[44]

It is difficult to imagine a more harmful practice for a profession that is supposed to provide health care for the good of others. Far from helping those who are ill or otherwise physically disabled, it puts them at risk of the sorts of unnecessary harms the poor California patient suffered—with the subsequent loss of autonomy because they do not have sufficient information to choose their physician.

I do not mean to pick on the heath-care profession or even on professions or professionals. Individuals can be equally at fault of obscuring or concealing the faults of other individuals. It does not take much imagination to write a letter to recommend someone you judge incompetent without opening yourself up to a lawsuit. "I'm sure he will work as hard for you as he did for me." Or "I would urge you to waste no time offering a job to this candidate."[45] You simply pass onto others the problematic individual.

So there are a raft of ethical issues that can arise regarding self-regulation. There is the question of whether the procedure used to assess other professionals is appropriate or, as with the Memphis case, faulty because it excludes pertinent information. There is the question of whether the judges can themselves be objective since they are fellow members of the same profession a miscreant taints. There is the question of whether the records of past problems with a professional are publicly available so that the public can know and make decisions accordingly. And there is the question of incompetent professionals simply skipping town and opening up shop elsewhere to harm other patients or clients—without other professionals knowing they are welcoming someone about whom there is "overwhelming evidence of unprofessional conduct."

There may well be other ethical issues that must be addressed in any system of self-regulation, and I do not mean to suggest that all self-regulation is faulty. My only concern is to note where ethical issues arise for any system of self-regulation. That there are so many may explain why it is easy to find examples of failures, but the aim is not to find fault, only to note the fault lines, as it were.

We may think that those within a profession are best positioned to understand its strengths and limitations, but those trained to a profession must engage in a further step to assess it. They must wrench themselves out of their professional position to view it as spectators who, because of their past training, are able to understand why things are done as they are done within the profession and to see where things can go wrong. It turns out that it is not so easy as we might imagine. We have no doubt all discovered some habit we have that passed us by completely unnoticed. I used to say, "Yes, I know," in response to a remark—even though I knew nothing about what it was that was being remarked on. It was my way of saying, "Oh, I see" or "Yes, I understand," but what it implied was that the person talking to me was not telling me anything I did not already know. It took a while to rid myself of that unfortunate habit, and I am not completely sure I have. I have no idea how many I upset by that apparently arrogant response. I failed to hear what I was saying, and it was only when someone said, "No you don't" that I was caught up and began to understand what I was doing. The situation for professionals is no different in kind.

§7 Norms

To become a professional, as we saw, a person must come to have special knowledge and special skills, and those differ from profession to profession. The special skills are captured in conditional statements that tell us that if we wish to achieve a particular end, we are to do so-and-so. A recipe is a simple example. If I want to bake a cake, a recipe tells me step-by-step what to do. If my cake does not turn out, my first question concerns whether I followed the recipe. "Did I put in two cups of flour?" "Did I forget the salt?" I appeal to the recipe first because it has presumptively been honed by experience, shaped by those who have baked to work it into its present form in response to the failures of past iterations. We presume it is correct because of that honing.

The same is true for the rules of skill that distinguish the various disciplines. These have been honed into their current forms by those in the various disciplines reworking them or replacing them in response to failures. So they presumptively provide us with a firm first step in assessing what a professional did or failed to do. They tell us, in short, not only how to achieve the particular ends of a profession, but how we ought to achieve such ends.

Some may be difficult to learn, requiring hours and hours of practice to get them right, honing one's own skills, as it were, to fit the rule one is trying to learn. But rules are not foreign to us. We have been learning such rules since we were little children. "If you want clean teeth, brush up and down, not back and forth." That is a rule of skill that tells us not only how to brush our teeth, but how we ought to brush our teeth to get them clean. It is a rule we have come to adopt because brushing up and down does the best job of cleaning.

A vivid *Sesame Street* vignette has Ernie asking as he comes in for a meal, "Do I take my coat off before I sit down or after I sit down?" A deep voice says, "Before you sit down." "Do I pull out the chair before I sit down or after I sit down?" The deep voice says, "Before you sit down." "Do I open my mouth before I put the peas in or afterwards?" The deep voice says, "You are on your own." And, of course, Ernie fails to follow the rule we all picked up early on, without having to be taught: "If you wish to eat, you open your mouth before you put food in."

We learn how to pour milk, how to make toast, how to throw a ball, how to add and subtract, and on and on. We learn rules of skill from our earliest childhood, that is, and so, by the time we come to learn the rules of a profession, we have had plenty of practice. The rules are different, and, as remarked, some may require a great deal of work and practice to master, but their form and function are the same. Just as we learn, as it were, the norms for civilized life on the playground and in our families and school, we come to learn the norms for the roles we come to play.

Those norms are conditional descriptive imperatives, telling us to do this to achieve that. They are normative as well, telling us what we ought to do to accomplish the end in question. "This is what you need to do to change a diaper to make sure the baby doesn't get a rash," "This is what you need to do to ensure you have enough savings for an emergency."

When we look to professionals, we find nothing different. They too learn rules of skill to practice their professions. A surgeon who fails to follow the proper rules of skill in removing a tumor and so causes a patient's death, a lawyer who fails to file papers in a timely manner or, filing them, fails to fill them out in accord with the requirements, an engineer who miscalculates the stresses for a bridge—these are failures to follow the relevant rules of skill. We accept that professionals will make mistakes from time to time, and we generally withhold ethical judgment when they do. They are human, after all, but we do not withhold ethical judgment when they are negligent or careless or when they display a pattern of incompetence.

When we are learning the rules of skill of a profession, we are learning the standards for that profession, what those within a profession ought to do. That was the basis of our criticizing Ambrose as a historian. Presenting fiction as history, rather than the fiction it is, is deceptive, neither characteristic nor worthy of a historian. A historian is to discover what is true about the past and report it, carefully marking what is discovered with the appropriate caveats when the evidence is less than sterling. The very nature of the profession requires that historians tell the truth, as best as they can.

The standards of a profession clearly have ethical weight. If a surgeon is being sued by a patient, the first question the lawyer ought to ask is whether the surgeon used the standard procedure, the norm for that type of operation. If so, the lawyer can argue that the plaintiff is not suing the surgeon, but the entire profession since the surgeon did exactly what any surgeon would do. But if the surgeon says, "No, I tried something new to see if it would work," the lawyer has a much different kind of case. The standard procedure may not itself be ethical, but the surgeon who follows it is in a better position ethically than one who "tries something different." It is then not the surgeon, but the whole profession that is making a mistake.

That is certainly possible. There is no guarantee that what has become the standard practice or norm in a profession is the right thing to do. If there were, we would have had no changes in medical practice since the days of rebalancing the humors by bleeding to trepanning, drilling a hole in the skull, in order to increase blood flow and treat a variety of ailments. What is standard changes as we make medical discoveries, create new medicines, and improve our technology.

We will need to justify the relevant norm because appealing to it amounts to saying, "everyone does it." That is not an acceptable premise when we are trying to determine if something is ethical. If I am pulled over by a police officer for going 75 mph in a 55 mph zone, I will still get a ticket even if everyone does it and the officer could have stopped anyone in the vehicles whizzing by for the same offense. My being unlucky enough to be picked out does not provide me any cover.

We have focused on the standards society imposes on professionals, and professionals impose on themselves, but those are not fundamentally different from those we impose on each other every day. We certainly ought not to accept as an excuse for some unacceptable behavior that everyone does it. If the norm in a firm is that females, even if they are senior executives, get the coffee or a bottle of soda for the boss, that does not make it right.[46] Many a norm is wrong, and so appealing to a norm, the standard way of doing something, can at best be a first step in any assessment.

Even that first step can be problematic. Appealing to the norms of a profession is not as clear-cut as the Ambrose example may make it appear. The norms may themselves be contested by the very professionals who are supposed to act in accordance with them, and we would need first to assure ourselves that the norm is in fact clear and unambiguous and descriptive of the common practice. We would then need to look at the reasons for the practice before making a final judgment because it is not the norm that justifies what we are to do, but the reasons for the norm.

We can no more determine what professionals ought to do by citing a norm of the profession than we can determine what we ought to do in our ordinary lives by citing a commandment or some moral rule like "always tell the truth" or some supposedly commonsense judgment.[47] We will at least need the reasons for the relevance of that norm or commandment or rule in the situation in question and, as we shall see, usually a great deal more.

§8 Grounding Ethical Judgments

Ethical considerations enter into our lives when we can raise a question about justice, or causing unnecessary harm, or doing good, or our autonomy. We do not have an ethical problem if someone is doing something good. We might think the person could do more, but that is not much of a problem. We do not have an ethical problem if someone is acting fairly. We do have ethical problems when individuals are acting unjustly or unnecessarily curtailing our autonomy, and when they do, they are causing unnecessary harm. So we can concentrate our attention on what causes unnecessary harm.

That is a test we can use to identify an ethical problem. Our autonomy is curtailed all the time by our relations with others, for instance. We cannot just run through a crowd as though no one else were there, knocking people down and causing injury. An ethical problem occurs when our autonomy is unnecessarily curtailed, thereby causing unnecessary harm. Just so, an ethical problem occurs when we are treated unfairly, causing unnecessary harm.

So, in addition to having identified the objects of ethical concern—a person's character, knowledge, intention, action or inaction, and the consequences—we now have a response to the first of the three requirements we laid out for making ethical judgments:

1. We need to be able to recognize when an ethical judgment is appropriate. What about a situation occasions an ethical concern?
2. We need to understand the situation from the point of view of everyone involved and, like a judge trying a case, back off to view the situation objectively.
3. We need to justify any judgment we make. Do the facts support it? Do we have good reasons that justify it? Is our judgment backed by an ethical principle?

We can identify ethical problems by examining the harms of any act or inaction and seeing if any are unnecessary.

We would then need to back off and look at the situation from the points of view of everyone involved to ensure, in part, that we have properly identified the harms and which of those are unnecessary, if any.

That leaves us with the last requirement, justifying the judgment we make. It might seem that we have satisfied that requirement by appealing to norms and the standards, or codes of ethics, of professions. In criticizing Ambrose, I appealed to the Standards of Professional Conduct of the AHA, what is effectively a code of ethics for those in the profession. I also appealed to the norms, stated or unstated, of various professions as we examined cases, and we saw that the norms have ethical weight. A practitioner is ethically far better off to follow the standard practice of the profession than simply to decide, on the fly, what to cut and where and when in surgery, or how much support a girder needs, or what the legal requirements are for writing a will.

But neither the norms of a profession nor the norms of our regular lives justify what we do, and even if norms are embodied in a code of ethics, we gain nothing in terms of justifying what we decide. That is not to deny that the norms or a code have some ethical weight, but appealing to a norm or a code does not in itself justify anything.

Appealing to a code of ethics amounts to saying, "this is what my profession tells me I ought to do." We need to know if what your profession has codified is indeed what you ought to do. Appealing to a norm amounts to saying, "everyone does it." We need to know if they are ethical in doing it.

When we look at disputes in our ordinary lives and among professions, we will find that appeals to norms and codes of ethics are all too prevalent. Perhaps individuals believe such appeals are an easy and quick way of ending disputes. But such appeals no more justify ethical decisions than appealing to a belief that they do. Getting clear on why they fail will clear the way to seeing how to justify our ethical decisions.

4

Norms and Professional Codes of Ethics

It is all too common in our daily lives and in professions to appeal to a code of ethics or the "norm" to attempt to settle an ethical dispute. "This is how we do it here." Or "Follow the rules: they're on the wall." Such appeals have some ethical weight, putting whoever is not following the code or the norm on the defensive, having to explain what is wrong about what the code or norm says ought to be done and why what the person is doing is right. But it is not the code or a norm that settles the matter, and we need to be clear why before we can proceed to lay out the proper method of settling ethical disputes.

We can readily summarize the problems we will examine. Appealing to norms is simply appealing to what everyone does, and that everyone is doing what you are doing does not make what you are doing the right thing to do. Appealing to codes does not help either. They can embody and hide disputes within professions, glossing over what can be intense disagreements even about the purpose of the profession.

To an outsider, those within a profession seem of a kind: historians are historians, lawyers are lawyers, doctors are doctors. But to those within a profession, the nature of what it is to be a professional of a particular kind can be contested—with interesting ethical implications. It is a continuing disagreement in law whether lawyers should be hired guns, doing whatever needs to be done, even pushing against the law, to help their clients, or whether they are guardians of the law, with a higher obligation to justice. This kind of internecine dispute is a neglected aspect of professional ethics, but worth exploring because it is unclear how we can resolve such a dispute and because different conceptions of a profession have competing ethical implications. Indeed, competing conceptions of what it is to be a lawyer are founded on competing principles about what a lawyer ought to do. We thus cannot simply appeal to the norms of the profession because those are precisely what is in dispute. If a professional is of such-and-such a kind, a hired gun, say, then the professional is acting properly, ethically, to follow one set of norms, but if a professional is of another kind, then another set of norms becomes relevant.

So neither norms nor codes of ethics provide us with what we need to justify our ethical judgments, let alone help us understand them or provide leverage to assess them. They are not going to prepare us for the kinds of ethical challenges we will face in our lives or chosen profession or even allow us to recognize all the ethical issues we will face. There is a reason why every profession has a historical record of having adopted and then modified and modified yet again and again its original code of ethics. New ethical challenges surface, and problems that were thought to be addressed turn out to be more complicated than originally thought. It can be insightful to pick a profession and look at the history of its particular codes,[1] but however that history unfolded, we will find that none of the variants can provide the backing we need when making a judgment about an ethical problem in the profession.

§1 Norms and Professional Codes of Ethics

Professional codes of ethics are at best a guideline to what, at some particular time, those, or some of those, in a profession think the profession and members of the profession ought to do. Even if all those within a profession have reached enough of a consensus at a particular time to agree on a code of ethics, the requirement that a profession reach agreement about its code pushes its provisions toward an acceptable generality that is of little help in specific cases. The requirement that engineers hold paramount the safety of the public is so vague and general as to be unhelpful, for example. We cannot determine in any particular case what engineers are to do to fulfill it.

The I-35W Minnesota bridge that collapsed in 2008 killed thirteen and fell because of "a metal plate that was too thin to serve as a junction of several girders." It was apparently not strong enough even given the original weight of the bridge, but additional weight was added over the years "as workers installed concrete structures to separate eastbound and westbound lanes and made other changes, adding strain to the weak spot."[2] When that metal plate failed, the whole bridge collapsed because there was no redundancy. It is hard to imagine how appealing to the admonition to hold the safety of the public paramount would have helped the engineers determine what thickness of metal should be chosen for the plate or justify adding what would be needed to ensure redundancy.

Another example concerns the Citicorp Center in New York. Its wind braces had been bolted together rather than welded, as specified. The result was that a wind of no more than 80 mph hitting the walls at a 45° angle could topple it.[3] Once the problem was recognized, the structural engineer and his group immediately set to work to strengthen the building, but the code of ethics gives no guidance about how to proceed in such a situation. Should those in the building be warned? Those nearby who would be killed or injured if the building did topple? The only information given to the public was in a brief press release by Citicorp stating that new data showed that wind velocities might be slightly higher than when the building was designed in 1973 and that remedial measures were being taken.

The engineers, with the city's Department of Buildings, did much to ensure that if disaster did strike, help would be quickly on the way, and they put stress tapes at various places on the building to warn them in real time of any problems. But they also worked diligently to keep the real problem to themselves. Although the repair work went on for some time, no one in the building or the environs was the wiser to the seriousness of the problem even as a hurricane was making its way up the east coast. The hurricane veered off, the wind braces were strengthened, and no disaster struck.

A code of ethics that says engineers should hold paramount public safety gives no guidance about what to do in any specific case to ensure that the public is safe. The engineer and his group certainly did not look to a code of ethics for guidance. A code is generally too general in its admonitions to be of any use in determining how to resolve particular problems. That is only one of many problems with using codes of ethics to settle ethical questions within a profession.[4]

In addition, the norms of a profession are not all captured in a profession's code of ethics, and the reason is fairly obvious. A professional occupies a role, and roles carry with them ethical implications. This is as true of professionals as it is for any other person in a role. A parent is in a relation with a child, a relation that empowers and obligates the parent to act in certain ways and to refrain from acting in other ways. I once saw a mother loudly slap her baby and, when people turned, looking aghast, the mother said, "I'm her mother, and I can do whatever I want with her." A mother is not licensed to slap her child. That role constrains as well as empowers. The mother would certainly have been entitled to chastise her child, or try to calm her down—something we onlookers were not entitled to do although we could certainly chastise the mother, or try to calm her down.

There is no code of ethics for parents or for many of the other roles we take on in our lives. Just as parents have obligations to their children, for instance, children have obligations to their parents that make it appropriate for someone to say, "You ought to help her because, after all, she is your mother." The point to make about that "ought," a point we could make about the "ought not" regarding the mother slapping her child, is that

> the obligation to help is said to follow from the fact of social relationship. But the fact is not a mere fact; it is a fact of social relationship. And the fact of social relationship is one about people occupying roles vis-à-vis each other. The notion of a role has built into it a notion of some conduct as appropriate. It thus provides a bridge ... between factual statements about social situations and conclusions that something ought to be done in them.[5]

Roles imply norms. Some may be embodied in codes of ethics; many are not. We are all familiar with such norms. There is no code of ethics about how to be polite, but we learn early on to respond politely to a stranger who asks, "So how's it going?" and not to mention our devastating illness. When the Chair of the president's Council of Economic Advisers was asked about the long government shutdown that left many people having to work without pay, he said that it was actually a gift to the ones being furloughed since they could go on vacation without taking any vacation time. The Chair's remark is telling. The kindest reading is that he does not understand that without a paycheck, many of those furloughed may be unable to pay their rent or mortgages, let alone afford a vacation. But even so, as Paul Kruger remarked about the

Chair's response, "You don't have to be a public relations expert to know that you're supposed to express some sympathy, whether you feel it or not."[6]

Many of the norms of a profession are unstated, practitioners coming to an implicit understanding of what is acceptable and what is not for their profession as they come to be professionals. Physicians, for example, are trained to learn how to look at patients as mechanisms, as it were, like bicycles that have some failing or other or have been in some accident and are mangled. We want that objectivity from physicians. The last thing we would want is for our physicians to turn red with embarrassment upon seeing us undressed for an examination. But physicians must also relate to us as human beings, not as mechanisms, with a bedside manner quite at odds with the attitude of a bicycle mechanic telling us about what needs to be done to our bike to make it serviceable again.

It makes a moral difference, obviously, how our physicians treat us. If our physicians cannot see us as mechanisms subject to breakdown and breakage, they will not assess our condition properly and will not provide us with the medical care we need. But if our physicians cannot communicate to us, person to person, with the care and compassion we rightfully expect from a caregiver, we will properly feel objectified—not a patient, but an object for inspection. The necessary communication between physician and patient will suffer accordingly.

Neither of us may have brought to consciousness the implicit norm that regulates our relations to one another. But a failure can bring the norm to the fore instantly. If we heard that a physician at Kaiser Permanente Medical Center in Fremont had informed his patient that "he would die within a few days," we would not have expected to discover that the patient was informed via tele-video by the physician sitting in an office somewhere. The patient's granddaughter said a nurse told her that "a doctor would be making his rounds," and a nurse then wheeled in the video device.[7] The granddaughter was stunned to hear the physician, via the device, telling her grandfather, "I got these MRI results back and there's no lungs left, there's nothing to work with," going on to say that with "no lungs left [the] only option is comfort care, remove the mask helping him breathe and put him on a morphine drip until he dies"—apparently then affronting the patient even more in speaking past him to the nurse in the room. The physician did not have the courtesy to come to the room or, apparently, determine whether the man's wife of 58 years was there with him. Perhaps worse, when the patient's wife arrived and complained about the way in which her husband had been informed about his impending death, she was told "by a nurse 'this is our policy, this is how we do things.'" The hospital then added, in apparent justification of its policy, "The evening video tele-visit was a follow-up to earlier physician visits. It did not replace previous conversations with patient and family members and was not used in the delivery of the initial diagnosis"[8]—as though having a physician at the patient's bedside at some time was good enough to justify informing him he would "die within a few days" by tele-video. As his granddaughter said, "I could tell by the look on his face what that did to him."[9]

We do not expect our mechanic to ask us to come in to tell us, person-to-person, "Your transmission is shot, and there's nothing to work with." A phone call would do. But a physician telling a patient via tele-video? And the hospital having as a policy that patients are to be informed of their medical condition when facing death by a tele-video? Apart from the ethical problems arising from the hospital's having adopted such a policy, that policy cannot let the physician off from doing what he is obligated as a physician to do—see the patient in person to deliver such news and check to see if any member of the family is there to comfort him. We rightly expect a different sort of relation between a physician and a patient, particularly one about to die, and we would expect the physician to ignore whatever policy the hospital might have that would preclude, or justify, his not telling a patient in person of imminent death.

To take a less striking example, but one perhaps more frequent than the physician's callousness at Kaiser Permanente, we expect those health-care providers whom we have seen before for some period of time to remember the pertinent details of our health. I expected my optometrist to remember that, when she prescribed progressive lenses several years ago, I could not adjust, given all the reading I do. I thus expected her to remember that we ended up with different glasses for different functions—reading glasses, computer glasses, driving glasses. So I was taken aback when she prescribed progressive lenses yet again, telling me, yet again, that they have improved. When she did that, it fundamentally altered my understanding of our relationship, giving me ample reason to find a new optometrist, one who could remember me from appointment to appointment—or at least take notes of issues and check them out before seeing me for a new appointment.

Whether remembering a patient's health is explicit or implicit, it is a norm of significance. It makes a moral difference what kind of relation we have with our health-care practitioners and a practical difference as well since a failure impedes the kind of relation we need to communicate well with one another.

The norms that mark our relation range from the significant to the trivial. It is perfectly normal for my physician to wear a suit. It would be a trivial matter were he to see me without his suit coat. It would not be a trivial matter were he to wear only his skivvies or pick his nose during the examination. It would equally not be a trivial matter were he to prescribe medicine which I failed to take. It would be even worse were I to return, after not taking what was prescribed, complaining about the same problem again. A patient's role is marked by norms as much as a physician's.

Such norms need not be written out anywhere to have power to regulate behavior. Indeed, we need not even be aware that we are following a norm, and calling them norms is not to bless them. They may be ethically neutral, beneficial, or harmful. To call them norms is to make a factual claim: this is what those in that role ought to do. Whether what they do, or do not do, is right or not requires another enquiry.

There are many examples of such implicit norms. For instance, defense lawyers often agree to share information with opposing lawyers when they have a common interest. The agreement allows them to pool information without waiving their right to assert attorney–client privilege. The agreement is conditional, however, on their having a common interest. Manafort and his legal team had such an agreement with the White House during the Mueller investigation, but once Manafort agreed to cooperate with the Mueller investigation, their interests diverged. Manafort's lawyer, however, continued to provide information to the White House, passing on what Mueller and his group were asking Manafort and so giving them inside information they were not supposed to be privy to. Their interests became adverse once Manafort agreed to cooperate, and that is why the lawyer's continuing to share information with the White House was "shocking and unprecedented, a brazen violation of criminal defense norms," according to one criminal defense lawyer and former prosecutor.[10]

In contrast, when Flynn was questioned in the Mueller investigation, his lawyers upheld their agreement, informing the opposing counsel "that they were no longer in a position to share information under any sort of privilege." The counsel was "indignant and vocal in his disagreement," but Flynn's lawyers upheld the norm.[11]

When Manafort's lawyers failed to abide by that norm, they did nothing illegal, but the effect for them is that "no federal prosecutor will ever trust them again." That is a huge loss for a lawyer who is now far less likely to work on a case involving federal prosecutors. As for Manafort, he lost his chance for a reduced sentence, having breached his agreement with Mueller to be a cooperating witness. The only conclusions to draw are that Manafort was not honest in his agreement to cooperate, but was looking for a pardon, and that his lawyer was willing to risk a reputation as honest and trustworthy to further Manafort's quest.[12]

If someone disagrees and argues that Manafort's lawyer had an obligation to do whatever Manafort asked him to do, provided it was not illegal, we are not going to settle the matter by appealing to "a brazen violation of criminal defense norms." We are going to need a discussion of the reasons for having agreements among lawyers to share information and whether there are conditions imposed on such agreements that prohibit certain forms of behavior such as, for example, sharing information about third parties.

We might think that some professions are immune to such disputes and that we could appeal to their codes of ethics and norms to settle ethical problems. Surely, one wants to ask, accountants must all agree on the value of a company being audited, for instance, and actuaries must agree on what they value. It might seem as if they are just adding and subtracting. How could they disagree? And if we are surprised by those professions, surely historians are immune from such disputes. They are to tell the truth, as best they can, about the past. How could there be room for disagreement?

The point of picking accountants, actuaries, and historians is that these would seem among the professions most likely to agree on what they do and least likely to be subject to internal disputes that put into doubt any appeal to their norms or codes of ethics. As it turns out, they are riven by internal problems that preclude our settling anything involving those professions.

§2 Accountants and Actuaries

We turn to accountants to provide us with an objective evaluation of what a corporation, say, is worth. If we are interested in purchasing stock in the company, for instance, we want to know if the company is doing well or poorly.

Accountants assess the value of a company in accordance with GAAP, the Generally Accepted Accounting Principles. The advantages are obvious. There is a single standard, supposed to be used worldwide, that allows investors and governments to compare the financial health of whatever accountants are providing an accounting for. The standard is also objective because GAAP requires that the value of a piece of property, say, be the price at the last transaction—an objective measure of what someone was willing to pay for the property. We know that the value of a piece of property does not stay constant: its value can go up or down depending on all sorts of variables, for example, whether the economy is growing or not, whether some undesirable neighbors have moved in, whether the property is kept up, and so on. But using the selling price as GAAP requires ensures that accountants do not have to estimate what a piece of property would sell for were it now on the market. Estimates can vary enormously, depending on what variables someone takes to be relevant and on what judgment is made about how the property's future will play out. The last selling price is a real number stating exactly what a buyer was willing to pay.

But that selling price need not reflect the true value of the property. Suppose a company purchases a piece of property for a million dollars only to find that it is the site of a toxic dump that will cost millions to clean up. An accounting firm must, by GAAP, figure the value of the property as an asset of a million dollars, not by any estimate of what it would cost to clean up. The company could not give it away, that is, but would have to fork out the cost of the cleanup to get rid of it. The one million asset on the books would become a multimillion dollar liability. Since an objective evaluation in accordance with GAAP requires accountants to use the last selling price of a property as its value on the books, the company would appear to have an asset worth a million instead of being in the red by millions. GAAP forces accounting firms to give inaccurate evaluations.

Accounting firms have found this a less than trivial problem. They have been sued for failing to provide investors with the information they need to know about a company's real, that is, market value. Audits indicated the savings and loan institutions in the 1980s were solvent because accountants calculated the book value, but the books hid the losses from properties those institutions purchased at prices significantly higher, in many cases, than they were worth. The institutions just kept the properties on the books and so looked solvent when, had their real worth been audited, they would have been seen to be insolvent.[13] Ernst and Young had to pay $400 million in 1992 because it "had improperly audited federally insured banks and savings institutions that later failed."[14] Klynveld Peat Marwick Goerdeler (KPMG) had to pay $97 million to the state of Victoria, Australia, after being sued by the government for a 1988 audit of "the Tricontinental Group merchant bank [that] failed to disclose its problems"—liabilities that totaled $1.85 billion when it collapsed shortly after the audit and shortly after the state of Victoria had deposited millions in it based on KPMG's audit. KPMG's defense was that it followed GAAP, but following GAAP failed to disclose the bank's market value. The state of Victoria lost its money when the bank collapsed.

Courts effectively held that the accounting firms had failed to act in the public interest—"clients, credit grantors, governments, employers, investors, the business and financial community, and others who rely on the objectivity and integrity of certified public accountants to maintain the orderly functioning of commerce."[15] It is in the public's interest to know the true worth—the market value—of a corporation, say. Investors cannot make reasonable decisions about where to invest without that knowledge.

The tension within accounting is between providing objectivity through GAAP's requirement to use the last selling price for the value of an asset and acting in the public interest to give its market value. Accountants cannot do both because they are bound, as accountants, to use GAAP. We cannot appeal to its code of ethics to resolve the problem because its code embodies the tension.[16] We cannot settle any dispute about a company's worth because we cannot provide an objective answer to the question, "What's the company really worth right now?"

We have a similar problem between members of the American Academy of Actuaries (AAA). Public pension funds keep two sets of books—the official record and the market value. The official record is the one that those with pensions and those responsible for pensions see. The book for the market value is kept private.

The two sets of books can obviously differ since the former is determined by a projection of what the interest rates will be for the pension funds and the latter reflects the actual interest rate. Problems arise when the market value is significantly less than the stated "official" value. Carmel-by-the-Sea discovered that the market value of its pension fund was $48 million short of what it owed the city's retirees—a very unwelcome and unexpected surprise since the official value showed the debt to be a quarter of that. Having two sets of books, one "official" and the other the true, or market value,

> raises serious concerns that governments nationwide do not know the true condition of the pension funds they are responsible for. That exposes millions of people, including retired public workers, local taxpayers and municipal bond buyers—who are often retirees themselves—to risks they have no way of knowing about.[17]

A small pension fund in California showed "far more money than it needed" and so decided to convert to a 401(k) plan, only to discover that it owed "more than half a million dollars."[18] The fund knew the book value, but not the market value—which the pension system kept secret. Those in the pension fund faced a risk they did not know about—and had no way of finding out until it was too late to make an informed decision.

There are two sets of books because one, the official one, calculates the value of a public pension's funds at an average of "7.6% a year" while the market value is calculated at a "riskless rate, currently below 3%." If a portfolio were to accrue in value by 7.6 percent per year, it would not take too many years for its apparent worth to be far more than it would be were it to accrue in value by less than 3 percent. Funds calculated at the higher rate are still one "trillion short of the money they will need to fund pension credits that workers have already earned. But if pension systems were required to use a riskless rate, currently below 3%, the shortfall would soar to more than $3 trillion."[19]

Using an optimistic rate of return has consequences far beyond keeping everyone but those who manage the pensions in the dark. Jeremy Gold is one of the authors of a paper that was to be published by "a 14-year-old task force on pension financing" of the American Academy of Actuaries and the Society of Actuaries (the AAA and SOA). As he noted, "Consistent lowballing of pension costs over the past two decades has made it easy for elected officials and union representatives to agree on very valuable benefits, for very much smaller current pay concessions."[20]

The thesis of the paper Gold and others wrote was that "many state and local retirement systems calculate their obligations using overly optimistic future rates of return. The authors want states and municipalities to adopt new valuation standards that would make projecting the cost of future benefits more predictable."[21]

The task force was shut down by the AAA and SOA and denied permission to publish the paper. The paper was "a work product of the joint PFTF," they said, "intended to be published by the academy and the SOA as a jointly owned and copyrighted paper." But the paper will not be published or endorsed by either group, and,

> because the paper was the work of the joint task force, we do not think it would be appropriate for members of the task force, as individuals, to take the existing paper and simply publish it somewhere else. We recognize that some of the individuals who have been on the PFTF have their own personal ideas and views on these topics, and the academy and the SOA encourage those individuals to express those ideas in other forums. But they cannot use the existing paper, with the particular expressions of ideas as developed by the task force, as the vehicle to do so.[22]

An internal tension between how to calculate the value of pensions has thus split actuaries, some arguing that overly optimistic projections of the value of public pensions leave governments and those who are to get pensions ignorant of the real value of their pensions, others arguing, it appears, that optimistic projections are justified because "governments don't go out of business the way private companies do, … [they have] a much longer window to recover from bad investments."[23]

Whatever the cause of the tension, it has significant moral implications. We would rightly object on moral grounds were a pension fund to lie to those expecting pensions, telling them they would be paid in full, say, when the fund was about to go insolvent. Those expecting pensions would retire and discover that the money they expected to live on in retirement was not there, exposing them and those dependent upon them to poverty and all the attendant ills. But the public pension funds might as well be lying given the effects of its failure to disclose the true value of funds. The perception everyone would have rests upon what is made public, and what is made public is an optimistic projection of what the fund could be worth if it paid a high interest rate, rarely if ever achieved.

We can see the effects of such optimistic projections in various municipalities across the United States. Dallas has "a hidden pension debt of almost $7 billion," the result of a decision in 1993 by state lawmakers who "sweetened police and firefighter pensions beyond the wildest dreams of the typical Dallas resident. They added individual savings accounts, paying 8.5 percent interest per year, when workers reached the normal retirement age, then 50. The goal was to keep seasoned veterans on the force longer." The actuaries involved pointed out that the assumptions the legislature was making "were shaky." So they did their duty. The legislature did not, and the mayor of Dallas now says "his city appeared to be 'walking into the fan blades' of municipal bankruptcy."[24]

The problem regarding accountants with which we began this section is far more difficult to solve than this tension regarding pensions. We cannot figure out any easy— or even complex—way to solve the accounting problem. Accountants cannot obtain objectivity by guessing the worth of a piece of property were it to be sold, but when they appeal to the price at which it was obtained, they achieve a specious objectivity which does not reflect the current value. The value they provide is the value the property did have, not what it does have.

Accountants are not going to split into opposing factions because of this problem. It is internal to accounting itself: the norm for achieving objectivity, GAAP, guarantees that accountants will not obtain an accurate accounting of a company's current worth. So appealing to the norms of accounting is not going to help us or help accountants.

The dispute between actuaries cannot be settled by appealing to the profession's norms because what is at issue is what the norm for calculating the value of pensions ought to be. That the dispute runs deep is evidenced by the AAA and SOA not only refusing to endorse a report of its own task force, but also insisting that the authors are not to publish it on their own.

It is more than a little unfortunate that the split has such implications for the public's ability to exercise their autonomy in making informed decisions about the future— especially for those individuals whose life savings are tied up in pensions. Their being able to live with some comfort in their old age depends upon knowing how much has really been put aside and thus whether they need to save more.

The bottom line here, so to speak, is that the dispute among actuaries is causing great harm. That is an ethical problem, obviously, but to settle it we cannot appeal to their code of ethics. It obscures the dispute. So one profession we might think would be clearheaded about what it ought to do is not at all clearheaded, causing harm that catches people by surprise when they discover they have far less for retirement than they thought that would have and discover it far too late to do anything about it.

§3 Historians

We might well expect historians to have a code of ethics free from the sorts of tensions that affect actuaries and accountants. After all, historians can all agree, and we can all agree, that historians are to write the truth about the past, as best they can. We appealed to that truth in criticizing Ambrose. The discovery that he never met with President Eisenhower alone and only met with him and others once or twice, and for less than five hours in total, meant that his biography instantly lost all credibility as a work of history.

The judgment implicit in that loss of credibility rests on our universal agreement that historians are to tell the truth about the past. Thucydides begins his histories by saying, "To hear this history rehearsed, for that there be inserted in it no fables, shall be perhaps not delightful. But he that desires to look into the truth of things done, and which … may be done again, or at least their like, shall find enough herein to make him think it profitable."[25] By the seventeenth century, the understanding that historians are to tell the truth was so embedded in the profession and elsewhere that in his extensive dictionary Pierre Bayle could ask, rhetorically, after remarking that historians can upset their readers with the truth, "Does this free a historian from the obligation he is under of relating the truth with all possible exactness?"[26] As David Hume puts it, "The first page of Thucydides is, in my opinion, the commencement of real history. All preceding narrations are so intermixed with fable, that philosophers ought to abandon them to the embellishments of poets and orators."[27]

However historians may agree about the necessity of a historian's telling the truth, they are in disagreement, sometimes vehemently so, about what a historian must do to tell the truth. We might think this is a disagreement about alternative ways of articulating the truth, but the disagreement concerns what historians are after in writing history, what is the focus of their concern. That disagreement is sometimes put as one between historians being analytic rather than writing history as narrative. As one historian puts it:

> The gradual withering of the narrative impulse in favor of the analytical urge among professional academic historians has resulted in a virtual abdication of the oldest and most honored role of the historian, that of storyteller.[28]

So it is claimed that Gordon Wood, one of the most honored of contemporary historians, has changed "from being an academic to a more-popularly-oriented historian,"[29] a difference which marks a major dispute about how a historian ought to write in order to be a historian.

The Glorious Cause: The American Revolution, 1763–1789 is volume II of the *Oxford History of the United States*, and in his review of that work, by Robert Middlekauff, Wood is unsparing in his criticism of Middlekauff for not recognizing "that society and culture transcend the particular aims and purposes of individuals, that people make their social and intellectual history but are at the same time bound by what they have made." Middlekauff thus writes of the Revolutionary War, Wood observes, as though people "are free-acting autonomous moral agents whose motives and actions have clearly defined consequences." Personal blame and praise is thus appropriate, and what is left out are all the social and economic forces that would explain why, for instance, "revolutionary Americans suddenly broke from English constitutional practice and effectively barred the subsequent emergence of parliamentary cabinet government." Wood sums up this particular criticism by saying, "Middlekauff's account of the formation of the Constitution virtually sets back scholarship on the issue at least a century."[30]

This is from one famous historian about another famous historian and is an indication of the depth of disagreement about the very nature of history. This has been referred to as the "split in the American historical profession between traditional narrative and quantitative social science" and raises, obviously, both the hackles of its competitors and serious epistemological questions about how we are to come to knowledge of the past.[31]

This split is not just between historians who write narratives and those who wrote "historical monographs," as Wood puts it, but between those who think history is created by the great individuals in history—for example, George Washington—who make all the difference and those who think social and economic and other forces are what matter in historical change.

One obvious ethical implication is that a citizenry primed with the former view is all the more likely to take seriously some self-proclaimed "great man"—like Hitler or Mussolini—who says, "I am the only one who can fix it."[32] If social and economic and other forces are what matter for societal change, then appealing to a "great man" means ignoring the causal factors responsible for the troubles or the successes a society is having.

This split between historians is by no means the only one. Barbara W. Tuchman once wrote that she writes history "not 'to instruct but to tell a story.'"[33] Some historians think one point of writing history is to instruct and could argue that there is no way historians cannot instruct when writing history. We are all familiar with the claim, "Those who don't know history are doomed to repeat it." As Thucydides said, the reason we are to "look into the truth of things done" is that they or their like "may be done again," and we can learn from knowing what happened in the past how to avoid mistakes others have made.

It should be no surprise, however, to find historians criticizing books of history that are written "not merely to impart historical information but to teach moral and political lessons." Such books "reflect an assumption that they are to serve as what are now called 'modes of socialization', as sources of values, aspirations, and models to follow whose influence lasts far beyond childhood."[34]

The ethical implications of such a view are obvious—with different values being hawked depending upon the differing views of individual historians. A historian who thinks Elizabeth I of England by far its best monarch is teaching moral and political lessons far different from a historian who thinks Henry VIII, with all his faults, the best model to emulate.

We hardly need any other examples of the contested conceptions historians hold about how to write history, but here is one more. From 1865 to 1892, Francis Parkman wrote a seven-volume history of France and England in North America, and though it was lauded at the time, it fell out of favor because, among other things, his

> histories were dominated by his belief in the inevitability of progress, by his acceptance of the Great Man theory of historical change, and by an anticlericalism so strong as to affect his judgment of events at crucial moments.[35]

We see again the charge that a historian has adopted the "Great Man theory of historical change," but two new charges are added. One is that historians should not assume that events proceed inevitably toward progress. The other is that an anti-religious bias has affected Parkman's objectivity.

As Gordon Wood puts it, "That we historians are telling the truth is what distinguishes us from fiction writers."[36] But we now see that the seemingly universal agreement that telling the truth about the past is the role of historians—part of their role morality, what they ought to do as historians—obscures serious disputes about how historians are to tell the truth. These disputes are internal to the discipline in the sense that historians disagree with each other about what they ought to be doing as historians, but the disputes have significant consequences for the public.

Some of these are epistemic. When we discover that a famous historian like Stephen Ambrose lied about events so central to one of his major works, a lie that undercuts its historical value, we ought to be at least moderately chary of taking historians at their word. When we discover, in addition, that even they disagree about how to fulfill their overarching aim to tell the truth, we ought to wonder what we are to accept as historically accurate and what not. We outsiders have no way to judge these disputes or to determine how they affect what various historians write. So we have no way of knowing whether what we are reading has been shaped by a contested conception of history and so no way of knowing how to protect ourselves from any biases that have entered into what we are reading.

But a second set of consequences is of more immediate concern. The differing conceptions of how historians are to tell the truth about the past have ethical implications. They are not just different ways of approaching the past—as though we could read a multitude of books about the Civil War, say, and simply pull their narratives together into a single coherent whole. They are different ways of understanding the past—as object lessons for what we ought to avoid, as describing individuals who model how we ought to behave, as evidence for the inevitable progress of humankind and so a directive about how we ought to behave to further that progress, and so on. These different understandings of the past have different moral implications, giving us moral guidance of different sorts.

These disputes within history are not ethically neutral, that is, and in some cases at least rest on competing ethical principles about what a historian's role is. Wood is not just saying that Middlekauff fails to provide an adequate understanding of why our constitution ended up as it did. He is saying that Middlekauff's account is harmful, setting "back scholarship on the issue at least a century." That is a moral claim, based on the principle that historians are obligated to further the study of history, not undermine it through carelessness or negligence or a mistaken understanding of the nature of history.

The dispute, to repeat, is not about how to write history, as though the dispute were about the different ways historians have of telling the truth. That characterization of the dispute does not capture what is really at issue. As Wood's scathing critique of Middlekauff makes clear, he thinks Middlekauff has failed in his primary obligation as a historian to tell the truth. It is not as though Wood thinks that there are two different ways of being a historian, his and Middlekauff's. It is not as though he thinks there are different ways of arriving at the truth in history, that is, but that how one writes history determines whether one is writing the truth or not.

So history is riven by internal disputes about what a historian ought to do. When we looked at the Statement of Standards of Professional Conduct of the AHA in criticizing Ambrose, we saw that historians are to honor "the integrity of the historical record." That sufficed for calling out Ambrose as a historian. But, as we now can see, the phrase obscures a deep disagreement about what historians ought to do to tell the truth about the past. Does the Great Man theory honor the integrity of history? Must historians examine the social and economic forces to do that?

However plausible it may have been to think that history, of all professions, would have an unambiguous code of ethics about historians telling the truth about the past, we have discovered disputes among historians that give the lie to that. So we have yet another example of why we cannot appeal to codes of ethics to settle ethical problems. They themselves are ethically problematic, burying competing conceptions in general vague terms.

§4 Tensions within Professions

The split among historians, as with the split among actuaries, cannot be settled by appealing to the profession's norms. Those norms are just what are in question. Is it a feature of an actuary's role to provide an accounting of public pensions that reflects a realistic rate of return or one that reflects, on average, an unrealistic 7.6 percent rate of return? Despite that question having a rhetorical ring to it, its answer will depend upon actuaries coming to grips with what it is to be an actuary—what obligations an actuary has to the public and how those obligations are best fulfilled. The answer depends not upon a clear understanding of an actuary's role that we have at hand, but upon the results of a reasoned discussion within—and without—the profession about that role and an examination of the ethical implications of choosing one understanding of that role over another.

This sort of tension between actuaries and between historians can be found in many other professions. When DNA revolutionized biology, biologists trained in the old style found themselves marginalized. A biologist at the University of Wisconsin complained that he had been a professor of biology, but after DNA-savvy biologists came to dominate the department, he found himself relegated to a "field biologist"—a downgrading of his status, he thought, and a source of tension about the nature of biology.

There is also the dispute among lawyers as to their fundamental role in defending clients: should a lawyer be a hired gun, doing whatever can be done to defend a client, including, for instance, allowing a client to lie before a jury or judge, or should a lawyer hold the integrity of the legal process as more important?

Such a dispute about the role of lawyers obviously has ethical implications, and the dispute is grounded on either side on moral principle. If the presumption of innocence has any importance, it is argued, then surely the burden must be on the state to prove guilt beyond a shadow of a doubt—within the existing legal framework. As long as a lawyer does not break the law, anything goes in defending a client, it is claimed, because it is an ethical imperative that guilt must be proved. Otherwise innocent people may be convicted. On the other hand, it is argued, although the legal system is an instance of imperfect procedural justice, with some guilty being found innocent and some innocents found guilty, the integrity of the system depends upon the trust that no one is trying to game the system and that a defendant's lawyers are doing their best to prevent a proof of guilt—within the confines of the existing legal framework. They are not to bribe the judge or members of the jury or coerce any witnesses into recanting their testimony or making up new stories. Our trust in the integrity of the legal system depends upon our trust that members of the legal profession—the lawyers, the judges, the court stenographer—are doing what they ought to do to maintain and further that integrity.

Such a dispute about the role of lawyers comes to a head when a lawyer is told by the client of an intent to lie upon the witness stand. The lawyer ought to try to convince the client that lying is a mistake, that the prosecuting attorney is bound to catch the client out, and that the consequence will surely be a conviction when the jury becomes convinced the client is lying. But if the lawyer is unable to persuade the client, what ought a lawyer to do?

Lawyers disagree, some arguing that a lawyer has what amounts to an absolute obligation to defend a client even if the client lies under oath, others arguing that as an officer of the court a lawyer cannot let a client lie without telling the judge of the client's intent, effectively ensuring a mistrial since the attorney–client relationship has then been breached and teaching the client the lesson not to tell the attorney the next time. We cannot appeal to a legal norm to determine who is right because it is the norm that is in question.

We can conclude from such tensions within professions that

- disagreements about the nature of a profession are not ethically neutral:

  - They often rest on competing ethical principles about what a profession's role is.
  - Taking one contested view of a profession's role over another will change how we understand, and settle, particular ethical issues that arise within the profession.

- how these disputes are settled, if they are, is a matter of ethical concern not just to those within a profession, but to the public at large since no matter how they are settled, they will have a great impact on the public, with some settlements causing great harm.

The norms of a profession thus do not provide definitive answers to what those within a profession ought to do. As we saw with historians over their disagreements about how to write to tell the truth and with actuaries with what rate of return is reasonable to project, the norms can be contested. Such contests cannot be decided by appealing to what is itself being contested, the norms of the profession. Those contests must be determined on other grounds, the reasons for adopting one conception over another.

Whenever we have a serious ethical issue, that is, we must provide reasons for making whatever decision we make, reasons that presuppose an objective understanding of what is at issue and do not just appeal to a profession's norms. At the very least, if we make such an appeal, we must provide the reasons that explain why that appeal is relevant to the particular case in question. That minimal requirement is enough to justify the claim that appealing to a profession's norms is not, in and of itself, sufficient to justify an ethical decision.

Serious ethical issues generally involve cases where both sides in the case have what they take to be good ethical reasons for deciding in favor of their side rather than the other. Making an ethical judgment requires that we be objective and consider only the reasons for and against any one decision. If we are a party to the case, objectivity requires that we hoist ourselves out of our own position to put ourselves in the position of those on the other side who think themselves in the right, letting go of the passion that underlies our commitment to our side to see how others could be as passionate about theirs. We must then maintain that objective position to examine and assess the reasons each party, ourselves included, have for their side.

Although judges are not parties to the cases before them, they must immerse themselves far enough into the parties' positions to understand why they care enough about the issue to spend the time, the energy, and the money to go to court and risk losing it all. They are then obligated to be objective in examining and assessing the reasons each side has for its view so as to adjudicate between the two. Making ethical judgments in serious cases requires the same of us.

That is a high standard for any of us to meet. It means that we are to strive for objectivity in regard to any moral situation, an especially difficult task when we ourselves are a party to it, and that we must then consider, objectively, the reasons for and against deciding one way rather than another—an equally onerous task when we may be inclined to downplay those reasons that do not support our own position and difficult even when we are spectators only judging what ought to be done. It no more suffices to appeal to a code of ethics or to norms than to appeal to one's gut.[37]

5

Virgin Eyes: Seeing from Other Points of View

The only real voyage of discovery consists not in seeking new landscapes but in having new eyes. —*Marcel Proust*

The power of an ethical condemnation is so great that we have an ethical obligation to be cautious in coming to judgment. If we think someone has lied to us, it will change our relations, and if we publicly condemn the person, we change that person's relations to all who know of the condemnation and must now wonder if it is true.

We have other reasons for caution as well. As Kahneman has noted, we often make, and must make, judgments without stopping to think. We are thus open to our beliefs biasing those judgments without our being aware of it. This is all the more likely when we are a party to the situation in question. Self-interest can trick us into thinking we are seeing the situation with virgin eyes, as it were, when, instead, we see it through the lens of of our own biases and interests.[1]

But given the harms a false judgment can create, we have an obligation that our judgment be as objective as it can be, and one way to help ensure that objectivity is to understand as best we can how others view the situation. Getting into such a position is a complex undertaking, however, requiring a capacity for objective observation, an imagination both rich with possible explanations for behavior and yet constrained by the real possibilities of situations, a talent for reconstructing plausible arguments given the conclusions, and the ability both to step out of one's own position and to step into another's, seeing what may be an emotionally loaded situation from another's point of view. Indeed, this first step already requires a sophisticated moral stance.

§1 Basic Ethical Judgments

What we learn on the playground about how we ought to behave becomes so ingrained in most of us by the time we reach maturity that we unfortunately have no hesitation calling out as ethically wrong someone's cheating, or lying, or breaking a promise. Ethical cases involving these ethical basics do not seem difficult at all.

Sometimes they are not just as, sometimes, we have no problem judging those who continually do what is wrong. A person who lies and repeats the lie over and over even after evidence shows that what is said is false is a liar. That is a character trait few aspire to. A person who constantly bullies others and continues to bully after being called on it is a bully. That is another character trait few aspire to. We also can have no problem calling out unethical behavior when the behavior is so egregious there can be no excuse for it. Shoving an old lady down the stairs is one example.[2] Police officers kicking and beating a suspect who has surrendered is another.[3]

The ethical judgments we make regarding such matters are relatively unproblematic and do not require much on our part. Things can go wrong, of course. We might not have realized, on the playground, that John was given the toy to play with. We might not have seen the other child offer to let Mary go first. We may be upset at a friend breaking a promise to meet for dinner and then discover the friend stopped to help someone in an accident, a good reason that outweighs keeping the promise.

Even such basic judgments are always conditional, that is. They hold only if we have got the facts right, we have correctly perceived what is going on, and so on. They are no different in that regard than other judgments we normally make. We may think we have served someone pure Kona coffee when it is a blend, or we may mistake the name of the book we are recommending. But those considerations aside, the judgments themselves do not require any special skills or special knowledge on our part. We should note, however, two features such judgments must have that are demanded of any ethical judgments.

First, if need be, compelling reasons can be given for them. Parents on the playground do this all the time: "How would you like it if she did that to you?" "You know that's not fair." The parents are appealing to basic principles of justice. Behind such basic judgments as it is wrong to lie are reasons that justify them. We need not appeal to them or appeal to any reason at all provided only that they are there, ready to be invoked if necessary. We all have come to understand that lying is wrong unless there are weighty ethical reasons making a lie the ethically best option, and we all have at least some understanding of why it is wrong. So we do not need to provide the reasons every time we make such a judgment.

Second, these basic judgments are not to be biased in any way. One requirement for an ethical judgment is that it be objective, independent of whatever we may wish or desire and independent even of any beliefs we might have that could bias our judgment. You may think a parent overprotective who complains that your kid is being a bully—"My kid?!"—but when yet other parents come to you to complain that "yes, your child is a bully," you have good reason to get past your self-interested regard for your wonderful child and try to look at the kid from other points of view. Of course, it may be that they are all biased against your kid, and then we have a different kind of ethical problem. Their agreement does not make it true that your kid is a bully, that is, but when others involved make the same judgment, that is evidence that the judgment is not biased by anyone's self-interest. The aim, of course, is to try to ensure, as best we can, that our judgments are not simply a reflection of our self-interest.

The situation regarding bias is quite different when we are a party to what others may see as unethical. It is always a delicate matter when one is involved in an ethical problem to separate oneself from one's own self-interest and see the problem objectively or even from the point of view of anyone else involved. We are particularly ill-placed even to see what the problem is, let alone decide what we ought to do. We see it through our eyes, with our interests and our beliefs, and not through the eyes of others involved. So we may see the problem in one way while others see it in another, but we cannot hope to have a reasoned solution without an objective understanding of the problem.

The problem of trying to see a situation with virgin eyes is particularly complicated when the problem arises because of some structural feature so deeply embedded within a system that it never occurs to anyone within the system that it may be causing problems or when the problem arises because the very way in which someone is trained to look at a problem as a professional precludes seeing alternative ways of viewing it.

At a teaching hospital in Memphis, a physician was standing by an elderly woman's bed explaining to a number of interns, all male, what her problems were and how they ought to treat her. She was not wearing anything and had her robe pulled up above her breasts and her bedclothes pulled down to her knees while a physician and interns were discussing her case. She was unable to speak, but the entire time they were there, she was moving her right hand up and down, up and down. The group thought what they called her "twitching" was a puzzling neurological difficulty somehow connected with her condition and went on about their business. They failed to realize, or even see, that she was trying to pull her robe down to cover herself up, but, unable to do that, was trying to tell them what she wanted by moving her hand continually. They saw her as a case, a set of problems to be resolved. They failed to see her as a patient, an elderly woman who was embarrassed to have herself fully exposed to a group of men.

A psychologist was with the group and, after we all left the room, asked the interns (and the physician) if they had noticed anything. The psychologist suggested that the woman was trying to tell us in the only way she could, given her condition, that she wanted to be covered rather than have seven men standing around staring at her naked body. He then went back in and covered her and told us when he came out that she stopped "twitching" when he covered her. The physician and interns were looking at the patient as an object to be examined, not as a person who was embarrassed to be exposed like that. Indeed, the physician was effectively showing the interns how to look at her as a case rather than an elderly woman needing help.[4]

The former problem, where some structural feature is missed, is far more common than we might expect. The tie between lending institutions and home mortgages was broken when banks sold off their mortgages to be diced up and mixed with other loans to become collateralized debt obligations (CDOs). The professionals in the field, including the head of the Federal Reserve, said that CDOs would make for a less risky investing environment. But once the tie was broken between lending institutions and mortgages, those providing mortgages had no incentive to ensure that customers could pay since the risks of default would be transferred to companies holding CDOs. Indeed, perversely, those providing mortgages had an incentive to provide mortgages for as many individuals as possible since they gained a commission and took on no risk.[5]

It is difficult enough to take account of one's own viewpoint and somehow see a situation as others see it. It is all the more complicated when others within your profession, because of their training, are as blind as you to seeing the real problem—for example, the interns not seeing the embarrassment of an elderly woman at having her body exposed. And it is complicated even more, obviously, when the problem is a feature of the system within which everyone is operating. Although the medical group had not planned on examining the patient and so did not need to see her exposed, it was standard hospital procedure to prepare such patients ahead of time for inspection, as it were, by pulling down the bed covers and pulling up the gown. No one in the medical group thought to wonder why the patient was exposed in that way when there was no need for it—especially when ill patients can get chilled if rounds are slow.

So despite its being incumbent upon us—we are morally obligated—to understand as best we can how others view the situation if we are to position ourselves to make a proper moral judgment, we have the delicate task of disengaging ourselves from our immediate intuitive response and of then figuring out how others in the situation can respond as they have, attributing to them whatever must seem plausible to make their view reasonable to them. Completing such a task does not guarantee complete objectivity, but it is a first important step to get out of ourselves so we can make a fully objective judgment, one independent of our point of view.

The step is not morally neutral, that is, requiring, as it does, that we take a point of view other than our own, and it is not easy, requiring, among other things, that we construct plausibly attributable arguments that would justify, when that is possible, the acts or omissions of others in the situation.

I shall concentrate on this last requirement here—constructing plausible arguments—pulling out a part, but only a part, of what is necessary to understand someone else's point of view and recommending a procedure to tease out the beliefs and assumptions of the participants. I will consider a case involving what was our health-care system. It has the virtue of illustrating how we can be tempted into mistaken moral judgments unless we understand the point of view of others in the case in question.

§2 Stepping into Someone Else's Shoes

Few should doubt that our health-care system, a complex artifact of our own making, suffers and has suffered some terrible moral defects. Among its more appalling features was that self-insured companies were entitled, by law, to cut benefits for employees they insured after the employees became ill and needed the benefits they thought they paid for:

> Among the most striking cases in which employees found they had insurance in name only were those of Richard Owens in Atlanta and John McGann in Houston. After Mr. Owens began filing thousands of dollars in AIDS claims with his employer, a furniture chain called Storehouse, the company cut its maximum

lifetime benefit for AIDS to $25,000 from $1 million. Similarly, Mr. McGann's employer, H & H Music, a Texas retail group, reduced its $1 million maximum to $5,000 for AIDS cases.[6]

These changes were retroactive so that neither McGann nor Owens received the health care benefits they had paid for.

This feature of the health-care system may seem so strange as to be incomprehensible. An employee for such a self-insured company signs on to the employer's health insurance plan, pays into that plan on a regular basis without fail, and is covered for health problems throughout the years, but, then, when the employee falls desperately ill and especially needs the health insurance the plan was to provide, the company is entitled to say, "Yes, we know you were entitled to coverage for that condition, but that was only until you were in that condition. Now that you need the coverage, you no longer have it."

McGann and Owens found themselves in the morally disquieting position of being denied coverage for a condition they had every reason to believe was covered, having signed a contract for coverage and then done everything required to ensure continued coverage. The companies reneged on their contractual obligations.

If we put ourselves in the position McGann and Owens found themselves in, this is what we would know:

- We had a clear and unambiguous contact with our employer providing coverage in case of catastrophic illness.
- We fulfilled our contractual obligations, paying our premiums in a timely manner on a regular basis.
- We were covered in all previous instances where we needed health care.
- We received no prior warning that our coverage would be changed.

"Given all this," McGann and Owens would say, "we would reasonably believe our coverage would continue. Indeed, given what we know, it would be unreasonable not to believe our coverage would continue." So it would seem that McGann and Owens were justifiably upset in discovering that they did not have the coverage they reasonably believed they had.

We have come to that judgment by doing what we should always do when faced with an ethical problem:

> Construct an argument that has as its conclusion what the participants could reasonably believe that would explain or justify their behavior.

When we construct such an argument, we have three concerns: do the premises reasonably support the conclusion, are the premises themselves reasonable, and does the conclusion explain why the participants did what they did?

It would have been quite reasonable for McGann and Owens to believe they had coverage. That belief would explain why they were surprised that they did not have coverage and explain why they had done nothing to provide for themselves if the company coverage did not materialize.

Our concern here, it should be emphasized, is not what they actually believed. It is certainly highly likely that they believed they had coverage. But for us to construct an argument that makes sense in the context, we do not need to determine what they actually believed. They may have been so ill, or so taken aback, that they did not know what to believe after being denied coverage.

In constructing an argument that would explain or justify their behavior, we are not describing what was going on in their heads, that is, but what could have made their behavior reasonable. Why, for instance, did they not take out extra coverage in case the company reneged on the coverage it was to provide? Because they had no reason to believe the company would renege. No reasonable person, in such circumstances, would spend extra money for coverage they reasonably thought they would never need. We are not reconstructing their thought processes, but constructing for them an argument that would explain or justify what they did. Whether they thought of that argument is irrelevant to the question of whether good reasons can be provided for what they did.

One way of putting this is to ask what we would know if we put ourselves in their position, and in doing that we were effectively asking, "What would we believe if we were in their position?" In answering that question, we are solving one of the major problems we have in making any moral judgment. When involved in a moral problem, we need to ensure that we are not just believing and doing what is in our own self-interest, and in constructing an argument to show that the relevant belief was reasonable, we are determining whether the belief was one anyone in that position would share.

Constructing that argument gives us their perspective, an understanding of how they look at the situation. We are looking at the situation not through virgin eyes, but the eyes of McGann and Owens, but that is a crucial step towards achieving the objectivity we need to come to a moral judgment. In their eyes, they had coverage—whatever anyone else involved may believe.

§3 The Moral Situation

Seeing the situation through the eyes of McGann and Owens allows us to see just how unreasonable a position they found themselves in:

First, they had AIDS, an obviously unfortunate illness to have, and they then discovered that they had only limited coverage. They had an illness that was likely fatal and, to their surprise, no way to pay for the medical costs of treating the illness and its accompanying effects. So they were significantly harmed by the loss of coverage. We need not go into the details of the psychological and physical harms to understand that the worse that can happen after being diagnosed with an illness that is almost certainly fatal is to discover that you have no real access to the health-care system, the only system that can support you in any way.

Second, and morally worse, the companies led the employees to believe they would be covered in case of catastrophic illness. The employees and the companies agreed to the contracts, the language was clear and unambiguous, the employees paid their premiums, and the sudden loss of coverage occurred without any prior hint of a problem. In reneging on their agreement, the companies caused the employees great harm, but in leading them to believe they had coverage, the companies deceived and wronged the employees. And that is morally worse.

When we break a promise to someone, we may harm them or benefit them: what we do depends upon the effects of breaking the promise. But whether we harm or benefit them, we wrong them just by breaking the promise. Suppose someone lies to you, but things work out well anyway. The lie turns out not to have mattered much—at least to something other than your relationship with the person who lied. For that relationship has now changed. You now know that this person cannot be trusted not to lie to you. That is a harm that a wrong can produce—independently of whether the effects of the lie are beneficial or harmful. This is not to say that telling a lie or breaking a promise may not be justifiable. It may be the only way to prevent great harm, but it is still a wrong. It is far worse morally if the wrong produces great harm—as it did for McGann and Owens.

Third, to understand how unreasonable their situation was, we may ask why they did not obtain additional health insurance to supplement the insurance their companies provided. Why did they not seek catastrophic health insurance from another company—in case their company did not honor their contract? The company wronged them by giving them every indication that they did not need additional catastrophic insurance, but had they signed on for additional insurance, they could not have known they had obtained it. They would be in no better position regarding any company that provided such additional insurance than they were regarding their employers. What they would know about their new insurance would be no different than what they thought they knew about their company's insurance. Their epistemic position would be the same, and they still might not have catastrophic coverage.

So we now know the following about McGann and Owens:

- They reasonably believed they had coverage for catastrophic illness.
- They were wronged by the company's leading them to that belief.
- After they became ill, they were harmed by the company's cutting their coverage from one million to $5,000 and $25,000, respectively.
- There is nothing they could reasonably have done to avoid their situation.

If they could have done something and failed to do it, then we would hold them morally liable for at least some of what occurred to them. Some might argue that they could and should have avoided getting AIDS, but we do not know how they got it. They might have gotten it, say, through a blood transfusion. In any event, the ethical problem arises whatever fatal illness the two had—provided that curing them or caring for them was expensive. And we cannot hold them morally culpable in any way for not having catastrophic coverage. They were clearly harmed, and wronged, and so it would seem that the companies are morally liable.

§4 The Position of the Companies

As usual, however, things are more complicated than they may seem. If we look at matters from the point of view of the managers who made the decisions to cut coverage so dramatically, we discover that they have a story to tell that makes their actions far more reasonable—and ethical—than they may at first appear.

Each of the companies involved—Storehouse and H & H Music—was large enough that they were permitted by law to self-insure. But when faced with an employee's catastrophic illness, such self-insured companies can lack the necessary resources because their base is only as large as the number of their employees. Those managing the health-care system for such a company can thus face a moral dilemma when claims for a catastrophic illness are made. AIDS is so expensive to treat that paying in one case can bankrupt a relatively small system and so preclude coverage for anything else for everyone else in the system.

From a manager's point of view, that is, the moral problem looks far different than it does from the point of view of an employee denied coverage. I assume that the case looks different enough as to make us reconsider, if not ultimately reject, our initial judgment. We no longer have a simple moral judgment to make but a difficult moral dilemma to consider.

Taking the managers' point of view also makes clear how their hands seem tied morally by their companies having chosen to self-insure. It is not that managers simply chose, without more ado, to deny coverage to those who have AIDS, but that they chose to deny coverage to those who had AIDS because their only other choice, we may presume, was to deny even basic coverage to all the other employees. If we make the judgment that the employees were treated unethically, the managers get little sympathy, but if we look at the situation from their point of view, we can see that they face a difficult moral dilemma not of their own making.

We do not know why the companies self-insured. We should perhaps presume economic reasons, but health security for their employees may have been a motivating factor. Whatever the motivation, the law permitted self-insurance for companies whose pool of payees is insufficient to cover the costs of catastrophic illnesses. The companies, and the managers, were in a health-care system whose structure provoked moral dilemmas whose resolution would cause great harm no matter which option was chosen.

The design of that health-care system thus puts at odds competing moral imperatives, and it also makes rational for corporations involved in providing health-care what would strike us all as immoral behavior if it were not that it seems rational in a system that permits and encourages it. Taking the managers' points of view thus opens up for view the intellectual and moral incoherence of that health-care system.

§5 So What Ought to Be Done?

The managers have dilemmas created by the structure of the health-care system. Their dilemmas might seem easy: is the relevant manager at each company to honor the company's contract with the employee with AIDS or ensure that sufficient funding is available so that other employees have basic coverage?

This sort of dilemma might seem easy because it appears to be a choice between the one and the many. A calculation of how many are being harmed and how many benefited by providing and not providing coverage for the employee with AIDS would seem to show that the needs of the many outweigh the need of the one. In addition, at the time a diagnosis of AIDS was a death sentence: there was no known cure and no known way to slow down the disease. So honoring the company's contract would at best only ease the employee's path to the inevitable while leading to the loss of basic coverage for every other employee.

But this form of calculation assumes that all the harms are of the same sort, and it is, at least, not obvious that is true. If I promise a friend to do something, I have an obligation to keep my promise, and my friend has a right that I keep my promise. It may be that nothing much hangs on my keeping the promise or not, but even if there are no significant consequences to my breaking the promise, I still will have wronged my friend. The loss of my breaking my promise is significant: my friend and I no longer have the same relationship we had before. My friend can no longer trust me.

Breaking the promise is wrong, and it has, at a minimum, the bad effect of changing our relationship, but it is not wrong because it had that bad effect. It would be wrong even if my friend never realized that I broke my promise. It is a wrong in and of itself, intrinsic to the act of breaking a promise and wrong no matter what the extrinsic effects. If my friend told me a lie so the friend could benefit by my doing something I would otherwise not do, my friend would have used me, and I would feel used once I found out. My friend would have turned our relationship from one of mutual respect into one where I became an instrument to benefit the friend. It is difficult to imagine a friendship long surviving such treatment, but, again, the harm is not the loss of the relationship, but the one person not respecting but using the other.

A contract is a form of promise, with each party obligated to the other and so each party having a right vis-à-vis the other. The employer has a right that an employee pay for the health care to be received in case of illness or disability; the employee has a right that the employer pay for the health care coverage to be provided when it is needed. Breaking the contract is wrong independently of the consequences of breaking it.

So the form of dilemma the managers face is not one where we can just count up the benefits and losses to the one and the many and then let the obvious weight of the many determine the solution. The managers must instead choose between harming many and doing a wrong to the one employee. The solution is not so obvious as it would be were we simply counting benefits and losses.

But we have gotten this far without delving very deeply into the details of the case, and we are not going to be sure we can make the right moral judgment without a great deal more detail than we now have. For instance, could this be a false dilemma? Is there, that is, another course of action that we have somehow missed because the problem presented itself to us as a dilemma? We can get so caught up in false choices that we fail to realize that there are alternatives. Parents take advantage of this when they say to a child, "Would you like to brush your teeth before you take your bath or afterwards?" They are giving the child specious control since the presumption behind the choice is that the teeth will be brushed. I once was audited by the Internal Revenue Service (IRS) after receiving a year-long fellowship—which constituted a business trip and left me paying little in taxes. As I left the room after an interview where I was chided for not having a receipt for one night's stay at a motel, the agent said, "Wait! You didn't pay your social security tax!" I was startled, and he continued, "Either you were employed or self-employed, and either way you have to pay. The funding agency didn't pay your social security tax. So you are going to owe, well, big bucks." It took me four months of sleuthing to discover that as a fellow, I was neither an employee nor self-employed, but initially, I was caught up in what turned out to be a false dilemma imposed on me by the IRS agent. Since I was getting money monthly, how could I not be employed or self-employed?

One thing we would need to do to make a judgment in this AIDS case is to determine if there was an alternative source of funding that was being overlooked or, perhaps, a less expensive form of treatment that would significantly reduce the cost to other employees. We are asking, in effect, "Did the managers have no other option but to forgo basic health-care for the rest of the employees if they provided catastrophic coverage for their one employee?" We would also need to explore whether the employees were at fault for not having explored the size of the insurance pool in their company and determining for themselves, if they could, whether the company was or was not likely to renege on its coverage for catastrophic illness.

There may well be other details we would need to explore, but we have enough to see that we have gains in moral understanding from taking the points of view of the participants and losses if we do not. The lesson is obvious, I should think, but too often unheeded— particularly in cases to which we are a party and cannot make a proper moral judgment without trying to understand the issue from the points of view of others involved in the case. However hard we may try to understand a case from other points of view, we are still trying to understand it from within our point of view, and that insidious bias may well infect our judgment. Unfortunately, there are no virgin eyes and so none regarding morality. We thus ought to practice at least moderate skepticism about our moral judgments.

§6 Background Conditions

One feature of this case that deserves special emphasis is the background condition that created the original dilemma for the managers—that both companies involved were self-insured, with neither having enough employees to provide enough funding for what their policies had promised, coverage for catastrophic illness.

This background condition raises a variety of ethical issues. We may applaud the companies for providing health care for their employees, but we can certainly fault them for committing themselves to benefits such as catastrophic health insurance when their resource pool was insufficient to meet even one claim. We can criticize the government for permitting self-insured companies with such insufficient resources.

There is much, that is, about the background condition for this case that is ripe for examination and critique, but what I want to emphasize is that there is a background condition that created the problem the managers and employees had. Whenever we see an ethical problem, we need to ask not just about the details, but about the frame, as it were, it sits within.

We all live and work within frameworks that condition our options. In some countries drivers must stay in the right-hand lane, in others, in the left. In some countries, the citizens speak English, in others, other languages. We cannot expect someone in Ukraine to understand us when we ask, in English, "What's the best restaurant in town?" Asking is not one of our options any more than driving on the right-hand side of the road is an option in England or Japan.

When we play games with children, part of what we are doing is teaching them that their moves are constrained by the rules of the game. They cannot move pieces in Monopoly whenever they want to wherever they want, for instance. The rules of the game frame and constrain our choices.

These sorts of background conditions are relatively easy to understand and perceive because other options are relatively obvious. It is easy enough to understand that not everyone drives on the right-hand side of the road or that not everyone speaks English. But some background conditions can be so pervasive as to be hidden from us. We find it difficult to get outside the conditions to see them.

We can get a sense of this problem by looking at an assignment sometimes given to engineering students. They are to figure out how to make the delivery of grain from a grain elevator more efficient. As things are now arranged, they are told, the grain comes down a chute into a 100-pound grain sack when a worker pulls a lever opening the gate holding the grain back. The worker has to judge when to close the gate so as to fill the sack without wasting any grain. Once the sack is full, the worker sews the opening closed and then pulls the sack across the loading ramp to load it onto a truck that will deliver the grain to a farmer. The edge of the loading ramp is about 25 feet from where the sack is filled. The truck bed is about a half foot above the height of the ramp, making it easier to lift the sack into the truck.

How, they are asked, can things be arranged to make it a more efficient operation? The answers concentrate upon obvious inefficiencies within the system. "Why not have a timer or some other measure on the gate that closes it after 100 pounds of grain has passed through?" "What about using staples rather than sewing the top of the sack? That should be easier." "What about putting the sack on a small cart before it is loaded so the cart can be pulled to the truck?" "What about moving the chute so that sacks can be loaded next to the truck?" "Why can't the chute be flexible enough that the sacks can be filled while they are in the truck?" Each of these answers presupposes the existing framework—grain to be loaded onto sacks which are then to be loaded onto trucks to carry to farmers, who must then, of course, move the sacks to where they can be stored safe from wildlife and weather and then move them again as they are needed to feed the livestock.

The point of the exercise is to teach the engineering students to think outside the box. Asking how to make the system more efficient puts the students inside a box, hunting for ways to make the system better by moving things around, all within the box. Students oblige, as it turns out, but they should be asking, "What is the end result we are trying to achieve?" That question opens up possibilities that the question asked does not. If we focus on the end of getting grain to the farmers efficiently, and ignore the question we were asked, we could design a much more efficient system that would be far better in many ways. Suppose we were to load tanker trucks with grain directly from the silos, using a loading spout.[7] The trucks are designed to drop their load through an opening between the truck's frame that the driver operates with the push of a button. We convince farmers to allow us to build a ramp with a bridge in the middle and a storage unit that we supply under the bridge. The driver goes up the ramp, stops in the middle, makes sure the top of the storage unit is open, pushes the button, empties the grain into a weather- and wildlife-proof unit, and drives back to the elevator for another load. The farmer does not have to handle any bags at all, and neither does anyone at the elevator. There are enormous savings in labor and equipment, and the elevator now has steady customers who have agreed to have ramps built on their farms.

The engineering students are constrained by the question being asked and so limit their solutions to the conditions imposed by the question: what changes in the existing system would make things better? The form of the question traps them within a box, and to get out they have to come to see that they were trapped. It is a good exercise to get the students to ask about any engineering problem, "What is the ultimate goal?"

The exercise illustrates a truth about how structural features of the world constrain our choices and how difficult it can be even to recognize those features. We can be so embedded in them that it never occurs to us to try to pull ourselves out and examine them to understand how they constrain us. So McGann and Owens were trapped inside a health-care insurance system that precluded their getting the catastrophic health insurance they thought they had. It might not have helped them much to understand the constraints of the system since there was no guarantee that they would not run into the same problem with additional insurance, but being aware of how structural features of our situation can create ethical problems, as it did for McGann, Owens, and their managers, can help us focus on those features rather than fret about the details of the ethical problems the system creates.

The lesson is clear: whenever we face an ethical problem, we need to back off and ask ourselves what structural features of the situation have made the problem possible. We may well discover that we have no way of resolving an ethical problem without changing the background conditions—or we may discover that once we become aware of how the background conditions are affecting how we think about the problem and any resolution, we can jettison them and think about the problem anew.

6

Understanding Cases

Trying to understand a dispute can be like entering a foreign country, with different customs and a different language. That difficulty comes into focus best when we look at cases within professions. Each profession has its own specialized knowledge and rules of skill and its own vocabulary, and if we are to come to understand a case involving a profession, we must become familiar with what it requires of its practitioners to understand any ethical problem they may have. The problem is no different in kind from that we face in trying to understand any dispute.

For we each have our own histories, both enlightening and burdening us. Those histories allow us to see and understand what others do not and prevent us from seeing and understanding what others can see and understand. A biologist, for instance, can see in a petri dish what others of us do not see. A photographer may see how a certain light will affect a photograph when others of us can only shoot and hope.

Such enlightenment comes from being trained into a profession, and we are obviously burdened when we lack that training. We will miss technical details that require that training even to see, let alone understand their significance, and we may miss the big picture that training in a profession would allow us to see.

That is a reason for at least moderate skepticism about our capacities to understand, still less settle, ethical disputes within and about professions. Constructing arguments for the participants in a dispute to understand how they see it requires knowledge that those within the profession have come to have because they were trained into the profession. An outsider is thus at a disadvantage even to understand the nature of the dispute—to see it as each party to it sees it. An outsider has the advantage of not being invested in the outcome of the dispute, but is at an obvious disadvantage in making an objective and fair judgment about how it is to be resolved.

This is not a problem unique to professional ethics, but common to any enterprise that attempts both to understand another's point of view and then make an objective judgment. As David Hume put it, "When I am at a loss to understand the effects of one body upon another in any situation, I need only put them in that situation, and observe what results from it." What happens, we might ask, when one billiard ball hits another just so? "But," he continues,

> shou'd I endeavor to clear up after the same manner any doubt in moral
> philosophy, by placing myself in the same case with that which I consider, 'tis

evident this reflection and premeditation wou'd so disturb the operation of my natural principles, as must render it impossible to form any just conclusion from the phaenomenon.[1]

Or consider trying to understand our pets or our studying animal behavior in general. We need to "empathize with the species under study. We need to get under its skin, ... or as we would nowadays put it, try to enter its Umwelt,"[2] and yet be able to back off to make an objective judgment that is not biased by our being within our own skin. Ethnologists face the same problem. How does someone from England, say, become an expert on the French without becoming, as it were, French, able to pass for French among the French, and yet also keep enough critical distance to make objective judgments about their way of life?

This problem of an outsider getting inside the skin of a professional and yet being able to make judgments that are not biased by the outsider's own skin is universal, and the first problem we will consider is how our training, or lack of it, can get in the way of our understanding an ethical dispute within a profession. We shall then examine in detail how badly things can go wrong by considering Edward Tufte's brilliant but fatally flawed analysis of what the engineers at Morton-Thiokol ought to have presented to NASA the night before the Challenger launch.

§1 What Professionals Learn to See

When you drive through the Columbia Plateau in eastern Washington state, you will see some remarkable geological features—"dry waterfalls, canyons without rivers that might have carved them ... mounds of gravel as tall as skyscrapers, deep holds in the bedrock that would swallow entire city blocks, and countless oddly placed boulders."

In 1923 a geologist named Harley Bretz argued that the oddities of the landscape were the result of "a massive flood, perhaps the largest in the Earth's history—'a debacle which swept the Columbia Plateau', ripping soil and rock from the landscape, carving canyons and cataracts in a matter of days." The paper was received with derision by the leading geologists of the day, convinced that geological changes occur gradually and, no doubt, that an appeal to a great flood "solved" the problem by a deus ex machina. Bretz's thesis was confirmed in 1940 with the discovery in western Montana of "a swath of current ripples 30 to 50 feet high" that could only have been formed by "a massive flow of water."[3]

As Glenn Hodges puts it, in telling Bretz's story,

It takes practice to see the world as a geologist does. When I got my first glimpse of [what is called] the Channeled Scablands more than 20 years ago, I was struck by their strange beauty, by the ways rolling hills could suddenly yield to a landscape of rocky buttes. I had no explanation for the terrain, and I didn't need one—I had that primitive eye that looks at rocks and just sees rocks. But when I returned to the scablands with Bretz's story in mind, suddenly I was in an entirely different world.

Standing in the middle of a broad swath of scablands extending from horizon to horizon, my mind's eye could clearly see—the floodwaters blasting through, like a raging inland sea, ripping up everything not strong enough to stay moored.

It is not just technical details we can miss, but even the very nature of what is right in front of us—"what was once the largest waterfall in the world ... three miles wide and 400 feet high—ten times the size of Niagara Falls."[4]

Getting someone who is not a geologist to see what Bretz saw requires an education about how to explain geological formations, how to see them as more than rocks. It may take no more than reading about what is at issue, but even that can be a problem.

Here is a description from my local weather channel about more snow being expected after a fierce blizzard because, it says,

> the latest 00z blend of model quantitative precipitation forecast has come in higher than older runs on the northwest quadrant of the surface low where enhanced low level convergence will occur. BUFKIT profiles are showing there will be period near midday into the afternoon hours near and north of Syracuse where heavy snow will be possible with a nice crosshair signature.[5]

A trained meteorologist may well understand what an 00z blend is, what a BUFKIT is, and what "heavy snow ... with a nice crosshair signature" amounts to, even, perhaps, why some crosshair signatures are "nice" while others, presumably, are not. But most of us are clueless, and that we are clueless illustrates two different problems:

1. If we are to see things as a professional sees them, we must immerse ourselves at least somewhat in that profession—enough to understand to some extent the relevant terminology and rules of skill definitive of that profession.
2. If professionals want non-professionals to understand what they are saying, they need to explain matters in such a way that mere mortals can understand.

The ideal when we have a problem in professional ethics is to construct arguments for the parties to the problem that would explain or justify why they hold the competing views they do. But we can see from the meteorological example how difficult it can be to understand what the various parties are saying. The most obvious marker for the impediment we face is strange terminology that has a distinct home in a particular discipline—"crosshair signature," for instance. Professional terminology is like a code, needing to be deciphered, and we need to understand enough of the context within which it makes sense if we are to understand what it means to a professional.

The problem arises in every profession. In an obituary for Maryam Mirzakhani, who won the equivalent of a Nobel for her work in mathematics, we get this description: "Mirzakhani specialized in theoretical mathematics that read like a foreign language by those outside of mathematics: moduli spaces, Teichmüller theory, hyperbolic geometry, Ergodic theory and symplectic geometry."[6] Outsiders can run into such a linguistic morass in the very ordinary intercourse we have with physicians, for instance. When a physician tells you when you are suffering severe pain, "Your piriformis is compressing your sciatic," you know you need a further explanation. What is the piriformis? The sciatic? How does the one compress the other? Why is it doing that? The questions may seem endless to your physician, but their point is to allow you to immerse yourself deeply enough into the discipline to understand the problem. Was there something you did that caused it? People can experience severe headaches by sitting with their chin on their knuckles: the upward pressure is sufficient to push the jaw out of alignment and produce headaches. The solution is obvious. Something equally simple may be possible for your sciatic pain—or not. You want to understand the nature of your problem at least in part to see if you can change the causal conditions that gave rise to it.

Just so, you want to understand an ethical problem that arises within a profession, medicine, say, or engineering, so you can resolve it. We have to come to understand the problem as each of the parties to the problem understands it and then back off and see it as it ought to be seen. That is the ideal, and it is obviously difficult to achieve. Someone within the profession in which the problem arises brings a history to it that may make objectivity difficult to achieve, and those outside the profession must immerse themselves deeply enough into the profession to understand the problem— with no assurance that they have learned enough to understand it or, in learning enough, have thereby biased themselves to see the issue one way rather than another. If we accidentally immerse ourselves in history as practiced by the "great man" school, we may well miss what all the fuss is about when another historian complains about thinking about history in that way.

So we have grounds for skepticism about our capacities to understand and settle ethical disputes within any profession, and we have even more reason for skepticism when we consider the many other impediments to achieving objectivity. Besides not having the expertise we need to understand the details of some particular profession, we should all presume, as I have noted, that we have false beliefs that can bias the way we understand and see something. These may be beliefs we have because we took someone at their word or, for instance, beliefs we came to as children and have never had the occasion to question.

I remarked about one of my students believing he literally could not see PG-13 films and only discovering he was wrong when, at 10 years old, he told his friends when they were choosing what to see at a multiplex that there was no reason to go to a PG-13 movie since, as he said, "It's a PG-rated film. You can't see it." He was astonished when they opened the door, and he looked in. He could see it!

We may not have our beliefs proven false so dramatically, but in a world full of false claims, it is easy for us to pick up false beliefs. So even when we have what we consider some success in achieving objectivity, we cannot be sure we have jettisoned our histories and not somehow privileged our position or the position of others involved. That is the reason for being at least moderately skeptical of our ethical conclusions.

We are going to examine a mistaken ethical conclusion in §2 that turns on a failure to understand some technical details within engineering. That examination will illustrate two additional matters that relate to professional ethics.

First, how we present data can raise ethical issues. It seems all too common for those presenting data to think, "Data is data." We present what we have, and that is that. So the president of a company who presents a graph of earnings leaves it for those present to applaud or squirm, their value judgments showing in what they do. The president is just presenting the data, that is, and considering whether the earnings are good, mediocre, or bad is another matter that requires evaluation. On this common view, no value judgments enter into the presentation of data. A sharp line separates data from any value judgment, what is fact, that is, from what we think about the facts. But, as we shall see, presentations embody values and can have ethical implications.

Second, any presentation reflects back on the person presenting. When we see misspelled words in a PowerPoint, or read a badly mangled sentence, or hear an obviously mistaken inference, we cannot help but make a judgment about the person's intelligence, knowledge, and standards of care. We tell much about ourselves by how we present ourselves in our writing and speech and other modes of communication. A student who cites Dick Clark as the author of "Cogito, ergo sum" as much as says, "I did not read the selection from Descartes or pay attention in class." When someone spells "honor" as "honer" over and over again in tweets, we cannot help ourselves from making a judgment about the person's intelligence and education. In short, how we present our message is as much a display of us as of our message. We display our intelligence or lack of it, our knowledge or ignorance, our competence or incompetence.

How we present what we have to say or show is thus not a trivial matter. A lawyer who presents the facts of the case in a closing statement by lacing the presentation with expletives or by ranting at the judge will be judged by the jury, the judge, colleagues, and onlookers to have blotched the presentation—even if the facts are exactly right and organized in just the right way. We present ourselves in everything we do, and though the medium is not the message, it can certainly alter it so we fail to connect with our audience.

§2 Tufte and the Morton-Thiokol Engineers

Edward Tufte's work on information design has been called "a visual Strunk and White."[7] Its main thesis is that we can present information in different ways and that some forms of presentation are significantly better than others in conveying the information with maximum impact and understanding. The thesis is simple, but its genius is in its application and the presumption that if you are unable to present perspicuously what you are thinking, you are not thinking perspicuously.

The examples Tufte gives throughout his books are generally wonderful illustrations of how we can represent something—or can fail egregiously. In *Visual Explanations: Images and Quantities, Evidence and Narrative*, he asks what the engineers at Morton-Thiokol were thinking when they recommended not launching the Challenger the night before the launch. Tufte is effectively asking the question we ought always to ask when assessing what others do: "What did it look like from their point of view? What were they thinking?"[8]

NASA had asked for a teleconference to discuss whether it should scuttle the Challenger launch scheduled for the next morning. Overnight temperatures were expected to drop into the teens—18°F or so—and the Viton used in the O-ring joints was certified down to only 25°F. NASA's query was whether it was safe to launch after such an overnight low. Morton-Thiokol was the contractor for the booster rockets and had to approve a launch outside the range of certification. The managers at Morton-Thiokol approved the launch, but, Tufte argues, they did it because the engineers failed to present their data properly.

The overarching principle behind every presentation, Tufte argues, should be a commitment to "finding, telling, and showing the truth." If we think data is data, we might think we would honor that commitment by leaving out anything that might smack of a value judgment. But how data is presented already embodies value judgments. The engineers' charts and graphs illustrate quite clearly their judgments about what is important and what is not—and reflect poorly on their judgment.

As Tufte points out, the charts and graphs the engineers faxed to NASA were confused and confusing. One example will illustrate his point. Here is one of the charts the engineers faxed:

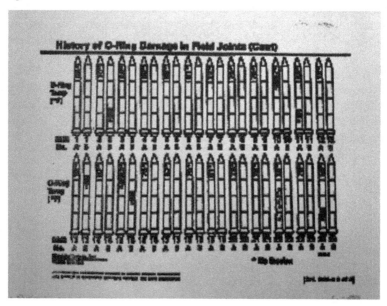

Figure 1. A Morton-Thiokol chart

This image of the chart is about as difficult to read as it would be when faxed, but that is only part of the problem. The chart would be difficult to read even if every single letter were crystal clear. The clutter is obvious, and the clutter prevents us from determining what we are supposed to see.

A powerful painting will direct our eyes to its main subject and usually do so in ways too subtle for us to notice. We just find ourselves looking at the painter's primary object of concern. All the elements in such a painting direct us to that object, and we can readily distinguish such a composition from those with clutter that impedes our focus and confuses us about what we are to see.

The chart Tufte examines is a classic example of how more is less. The detailed drawings of the rockets are not there to tell us about the rockets' details: they are simply place holders for the various launches. The problem of clutter would be clearer, perhaps, if instead of rockets, the chart had images of bicycles, for instance. We would ask, "Why bicycles?" And in seeing no good reason, we ought to see there is no good reason to have rockets. The drawings convey no information that is helpful in understanding whatever the engineers are trying to convey to NASA, but, instead, impede our understanding by diverting our attention from determining what they mean to say. The rest of the details in the chart are, again, so much clutter. Instead of directing us to what is the main object of concern, they prevent us from seeing what the main point might be.

The engineers made matters worse by providing many more charts and graphs, thirteen in total, making it unclear which chart was most important, if any, and which conveyed the information directly of concern, namely, the relationship between cold weather and the resiliency of the O-rings.

No wonder, Tufte claims, the engineers failed to persuade NASA not to launch. They recommended that shuttles not be launched when the temperature was below 53°F, the calculated temperature of the O-rings at the launch the previous January when significant erosion of the primary O-ring was observed. There are two O-rings between the sections of the booster rocket, the primary and secondary. If the primary should fail, the secondary is all that is left to prevent hot gases from continuing. The previous January, the primary O-ring had not sealed, and hot gases had blown by and significantly eroded the secondary O-ring. Had that O-ring been breached, the consequence would have been catastrophic. The engineers were concerned that the low temperature had diminished the resiliency of the Viton, but, as Tufte puts it, when we argue causally, "Variations in the cause must be explicitly and measurably linked to variations in the effect."[9] The engineers failed to chart the link.

What the engineers should have done, he claims, was provide a scatterplot correlating the temperature with O-ring damage. Such a chart would have convinced NASA not to launch. Here is the chart Tufte thinks the engineers ought to have presented:

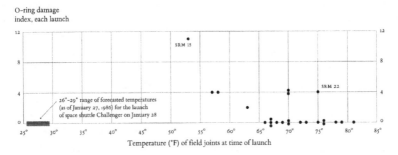

Figure 2. Tufte's chart

We can see the correlation between temperature and O-ring damage, Tufte claims, and as he puts it, "Clear and precise seeing becomes as one with clear and precise thinking."[10] Put negatively, we can say that "poor representation mirrors poor reasoning and encourages and sustains it."[11]

The power of Tufte's representation of the data becomes immediately clear if we consider the upward trend of what he calls O-ring damage as the temperature drops:

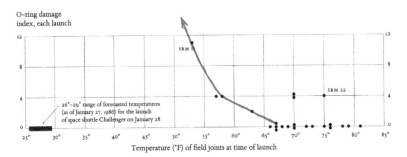

Figure 3. The ascending curve of risk

The ascending curve of risk is there for anyone to see. Because the projected range of launch temperature is on the chart and the amount of O-ring damage is not, we end up following the ascending curve in our imagination, wondering just how high on the O-ring damage index it will go. It is clearly off the chart—no doubt just the thought Tufte wants us to have. Rather than chart the obvious, he designed the chart to force us to realize that the potential O-ring damage would be enormous and that we have no way of knowing just how bad it would be—or, obviously, what its effects would be on the shuttle.

Tufte draws three conclusions from his analysis of the charts the engineers provided. The first was that, as he starkly puts it, "In designing those displays, the chartmakers didn't quite know what they were doing, and they were doing a lot of it."[12] They should have been trying to show a causal relation between falling temperatures and rising O-ring damage, but, Tufte argues, the "discrepancy between the intellectual tasks at hand and the images created to serve those tasks" was "scandalous."[13] So his first conclusion is that the engineers were incompetent at representing what they were trying to convey.

But Tufte thinks poor representation mirrors and encourages poor reasoning, and so, second, Tufte is also accusing the engineers of not thinking clearly—to a "scandalous" degree, as he says. It would be a leap to infer from someone's making a mistake, however scandalous, that they were incompetent. Even the best can make a mistake, but the leap is encouraged by Tufte's language. In saying that the engineers did not "quite know what they were doing" and did a lot of it, that it was more than just a casual mistake, Tufte is saying that their confusing charts reflect their confused thinking. He seems to be saying that none of their thinking was clear, a conclusion supported by their providing so many charts and none that correlated temperature and O-ring damage.

Third, and most important, Tufte says, "Had the correct scatterplot or data table been constructed, no one would have dared to risk the Challenger in such cold weather."[14] He is claiming that the engineers were responsible for the Challenger being launched and thus for the astronauts' deaths. Had they done the intellectually respectable job by providing NASA with Tufte's scatterplot, NASA would have seen how dangerous it would be to launch and not have risked it. By not presenting Tufte's chart or its equivalent, the engineers failed to prevent the launch—and so are responsible for the launch and the deaths.

Tufte thus makes three judgments about the Morton-Thiokol engineers: they failed to represent well what they were needed to convey to NASA; they were not thinking clearly; and they were ethically responsible for the Challenger disaster. Each of these three judgments is a result of the scatterplot Tufte offers. When we see the ascending curve of risk, we cannot help but wonder how the engineers could have failed to provide such a scatterplot. If they were trying to represent the relation between temperature and O-ring damage, why did they not do that, tying the two together so we could readily see how O-ring damage increased as temperatures dropped? The judgments Tufte draws leap out from his scatterplot. The engineers had such a simple task—which they so bungled that no one looking at their charts would be able to determine what they were trying to show, let alone see the purported correlation between increasing O-ring damage and declining temperatures.

So Tufte's chart is not value-neutral. It leads us to make value judgments about the engineers—about their representational and intellectual capacities and about the ethical implications of how they used those capacities to say what they needed to say.

I do not mean to criticize in saying that Tufte's chart is not value-neutral. We should instead presume that all representations embody values of some sort—about the best way to make one's point clear, if nothing else. The nice point about Tufte's chart is that it makes clear just how value-loaded a representation can be in presenting what would be accepted in engineering circles as "just data." We have no problem seeing some representations as bearing values. Political cartoons are full of images representing individuals as pigs, for instance. Data are no different in kind, I am arguing—however difficult it may be to see that regarding some data. The advantage of choosing Tufte's representation is that the value judgments are clearly a result of his scatterplot showing how the engineers ought to have presented their data. Tufte has presented his views about the mistakes made by the Morton-Thiokol engineers as clearly and concisely as, he claims, every presentation ought to be. But he has made several crucial mistakes in representing the engineers' position.

The first comes in how he describes the independent variable in his scatterplot, the temperature. He mixes together ambient air temperature and the temperature of the O-rings, apparently under the false belief that they were identical or that distinguishing them was not relevant. We can see this instantly by moving SRM 15, the flight from the previous January that had unexpected O-ring erosion, to where it would be if we were measuring only ambient air temperature. It was launched when the ambient air temperature was 64°F. The 53°F Tufte has for it on his scatterplot was the calculated temperature of the O-rings. SRM 15 had been out on the launch pad when the ambient air temperature was what was then described as a hundred-year low, and so the O-rings had become chilled. Roger Boisjoly happened to be the engineer responsible on that launch for being at Cape Kennedy and checking out the recovered booster rockets, and when he saw the O-ring erosion, he calculated the O-ring temperature.

If we move SRM 15 to the correct temperature at launch, we get this version of Tufte's scatterplot:

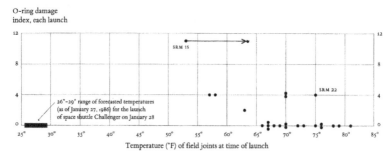

Figure 4. Correcting Tufte's chart

This scatterplot is still not right, however, since it describes the independent variable as "Temperature of field joints at time of launch." The engineers had only calculated the temperature of the field joints for two flights, SRM 15 and SRM 22. SRM 22 was a flight where the ambient air and field joint temperatures were identical, 75°F. There had been significant erosion on that flight as well.

We could no doubt retroactively determine the temperature of the field joints for those flights where the shuttles had been on the launch pad only during relatively stable weather so that we could safely say that the O-rings had not been chilled prior to launch. But Tufte did not do that. He assumed, I assume, that the O-ring temperatures corresponded in every case with the ambient air temperature. We know that temperature, but we cannot simply equate that temperature with the temperature of the field joints—as Tiufte does. The O-ring temperature may be hotter or colder depending upon how long the shuttle has been on the launch pad and, obviously, the temperature preceding the temperature when the shuttle was launched.

When we clarify what is being measured by the independent variable by changing everything to ambient air temperature, we get the following chart:

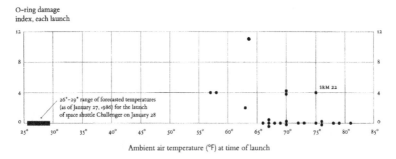

Figure 5. Ambient air temperature at time of launch

The first thing we ought to see from Tufte's corrected scatterplot is that the ascending curve of risk is gone. What the chart tells us is that there was a risk of what Tufte calls O-ring damage at any temperature of 64°F or below.

Had the Morton-Thiokol engineers presented this chart, it would certainly have failed to persuade NASA. The engineers had recommended to NASA not to launch below 53°F and were chastised for introducing a new and unreasonable launch criterion. The engineers were in fact retreating to their experiential base because they thought their experimental base inaccurate. They were saying that if NASA insisted on a launch, it should only launch within the experientially acceptable window. SRM 15 had experienced severe O-ring erosion at 53°F, an occurrence completely unexpected from the experimental data they had which showed no problem at all for the O-rings when the rockets had been tested. The rockets had been strapped down and fired on the ground, bouncing around and putting all kinds of unusual stresses on the joints without a single mishap. Those firings had occurred when the temperature was in the forties. So to have O-ring erosion at 53°F was shocking and put the engineers in doubt about their experimental data. That is why they retreated to their experiential data. Not knowing why O-ring erosion occurred at 53°F, they were cautious about recommending a launch outside the margin of safety—or, at least, moderate safety—provided by their experience with O-ring damage and temperatures.

There is another way to cleanse the independent variable in Tufte's scatterplot of its mixture of apples and oranges. We could mark just those flights where the engineers actually had information about the O-ring temperatures. We might expect such a chart to have marks at 53°F and 75°F, but the engineers had already determined that the O-rings in the SRM 22 flight at 75°F must not have been properly seated in the first place.

The O-rings are put in place in an isolation chamber, with negative pressure and those assembling the rocket segments wearing clothing designed to prevent any stray dust or dirt from getting on the O-rings, the grease which surrounds it, or the putty inside the rocket that covers and is to protect the joints. Even a small piece of hair may cause problems, and when the engineers examined the damage in the SRM 22 booster rocket, they determined that it was caused by something having gotten on the O-ring or in the grease and was not a fault of the basic design. So SRM 22 is properly put aside as not relevant to their concerns about the relation between O-ring temperature and damage.

A chart with the relevant O-ring temperature marked looks like this:

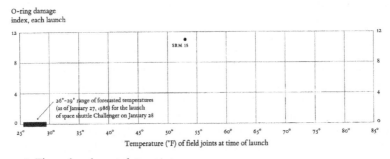

Figure 6. The only relevant data point

This chart has the wonderful advantage of directing our eyes to the only thing that matters, but, of course, it is not a scatterplot. It gives us one item of information. Tufte says that engineers' data was very thin.[15] This chart shows just how thin the data really is.

Yet even when we correct the independent variable so it shows only the calculated O-ring temperature, we do not have an accurate chart. What Tufte has marked as the dependent variable, O-ring damage, is as confused as his independent variable. He describes O-ring damage as "erosion, heating, and blow-by" and then references "soot" in explaining what he calls the Damage Score for one flight, apparently under the false belief that soot is on a par with erosion, heating, and blowby or identical to one of them.

Tufte combines erosion, heating, blowby, and soot as though they were all equally relevant to the problem the engineers had, but their only concern was with blowby of the primary O-ring producing erosion of the secondary O-ring. Soot? That occurs when there is erosion; it is a by-product. There is no reason to treat it as a separate problem from erosion. Heating? If the O-rings did not get hotter, that would be a surprise indeed. Heating itself was not a problem. What was a problem was heating sufficient to erode an O-ring.

In addition, Tufte's damage scores make no sense. He has SRM 22 with a score of 4 for two incidents of blowby. So one incident of blowby apparently equals 2 points. SRM 15 gets the highest score, 11, with three incidents of erosion and two of blowby. Two incidents of blowby apparently equal 4 points; so the three incidents of erosion must equal 7 points. But elsewhere in the chart one incident of erosion is given a score of 4. If there are three incidents of erosion, and you multiply that by 4, you get 12. Add 4 for the blowby, and you get 16, not 11, as the score for SRM 15. It is impossible, that is, for anyone to reproduce Tufte's chart accurately using the index he provides for measuring damage. It lacks the objectivity necessary for replication. We can perhaps understand this problem more fully by asking what damage score we would give a flight with three incidents of blowby and two of erosion. Three incidents of blowby equal 6 points, but what score do we give the two of erosion? Three incidents equal 7 at one point and one incident equals 4 at another. So what score are we to give two?

Indeed, none of the scores are helpful. What does a score of 4 tell us? Or a score of 2.33 (7 divided by 3)? Without some way of measuring the extent of erosion and the risk various incidents pose to the booster rocket's integrity, such numbers tell us nothing of value. Tufte has not provided us with any way of understanding the impact of the scores he provides to the risk of O-ring erosion. Tufte has done exactly what he accused the engineers of doing: he has failed to provide a scatterplot, or anything at all, mapping out the variables in what he calls damage with the scores he provides. That would need to be supplemented, of course, with an explanation for why each damage variable was given the score he provides for it.

In any event, the Damage Scores are not relevant. The only relevant variable—what should be the dependent variable—was blowby of the primary O-ring sufficient to erode the secondary O-ring. That occurred only in one relevant flight, SRM 15.

Tufte's scatterplot thus fails the test he sets: it fails to show what is true. Indeed, as he himself argued, mistaken representations not only fail to convince, but mislead us into making other errors. In providing a scatterplot, Tufte was led to confuse O-ring temperature with ambient air temperature and to jumble together, as though equally relevant, four different variables—soot, blowby, heat, and erosion—of very different significance. It would be bad enough to get the independent variable, the temperature, wrong. Confusing the O-ring temperature with the ambient air temperature obviously throws off the distribution of data points from what they would be were either O-ring temperature or ambient air temperature alone taken as the independent variable. But Tufte has not only mixed the two very different variables on the horizontal axis. He has also failed to isolate the one crucial variable for the vertical axis, blowby of the primary O-ring leading to erosion of the secondary O-ring, and instead has mixed in with it other variables that fail in "explicitly and measurably" linking "variations in the cause ... to variations in the effect."

Tufte's scatterplot has done exactly what he says mistaken representations will do: misdirect us and compound our mistakes. The Morton-Thikol engineers would have been intellectually incompetent and morally at fault to have used the scatterplot Tufte provides.

Tufte's failure is powered by at least two false beliefs:

- that soot, blowby, heat, and erosion are all of equal causal significance and
- that there is no causally relevant difference between the ambient air temperature and O-ring temperature.

Those two false beliefs power his scatterplot, and once we correct those beliefs, we end up with no scatterplot at all, only a single data point. Tufte is correct that the engineers failed to provide evidence of a causal link between O-ring erosion and temperature. But there is a good reason for that.

Tufte's analysis fails to take into account the history that the engineers, the managers at Morton-Thiokol, and NASA all shared. Tufte says at one point that history does not matter: "I'm not particularly interested in who did what first, or development. Because it is one damned thing after another."[16] But there are causal threads in history that can explain why we do what we do. These threads can be particularly relevant when we are judging someone's actions morally. In the Challenger case, history matters a great deal.

First, we would misunderstand what the engineers were doing if we failed to note that NASA was already well aware of the engineers' concerns about the relation of erosion and cold weather. NASA had agreed the previous August to a redesign of the booster rocket to obviate the problem, but had insisted on using up the existing rockets. The engineers were not telling NASA anything new with their various charts and graphs. They had already convinced NASA that cold weather posed a problem for the O-rings. That is why NASA agreed to a redesign. On the night before the Challenger launch, the engineers were simply reminding NASA of what they had said before.

Second, Tufte's scatterplot directs us to the engineers' supposed responsibility in the Challenger disaster. But the engineers did not make the final decision to approve the launch. That was made by the management at Morton-Thiokol over the strenuous objections of the engineers. The engineers were in fact excluded from taking part in that decision, and at one point, Boisjoly has said, he was pounding the table telling the managers to look at the photos of the erosion damage from SRM 15—all to no avail.

The managers knew what NASA and the engineers knew. They did not need to be convinced by any charts. They had already been convinced, but approved the launch anyway.

Tufte's chart points us at the wrong objects of concern. We should be concerned about why the managers at Morton-Thiokol decided as they did and especially why the VP for engineering, himself an engineer who had just before agreed with his fellow engineers not to recommend the launch, changed his mind and voted with his fellow managers—upon being told to take off his engineer's hat and put on his manager's hat. We should be concerned with why NASA insisted on pushing for a launch despite already having been convinced that the current design was problematic because of the impact of cold weather on the O-rings. As Tufte says, "'If the matter is an important one, then getting the displays of evidence right or wrong can possibly have momentous consequences."[17]

None of this would matter if Tufte's scatterplot were not so compelling. It is as powerfully conceived as a masterful painting, and because of its power, it has dominated discussions about the Challenger disaster and about determining responsibility.

It serves, however, as a powerful example of one thesis of this section: presentations are value-laden. Paradoxically, Tufte's scatterplot is ethically loaded in three ways:

- Taken at face value, it initiates judgments about the engineers' culpability. How could anyone have failed to see the incredible risk of launching the Challenger after seeing such a scatterplot? Failing to provide it was, on this view, an ethical failure, causing the death of the astronauts.
- It is itself ethically faulty. It purports to show the truth, but fails because, most obviously, both its independent and dependent variables mistakenly mix the proverbial apples and oranges. It also fails because its dependent variable not only mixes different variables, but misdirects us to what Tufte calls "O-ring damage" rather than to the crucial variable, blowby leading to erosion of the secondary O-ring.
- Because it is faulty, it misleads Tufte—and may mislead us—into blaming the engineers. A false accusation is itself an ethical fault.

It was surely not Tufte's intent to illustrate my thesis so well. His scatterplot leads us to make an ethical judgment and is itself mistaken, misdirecting us away from what ought to be our object of concern. It fails his own test, that is, of "finding, telling, and showing the truth" and illustrates how difficult it can be to get things right—even when we are only dealing with data. And it illustrates all too well how value-laden presentations of data can be.

The problems with Tufte's scatterplot do not affect his concerns about the various graphs and charts the engineers provided. They were ill-conceived, however effective they may have been in originally convincing NASA of the risks of cold temperature and O-ring erosion, and Tufte has properly criticized them. But providing a scatterplot with a single data point is no more help than simply insisting there be no launch below 53°F—as though it were enough to argue by analogy, as Tufte claims the engineers argued, that because they had erosion at an O-ring temperature of 53°F the previous

January, they will have erosion at the lower O-ring temperature the Challenger would certainly have if launched the next morning.

But the engineers were not arguing by analogy. Tufte claims that they did not know what they were doing, but that is not accurate either. They were in a quandary. There had been so many successful launches until the risk of catastrophic failure made its presence felt the previous January. As we saw, the erosion that occurred then was completely unexpected, and so they responded as good engineers should: they tried to figure out what had happened given that their experimental data with the engines being fired in temperatures in the forties was strong evidence it should not have happened.

Immediately after the discovery of erosion on an SRM 15 O-ring, Arnie Thompson tested the resilience of O-rings and discovered that the O-rings rebounded at 100°F, but failed to rebound for 2.4 seconds at 75°F and for more than ten minutes at 50°F.[18] These were shocking results. The tests showed that the O-rings would not fill the gap between the booster rockets created at launch even at 75°F—at temperatures, that is, where the O-rings had suffered no unexplained damage in previous launches.

The engineers were stunned. The tests showed that the O-rings were not working the way they thought they were working, that something else was at work to close the gap created by the movements of the booster rocket sections at launch. The tests also showed that the experimental data gathered from the test firing of the booster rockets was questionable: if it was not the O-rings rebounding that precluded erosion, what was it? The test firings gave no hint. The engineers asked for funding to determine what was really happening, but the management at Morton-Thiokol refused. So when they presented their findings to NASA in August after the January launch, they were effectively telling NASA that the O-rings were not doing what they thought they were doing and that they had no clear idea what was preventing blowby and the subsequent erosion—the putty which lined the inside of the joints? They just did not know.

So they were unable to present a chart showing the relation between erosion and temperature because their experiment showed that any data they gathered from the launches was untrustworthy. It is easy in retrospect to suggest a solution for how they should have proceeded the night before the launch. The engineers should have eschewed charts and simply restated their concern about the relationship between low temperature and erosion. That statement would simply say:

- We had the worst erosion ever experienced when the O-ring temperature was calculated at 53°F.
- That erosion was completely unexpected given the experimental results with the engines locked down and fired when the temperature was in the forties.
- After the unexpected erosion, we did tests on the resiliency of the O-rings at 100°F, 75°F, and 50°F and found that the O-rings failed at the latter two temperatures.
- That failure and the failure at 53°F makes us uncertain now about how the O-rings function in the joints and makes us question what has produced successful flights.
- We thus cannot trust our experimental data.
- We can only appeal to our experiential data, and that urges us not to launch below the temperature of the worst case of erosion we have experienced—53°F.

- Since a launch can be delayed until the O-rings are warmer, we see no need to risk a catastrophic failure.
- In any event, a launch below 40°F would breach launch criteria since the engines are not certified below that temperature.

If the first bullet points were unconvincing, the last should certainly have caused NASA pause. NASA criticized the engineers for introducing new launch criteria in recommending no launch below 53°F, but it did exactly that in launching Challenger below 40°F. It is difficult to understand what engineering reasons they could have for breaching accepted launch criteria.

It is a criticism of the engineers that NASA's query about the relation between temperature and erosion so focused their concerns that they failed to back off and ask whether other launch criteria would be met given the expected range of temperatures at launch. As I have noted before, it is a common ploy that we use with children to ask them a question that captures their attention so that they fail to see that they do not need to answer the question at all: "Do you want to drink some milk before you take a bit of your veggies or after?" NASA was not purposefully obfuscating the issues, but the engineers did fail to extract themselves from the parameters of the question that bracketed their thinking.

Unfortunately, it is with presentations as it is with other ethical issues: we must succeed "at the right times, with reference to the right objects, toward the right people, with the right motive, and in the right way."[19] We can go wrong in so many different ways, that is, that no rule or rules can determine how best to present our findings—to a particular audience, at a particular time, on a particular occasion, and in the right way. But we can minimize our mistakes by recognizing that however we decide to present our data, we are choosing a mode of presentation that is value-laden, and we should ensure that the values present or implied by that mode are those we can support.

§3 Moderate Skepticism

One lesson from examining Tufte's analysis of what the Morton-Thiokol engineers did the night before the Challenger launch is that you need to check what you think with some in the profession, preferably some not involved in the issue under examination. This is particularly so if you are an outsider, not a member of the profession and so not conversant with the relevant terminology and not trained in the relevant skills. As we have seen, it is easy to make mistakes. Tufte's mistakes illustrate just how difficult it can be for us to put ourselves in someone else's shoes, especially the shoes of a professional with the special knowledge and skills and ways of thinking that mark out that profession from others.

Tufte failed to check his analysis with anyone familiar with O-rings and the problems with the booster rocket design that necessitated their use. Roger Boisjoly or Bob Ebeling[20] or Arnie Thompson would have quickly pointed out to Tufte where he had gone wrong. He may have been hesitant to consult with them, given his claim about their moral culpability and their not thinking clearly, but other engineers not involved in the launch could have pointed out the obvious: that the ambient air temperature at time of launch is not necessarily the O-ring temperature at time of launch and that the crucial effect that concerned the engineers was the erosion of O-rings because of blowby, not Tufte's catch-all phrase, "O-ring damage."

One consequence of the sort of mistake Tufte made is that it gets picked up and becomes "gospel." This is particularly so when the mistake is so elegantly presented, but even when it is not, it can lead to a thorough muddling of the factual situation and to policy decisions that can cause great harm.

In a 2003 case, Smith v. Doe, Justice Kennedy wrote that the recidivism rate for sex offenders is "frightening and high," citing an earlier case, McCune v. Lile, where he claimed it "has been estimated to be as high as 80 percent." That figure "has appeared in more than 100 lower-court opinions, and it has helped justify laws that effectively banish registered sex offenders from many aspects of everyday life." But the figure comes from "an offhand and unsupported statement in a massmarket magazine," not from any research. The research supports a significantly lower percentage, but that 80 percent has taken on a life of its own and captured the attention of those setting policy.[21]

In an era of "alternative facts," we need to be careful that claims without any factual support are not taken as true, but, obviously, we are not experts in every field of human inquiry and do not have the time even if we were to check everything out. So we tend to give credence to experts—who must themselves be checked out. Not every supposed expert is an expert, and even experts can be mistaken—as can those touted as experts. In a report on Germany's success with solar energy, Fox Business reporter Shibani Joshi said, "They're a smaller country, and they've got lots of sun. Right? They've got a lot more sun than we do," adding that although California gets sun, "here on the East Coast, it's just not going to work."[22]

According to the US Department of Energy's National Renewable Energy Laboratory, Joshi is mistaken—and so mistaken that we must judge that she is no expert. Even "the sunniest part of Germany" gets less sun than "virtually the entirety of the continental United States." Alaska has "the lowest annual average of direct solar energy" in the United States, and "Germany's solar resource is akin to Alaska's."[23] So if you heard Joshi and did not check out what she said, you might end up with a false belief about the amount of sunshine in Germany, a false belief about why it has been so successful in producing solar energy, and, worse, a false belief about the viability of solar energy on the east coast of the United States. The Fox news anchors did not correct or question her, and so, presumably, they were as taken in as viewers might be.

Mistakes can take on a life of their own, especially in this digital age where a tweet can go round the world in a moment. Such wide and quick dissemination is particularly unfortunate when we have made a mistaken moral judgment. Corrections are not so widely disseminated, unfortunately, and a mistaken moral judgment can affect a person's life for the worse in all sort of ways.

So we need to be as careful as we can not to make mistakes. We should be equally careful about how we present what we know. We should think of a presentation as a solution to a design problem. What are we trying to accomplish, and what is the best way to do that? If we are conveying information, we will want our presentation to maximize clarity and minimize misunderstanding. If we are trying to convince someone of something, we will want our presentation, at the least, to leave a memorable and pleasant impression. If we are trying to mislead someone, we can do no better than President Nixon after losing the gubernatorial election in California. He was asked if he would run for president and said, "I will not run for any other office." The headlines had him saying that he was quitting politics, but what he meant was that he had made a mistake running for governor and would concentrate now on running for president. His answer to the reporter's question was ingeniously ambiguous, a nice solution for a politician, but clearly false in the sense in which he thought it would be taken.

That example is a sample of how a representation can be value-laden—both by being false on its natural reading in that context and by misleading us into an unwarranted assumption about Nixon's future plans. The example illustrates another point about presentations. They reflect back on the person giving the presentation. A professional can come off looking unprofessional in a variety of ways, but one sure way is through a blotched presentation. Nixon comes off looking decidedly political. Joshi comes off looking decidedly unprofessional.

So we need to check the claims of experts and supposed experts and check on our own even deeply-seated beliefs as well. The aim is to ground any judgment we make in the facts, and we surely want to ground moral judgments in the facts as best we can. The last thing we should do—if we are to be moral—is to judge someone as morally wrong, or morally right, when we have not got the facts right.

But as we saw with Tufte's mistake, getting them right is no simple task. We are like generals who want a bird's-eye view of a battlefield. They are disadvantaged in making the right choice just by being on one side, and they would be better off if they could see it as someone outside the battlefield saw it. Just so, someone within a particular discipline trained to look for particular kinds of problems—those relevant to the discipline—may well miss other features of the situation that turn out to be relevant. We are thus to look at a situation as best we can from within the boundaries of a profession, so as to understand its technical or specialized features, and from outside those boundaries, so as we can see any features a professional may have missed because they were not thought professionally relevant.

As I have argued, the aim is to construct arguments for the participants that would make sense of what they do or fail to do, and in trying to achieve this aim, we are subject to all the problems anyone has in hypothesizing what someone might give as the reasons for their behavior—when they might not have been thinking at all, let alone thinking through the reasons for behaving one way rather than another. The dangers are augmented when we construct an argument for a group of individuals who may never have put their thoughts to paper or even come to have shared their thoughts.

So the suggestion I am making about how to proceed to understand morally difficult cases is itself fraught with problems. But these are problems, I think, endemic to understanding anyone's acts or omissions, even one's own, and I take these problems as cautionary for particular cases, not as criticisms of the procedure itself.

7

Kinds of Ethical Problems

We now know that

1. We need to be able to recognize when an ethical judgment is appropriate. What about a situation occasions an ethical concern?

    - We have identified one way of recognizing when an ethical judgment is possible and necessary. We are to look for unnecessary harms.

2. We need to understand the situation from the point of view of everyone involved and, like a judge trying a case, back off to view the situation objectively.

    - But the ethical problems some face arise not because of anything they did or failed to do, but because of a systemic feature over which they have no control. The managers who denied health-care benefits to employees who had paid for them faced a terrible choice because of a faulty health-care system.

3. We need to justify any judgment we make. Do the facts support it? Do we have good reasons that justify it? Is our judgment backed by an ethical principle?

    - We cannot justify any ethical judgment we make by appealing to what we believe, no matter how deep our belief.
    - We cannot justify an ethical judgment just by appealing to codes of ethics or norms. Even in the case of Ambrose's lying, we provided reasons for historians telling the truth as best as they can, noting the unnecessary harms that occur when they do not.
    - To understand and, if we can, eventually resolve an ethical problem, we need to construct arguments for the participants that would make sense of what they did or failed to do.
    - One condition for constructing such arguments is to get a deep enough understanding of the situation to appreciate and assess the arguments those involved are making. Tufte's failure to understand the engineering data he was examining illustrates the problems that arise when we fail to get deeply enough into a situation to understand it fully.

When we are involved in a contentious ethical issue, we can easily get stuck and want to throw up our hands and say, "We just disagree"—as though there were no objective way to resolve ethical problems. But we ought to presume that however difficult an ethical problem may seem, we can settle it somehow and settle it ethically.

There are certainly impediments. We may not get deeply enough into a situation to understand it properly. Or our self-interest may blind us to a reasonable resolution. Or we may misidentify the kind of ethical problem we face. Not all ethical problems are the same, and the strategies we must use for one kind of ethical issue will fail for other kinds and mislead us in trying to understand and resolve them. In particular, the procedure we adopt for deciding what to do, our decision procedure, will vary as the sorts of ethical problems vary, and if we are not to make the wrong decision, we will need to be sure that, among other things, we have tailored our decision procedure to the kind of ethical problem we have.

§1 Kinds of Ethical Problems

It seems to have become standard practice for those examining ethical issues to refer to them as dilemmas—as though ethical dilemmas were the only kind of ethical problem there can be. The practice may stem from ethical issues requiring a decision between, as it is often put, what is right and what is wrong. But facing a choice between right and wrong is not facing an ethical dilemma. An ethical dilemma occurs when "a difficult choice has to be made between two courses of action, either of which entails transgressing a moral principle."[1] We face an ethical dilemma when we cannot, as it were, do right without doing wrong.

We looked at an ethical dilemma facing the managers of the two employees who were diagnosed with HIV. They could provide health-care coverage for those employees or for the rest of the employees in the companies. They could not do both, but doing either would harm those who would then not be covered.

We face dilemmas all the time in making ordinary decisions about everyday matters. We want another cup of coffee, but know it may upset our stomach. What should we do? We face the same kind of difficulty when we must choose between honoring an invitation and helping a frantic friend who calls just as we are leaving. In both cases we have dilemmas. That is one kind of problem we regularly face, and sometimes the dilemmas are moral—as in the case of McGann and Owens being denied health-care coverage. Sometimes dilemmas are easy to resolve and, obviously, sometimes not when the alternative courses of action are relatively balanced ethically so that it is difficult to find an ethical reason to favor one over the other.

But not all ethical problems are dilemmas. It is not even clear that dilemmas make up the bulk of the ethical problems we face. Problems that may present themselves as dilemmas often turn on other matters that will be missed and not resolved properly if the problems are treated as dilemmas. We need to distinguish what I call factually problematic and conceptually problematic ethical issues from dilemmas.

A factually problematic ethical issue occurs when the information on which we think we must base a decision is, well, problematic. We may know we are missing some data we need. Or we may have so much information that we cannot figure out how to sort it into what is relevant and what is not. Or we may suspect that some of what we have is false or at least not well-supported. Any of a number of problems may arise regarding our epistemic basket, if I may call it that, and any one of those problems ought to make us hesitate in making any judgment.

The worst case scenario occurs when we must make a judgment with a problematic epistemic basket, and that scenario occurs all too often. More, or better, information might make the answer obvious, but in the worst case scenario we must make a decision before we can know that we have all the information we need to justify a choice. We need only consider emergency medical decisions to find case after case where a particular judgment seemed reasonable, but turned out to be wrong given further information that came to light as the patient got worse and worse. Every flu season brings cases where a patient is mistakenly diagnosed. A 12-year-old girl diagnosed with the flu died of "cardiac arrest and septic shock after a bacterial infection … had somehow entered her bloodstream and quickly shut down her organs."[2] An Arizona woman diagnosed with the flu died of flesh-eating bacteria, caused by her eating raw oysters.[3] In both cases, the original symptoms were consistent with the flu, and since the flu was so prevalent at the time, the physicians presumably went with what seemed fairly certain at the time.

The point is not to question the decisions of the physicians, but to point out that they made decisions in factually problematic situations—whether they realized that or not. What becomes prominent in such situations is the procedure we adopt for deciding what to do in the face of uncertainty. Without knowing for sure what to do, are we to flip a coin? Choose the option with what appears the least worst outcome—or the best outcome even if the chances of a terrible outcome are increased?

In neither of the cases regarding the misdiagnosis of flu did the physicians order a blood test to ensure they had the correct diagnosis. They instead chose a decision procedure we are all familiar with, what is sometimes called the duck test: "If it looks like a duck, swims like a duck, and quacks like a duck, it's a duck." We make decisions on the basis of characteristics which provide strong, but not completely decisive evidence for the judgments we make. Without some compelling reason to treat a new case any differently from how we have treated others that display just the same characteristics, we move on to the next case—even though we know we might be mistaken. It is arguable, in fact, that we are always making decisions without knowing that we have full knowledge and are thus always open to second-guessing our choices. As we shall see, different decision procedures have their strengths and weaknesses, and the choice between them is an ethical choice.

We face a different kind of ethical problem when the issue is conceptually problematic. That sort of issue arises when we have a disagreement about, we may say, what something means. A lawyer is obligated to give due diligence, but a client may think that requires a set of actions significantly richer than the lawyer thinks is required. The facts are not in dispute: the lawyer and the client agree that the lawyer did whatever the lawyer did. Their disagreement is conceptual: what constitutes due diligence? The disagreement will not be settled by additional information about what the lawyer did. Such cases are to be distinguished from those in which the information we have is more than sufficient to justify a judgment: a lawyer who sleeps through a client's trial is not giving due diligence.[4] In conceptually problematic cases, the disagreement seems intractable: no agreement seems possible because the concept is so contested, with compelling reasons given for each of the opposing conceptions and with no relevant facts to tip the balance one way or the other.

We need to keep in mind these distinctions between different kinds of problems so that when we are trying to resolve a problem, we will look in the right places. When our problem is conceptual, piling on more facts will not help resolve it. When it is factually problematic, we need to pay careful attention to what decision procedure we choose since that will be primary. If we mistake the nature of the problem, we may cause harm by spinning our wheels or misdirecting our attention to what is irrelevant.

But when we look at cases that arise for professionals, we find that dilemmas and factually or conceptually problematic cases can enter into a professional's practice in two different ways, as something internal to the practice and something external. An external ethical problem arises most obviously when a professional wears two hats. An engineer may be told by a manager to do something that seems unprofessional, and the engineer then has an ethical problem, but it is not an ethical problem in engineering. It is an ethical problem that arises because the engineer is also an employee. The same sort of problem could readily arise for any other professional who is employed or in a partnership. Such problems are not internal to a profession.

An internal problem arises within a profession. An engineer makes ethical choices every time a design problem needs to be solved. How should we build a bridge over the Tacoma Narrows, for instance? That design problem led to a solution called Galloping Gertie, a bridge that acted like a wing and undulated up and down until its ultimate collapse in response to the winds that came into the Narrows.[5] How do we fasten three-ton sections of concrete to the ceiling of the Boston Tunnel? That problem led to the use of metal ties fastened with an epoxy that failed to hold, resulting in the death of a woman when the car she was riding in was crushed by concrete sections coming down.[6] Engineering design solutions have effects, that is, whatever they are, and so solving a design problem is an ethical as well as technical enterprise. When some of the effects produce unnecessary harms, we have an ethical problem.

There is yet a third feature of ethical problems we need to distinguish if we are to position ourselves to make a moral judgment. A person takes on different kinds of moral relations in becoming a professional, and the kind of moral relation or relations at issue in an ethical problem will make a difference to our understanding and the potential resolution of it.

A police officer, for instance, is empowered to make arrests and must use discretion when making a judgment about whom and how to arrest someone. When a plain clothed police officer tackled and then handcuffed the tennis star James Blake when he was "leaning against a pillar outside the Grand Hyatt Hotel" in New York, he was exercising his discretion—poorly, we should add. The officer mistook Blake for a suspect, but he failed to identify himself as an officer or to say anything to Blake. Without any warning, the officer roughed him up by charging him and forcing him to the ground to handcuff him.[7]

A poor exercise of discretion is a different kind of ethical problem than, say, a surgeon who refuses to operate on a patient on the morning of the scheduled operation. Having committed himself to operate on the patient, who had been prepped and prepared for the operation, including medication, the physician failed to fulfill his duty to the patient—and, of course, his obligations to the hospital and the rest of the staff.[8]

These two cases involve different ethical relations these professionals took on and require different sorts of responses. We will fail to understand an ethical situation correctly if we assume, as is often the case, that professionals only take on obligations, only differ from one another by the kind of obligations they incur, and only face ethical dilemmas.[9]

So we divide the moral problems professionals face in three ways. Some are internal to a profession, some external, and whether internal or external, problems arrive as dilemmas or as conceptually or factually problematic. Last, they can differ because of the different ethical relations at issue. We will find that we face the same array of ethical problems in our ordinary lives and need to take the same care in how we resolve them as professionals should. We will also find that, as with professionals, we face internal and external problems and enter into ethical relations as soon as we are born.

We will consider conceptually and factually problematic cases in this chapter, turn to the internal/external distinction in the next, and then lay out the different kinds of ethical relations a professional takes on.

§2 Factually Problematic Cases

We might think we should do an epistemological inventory as a first step when we face an ethical problem: what do we know and what we do need to know but do not know? Unfortunately, the state of our knowledge when faced with an ethical problem is always itself problematic. If we were to have asked McGann or Owens if they had health insurance, they should have responded with surprise: they knew they did, having paid for it all those years. They not only thought they knew; they had the best of reasons for thinking they knew.

We cannot know, facing any new ethical problem, whether we shall be surprised like they were, and any inventory can at best only be preliminary, subject to revision and correction as we proceed. We are faced with that problem in any event since we may well discover, as we proceed into a case, that what we thought we knew was relevant turns out not to matter or to be false, as with McGann and Owens, or that what never occurred to us as important turns out to be crucial. Untangling an ethical problem is like solving a mystery: we may not realize until we are far along in the process that what matters most is, as Sherlock Holmes discovered, the dog that did not bark in the night.[10]

We often face such epistemic shortfalls and in situations where we must make decisions when we would like more information, but cannot get it. We face these almost every day when we drive. The car ahead of us is going significantly slower than the speed limit permits and meanders, going slightly off both right and left. The driver could be texting, inebriated, falling asleep, drinking a Big Gulp, showing kids how not to drive—any of a number of things. The driver may be risk averse and afraid of having an accident. Or the driver may be working always to keep the car on track since unaligned wheels keep pulling it awry. We do not know and cannot find out in time to decide whether we should do anything. Pass quickly when we can to get around the slow poke? Honk to wake the driver up and risk road rage? Call the police to report the vehicle?

We will have done something even if we do nothing but stay behind the car, but we cannot know whether what we do is the right thing to do. If the driver needs help, we will not have helped. If the driver is a danger to others, we will not have mitigated the potential harm. In any event, we will have made a decision and thereby made use of some decision procedure in making it.

We are all familiar with decision procedures—flipping a coin, drawing straws, plucking petals from a daisy one by one. We also know, implicitly at least, that they are each conditioned, to be used, that is, only when certain conditions are satisfied. So if I steal your car, and you catch me with it, you would think me quite mad—or joking in some perverse way—if I offered to flip a coin for it, giving you a 50/50 chance of getting back what is yours. Flipping a coin is ethically wrong when you are flipping for something that belongs to someone else. My 5-year-old daughter quite rightly refused to settle a dispute between her and her brother about the ownership of a toy by asking me, in effect, "Why should I give him a chance to have what's mine?!" In brief, when the conditions appropriate for a decision procedure are not met, using it raises an ethical red flag.

So choosing the correct decision procedure to use in a situation where we have an epistemic shortfall is a choice with ethical implications. My daughter could have lost her toy had she agreed to flip for it—assuming she was right that it was hers. The difficulty, obviously, is determining what decision procedure to use where.

Unfortunately, there is no decision procedure to choose which decision procedure to use in any particular case. The two extremes seem obvious: when it does not much matter what is decided, almost any decision procedure will do, and when it matters enormously because making the wrong decision is likely to produce catastrophic results, great caution is called for. The cases in-between are the troublesome ones. We can get a better handle on those by considering a case where the professional should have gotten more information, but did not seek it and a case where the professionals involved had enough information, but did not use it.

The former case involves a social work agency whose mission was to provide counseling to those with low incomes and limited access to counseling. It had a long waiting list of individuals needing counseling, but was asked to provide substance abuse and mental health counseling for a number of local businesses. The businesses paid the agency for its services, and so the agency took them on, putting the employees of the businesses at the head of the line. The director of the agency said that they were treating everyone the same as before and asked what could be the harm if adding paying clients did not change the way anyone was being treated and provided the agency with more money. "Those who pay up-front get quick service, and those who cannot continue to wait, just like before."

Yet everything was not "just like before." The agency's treatment of low-income clients had become unjust in two different ways. Those waiting had to wait that much longer as "full-cost reimbursement" clients went ahead of them, and they were daily reminded, as they were not before, that they are second-class clients. In addition, the agency's mission no longer focused exclusively on the poor.[11]

Before we can assess the director's decision, we need to know a great deal that the director failed to find out before making a decision. How many paying clients would be coming to the agency? And so how much longer would those waiting have to wait—an extra hour? Or a day? Or two weeks? And how much money would be coming to the agency? Would it be enough to allow the agency to serve more low-income clients? Or serve them more quickly? Would the agency's taking on paying clients harm its chances of getting more public funding? Would its focusing less on low-income clients harm its chances of getting charitable contributions? Did the agency ask the businesses if their employees were willing to be added to the waiting list—or pay more for the privilege of being first in line? Or pay enough to cover one or more low-income clients?

We do not know the answers to these questions. The agency director did not ask them. So we have no way of knowing if the decision to accept paid clients was the right decision. Making clients who need counseling wait is not a good practice in any event. Some may need help quickly. Making them wait even longer is worse. So the gains from taking on paid clients who went to the front of the line would need to be significant enough to justify treating low-income clients worse than they were being treated. But without information about how taking on paying clients impacts low-income clients and the primary mission of the agency, we cannot know if the director's decision was justified—and neither can the director. The situation was factually problematic, and the director, a social work professional, should have gotten more information before making a decision.

We can contrast that sort of case with any of a number of mistaken decisions that various professionals made to create and then aggravate the Flint water crisis. At least one was made as though there was insufficient information.[12] When the city switched from Detroit water to water from the Flint River, federal law required that phosphate be added to the Flint River water. Flint's population was over a hundred thousand, and the law requires that addition for cities of that size and over. But the city did not follow the law. Instead, professionals at the Michigan Department of Environmental Quality (MDEQ) decided that the water should be tested twice over a twelve-month period to determine if it was dangerous. As the Flint Water Advisory Task Force's final report puts it,

> A critical element of that treatment—corrosion control, as required under EPA's Lead and Copper Rule (LCR)—was (incorrectly) determined by MDEQ not to be required immediately; instead, Flint could complete two 6-month monitoring periods and MDEQ would then determine whether corrosion control was necessary.

If we construct an argument to understand why the MDEQ decided to test the water over a twelve-month period, it would presumably look something like this:

1. We are not required by law to treat the water.
2. There is no reason to think the water is not fit to use.
3. Were we to require that the water be treated with phosphate, the Flint Water Plant would have to install expensive equipment.
4. Without knowing that untreated water would have harmful effects, there is no sense wasting money to treat the water.
5. Even a discovery six months in that the water was corrosive would not suffice to justify treating it because that test might be an outlier, not indicative of a persistent problem.

With such an argument, we can at least begin to understand why the MDEQ adopted the decision procedure it did, and we can also expose the two major false assumptions it made—in the first two premises. Without phosphate treatment, the water was so corrosive that it ate through the protective film on the city's water pipes, exposing citizens to lead. The corrosive effects were so bad that a GM plant was allowed to switch back to Detroit water because Flint River water was corroding machine parts. When Marc Edwards at Virginia Tech tested a sample sent to him by a Flint resident, he found that "the amount [of lead], 13,200 ppb, qualified the water as toxic waste."[13]

Anyone familiar with the Flint River should find it incredible that the residents of Flint were expected to drink it and use it to bathe, shower, and wash their dishes and clothes. The river is known to be polluted by industrial chemicals, sewage, and road salt, and you can see it is filthy, the river bottom hidden by the debris and trash and the films of oil and other pollutants. There were facts enough, that is, to justify a decision not to use the river water, but the MDEQ treated the situation as factually problematic and then adopted a decision procedure that ensured the most amount of harm to the residents if the water was corrosive.

A nice contrast with the decision procedure the department adopted can be found in the way fifty-six nations responded to the evidence that chlorofluorocarbons (CFCs) were depleting the ozone layer. The explanation for how CFC's chlorine atoms destroyed ozone molecules was still an open question in 1987 when the nations acted, but the correlation was high enough, and the danger great enough, that the nations signed the Montreal Protocol agreeing to cut CFC production and use in half, a cut they later made deeper. The danger was not just that the ozone layer would be depleted, but that if they waited to obtain more information about how CFC's worked to deplete it, it would be too late to reverse the rising curve of depletion. They risked making a mistake since it might have turned out that CFCs were not responsible, but the harm that decision would cause was small compared to the much greater harm if nothing was done.[14] In the face of the real possibility of great harm, the nations eschewed more research to minimize any harm that could occur.

What has happened since proved them prescient. We now understand how CFCs destroy ozone, and it has been reported that the upper ozone layer, at least, has recently stopped expanding. It is shrinking and healing.[15] But even if the Montreal Protocol had been a mistake, it was a prudent decision in the face of potentially great harm. We make such decisions all the time in our ordinary lives, as I have suggested, and although we may sometimes act too cautiously in the face of a harm that does not materialize, we would live very different lives if we were all high fliers, like Jack trading the family cow for supposedly magical beans. The likelihood of our always lucking out is close to nil, and knowing that, we are generally much more cautious than Jack.

The professionals at the MDEQ did not face a factually problematic situation, but the advantage of examining the case is that it illustrates all too clearly how choosing one decision procedure over another has ethical implications. It is wrong to cause unnecessary harm, but in treating the situation they faced as factually problematic, that is exactly what those at the MDEQ did in choosing to monitor the water for a year before acting. Their decision caused the harm they should have acted to prevent.

It may seem like the rational and reasonable response to any problem to fill our epistemological basket by gathering as much information as we can before we act, but delaying a decision until after gathering more information is itself a decision and requires reasons. When delaying can cause great harm, the harm acting immediately would cause had better be significantly greater. That was certainly not the case in Flint. The professionals in the MDEQ could have refused to permit the use of the Flint River water until it was treated properly. That would have been the right decision—ethically and legally—and the only harms were that Flint would have to renegotiate with Detroit to return to its original supply and pay for it as before.

Deciding to test over a twelve-month period was a mistake, but it was only one of many decisions, some of which could hardly be called mistakes since they were intentional and even more egregious. It is a measure of how egregious some of those decisions were that they led to indictments. An engineer at the MDEQ was charged "with misconduct in office for authorizing use of the Flint plant, 'knowing that the Flint water treatment plant was deficient in its ability to provide clean and safe drinking water.'" A district supervisor in the same department and the city's utilities manager were also charged, the three facing "a total of 13 charges, a mix of felonies and misdemeanors."[16]

What is most egregious is that the engineers and supervisors responsible for testing the water in the homes of Flint residents skewed the procedures and then fudged the results. They took samples only from a limited number of homes, most in new subdivisions that had newer water mains that were unlikely to contain lead, and, among other ways they skewed the procedures, they told residents to run their taps before taking a sample, guaranteeing a lower level of toxicity.[17] They then took out two samples whose disappearance just happened to ensure that the results fell below the level of toxicity that would require remedial action.[18] They treated the situation as factually problematic when it was not, and then they made it so.

It is difficult to convey how deeply unethical it is for those charged with discovering the facts to pervert the procedure for gathering them and then fudge the results when rigging the procedure fails to produce the result they want. That would be wrong in any case: we cannot make decisions to solve a problem if we do not know what the problem is. It is particularly egregious when professionals charged with gathering the necessary data purposefully undermine what they ought to be doing. They are the ones specially trained to test the water. They did not make a mistake. They purposefully ensured that those charged with making decisions had false information.

They might as well have fabricated the "data" out of whole cloth. They would not be the only professionals to do that. An anesthesiologist at Baystate Medical Center, Dr. Scott S. Reuben, published a slew of articles on the proper treatment for postoperative pain. He owned the field, as it were, with his articles citing trials that supposedly proved beyond a doubt that patients should have "aspirinlike drugs and neuropathic pain medicines after surgery." The Pfizer drugs Celebrex and Lyrica were the recommended choices, and it turned out to be no coincidence that Pfizer funded his supposed research. He had performed none of the clinical trials he referred to in his research, having made them up. "Baystate investigators determined that Dr. Reuben had concocted data for 21 studies, and the health system asked the journals in which those studies were published to withdraw them."[19]

What he did was wrong in and of itself, but he also caused great harm. First, his extensive publications, supposedly backed by so many clinical trials, dissuaded others from doing research in the area. Research was thus set back at least a decade, from the date of his first publication in 1996 to 2008 when Bayside made its determination. Why would anyone waste their research time investigating a problem that had already been solved? Second, the revelation that he had concocted data and that reputable journals had accepted his articles, stating findings supposedly based on that data, creates distrust of the journals and, unfortunately, research itself. If those charged with vetting articles for publication cannot discover that the research was concocted, certainly those who rely on the articles for advice about how to treat patients, for instance, cannot be expected to discover that. They ought to have at least some hesitation trusting what they read in those journals in the future and wonder if the same problem does not occur in other journals.

Third, he misled all the physicians who prescribed the Pfizer drugs to their postoperative patients. Those physicians thought they were prescribing the best drugs available, but no one could know that. And, fourth, he may have caused harm to those patients, for all he could know. They were getting drugs that may not have been as effective as other drugs they could have received. Dr. Reuben thus set back research, sowed distrust of supposedly vetted articles, misled physicians, and may well have caused postoperative patients unnecessary pain.

Faking data is not only intrinsically wrong, that is, but extrinsically harmful as well, causing injury not only to individuals, but to the institutions upon which we all depend—local governments and agencies charged with providing us with clean water, for instance, government agencies responsible for ensuring that our water is safe, research scientists whom we trust to provide us with discoveries about how best to care for ourselves and our planet, and the scientific process itself, which depends upon trust between researchers that findings in reputable publications have been properly vetted.

With that in mind, and the examples provided, we can understand why our knowledge when faced with an ethical problem is itself always problematic or, at the least, should be presumed so. That ought to provide the drive to ensure that our data is as accurate as possible and also makes it clear why the choice of a decision procedure is the most ethically significant step in resolving the problem or precluding its recurrence.

That leaves unsettled the matter of what decision procedure to use when faced with any factually problematic case, but, to emphasize the point, there is no decision procedure for determining which decision procedure to use when. We have learned that we ought always presume we are in a position of uncertainty—with uncertainty about how much uncertainty we face.[20]

But as we know from the sort of research Daniel Kahneman has done, we all tend to be more certain of what we think we know than we have any right to be and make all sorts of simple mistakes in reasoning that lead us astray.[21] "We hear that the price of something rose by 50 percent and then fell by 50 percent, and we reflexively, mistakenly conclude, 'Oh good, we're back to where we started.'"[22] The gambler's fallacy, false dilemma, the slippery slope—the list is long, but each fallacy marks a way in which we make mistakes in reasoning.

Of particular concern here is that we are overconfident. We tend to have more confidence than we are entitled to,[23] and when we are in a position of uncertainty with uncertainty about how much uncertainty we face, such overconfidence can lead to harmful mistakes. When a frog wanted to get across the river and a scorpion offered to give it a ride, it asked if the scorpion would sting it. The scorpion said no, but then, midway across, stung him. When the dying frog asked why, the scorpion said, "I could not help myself. It is my nature."[24] The frog had more confidence in its ability to read the scorpion than it was entitled to. Let that be a lesson for all of us as we face factually problematic ethical issues.

§3 Conceptually Problematic Cases

When people argue about who is the best baseball player or whether an Akane apple is better than a Kidd's Orange Red, they might be arguing about something that could be settled by more information. "He hit .327 in his final season?! I didn't realize that." But often additional information does not seem to help. What may be at issue is what each considers "the best," and their understandings of that may so differ that agreement becomes impossible.

If someone considers batting more essential in baseball than fielding, a strong hitter will rise to the top above a great fielder, and the dispute about who is best will turn not on facts about batting and fielding, but about the standards for determining what makes baseball better—better fielding or better batting or something else entirely.

We find such disputes almost everywhere. Akane apples have a strawberry and raspberry taste and, like the Kidd's Orange Red, are sweet and aromatic with a bit of a bite to the taste. The Kidd's Orange Red, however, has a honeyed flavor and is heavily scented. Which is better? It is easy to say that it is just a matter of taste, but judges in country fairs must make a decision about which is best—think here of the Westminster dog show and which dog is, well, top dog—and what will matter in any disagreement are competing conceptions of the best apple, or best dog.

The disagreement will not be settled by any additional information. "Take another bite. Isn't that just the best?" There is no obvious way of resolving disputes where what is at issue is the standard for what constitutes the best.

That is the problem with disputes within the professions about what constitutes due care, or due diligence, or anything else that involves what it is for a professional to have done a proper job.

> "Didn't your agent check on whether there were liens on the property?" "That's the seller's obligation."[25]
>
> "Wasn't the clerk aware of the new form needed to make the divorce legally valid?" "It's the legislature that's at fault for not requiring that the new forms be printed."
>
> "Why would your physician prescribe Risperdal for your son's hyperactivity? Despite what Johnson & Johnson says, it is not supposed to be used for children." "But it's advertised for them, and I've had good success prescribing it."[26]

Each of these situations seems to involve competing conceptions of what it is for a professional to do a proper job. At least that is the starting point. A discussion may help clarify the disputes, but the dispute about what constitutes a professional's responsibility may well remain unsettled, with different professionals using different conceptions of what they are to do as professionals.

We should not confuse conceptual misunderstandings with cases that are conceptually problematic. An acquaintance found herself in the middle of a dispute between engineers arguing about whether what they had installed was transparent or not. One group thought it obvious that it was and was taken aback by the other group, who said it was not. "How can it not be transparent?! It's right there!!" "That's the problem!"—and you can hear in the last remark the "What? Are you an idiot?!" It turned out that they were working with different conceptions of transparency. For the one group, something was transparent if you could see it; for the other group, it was transparent only if you could not see it, but see through it as though it were not there.

The two groups had a disagreement about what "transparent" means, but once they became clear that they had defined it in different ways, they were able to resolve the dispute. The dispute was not conceptually problematic because neither side ended up insisting that their understanding was the right one, the only way "transparent" ought to be understood.

When a client disputes whether a lawyer showed due diligence and the lawyer claims due diligence and lays out all that was done for the client, without the client being satisfied, we have a dispute over what due diligence requires—not about what the lawyer did, but about whether the lawyer did enough, or did enough in the proper way, to claim due diligence.

Both parties in this case have an option that would allow for a resolution. They can look at what other lawyers consider due diligence and at past disputes regarding the matter between other lawyers and clients. Looking there will provide at least a base line for what counts as due diligence by a lawyer, and the lawyer and the client can then compare what was done for the client against that baseline.

If there is still disagreement, they might be able to work it out with a frank and open discussion about what the client expected and what the lawyer did and did not do and why. These sorts of conceptual cases are frustrating for the parties involved because they appear essentially unresolvable and the source of the disagreement may not be at all obvious.

Obviously, trying to resolve a disagreement while not understanding its source is clearly an impossible task that will frustrate the parties involved. The situation we find ourselves in is, regarding the level of frustration, like that described by Deborah Tannen about her and her former husband. In his family, asking "Do you want X?" meant that the person asking wanted X and was checking to see if you did too. In her family, asking that was simply a question with no implications about your desires. So she would ask her former husband, "Do you want to visit my parents this weekend?," and he would hear, "I want to visit my parents this weekend. Do you?" Being a nice guy, but not particularly interested in seeing his in-laws, he would respond, somewhat wearily, "Sure. That's O.K." She, hearing his hesitation, would ask, "Do you really want to visit them?" He would hear, "I don't want to visit them. Why do you?" And then he would explode, asking her why she could not make up her mind about what she wanted to do, leaving her completely dumbfounded because all she had done, from her point of view, was ask what he wanted to do. They were never able to get past this sort of disagreement because she would ask, "Are you angry?" And he would hear, "I'm angry. Are you?" And so he would respond, "I wasn't before, but I am now." And the conflict would simply continue, unresolved and unresolvable because they could not sort out what underlay the failure to communicate. It was only after a divorce that Tannen was able to figure out the source of the dispute.[27]

Just so, conceptual disagreements can go on without any party being aware of the nature of the disagreement, and the frustration will grow as the parties do what we all seem to do when we have a disagreement. We each pile on new information to convince the other party. Or we repeat ourselves in different ways, thinking that somehow the others must not have understood what we were saying—which seems so obvious to us. None of these maneuvers will help, but only aggravate the situation and make it harder to see what the problem is. Pretty soon we are overwhelmed with information and explanations that are of no use and with so many variations of each party's position that we have confusion instead of clarity. The disagreement is made much the worse because the competing parties each generally claim the high moral ground, backing their understandings with claims about theirs being the morally right way of understanding what is at issue.

Tannen and her former husband had not exhausted all their options in coming to an understanding, and that may well be the problem with a dispute that seems to turn on different understandings of a central concept. But there are conceptual disputes that are essentially contested. That is, they are disputes about a concept—the best dog, due care—that are "not resolvable by argument of any kind," but "are nevertheless sustained by perfectly reasonable arguments and evidence."[28] They are hard to discern and are marked by the sort of frustration Tannen and her former husband experienced, but unlike that issue, they are essentially unresolvable.

If you wish to start a conceptually problematic disagreement, ask a group of new parents whether they ought to sleep with their newborns. You will have each side piling on information, providing alternative and sometimes even incompatible statements of their position in the hope that perhaps this will penetrate the brains of those on the other side. You will find appeals to the high moral ground by both parties.

You will hear, on the one hand, that it is cruel to leave a newborn bawling away when what the newborn needs is a loving caress next to its mother's beating heart. The tone is an almost incomprehensible outrage that any caring parent would fail to do that for an infant. On the other hand, you will hear that it is dangerous to the infant. It is unfortunately not all that unusual for infants to suffocate while sleeping with a parent. Steve Eisman writes that his wife, "sick with the flu, had been awakened by a night nurse, who informed her that she, the night nurse, had rolled on top of the baby in her sleep and smothered him."[29] So you will hear those who let their infants bawl saying that bawling is better than dying—again, with that tone of almost incomprehensible outrage that brooks no response.

What is at issue in such an exchange is what is proper care for an infant, a contested concept if there ever was one. The most difficult of these contests occurs not when the parties hold their positions for different moral reasons, but when they hold different positions for the same moral reason. In the case of the proper care of an infant, the moral imperative is to help the infant. What is at issue between the parties is the morally right way to understand that imperative. One party takes the imperative to license, or even require, sleeping with the infant to calm it down, and the other takes it to mean trying to ensure that the infant does not suffocate.

There may be options here to settle this dispute, evidence, for instance, of the likelihood of suffocation. But without such options, the dispute looks to be irresolvable. The imperative in contention is that we are to help the infant. We might try appealing to some general moral principle to determine which of the two conceptions in contention is right, but, as we might expect, any moral principle would be as contentious as the imperative at issue. We might appeal, for instance, to the principle that we are to do no harm, but then the issue is which is more harmful, letting the infant cry without the comforting touch of a parent or comforting the infant in the parent's bed at some risk. We might appeal to the principle of beneficence, but, again, we will end up with contentious disagreement about what is most beneficial to the infant.

So we cannot appeal to some higher moral principle to settle the matter, and once the discussion has gone through all the ways in which an infant is harmed or benefitted by sleeping with a parent or crying itself to sleep, no additional information about how an infant may be harmed or helped by being held or ignored seems to make any difference to the disagreement. We can give additional reasons for whichever view we hold—for example, that it is easier for a mother to nurse if the infant is in her bed or that a crying baby makes sleep impossible. "It is easier to nurse, but at such a risk!," the other party will say. "Letting the baby cry itself to sleep is much better for your sleep later than habituating it to being picked up whenever it cries." Adding such reasons will not tip the balance one way or the other.

The dispute does not seem to depend upon a lack of information or any misunderstanding about the information available, and we can rephrase the contested positions however we wish without resolution. Rephrasing our view in the hope that the other party will now understand what we are saying seems merely to open the disagreement to further misunderstanding.

As is the case with all situations where we seem to reach a stalemate, we may simply have overlooked something or failed to realize the competing parties are not seeing the problem in the same way or even thinking of the same problem. So we should be hesitant to throw up our hands and say, "It's conceptually problematic," and let that be the end of it. If we do have a conceptually problematic ethical issue, we will find that it is not open to the usual modes of dispute resolution. If we have a dispute of this form, we will just spin our wheels if we pile on more information or rephrase our position in the vain hope that saying it differently will make it clearer. It can certainly be frustrating to find oneself in such a dispute, but that there are such disputes tells us to be chary of the assumption that all moral disagreements can be settled.

We might expect such conceptual disputes between lawyers and clients, for instance, but they can occur within professions as well. In October 2007, a surgeon in Florida removed a kidney instead of the gallbladder that was to have been removed. That sort of mistake is not common, and the surgeon in question had over two thousand "successful operations over 15 years." The surgeon and the Department of Health agreed to a $5000 fine and a letter of concern, but the Florida Board of Medicine rejected their agreement and imposed "a reprimand, $10,000 fine and other standard penalties, such as community service and taking classes." The facts of the case were not in issue. What was at issue was what constitutes due care on the part of a surgeon,[30] and the Department of Health and the Florida Board disagreed. It is not at all obvious how we might go about determining which judgment was correct.

We seem to have in this case an essentially contestable disagreement over what amounts to due care. I say "seems" because it would take more detail to be sure that there is not some new fact that convinced the Florida Board of Medicine to increase the penalty, and that concern about being sure that we have got an essentially contested concept is always an issue. We need to be sure we have exhausted other possibilities before deciding we have a conceptually problematic case. Tannen and her husband gave up when the issue that separated them could have been resolved. So we need to be careful not to give up on resolving a dispute when it could be settled.

We should note, however, that those involved in such disputes often "solve" the problem by redescribing what they do, changing the terms of the disagreement so that they can get off any ethical hooks. Financial advisors chastised by clients who do not think the advisors acted in their best interest can argue that they are not really advisors, but salespersons. They are thus under no obligation to advise their "customers." They are, after all, just selling stuff. A salesperson may advise a customer about what to buy, but is under no obligation to give the best advice, the advice that best benefits the customer. So we can hardly fault "financial advisors," they would argue, for not elevating their customers' interests above their own.

This sort of redefinition is a common—perhaps all too common—response to what we would consider conceptual disputes. With no way to win a conceptual disagreement about what a professional's obligations are, and with a profession's—and a professional's—reputation on the line, the preferred move seems to change the terms of the discussion. "You can't fault us for not providing advice to clients because we are salespeople with customers who can decide for themselves what they want and don't want."

In *The Big Short*, Steve Eisman remarks in regard to the financial crisis of 2008 that the rating agencies failed to do due diligence regarding collateralized debt obligations (CDOs).[31] The objection is that the ratings the agencies provided for such CDOs could not be relied upon for investment purposes when, presumably, the whole point of the rating agencies giving ratings is supposedly to provide accurate information to potential investors about the worth of CDOs, among other things.

One problem is that the rating agencies have a conflict of interest. They are being paid by the investment banks to rate their offerings. So they have an incentive to provide good ratings in order to keep their business. In a congressional hearing, Waxman said to Raymond McDaniel, CEO, Moody's, "In 2005 you said, 'we believe we have successfully managed the conflicts of interest and have provided objective, independent and unbiased credit opinions.'" McDaniel replied that "we seek to maintain the highest levels of objectivity, independence, and professionalism in assigning our ratings."[32] But, he added, the ratings we give are just "our opinions."[33] In the same hearing, Deven Sharma, CEO, S&P, said that "the only thing we do is to opine on whether they meet our criteria or not." Since he did not specify the criteria, his response leaves open the possibility that their opinions are based on an objective evaluation of the offerings, but he made it clear that he did not mean that. He added that our opinions "do not speak to the market value for security, the volatility of its price, or its suitability as an investment." Stephen Joynt, CEO, Fitch, made it unanimous among the three rating agencies by agreeing that "our ratings are our opinions."[34]

So, the rating agencies claim, they cannot be faulted for failing to do due diligence in assessing the value of CDOs. If the ratings are only opinions, then there is no claim that they meet or fail to meet any criteria at all and certainly no claim that investors should take the opinions as judgments on a CDO's "suitability as an investment."

We saw that financial advisors represent themselves as advising investors—hence their title—but when pressed because of failures to provide advice that is advantageous to the investor rather than the advisor, they switch and say, "We just sell stuff." The title "investment advisor" does not describe what they do. Just so, we now see, for ratings agencies. They represent themselves as providing accurate information for investors, and, indeed, investment banks pay them to do that. But when pressed because of failures to provide accurate ratings, they switch and say, "We are just giving opinions. You shouldn't rely on them when making investment decisions."

Such switches certainly fail to resolve conceptual problems that arise about such matters as due diligence, and they need to be noted because they are deceitful. An investment advisor who claims to be a salesperson and rating agencies that claim their ratings are only opinions that cannot be relied upon are deceiving us when they represent themselves as being investment advisors and rating agencies. And that is a moral wrong. The best we can do in what may turn out to be conceptually problematic cases is to be sure we have properly identified the issue as conceptual and so have laid aside any attempts to resolve it by providing additional information or restating our view. We can come to agreement that we disagree, and that is far better than dissimulating and so confusing matters that much more.

§4 Summary

We can face three different kinds of ethical issues, and if we fail to identify the kind of issue we face, we will fail to resolve it in the right way, if at all. When a case is factually problematic, we need to try to have the facts necessary to make a reasonable decision, knowing that we may be missing something without realizing it, have data that was fabricated, or be unable to obtain in a reasonable amount of time data we would like to have before proceeding. Knowing how unlikely it is that we can know we are in the best epistemological position we can be, what will be crucial in deciding what we ought to do is the decision procedure we adopt. Do we decide cautiously, knowing that we may well be making the wrong decision? Do we decide like Jack in the beanstalk, taking a great risk for a supposedly great benefit? No matter what procedure we use, we ought to be cognizant that we are making a choice and try, as best we can under trying epistemic circumstances, to choose a procedure that gives us the best chance of doing the right thing. We have little guidance in such matters, there being no general decision procedure for choosing decision procedures.

When a case is conceptually problematic, more data only confuses matters, making the case appear factually problematic when no additional facts are going to settle the matter. We can easily get caught up in a dispute, thinking that the other parties to the disagreement are simply missing what we are saying and so recasting our position and also adding more information if we can. But all that will be fruitless in a conceptually problematic case and only make it that much harder to see that we are in a dispute that has no obvious ending.

If we find ourselves in a dilemma, a situation where no additional facts are going to help resolve the problem we face, we will need to make a morally difficult decision and ought to be sure, before deciding, that we have no morally relevant reason for making one choice over the other. The situation faced by the managers of the companies McGann and Owens each worked for found what arguably was a morally relevant reason, the number of employees who would be without health insurance if McGann and Owens were each provided the money they had a right to under their health insurance policy. We will not pursue here the issue of whether that reason led to the right decision. We would have to determine whether there were other sources of funding, such as the companies providing for the shortfall the managers assumed would occur, and we would have to examine their assumption, assessing how much funding would be necessary to cover projected future costs for the other employees based on their numbers and their past histories of need. In any event, whatever we discovered would have no effect on the managers' decisions since those had to be made without access to such data.

8

Internal and External Moral Problems

An actuary has to make ethical decisions about whether to be a party to giving unrealistically optimistic projections of interest rates for pensions and having two sets of books, one for the public and one not. The actuary must make those decisions to be a member of that profession. It is an ethical decision since agreeing to unrealistic rate projections harms those who have pensions and yet cannot tell how much they are worth, and it harms those companies and institutions providing pensions since they cannot know what they have agreed to.

Those decisions are internal to the profession. The same is true for a historian who writes history as though great men were the main actors, carrying everything and everyone along with them. That is an ethical decision, having harmful consequences for our understanding of how we got where we are and for the lessons we could learn from a more nuanced history.

Such internal decisions arise for professionals in their profession, affecting them as they go about their normal professional business. They can also face very different kinds of ethical problems that do not arise within their professions, but between them and their employers, for instance, because they are not just professionals, but employees as well. These are external ethical problems and can arise for any professional with competing responsibilities. Recognizing such problems and resolving them, if possible, may not depend upon much, if any, of the details of the profession in question. Internal problems, however, depend very much on the details and arise because some of those details, at least, are ethically loaded. The way in which we respond to an ethical problem will vary depending upon whether it is internal or external to a profession.

§1 Internal Ethical Problems

It is not at all unusual for professionals to resist the claim that there are ethical problems within their professions. We become trained into the ways of the profession, and as with any complex system, we can fail to see systemic features that have become second nature as we have become adept at our profession.

An analogy may help. We have rules for walking on sidewalks that few ever think about despite following them with enough regularity to make them rules. The first is that we avoid bumping into one another even while staying close. The second is that we follow those in front of us, and, third, we keep up with those next to us, speeding up or slowing down as the situation requires. These rules of pedestrian traffic have become so second nature that we are only likely to note them, if then, when they are breached. We can use our measure of irritation at someone stopping dead in front of us to make a phone call or send a text as a mark of how deeply engrained within us are these norms for walking crowded sidewalks.[1]

We have internalized the norms for walking sidewalks in the way in which, say, a historian trained in the great man school of history may be completely unaware of writing an ethically charged history that other historians would dismiss as not being real history. Having written a PhD thesis within that school and having published articles and books about how great men have shaped history, such a historian is likely to be more than a little surprised at criticism for doing what is second nature for historians within that school—as the Preston Hotchkis Professor at Berkeley, Middlekauff, was no doubt taken aback by the Alva O. Way University Professor and Professor of History at Brown, Gordon Wood, saying, as we saw, "Middlekauff's account of the formation of the Constitution virtually sets back scholarship on the issue at least a century."[2] This dispute is internal to the profession of history, and as we have seen, it is an ethical dispute not only about the right way to do history, but about what history is to tell us. As we saw, a citizenry primed with the view that history is made by great men is more likely to listen to some self-proclaimed "great man" who says, "I am the only one who can fix it." That is an ethically loaded implication.

So becoming one kind of historian rather than another is itself an ethical choice. Middlekauff may not have been aware of alternative ways of doing history, and so he may not have been conscious of making a choice to become a member of the Great Man school. But it is an ethical choice nonetheless, with his writing and teaching having ethical implications. When the historian puts a "hero" at the center of the narrative, the historian is making an ethical choice, eschewing the social and political and economic details other historians take to be central to a historical narrative. That "great man" narrative consists of numerous choices about what is thought historically important and what is not, the choices dependent upon a commitment to the Great Man school and eschewed by historians of another school.

Ethical decisions are thus internal to professional historians. One cannot be a historian, that is, without making decisions that are themselves ethical or have ethical implications. As just noted, a historian need not be aware of making ethical decisions any more than pedestrians need be aware of the norms for walking sidewalks, but they are ethical decisions nonetheless. They embody judgments between competing visions of how to do history properly and between the resulting ethically loaded implications.

History is no different in this regard than any other profession—even professions that pride themselves on being wholly objective. Engineering, for instance, has long considered itself a purely quantitative discipline. On this view, it is thus purely objective and not marred by the subjectivity of value judgments that supposedly mark ethics. The Accreditation Board for Engineering and Technology (ABET) requires a consideration of ethics, but that requirement tends to find expression within engineering colleges in an extra course in engineering ethics, or an examination of the relevant code of ethics, or a discussion of some significant cases that raise ethical issues. The requirement is not thought to require any changes in the core courses of the engineering curricula because ethical considerations are not thought central to engineering's intellectual core.

Yet one cannot be a practicing engineer without making ethical judgments when solving the design problems that are engineering's particular province. We can use as our measure of how ethical considerations enter into engineering choices one ethical principle: do no unnecessary harm. There is no doubt that the artifacts of engineering cause harms as well as produce benefits. We would not have any fatalities from automobile crashes without automobiles. But the ethical principle is not that we should cause no harm, but that we ought to cause no unnecessary harm. And it is not that other ethical principles are not relevant to engineering, but that to show that ethical considerations enter into the core of engineering we only need to show that this one principle—cause no unnecessary harm—is central to engineering practice.

That turns out to be easy to show—in a variety of different ways. For instance, if we look at some of the standard examples of how engineering decisions have gone wrong, we can readily find instances of situations in which a different decision would have avoided unnecessary harms. One of the more depressing examples was the failure of engineers at Guilant to determine if the design of their defibrillators permitted leakage of bodily fluids into the electrical wiring so it could short out just when it was needed. The devices failed because of the deterioration of the polyimide coating on the electrical wires "in a component that sits atop the sealed part of a heart device. The component, called the header, is essentially a junction box connecting a unit's computer and power supply with cables, or leads, that carry electrical impulses to the heart." But the header was "not hermetically sealed" and so "body fluids can slowly seep into the header, … and cause [the] polyimide to deteriorate."[3]

The harms were not just to those who died when their defibrillators shorted out when needed, but to all those who had them implanted and were at risk of just the kind of death the defibrillators were implanted to prevent. Hundreds of thousands of people had to live with that risk of death—although Guilant decided early on not to inform patients or surgeons of the potential for the device to short-circuit. So hundreds of thousands were at risk while thinking they were safe.

Artifacts can cause unnecessary harms, that is, and it is an ethical decision to design an artifact that causes unnecessary harms—whether the engineer responsible realizes it or not. We can most readily see how ethical considerations enter into the intellectual core of engineering by looking at what I call error-provocative designs. These are design solutions that provoke errors even for the most intelligent, well-trained, and highly motivated in the most pristine of conditions.

To see how a design can provoke errors, we should consider both the circumstances in which the error occurred and the operator who caused the error. Suppose that the circumstances are pristine. There is nothing about the situation, that is, that could be at fault for the error. We generally hold a driver who goes off the road because of black ice innocent of any harm that may occur. We fault the black ice. But suppose that the operating conditions are pristine and that we have the best of operators, someone who is intelligent enough to know how to operate the artifact in question, has learned how to operate it and how to respond to any problems that occur, and is "in the zone," as it were, in terms of being alert and paying attention to the operating conditions. An error can occur because someone simply lacks the smarts to know how to operate the artifact in question, has the smarts but lacks the knowledge, or has the smarts and the knowledge, but is otherwise engaged—in texting, for instance.

But if an error occurs that is not due to the operating conditions or the operator, then it is due to the artifact having somehow misled the operator. We have all run into examples—doors that appear to open one way rather than another, knobs that look as though they are to be turned when they are to be pulled, and on and on. I had a friend with a very expensive gas stovetop that had the burners arranged in a semicircle around the center of the stovetop with burners at 8 o'clock, 11 o'clock, 1 o'clock and 4 o'clock. The knobs were similarly situated, with each knob placed just in front of the burner it supposedly controlled. While he was cooking lobster and pasta, I noticed that he turned off the burner with the lobster when he meant to turn off the one for the pasta. "Didn't you just turn off the wrong burner?" "Geez. I'm always doing that. I'm so stupid!" I went to look and, sure enough, the knobs for the burners at 11 o'clock and 1 o'clock were the reverse of what we would expect from looking at the stovetop. The 11 o'clock burner was controlled by the knob in front of the 1 o'clock burner and vice versa. My friend was taking the blame for an error-provocative design.

We owe to ethical engineers that the world is not filled with error-provocative designs. An evil genius of an engineer could no doubt have a great deal of diabolical fun from designing artifacts that would cause unnecessary harms, but engineers are not evil geniuses. They for the most part do what we all do in our daily lives, avoid doing what cause unnecessary harms. They need not make a conscious choice not to cause unnecessary harms. Doing the right thing is doing the right thing regardless of our intentions, and engineers deserve ethical credit for doing what is right.

Just so, we judge the Guilant engineers ethically at fault even though it is unlikely that they made a conscious choice to cause unnecessary harm. It is more likely that they just did not think through what would happen to the junction box when it was put in place and subject to bodily fluids. We do not need to assume, that is, that they considered possible solutions and deliberately picked one of the worst. We hold them ethically responsible because they failed to ensure that what they were designing would actually work when it was needed. That they presumably did not intend to cause unnecessary harm is irrelevant to our judgment that they were ethically at fault for failing to choose a design with a hermetically sealed junction box.

That the choice of a design solution is an ethical choice ought to be obvious to practicing engineers who constantly consider alternative solutions and compare them against each other in terms of all the criteria normally used—ease of use, cost of manufacturing, reliability, and so on. Criteria are always weighed against one another, and in the weighing, perhaps without being conscious of it, engineers are making ethical judgments. The Guilant engineers surely considered what battery to use—what size, for instance, what life-span, what cost, and what possible harmful effects the battery itself might have on the health of the recipient. In making their choice, they would weigh longevity against cost, for one thing. A battery with a two-year life span presumably costs less than a battery with a six-to-ten-year life span, and it should be obvious that the choice between the two is an ethical one, given the higher risk of earlier failure for the former and the need for an operation for a replacement.

The bottom line is that ethical considerations enter into the intellectual core of engineering through the choice of a design solution. To choose a particular solution is to make an ethical choice. So when Cadillac engineers decided to design a trunk that closed itself automatically once it was within a foot or so of being latched, they made an ethical choice. We need only think through what would happen with such trunks to understand the harms it would produce. All it takes is one person slamming down the trunk lid in the usual way we close such lids for the mechanism to break. Once the mechanism is broken, the trunk cannot be latched, and the repair requires taking out the back seat and replacing the motor. We know just how likely it is that someone will shut the trunk the way we usually do—a bellhop at a hotel, a helper at a supermarket, a forgetful owner. The harms were there to be seen, as it were, and they were unnecessary.

What is true of engineering and of history is true of every profession. No professional can avoid making ethical choices in going about the work of the profession: a physician's choosing a regular delivery rather than a Caesarean and so causing the infant to be decapitated,[4] or a lawyer choosing to tell the jury, against his client's will, that his client was guilty, resulting in a guilty verdict and a death sentence,[5] or a TV reporter who announced, without verifying the claim, that Michael Flynn would testify that "Trump had directed him to make contact with Russian officials while Mr. Trump was still a candidate."[6]

We know about such choices because they make the news because of the harms they cause, but the judgments that do not make the news because they cause no unnecessary harm are ethical judgments as well—the right ones—and they are internal to the professions in question, ethical judgments that must be made in order for the professional to be a professional.

§2 Internal Ethical Tensions

We have considered two different ways in which ethics enters into professions. The example of competing ways of doing history displays a tension within the discipline of history about what is it to be a historian. The engineering examples are not about competing views of engineering, but about how ethical considerations enter into the core of engineering. The former tension plays itself how in ethical judgments about what to consider and highlight in any history. So it has an effect on the everyday practice of history—on the kind of data considered historically relevant, the kind of historical documents worth examining, the kind of events worth emphasizing, and so on. The engineering examples are completely independent of anyone's view of how to be an engineer. Whatever one may think one is doing in being an engineer, one is making ethical choices.

Another example may help with the latter point. If I were a professional photographer, took a black and white photograph of the moon over Half Dome, and then entered my work in a show, I would remind the judges of Ansel Adams's famous photograph. Whether I called my entry "Moon and Half Dome" or not, they would consider my entry in relationship to that iconic photograph whether I wished them to or not. As a professional photographer, I am working within a profession with a history, and that history constrains what I can do and so forces those who look at my work to consider it in certain ways. Adams got there first, and so the judges cannot see my work except against that historical background. That background changes the terms of criticism.[7]

They would normally judge the composition, the lighting, the exposure, the focus, and so on, coming to a judgment about the quality of the photograph and either accepting it into the show as worthy or rejecting it. Those criteria are among the normal terms of criticism for a photograph, but for my entry? The very first query the judges must ask is whether the work, being so obviously derivative of Ansel Adams's iconic photograph, is intended to be ironic, is being entered as a joke or is just a stupid appropriation by someone somehow unfamiliar with Adams or with his stature within the canon. The terms of criticism will change, that is, and my photograph will no doubt fail to merit entry.

My work and the judges' judgments are ethically loaded. My photograph cannot be a "great photograph," but might be "a nice imitation." I cannot be a great photographer for taking the photo, but might be good at mimicking one. But in either case I am to be faulted. I either tried to foist my photograph off as an original, or I am somehow ignorant of the works of one of the world's greatest photographers.

This kind of example is not about tensions regarding the nature of a profession, and it does not show that ethical judgments are at the core of photography. But it is an example of a kind of internal tension, and we can find other such examples in many professions. For instance, physicians live what we may call a tensed life. They must look at a person's body as a mechanism, subject to faults and failures, but also look at the person as a human being with feelings and concerns and worries. The capacity to embody both capacities is vital to being a good physician and cannot be easy to master.

We saw how difficult it must be when we examined the case of the elderly woman in Memphis who was trying to cover herself while a physician, with a number of interns, discussed her case. They saw her as a case, not an elderly woman embarrassed in front of all those men.

Physicians have to learn how to see a patient as a person and an object to be examined. A colleague of mine at Michigan State heard tittering in the hallway outside his office and when it continued, went to investigate. He found it was coming from an examination room down the hall where second-year medical students were learning how to examine patients without getting embarrassed or embarrassing the patient. There were twenty students, and they were taking turns examining each other in ten cubicles. Some had dated, some wanted to date, some were indifferent, but all had to learn how to look at a naked body without tittering in embarrassment. What my colleague heard was the beginning of that training, with lots of embarrassed "patients" and "physicians." The hardest part no doubt came afterwards when the students then had to discuss with the "patient" what had been found in the examination and so had to be able to see the person as a person not a mechanism.

Similar examples of internal tension can be found in other professions as well. Journalists are trained to report what is said and done by those in government, for instance. One effect of their reporting is that they repeat what those in government say. But, as George Lakoff points out,

> Language works by activating brain structures called "frame-circuits" used to understand experience. They get stronger when we hear the activating language. Enough repetition can make them permanent, changing how we view the world.

Framing can be powerful—"as when Nixon said 'I am not a crook' and people thought of him as a crook." So a President first frames what he attacks—"crooked Hilary"—and then repeats it often. He thus leads "others to repeat his words … within his own frame."[8] Thus, when the media reports on what is said, they strengthen the frame he has created, furthering the false narrative.

So we have professional journalists doing what they have been trained to do in journalism school and so undermining their profession when they report that a president tweets that they are reporting "fake news." They repeat his frame, and his constant repetition and their constant reporting makes his claim harder and harder to dislodge.

We might think journalists reporting that the president says they are reporting "fake news" would undercut the message they are reporting. How can the fake news be trusted when it says it is fake news? But our minds do not work that way: repetition drills it in, whatever the source.

The ethical tension is that the standard way in which journalists convey the news serves the purpose of undermining them and thus the free press. They hold themselves to a high ethical standard of searching out what is true and discarding what is false only to find their high ground cut out from under them by reporting what such a president truly says.

Lakoff suggests a solution, that journalists provide what he calls a "truth sandwich." Instead of reporting what a world leader says, they should begin with what the world leader does. For instance, they could write, "Here is what resulted from the meeting in Singapore between the two world leaders—not much. Here is what our leader said resulted from the meeting. And here is an analysis of how much of what our leader said resulted from the meeting is true and how much is false." Journalists would still report what a world leader said, but only after stating another set of facts, what actually happened, and only by following it with an assessment that readers themselves can now make between what the world leader said resulted from the meeting and what actually resulted.

We examined a different sort of internal tension when we looked at the problem accountants have using GAAP. Accountants are required to evaluate whatever they are assessing by what it cost the last time it was bought or sold, but, as we saw, that requirement all but ensures that they cannot serve the public good by telling us the worth of what they audit. That audit informs decisions about investment, but GAAP prevents accountants from determining the true worth.

The accounting principles cause real harm, that is, and mean that we cannot be sure that we are getting an accurate assessment of a company's financial state, but it is not clear how accounting can come to grips with that problem and still maintain the objectivity provided by using an asset's price when it was last bought or sold.

The situations with the accounting profession and with journalism both involve a profession's failure to achieve the public goods that would presumably justify their professionals receiving the special standing they have as journalists and accountants. Although it is difficult to see how accounting can maintain objectivity and yet give the public what it needs to make investments, journalists can resolve the tension within their profession by changing the way they report the news, using truth-sandwiches rather than just repeating what a populist says.

We have gone through a number of different kinds of internal ethical problems. The set is not meant to be exhaustive, but illustrative of the many different ways in which ethical tensions can occur within a profession. Just as we need to determine whether the ethical problem we have is a dilemma or factually or conceptually problematic if we are to come to understand it aright and resolve it in the right way, we need to determine whether an ethical issue is internal or external if we are to come to grips with it properly.

§3 External Ethical Problems

It is a measure of how difficult it can be for professionals to see ethical problems that are internal to their profession that when we query practicing professionals for examples of the ethical problems they have faced, we are far more likely to get examples of external ethical problems than internal ones. In the early 1990s, Michael Pritchard interviewed a number of working engineers and produced a series of cases about the ethical problems they told him they had faced. It is not particularly remarkable that the bulk of those cases involve what I call external problems, arising not because of what those he interviewed were doing as engineers, but because of some conflict between what they are doing or thought they ought to do as engineers and others—their employers, suppliers, and so on.

Here are samples that illustrate that point:

3. *Gifts from a Supplier*
Scott Bennett is the engineer assigned to deal with vendors who supply needed parts to the Upscale Company. Larry Newman, sales representative from one of Upscale's regular vendors, offers Scott a chance at a good deal on a condo.

8. *Requested to Falsify Data*
Stephanie Simon knew Environmental Manager Adam Baines would not be pleased with her report on the chemical spill. The data clearly indicated that the spill was large enough that regulations required it to be reported to the state. Adam Baines asks Stephanie to change her report.

10. *Disposing of Toxic Waste.*
Just moments ago, Bryan's supervisor, Max Morrison, told him to dump half of the used coolant down the drain. Bryan knew the coolant was toxic, and he mentioned this to Max. But Max was not swayed.

11. *Hospitality from a Vendor*
Paul Ledbetter decides to accept hospitality from a vendor in the form of a country club membership.[9]

The first and last involve outside vendors seeking to ingratiate themselves with engineers who are involved in purchasing supplies for their companies. The middle two involve engineers who are told by their managers to do something they thought was wrong, but the relation is manager to employee, not engineer to engineer.

These examples clearly illustrate ethical issues, but they are not unique to engineers. They are the sorts of problems any professional might have who is an employee or has to deal with outside vendors. That is not to say, rather obviously, that other professionals would be writing a report on a chemical spill or disposing of toxic coolant down a drain. At issue in these two examples is the relation between managers and employees, and the problem for the professionals is that their managers are telling them to do something they think is wrong. This sort of problem is common to all professionals who are also employees. That situation is necessarily in tension with one's professional responsibilities being put to the test by a manager who challenges the professional's judgment.

The same sorts of examples may thus be found in other professions. A physician may receive benefits from a drug company with the implicit understanding that the physician will prescribe the drug company's products.[10] The ethical problem is not internal to the practice of medicine, but results from the physician's willingness to be bribed by an outside vendor, a character flaw of the particular physicians willing to have their decisions about what to prescribe for patients determined by a drug company's largess, decisions resulting in a huge cost to the medical system when the drug being prescribed is expensive—as it generally is.[11]

The engineer ordered by her manager to change her report and the engineer told to dump toxic waste down the sink may have difficulty refusing to do what their managers tell them to do. A refusal may well result in disciplinary action or even dismissal, but although both engineers are doing what they ought to do—keeping accurate records and not causing unnecessary harm—their problems do not arise because they are engineers. They arise because their managers are telling them to do what they know is wrong. These cases and the others do not pose difficult ethical issues within a profession, that is.

They are ethical problems professionals may have, but they are problems non-professionals may have as well. When a line worker refuses to do what the line boss orders the worker to do, they have an ethical problem. Why is the line worker refusing? Is what he is being told to do unsafe? Against regulations? Wrong for some other reason? Did the line worker understand properly? Was the line boss unclear? Overly aggressive? Acting beyond what was permitted of a line boss? We cannot begin to resolve the problem the two face until we are clear why the line worker is refusing the order, and then we can assess the problem the way we assess ethical problems. We must construct arguments that have as their conclusions what the participants could reasonably believe that would explain or justify their behavior, and once that is done, we can ask whether the premises reasonably support the conclusions, whether the premises are themselves reasonable, and whether the conclusions explain why the participants did what they did.

Such problems do not pose any special issues, and although understanding them and how to resolve them may tell us something about how to be ethical, or not, they tell us nothing about any profession. Internal ethical problems open up for us the ethical underpinnings of professions, on the other hand, telling us what ethical choices professionals have to make and why some choices that may seem mundane are deeply problematic. The dispute between historians about the great man theory of history illustrates that point.

That is not to say that those professionals facing such problems have an easy time making decisions. The case of the Flint engineer who agreed to use the Flint water treatment plant when ordered to do so is a case in point. He knew that the plant could not adequately treat the water from the river. Among its other problems, the plant had "ozone and clarifying equipment that were not functioning properly and new hires who had little background in water treatment."[12] He told those in the city responsible for the decision that the plant was not ready to treat the water and contacted the MDEQ, but got no response. He said he was given "his marching orders" to use Flint River water. He obeyed and was charged "with misconduct in office for authorizing use of the Flint plant."[13]

It cannot have been easy for him to follow "his marching orders," given what he knew, but it would not have been easy for him not to follow them, given the likelihood that he would be fired. These are not easy decisions for anyone to make, but professionals, especially engineers, have a special obligation to put the public good above their self-interest. So although it cannot have been easy for him to make the decision, it is easy to see which decision he ought to have made.

§4 Oddities

The distinction between internal and external ethical problems is not as clear and, well, as distinct as the contrast we have just laid out may make it appear. There are some cases that do not fall easily into either category.

One sort involves situations where what one does as a professional is at odds, to put it oddly, with oneself. One example concerns Ted Kennedy when he was senator from Massachusetts. The nation's Roman Catholic bishops issued a document saying "that faithful and serious Catholic public officials cannot advocate or support direct attacks on human life." It was thus wrong, they were claiming, for Senator Kennedy to support a woman's right to choose abortion. As Francis Cardinal George of Chicago put it,

> Ultimately, the conflict is not between the bishops and politicians. The conflict is between Catholic politicians and their own faith, and that's an internal conflict,

because their faith tells them that [they] are not accountable to us, nor even to the electorate or the Constitution. When all is said and done, they are accountable to a Lord who will ask them, what they have done to the least of their brothers and sisters.[14]

The bishops were asking, "How can you live with yourself, Senator Kennedy?"

They decided "not to recommend any sanctions against public officials who violate church teachings and instead will seek to educate them," but that they considered sanctions indicates how wrong they thought Senator Kennedy's position to be. His defense was that he was elected by the people of Massachusetts to represent them and that in supporting a woman's right to choose abortion, he was acting as their representative. But the query still lingers: how can you act as their representative when you are supporting what in conscience you cannot support? You cannot be Catholic, the bishops are saying, and somehow separate your conscience from your position as a senator:

> We urge those Catholic officials who choose to depart from Church teaching on the inviolability of human life in their public life to consider the consequence for their own spiritual well-being, as well as the scandal they risk by leading others into serious sin.[15]

The issue they raise is generalizable and, in this case, illustrates concerns citizens have voiced about whether a Roman Catholic politician will represent them or answer to the Pope. Until the election of John F. Kennedy, the latter was a damning charge. We find the same query about other elected officials. One says, for instance, that he is a Christian first and then a politician. Will his Christian beliefs trump what he ought to do as a representative? We can see how any professional may face the same sort of problem.

The issue of bakers who refuse customers or pharmacists who refuse to provide medication because of what they call their "personal ethics" are cases in point. A woman whose nine-week fetus was without a heartbeat had a prescription from her physician for Misoprostol, but the pharmacist refused to honor it—despite the woman's explanation that she wanted to be pregnant and that the fetus was dead.[16]

As she wrote,

> If you have gone thru a miscarriage you know the pain and emotional roller it can be. I left Walgreens in tears, ashamed and feeling humiliated by a man who knows nothing of my struggles but feels it is his right to deny medication prescribed to me by my doctor.[17]

This is a problematic example for two reasons. First, one's personal beliefs—what some call the person's morals—have no ethical weight at all unless they can be justified ethically. That the pharmacist has a "personal ethics" makes no sense: ethical principles do not vary from person to person, but hold for all persons. Second, even if the pharmacist's "personal ethics" are justified ethically, presumably by the principle that it is wrong to take a person's life and the assumption that the fetus is a person, providing Misoprostol to the woman would not violate that principle. The fetus was dead, after all. So it is a puzzle what ethical principle the pharmacist thought he was upholding.

In any event, the sort of problem the bishops raised for Senator Kennedy has parallels in professions such as medicine, law, and accounting, to name just a few, and it is unclear how a professional is to come to grips with it. An argument we might construct for Senator Kennedy that would justify his supporting abortion rights must have as a premise that the obligations he took on as a senator outweigh any obligations he has as a Catholic. His situation is different from that of the bishops. They have, as it were, a professional obligation to oppose abortion rights because of the position they hold in the Catholic hierarchy. A bishop who was elected senator would have a conflict between the obligations his two roles would create, and to settle that conflict, we would need to find some ethical reason for preferring the obligations of the one role over the other. Senator Kennedy is not an official of the Catholic Church, and so the conflict is between his obligations as a senator and how he can reconcile those obligations with his being a Catholic.

We do not need to determine which church doctrines are essential for someone to accept to be a Catholic, but the bishops want to impose on him as a "public official" the obligations they have as officials of the Church. It is not obvious that Catholics have an obligation to further church doctrine in fulfilling whatever role they play in society any more than it is obvious that Catholics who fail to follow church doctrine—as in using birth control, for instance—are thereby condemned by having committed "serious sin."

It is unclear how we are to go about resolving such a problem where one is, as it were, at odds with oneself and equally unclear how to categorize it. It is not internal to being a politician, given that that is a profession, since not all politicians have such a problem. It may appear to be external because Senator Kennedy is being told by others, the bishops, what it is he ought to do, but their position is not that he ought to do what they tell him to do, but that he ought to do what being a Catholic requires him to do. As Francis Cardinal George of Chicago said, " 'That's an internal conflict, because their faith tells them that [they] are not accountable to us, nor even to the electorate or the Constitution." So this is an oddity.

A second kind of oddity can occur when a professional is wearing two hats that may require the professional to act in ways that may be at odds with each other. Not recognizing that one is in such a position can cause the professional to make what may be catastrophic errors—as the Challenger disaster makes clear.[18]

As we saw, the engineers at Morton-Thiokol recommended against launching the Challenger because, with an overnight temperature in the teens, they were concerned that the Viton would be too cold to close the gap between the segments when they wobble at launch. The risk of failure was too high, and they thought the flight should be postponed.

NASA insisted that Morton-Thiokol revisit its decision, and after more discussion, Mr. Mason, senior vice president for Wasatch Operations at Morton-Thiokol, said, "Well, it's time to make a management decision. We're just spinning our wheels."[19] The engineers were excluded from the discussion with the exception of Bob Lund, the vice president for engineering. He hesitated when Mason asked him his opinion, and Mason then told him, "It's time to take off your engineering hat and put on your management hat."[20] Lund then agreed with the other managers that they should go ahead with the launch, and that decision was relayed to NASA.

Mason was asking Lund to think like a manager, not an engineer, and Lund did. He did not look at just the risk to the shuttle from the cold weather, but all the risks involved if the company told NASA not to launch. There had already been many delays; NASA had only weeks before solicited contracts from other manufacturers for the rockets; NASA's budget was up for review the next day in congress with a main concern being the constant delays in launching.

So Lund did what managers do: he did a cost/benefit analysis. The shuttle had flown often without problems, and although a failure would be catastrophic, the chance of failure was small. But the likelihood of losing their shuttle contract was high if they did not keep to their launch schedule—particularly since the president was to deliver his State of the Union message the evening of the launch and was planning on talking to the teacher in space. The cost of not launching was high.

But in changing hats Lund changed the decision procedure he had used as an engineer when he agreed with his fellow engineers that a launch was too risky. Michael Davis has put this well:

> First, engineers would not normally include in their calculations certain risks—for instance, the risk of losing the shuttle contract if the launch schedule were not kept. Such risks are not part of their professional concern; such risks are properly a manager's concern. Second, engineers are trained to be conservative in their assessment of permissible risk ... Engineers do not, in general, balance risk against benefit. They reduce risk to permissible levels and only then proceed. Managers, on the other hand, generally balance risk against benefit. That is one of the things they are trained to do.[21]

The engineers were looking at the risk to the shuttle from the cold, but the managers were to look at all the risks.

Lund was unaware that he had changed his decision procedure, but changing it made all the difference. He took off his engineering cap, which would urge caution, as it did when he was meeting, as an engineer, with the engineers, and he put on his management cap, which took the risk of a catastrophic failure of the Viton as just one risk among many that a manager had to consider, including the risk of losing the NASA contract that paid for his position. The result was that the Challenger was launched the next morning.

Perhaps Mason's "take off the one and put on the other" led Lund into doffing the one and donning the other, but that was a false choice. There was no need for him to stop being an engineer in order to act as a manager. He was, after all, the vice president for engineering, and his role was to wear both hats, as it were, acting as an engineer who managed the engineers and so represented them and the position he himself had adopted as an engineer. Instead he acted as just another vice president—as though he were just like the other vice presidents and not an engineer.

There is no pat answer about what someone who wears two hats ought to do when faced with a problem that creates a conflict between the perspectives of two different professions. But we should hope that one would think about how one was thinking while wearing each hat and recognize that a conflict between what one ought to do while wearing one hat and what one ought to do wearing another is not to be resolved just by choosing to wear one. It can only be resolved by considering the reasons for choosing one over the other.

9

Fundamental Moral Relations

We have referred generally to our responsibilities, noting our obligations or duties and rights, but our relations with others are not exhausted by our having rights and obligations. For instance, we entrust our health to physicians, our teeth to dentists, our legal matters to lawyers, our financial affairs to accountants, and in each case it is true that we have a right. We have a right to proper care, say, and the physician has an obligation to provide it. But in entrusting our health to physicians, we empower the physicians to do what the physician judges is best for our health. "Take two of these in the morning." "Stop smoking if you want to stop coughing." The physician is not duty bound to give such advice, but empowered by us, and by the law that licenses physicians, to give whatever advice the physician decides is best. Ethical issues arise regarding being empowered that we would fail to recognize if we limited ourselves to looking for rights and duties.

We have made extensive use of those concepts in analyzing various cases. McGann and Owens both claimed a right to health-care coverage for their AIDS because they had dutifully paid their premiums since they had started work, and they thought that the companies had a duty to provide coverage. The companies hesitated because they had competing duties, to McGann and Owens on the one hand and to the other employees on the other, and they could not afford to give everyone their due.

When duties are invoked, rights ride along as correlatives, and vice versa. My having a duty to keep a promise to you means that you have a right that I keep my promise, and your having a right means I have a duty. There is a single relation, a right–duty relation, seen as a right from one point of view and as a duty from the other point of view.

Such relations are always about something. I can hire someone to mow my lawn. I then have a right that the person mow my lawn, and that person has a duty to mow my lawn. We are in a right–duty relation regarding the mowing of my lawn. McGann and Owens and the other employees all presumably had a right to health care, having paid their monthly premiums, and their companies presumably had a duty to pay for it.

We might think that analysis would suffice to explain the ethical dilemma the relevant managers faced. How could they provide the health care everyone had a right to? But what we missed, since we stopped there, is whether the managers were empowered to make decisions about paying for employees' health care. To assess whether they acted ethically in denying McGann and Owens what they claimed they were owed, we would need to determine whether the managers were indeed empowered to refuse to pay for medical bills the employees had and whether, if they were, they exercised that power ethically. We would certainly fault them ethically if they displayed a history of bias, having refused to cover the expenses of their female employees, for instance, or if they refused the claims of McGann and Owens because they assumed they were gay. We need some relation other than the right–duty relation if we are even to raise the question of how they exercise their power.

§1 Power–Liability Relation

As Wesley Hohfeld said of analyses of cases in the law, "One of the greatest hindrances to the clear understanding, the incisive statement, and the true solution of legal problems frequently arises from the express or tacit assumption that all relations may be reduced to 'rights' and 'duties', and that these latter categories are therefore adequate for the purpose of analyzing even the most complex legal issues."[1] His concern was that assimilating all sorts of legal relations to the right–duty relation prevents us from fully understanding legal cases and so precludes our resolving them properly.

It might sound as though the right–duty relation would suffice for us to understand our being liable for jury duty, for instance. After all, once called, we have a duty to appear, and those who called us have a right that we appear. But our liability to serve as jurors is not a duty to serve, but "a liability to have a duty created" to serve. We will only have a duty to serve once the proper parties exercise their power "to impose a specific duty to perform the functions of a juror."[2] We cannot make sense of someone's having the power to create a duty if we only have at our disposal the right–duty relation.

So Hohfeld introduces what he calls the power–liability relation. In the law, and in ethics, I will argue, we empower individuals to create and change relations. So a state legislature is empowered to make individuals liable for jury duty, and if it passes legislation making any citizen over 18, say, liable for jury duty, we come into that liability upon turning 18 and carry it with us throughout our lives. At some point someone the legislature has authorized and so empowered to call us for jury duty may exercise that power and change our legal relation from being liable to have a duty to having a duty.

We come to have ethical duties in the same way. I bribe my son by promising him a cookie if he behaves while at the store. He behaves. I now owe him a cookie. He has a right to it, after all. He and I are in a right–duty relation because I made a promise, and I can only make a promise if I am a moral agent. That empowers me to make promises. A parrot can say, "I promise you a cookie!," but cannot make a promise.

My power as a moral agent is limited, of course. I cannot really promise him the moon. I can only promise what is possible. And I cannot make promises to just anything. I cannot make a promise to an iPad, but I can promise my son an iPad because he is a moral agent.

What makes my son and me moral agents is a nice question, but however we determine the features of a moral agent, the right–duty relation captures only one ethical relation we can be in. We can fail even to recognize that we have an ethical problem if we are blinded to any other relation by looking only for duties and rights, and we will certainly fail to resolve some ethical problems we face if we do not recognize that other ethical relation, the power–liability relation.

We can get a sense of how we are all empowered by considering a legal example Hohfeld uses. Suppose someone stops for the night at an inn. The traveler is asking for a room, and the question is whether the innkeeper has a duty to provide the traveler with a room since the innkeeper has "a public calling." Yet if we limit ourselves to rights and duties, the only way of creating a duty on the part of the innkeeper to the traveler would be for the legislature to impose a duty on the innkeeper, thereby creating a right on the part of the traveler to be a guest. That makes the traveler's right a function of the legislature's imposing a duty, and Hohfeld argues that understanding the issue in that way would short-circuit the legal issues involved. The innkeeper does not have a duty because of the legislature, but because the traveler "has the legal power, by making proper application and sufficient tender, to impose a duty on the innkeeper to receive him as a guest."[3] The traveler has an independent status as an agent to create a right by imposing a duty on the innkeeper. The difference is crucial, legally and ethically.

We need only think of how difficult it was for African Americans, as Blacks were then called, to travel in this country before desegregation empowered them to create duties on innkeepers—or any who owned or managed motels and hotels. African Americans had no power before to create such a duty. What desegregation did was not to impose a duty on the innkeeper, but to empower African Americans. Imposing a duty changes the innkeeper's relations, forcing the innkeeper to accept African-American travelers. Empowering African Americans recognizes them as agents, a recognition with profound implications legally and ethically. It puts them in a position of power over the innkeeper and accords them the respect all people deserve.[4]

This example gives us a sense of how empowering, as it were, the power–liability relation can be for individuals and for our understanding of the ethical issues involved in such cases. Individuals need to be empowered to be able to create rights and duties, and they cannot be moral agents without being empowered. The power–liability relation is a necessary condition for moral agency as well as for the right–duty relation.

We not only have rights and duties, that is, but can create rights and duties. We are, as it were, mini-legislatures, empowered and so entitled to create contracts, for instance, buying and selling goods and services, helping others when in need, making promises, taking care of our patients if we are physicians and our clients if we are lawyers.

H. L. A. Hart made this same point about what he calls power-conferring rules in response to such legal positivists as John Austin who hold that the law consists of the commands of a sovereign, the commands creating a right on the part of the sovereign and duties on the part of the subjects. As Hart points out, that understanding of the law leaves out the crucial feature that would empower a sovereign to issue commands, if that were what a sovereign did, and the feature that allows individuals within a legal system to make contracts, for instance. They must likewise be empowered—just as moral agents are empowered. What the power–liability relation adds to our ethical toolbox is what Hart's power-conferring rules add to our understanding of the law.[5]

§2 A Fundamental Moral Relation

The power–liability relation is thus a fundamental moral relation for at least two reasons:

- If we are to understand what it is to be a moral agent—as persons and as professionals—we need to suppose the power–liability relation. Moral agents are empowered.
- The right–duty moral relation is created by moral agents empowered to create such relations by, for example, making a promise, taking on a patient, and so on.

The power–liability relation is an ethical relation as well as a legal one, that is, and we can find examples of it in our ordinary lives as well as in different professions. We are always in many relations. We have siblings, mothers, fathers, uncles, aunts, friends, acquaintances, partners, children, colleagues at work, neighbors, and on and on. Certainly, in some of these relations we exercise power over others, legally mandated or not. Parents have power over their children, and though we may wince sometimes at how a parent admonishes some child, we recognize the parent's power to discipline the child as he or she sees fit—within limits, of course. Were I to discipline the child, I would have overstepped a boundary. Nothing empowers me to do that.

Were I to see the child about to drown in a pool, however, I would fail to exercise the power I have as a moral agent were I to do no more than wince. We all are empowered as ethical agents, and we can use that power well or not. Perhaps it would be better to say that we do use that power, well or not. We are gracious to others, or not; we are kind to others, or not; we bully others, or not; we shun some, or not; we are polite to others, or not; we shame others, or not. We are in a myriad of relations all the time, and we are empowered— as moral agents if nothing else. We can care for our parents when they become old and frail, or not. We can change our child's diaper with care to ensure a clean and dry bottom, or not. We can help a sibling with homework, or a household chore, or not. We can say something, or not, when a bully picks on others by calling them demeaning nicknames.

We encourage or discourage such behavior by the way we respond. We can smile when someone is bullied, sharing in "the fun." We can applaud when someone picks on others, adding to the demeaning nicknames, for instance. We can do nothing when someone offends another, failing to discourage such behavior and so sharing the ethical responsibility for its continuance. We use public opinion as a way of sanctioning unethical behavior and encouraging ethical behavior, and we all shape public opinion by speaking up or staying silent.[6] We can help empower bullies—or not.

Bullying is wrong, and although no one has a right to bully others, a person is empowered to be a bully, or not, and others are in a position of power to stand up to bullies—or not. We will fail to fasten on the proper remedy for bullying if we only have at hand the right–duty relation. If we only have a right not to be bullied, we can do nothing ethically when we are bullied except point out that the bully has a duty not to bully us and, correlatively, we have a right not to be bullied. But that we can speak out implies a power to chastise the bully and belies a failure to respond in any other way. When we speak out, we are exercising our power as moral agents, a power we can also use not just to call the bully out, but to stand up to the bully and refuse to be bullied.

In appealing to our power as moral agents, we are not conjuring up some exotic creature, but appealing to a relation we have used since we were little children complaining about not getting our share of cookies or the same allowance our older siblings were getting. We were then acting as moral agents, calling parents to account as moral agents who have failed, we think, to act morally in treating us as they treat our siblings and so became liable to be held to account.

"Liable" may be confusing here. "Careful, she's liable to fall!" can mean both that the toddler may fall, given her position standing on the table like that, and that she is likely to fall. But we are not using "liable" to mean "likely." A kid who steals a sibling's cookie is liable for punishment, but may have done it so surreptitiously as to avoid discovery. I am liable for jury duty even if it is unlikely that I will ever be called. I am liable to be stopped for going 65 mph in a 55 mph zone in upstate New York, but it is not likely that I will be stopped since everyone goes at least 8 to 10 miles over the speed limit. I am liable to be stopped by the Border Patrol anywhere in the United States within 100 miles of the external boundaries. That does not mean that it is likely that I will be stopped, only that I can be and am not in a position to protest if I am.

All "liability" means here is that someone is subject to someone's exercise of power. The state can make me liable to serve on a jury. My driving makes me liable to be stopped by those charged with enforcing the law. So a police officer is empowered by the state to give me a ticket if I am speeding, and I am liable for a ticket if I am speeding.

§3 Power and Discretion

My mother-in-law got her first speeding ticket when she was 78. She was clocked going 79 mph in a 45 mph zone. The police officer was probably not surprised that the car was speeding. It is a hot-rodded 1964 blue Chevrolet station wagon with a louvered hood, heavy-duty mufflers that make a deep roar, and an engine sufficient to make it roar, with at least 375 horsepower. He probably was surprised when he got to the car, no doubt expecting a young man and finding instead a gray-haired grandmother who, with her short height and bad back, sits on a cushion to drive. When he told her he had stopped her for going 79, she corrected him.

"But you're wrong. This is calibrated. I was going 81."

Even more perplexed at such honesty, the officer asked, "Where were you going in such a hurry?"

"To my quilting group."
"And you had to speed?!"

"I like to speed."

"You like to speed?! When did you start speeding?"

"When I was sixteen."

He had the good sense not to ask how many years ago that had been, but asked instead, "How many tickets have you gotten?"

"None. I don't speed if there is traffic around. It's too dangerous."

He then told her he had to give her a speeding ticket, but cut it to 69 when she said she had promised herself that if she ever got a ticket, she would stop speeding.

When she went to court and the judge questioned her about going 69 in a 45 mph zone, she explained that she had been going 81, that the police officer clocked her at 79 ("and you really ought to make sure those meters are calibrated properly"), but gave her a ticket for 69. The judge was more than a little surprised, as we might imagine, but after a discussion like that she had with the officer, he cut her ticket to 59. She had to pay a fine, but lost no points.

When we begin to unpack the legal and ethical aspects of this, we will find a right–duty relation. The officer had a right to stop my mother-in-law for speeding, and she had a duty to stop. No one can fault the officer, legally or ethically, for stopping her, and, obviously, no one can fault her for stopping. She might complain about the failure to clock her speed accurately, but she would have no right to complain about being stopped.

We cannot capture all the ethical aspects of the case, however, if we limit ourselves to rights and duties. The officer had a right to stop her and she had a duty to stop because police officers are empowered to enforce the law. The state legislature has given them that power and not given it to professors, say, or surgeons, or lawyers. The police having that power makes all of us liable. Just as we carry the liability for jury duty throughout our adult lives, we carry the liability of being stopped whenever we speed.

What we will most obviously miss if we consider only rights and duties is the discretion the officer and the judge exercised in lowering her speed, in effect, from 79 to 69 to 59. It is a fiction that she was going at any of those speeds, but the officer and the judge have the power to create that fiction for the purposes of the law. She was treated very well by them. They exercised their discretion to lower her speed and so saved her money and points.

Nowhere in any right–duty relationship is discretion found. When you make a promise to me, I have a right to what was promised and you have a duty to keep your promise. You do not have any discretion in the matter. You either keep your promise or not. But when discretion is involved, we can always ask, among other things, whether it ought to have been exercised as it was.

Our assessment of the treatment of my mother-in-law will depend in part on how the officer and the judge treat others similarly situated. The most obvious way in which they could have acted unethically would be to be less than evenhanded, treating my mother-in-law differently than anyone else going 81 mph in a 45 mph zone. Had it been a black male in that hot-rodded car, would he have been treated so well? The question answers itself. My mother-in-law was treated well almost certainly because she is a little old lady—despite her insistence that she was going 81, not 79, in a 45 mph zone and her admission that she was speeding because, as she said, "I like to speed." Being less than even-handed in how we exercise discretion is one way in which we can go wrong regarding a power–liability relation. We would be wrong legally and ethically as well in this case.

We cannot, in other words, come to any conclusion about whether the officer and the judge acted ethically if we consider only rights and duties. It is in the exercise of their powers to enforce the law that their discretion comes into play, and, to repeat the point, the ethical question is whether they exercised their discretion properly. We cannot even recognize that ethical problem if we do not have the power–liability relation at hand.

Cases involving police and judges are no different from those involving other professionals. We will need the power–liability relation if we are to recognize and respond to them appropriately. A lawyer is empowered to take care of legal affairs— represent a client in court, write wills, check contracts, and on and on. When I hire a lawyer, I am creating a right–duty relation: I now have a right that the lawyer represent me, and the lawyer has a duty to represent me. That right–duty relation would not exist if the lawyer were not empowered to take care of legal matters and if I were not empowered to hire the lawyer. The same power/liability relation underlies all the relations we have with professionals and they have with us.

We now have a third reason for the power–liability relation being a fundamental moral relation:

- We cannot properly understand at least some ethical issues (like those involving my mother-in-law) without making use of the power–liability relation.

There are thus at least three ways in which the power–liability relation functions morally. We are, first, empowered as moral agents. Second, it is only as moral agents that we can create right–duty relations. And now, third, we have at least one kind of ethical problem we would not even see were we not to have that relation at hand—the exercise of the discretion that goes with being empowered.

§4 Additional Ethical Relations

Hohfeld introduces two other kinds of relations he thinks are necessary complements to the right–duty and power–liability relations. The privilege–no-right relation is the complement of the right–duty relation. We are privileged when we are at liberty to, say, pick up a coin we see laying on the sidewalk. We do not have a right to the coin any more than anyone else does who did not drop it, but we may pick it up. So may anyone else, for that matter. We are all privileged, at liberty, to pick it up, and that means that no one else has a right that we not pick it up. My privilege to pick it up is your no-right that I not pick it up.

We can perhaps get a better sense of the difference between a right–duty relation and a privilege–no-right relation by considering the following scenario. I will sell you the privilege of eating the very best meal you could ever possibly have. Indeed, I will advertise it widely and sell the privilege to anyone willing to fork up the low price of $19.99. This is to be a grand meal, one that will merit a glowing review. It will have the best of ingredients, properly seasoned, properly prepared, properly cooked, properly presented. You will never again be privileged to have such a wonderful experience— and at such a price!

If you purchase a privilege to have this meal, you are at liberty to eat the meal and no one has a right that you not eat it. Indeed, everyone who has purchased a privilege is at liberty to eat it. No one has a right that anyone not eat it. Of course, buying such a privilege does not give anyone a right to the meal. No one has a duty to allow you to eat it. So buying a privilege to the very best meal you could ever have gives new meaning to "first come, first served." If I sell myself a privilege and eat the meal before you arrive, tough. You bought a privilege, not a right, and if you somehow mistook the one for the other, that is your problem, not mine.

The example works not only for the law, but also for ethical matters. We can find ourselves at liberty to do something, where no one has a right that we not, and ethical problems can arise when someone tries to prevent us from doing what we are privileged to do. There have been a series of incidents where blacks have had the police called because they have been perceived to be doing something they are not at liberty to do.

A white man called the police on a black family using the pool in the neighborhood where they lived because, apparently, he did not think they could afford to live there— despite their having a card that gained them entry to the pool.[7] They were at liberty to be there; no one had a right that they not be there; and yet they were treated as though they were not at liberty to be there.

A black graduate student fell asleep in the common room in her dorm, her books and papers spread out around her, and a white student called the police. The other student said "I have every right to call the police," but, in fact, she had no right that the black student not sleep in the common room.[8]

It is unfortunate that the list of examples goes on and on. Napping can now be added to the

> still growing list of things it is unacceptable to do while black. Other entrants include: couponing while black, graduating too boisterously while black, waiting for a school bus while black, throwing a kindergarten temper tantrum while black, drinking iced tea while black, waiting at Starbucks while black, AirBnB'ing while black, shopping for underwear while black, having a loud conversation while black, golfing too slowly while black, buying clothes at Barney's while black, or Macy's, or Nordstrom Rack, getting locked out of one's own home while black, asking for the Waffle House corporate number while black and reading C.S. Lewis while black, among others.[9]

In each of these cases, the blacks involved were at liberty to do what they did, and yet others, with no-right that they not do what they were doing, called them out, claiming they had no right to do what they were doing.

The standard way of analyzing such cases is that the blacks had a right to do what they were doing, but, I would suggest, a better way of understanding the problem is that they were at liberty, privileged, to do what they were doing and were treated as though they had no right to do what they were doing. It is just Hohfeld's point about legal relations that we tend to reduce them all to someone having a right, and that reduction prevents us from fully understanding what is at issue. In particular, it prevents us from seeing that others had no right to complain.

I will not pursue this relation in more detail here since we will have enough to handle showing how the power–liability relation enters into ethics. Needless to say, more needs to be said about this privilege–no-right relation and also about the other relation Hohfeld introduces, the immunity–disability relation. That relation complements the power–liability relation. Diplomats are typically immune from police citing them for traffic violations. A diplomat who parks illegally is thus in an immunity–disability relation with the police. The police are unable—have a disability—to issue a ticket because the diplomat has an immunity.

We can readily see how that relation operates in our ordinary lives. A parent says to a child, "Just tell me what you did. I'm not going to punish you for it." The child then explains what happened, expecting immunity from punishment. It would be ethically wrong for the parent to say, "Geez! No TV or cellphone for a week!" When you promise immunity, you disable yourself, as it were, from punishing the child. So if you punish the child, you are doubly at fault ethically: you broke your promise and in doing that, you changed the relation you had created, an immunity–disability relation.

We can find the same relation in professional settings when, for instance, a district attorney offers immunity to a suspect in exchange for testimony. If the offer is accepted, the district attorney and the suspect are now in an immunity–disability relation. The district attorney is unable later to bring charges against the suspect—even charges about matters that were only revealed through the suspect's having immunity. It would be an ethical breach for the district attorney to proceed to charge the suspect despite the previous agreement.

Both the immunity–disability relation and the privilege–no-right relation deserve a fuller examination, but for now we will focus on the power–liability relation and the sorts of ethical problems that can arise because of it.

10

Discretion

One consequence of seeing the power–liability relation as an ethical relation is that we can now understand and assess exercises of discretion. Each of us has discretion over a variety of matters, and it is always relevant to ask when it is appropriate to exercise that discretion and how it ought to be exercised. Those questions can raise a variety of ethical issues that require different kinds of responses than those we have seen so far in the ethical problems we have been examining.

§1 Discretion

Health-care practitioners are empowered to provide such public services as health care, and in exercising that power, they have a great deal of leeway, discretion, that is, to determine how to proceed among the various options possible for an injury or disease. A physician with a sick patient may require some blood tests, one or several, or may not. The physician has options, as does everyone with discretion, and whatever option they choose, even deciding not to do anything, they are exercising discretion. They are at liberty to do what they decide is the right thing to do in the situation in question.

The operating field for their discretion is limited by what is medically feasible, both by what they as physicians are empowered to do and by the circumstances. So the physician is not empowered to test the patient on Cartesian physics. A historian of physics might test a student, but such a historian could not order a blood test. Such limits, however vague their extent may be, are part of what it is to be a historian or a physician. But the operating field is also limited by the circumstances, in this case by what the physician judges this particular patient needs. So the police officer who clocked my mother-in-law going 79 mph in a 45 mph zone had a number of options, from not bothering to chase her down to chasing her down and then letting her go without a ticket to giving her a ticket for going 34 mph over the speed limit or what the officer did decide to do, giving her a ticket for going 24 mph over the speed limit. These are judgment calls.

Officers are charged with enforcing traffic laws, and that charge carries with it a charge to use their own judgment in deciding what to enforce and what not. A police officer in Cook County, Illinois, used his discretion in refusing a request to intervene when a man harassed a woman trying to celebrate her birthday in an Illinois park. The man harassed her "for wearing a shirt with the Puerto Rican flag, saying it was un-American."[1] The man apparently did not know that Puerto Ricans are American citizens. He was eventually arrested and charged with "two felony counts of hate crime." The harassment was that serious, that is, and the police officer displayed poor judgment in failing to intervene. The officer may have thought it a minor problem, but was wrong and has since resigned.[2]

Police often turn a blind eye to minor infractions, and though my mother-in-law's infraction was not minor, the officer was not duty bound to stop her. Had the officer gotten a call to rush to an accident and have driven off, she would not have gotten a ticket. In empowering the police to enforce the law, the legislature necessarily gave police officers discretion. We leave it to particular officers to enforce the law. We assume that they will show good judgment, but as we know all too well from too many cases, police officers sometimes fail to exercise their power properly.

Too many of those cases end in fatalities, but one that did not stands out if only because the police involved found themselves in the awkward situation of having stopped their boss, a Florida state attorney—for no good reason. When one officer looked at her license and asked, "What agency you with?," she replied, "I'm the state attorney." The officer was taken aback and said that running her license plate "didn't come back to anything" and that, besides, her windows were "really dark" so they could not see how many were in the car. As she noted later, "The license plate, while confidential, was and remains properly registered. The tint was in no way a violation of Florida law,"[3] and Florida law permits officials to have the Department of Motor Vehicles "withhold personal information contained in their driver's license and vehicle."[4] She should know.

What is most telling is that when asked why they had stopped her, they explained that they run license plates all the time to check on stolen cars—although she was driving a Ford Fusion, not an obvious choice for thieves. It appears they stopped the car because it was driven by an African-American woman and had tinted windows that prevented them from seeing who was with her.[5] She was by herself, having just finished teaching a class at Florida A&M University College of Law. It appears to be a classic case of being stopped for driving while black.

But, as she noted, the "stop appeared to be consistent with Florida law," and that is the point here. The officers were empowered to do what they did. What is at issue is not that, but how they exercised that power. They ran a check on her license plate. Why? It takes time to do that, and why waste their time on a Ford Fusion? Did they seriously think the car was stolen? It certainly looks as though they exercised that power in a discriminatory way: they checked the car because the driver was black, and they could not see who else might be in the car. Once it was checked and failed to come "back to anything," we might understand why they stopped the car, not assuming it was driven by a state official, but, again, we ought to wonder why. Had it been driven by a white man in a power suit, would they have proceeded to stop it? We cannot know, but we have some evidence that they stopped it because the driver was black. For instance, the officer in the passenger seat got out and went to the passenger side window of the state attorney's car, apparently prepared for more than just a routine traffic stop. And the claim they made that the windows were darkly tinted and so a reason for stopping her was met with a knowing smile: she knew they were blowing smoke.

We have here the same sort of problem we laid out regarding James Blake being tackled by the New York City police officer—a paradigmatic example of a poor exercise of discretion. The Blake case is particularly egregious because the officer gave him no warning. He got tackled out of the blue, without a clue. But both cases display a less than even-handed approach to enforcing the law.

§2 Good Judgment

It is an abuse of power to exercise discretion in ways that discriminate—against any particular group. Having discretion means using one's own judgment, but one is not empowered to do anything one wants. Discretion requires good judgment, and good judgment must have some factual basis. So police in Georgia who used a coin-toss to decide whether to give a speeding ticket to a driver were not displaying good judgment—or any judgment at all except to outsource their judgment to a coin-toss instead of deciding on the basis of the driver's speed and past history. As the police chief said, "This isn't a police procedure, to bring a coin flip—whether it's an app or an actual coin toss—that's not part of that decision making to decide to take someone's freedom." The driver put it well after the charges were dismissed: "These are people who are supposed to protect us, and instead are treating our freedom and our lives like games."[6]

Instead of outsourcing their judgment to such a decision procedure as flipping a coin, the police officers ought to have made a judgment based on reasons. They needed to construct an argument, even if not self-consciously, that took into account such matters as how fast the driver was going over the speed limit—81 mph in a 45 mph zone? Those reasons ought to provide guidance as to what discretion they had. If the driver was going 52 mph in a 45 mph zone, it would not be unreasonable to let the driver go with a warning. If the driver was in a hurry for an emergency, it would not be unreasonable to let the driver go. Many different factors that may or may not be relevant in the case need to be taken into account if the officers are to exercise good judgment.

What we are entitled to expect from professionals as they do what they are empowered to do is that they show good judgment. Police officers, physicians, lawyers, accountants, judges, engineers—they are all empowered to make decisions affecting our lives, and they are ethically obligated to exercise that power well by providing good reasons for what they decide to do. Flipping a coin to decide whether to weld or bolt a bridge strut is not an exercise of good judgment.

"Good judgment" is a complex concept that can differ from profession to profession and embody different virtues in different professions. We can go wrong in many ways—by expressing the wrong virtue, at the wrong time, toward the wrong person or object, for the wrong reason, in a wrong manner, and not in the proper degree. It is thus difficult to exercise a virtue properly. "It is possible to fail in many ways …, while to succeed is possible only in one way."[7]

We have already at hand examples of ways in which we can go wrong. Toward the wrong person or object? The police officer tackling James Blake is a good example. The wrong manner? The police officer asking the state attorney "What agency you with?" comes off as pushy, skeptical that the driver is high enough up the state's food chain to merit having personal information withheld. The wrong reason? Tinted windows are not a good reason for stopping a driver. Being black leaning against the side of a four-star hotel is not a good reason for being tackled and taken to the ground without warning.

It is easy enough to find more examples of less than stellar conduct on the part of professionals. A police officer in Lorain, Ohio, pulled over his daughter's boyfriend, and when the boyfriend asked what for, he said, "Have a seat in my car. We'll make [expletive] up while we go." The officer's dash cam captured "the 26-year patrolman's transformation from concerned father to authority-abusing police officer."[8]

In asking professionals to show good judgment, we are not asking anything more or less of them than we ask of ourselves as moral agents. It is sometimes perfectly appropriate to get angry, for instance, but we

> can display anger too frequently or not frequently enough, too mildly or too violently, for too short a time or for too long a time; one can feel anger toward people who have done nothing to make anger appropriate or fail to feel anger toward people who have done something to which anger is a proper response; one can feel anger at insignificant things or fail to feel anger at important wrongs.

And even if we had all that right, we would still fail to do what we ought to do were we not to be angry "for the right reasons, in the right spirit."[9] What holds for anger holds for all other virtues both for us and for what we are entitled to expect from professionals. We want our lawyer to be indignant, even angry, for instance, at what we take to be an injustice, but the anger should be expressed properly. A lawyer's screaming at a judge is no more appropriate than a parent screaming at a toddler or a physician screaming at a patient. These are not examples of good judgment.

We expect all professionals to show good judgment both in regard to virtues they share with other professionals and virtues that distinguish them from other professionals. We expect all professionals to be honest, to be committed to the ideals of their profession, and to have integrity, for instance. But some virtues seem uniquely tied to particular professions. An accountant gets no credit for *trying* to balance the books. We expect accountants to persevere until the books are in fact balanced. So it was beyond belief when a president proposed a budget with a two trillion accounting error. "How could the secretary of the treasury, the director of OMB and the director of the National Economic Council allow such an elementary error?"[10] Even a much smaller error would justify a judgment of accounting incompetence.

But whereas we fault accountants who do not succeed, we give credit to a member of a medical emergency team who tries but fails to resuscitate someone. We would fault the person for giving up after one or two tries, but we do not require success at resuscitating the patient to warrant praise.

What is different from profession to profession, that is, is that different professions are to show good judgment about different things. In a recent political imbroglio in Connecticut about confirming a justice of the state court, the president of the

> Connecticut Trial Lawyers Association, suggested a rubric for weighing court nominees: "Does he demonstrate patience, calmness and attention? Does he demonstrate courtesy, civility, open-mindedness and compassion? Is he committed to professionalism and improving availability of justice to all? Is he skillful in the administration of justice?" ... "These are the standards by which ... all judicial appointments should be measured."[11]

A physician need not have any interest at all in improving the availability of justice for all although we would expect patience, calmness, and attention. Engineers are to be risk averse. Financial advisors are to take some risks with our money, but usually not too much. Police officers are to put themselves at risk if that is the only way they can prevent further harm. Although there are, as I said, characteristics like honesty we expect from all professionals, we can readily sort out professions and professionals by the different characteristics we expect from individuals within each profession.

We can get a sense of how different professions and professionals are from one another by imagining a professional crossing professional boundaries. If I may repeat an example, were a professor to examine students the way a physician examines patients, giving them a passing grade or flunking them depending on how healthy the professor judged they were, the professor would soon be without a position. Were a physician to examine patients by giving them essay questions, patients would seek a new physician without hesitation.

In entering into a profession, we commit ourselves to a certain form of life, as it were, a way of thinking about the world in which we have mastered the skills those in the profession must have and have learned what is idiosyncratic to the profession— "moduli spaces," "Teichmüller theory," "BUFKIT," "heavy snow with a nice crosshair signature." We generally take on the characteristics that are necessary to succeed in the profession—being risk-averse for engineers—and thus the character we associate with particular professions. Jokes about engineers, lawyers, psychiatrists, and other professionals depend upon these standard conceptions of their characters.

We will need to keep such differences in mind as we zero in on particular cases from different professions. As we have seen with the Tufte example, it is not easy learning enough about a profession to be able to understand the details of a case, let alone resolve it. But there are some general ethical issues that arise regarding the power–liability relation, and keeping these in mind as well as the professional character of individuals will help us recognize and unravel otherwise obscure and confusing cases.

We also need to keep in mind variables that affect discretion in any profession. A police officer is constrained, legally and ethically, in how to respond to a traffic violation. There is a range of possible decisions, that is, with limits that are fairly obvious. An officer is not to shoot someone who has been stopped for a speeding ticket any more than a physician is to sever an artery to end an operation for, say, lunch. A judge is not to solicit sex from a speeding offender in exchange for leniency any more than an accountant is to cook the books for a percentage of the proceeds gained.

So one variable to keep in mind is the range of possibilities. Sometimes a decision arguably within the acceptable range is not the best decision. Our concern with the police cases was with the exercise of discretion, a virtue that spans many professions, and we can get that just right or be too lenient or too strict.

Some Burger King workers asked a woman to leave because "her barefoot baby violated the company's no shoes rules" as well as, they claimed, the health code.[12] They were wrong about the health code, and although all rules require interpretation, it is presumed that those interpreting them will exercise common sense. Few babies wear shoes, and so if the rule were as strict as those workers interpreted it, Burger King would exclude those with babies. And if babies are to be excluded, what about those wearing sandals, not shoes? Their feet are bare: that is the point of wearing sandals.

No great harm was done in this case, but professionals exercising their discretion much too strictly can cause great harm. A family who took photos of their young girls, aged 5, 4, and 1 1/2, found themselves the subject of a sex-abuse investigation because a Walmart employee "flagged the photos as pornographic." The most revealing of the photos showed the children on their stomachs lying on towels, and there was nothing pornographic about the photos, a court said—ten years later. Their children were taken into protective custody for a month while the couple's friends and families were interviewed about whether they were "child sex offenders." The court found that "the social workers presented no evidence that the children were in danger of being abused" and abused their authority in taking custody of the children. Meanwhile, the mother was suspended from her job for a year, the couple's name was listed on a sex offender registry, they "underwent psychological evaluation," and their home was searched with the police "seizing computers, cellphones, undeveloped film and other materials relevant to a child pornography probe."[13] The social workers were responsible for all sorts of harms through their failure to exercise good judgment.

§3 Raising the Bar

Some strict applications of discretion depend not upon the mistakes of the zealous, but upon external constraints that can raise or lower the bar for those exercising discretion. If the Border Patrol knows that terrorists are trying to enter the country by crossing from Canada, say, to the United States, those trying to enter are going to be subject to much stricter scrutiny than usual. No one wants to be known as the Border Patrol agent who failed to realize a traveler was a terrorist, and, rightly, no one wants to be responsible for the harms such a terrorist would presumably cause. Agents are much less likely in such a situation to let little things pass than usual.

The increasing number of examples of agents from Immigration and Customs Enforcement (ICE) detaining and trying to deport law-abiding residents of the country is a response to the judgment that any criminal history suffices as a ground for deportation. The bar for legal residency has become higher, and ICE agents have responded accordingly.

Those caught up in the increasingly strict interpretation of who is entitled to be in the United States and who is not include the professor with "graduate degrees in molecular biosciences and pharmaceutical engineering" he received during his thirty years in the United States, with a wife and three children who are citizens, and with no criminal record;[14] the landscaper in Michigan with no criminal record, an American wife and two children, deported to Mexico after twenty-nine years in the United States;[15] the 43-year-old physician in Michigan, brought to the United States from Poland when he was 5, detained because of two misdemeanors twenty-six years ago, to be deported to Poland despite speaking no Polish;[16] "the airport arrest and deportation of a 22-year-old female college student from Spain, visiting the United States for a vacation at the invitation of a librarian at Oregon State University, on grounds that she would give Spanish lessons to the librarian's young son for a few weeks—work for which she lacked the right visa;"[17] and on and on with "more than 28,000 'non-criminal immigration violators'" in the first seven months of 2017.[18]

What this list indicates is that the range over which someone can exercise discretion is not fixed, but flexible depending upon a variety of factors which raise ethical issues. Suppose we have as our priority deporting illegal residents "based on the severity of immigrants' criminal offenses."[19] An ICE agent would exercise discretion covering only those individuals with a criminal record, and we would certainly judge the agent too lenient not to arrest someone who had committed armed robbery and too strict to arrest someone because of a misdemeanor from, say, twenty-six years ago.

But suppose that instead of having agents measure their enforcement by the severity of an immigrant's criminal offense, we raise the ante, as it were, and set as our priority deporting illegal immigrants who have any criminal offense. Now an agent would be derelict not to arrest someone with even a minor offense. Given that no group is a priority, residents "who committed crimes long ago and satisfied their obligations to the American justice system have learned there is no statute of limitations on ICE's ability to use the immigrants' offenses as grounds to arrest and deport them."[20]

We would expand the scope even more were agents to measure their enforcement by someone being here illegally. But if we make no group a priority, then an ICE agent would be too strict only for arresting someone who was not an illegal immigrant and too lenient to fail to arrest someone who was. All immigrants are treated in the same way, and that has a number of ethically problematic consequences—for the immigrants, for the agents, and for the system that handles deportations.

It creates fear on the part of those who have lived here for years—thirty-eight in the case of the Michigan physician—that they could be deported at any time. They read stories about the man who called 911 because he saw an intruder on his lawn and was worried about his three-year-old twins and one-year-old son. The police came and took him away to detain him for deportation.[21] They read stories about the woman on her way to visit her new granddaughter and was detained after border patrol agents boarded the bus and asked all the passengers for identification.[22]

Immigrants are liable at any time to be arrested. They carry that liability with them all the time and everywhere. Unlike a citizen's liability for jury duty, this liability creates fear among immigrants and ensures that they will come to live in a shadowy world, unable to access even the most basic services, like police protection.

It has an effect on the agents as well. As former acting ICE director John Sandwerg puts it, "It diminishes the incentives on the agents to go get the bad criminals. Now their job is to fill the beds," and the more you fill, the more you fill the deportation system with individuals who are no threat at all. "If you apply that logic to local police forces," Sandwerg adds, "you're saying that every robber and rapist is the same as a jaywalker. And then you're clogging your courts with jaywalkers."[23] So it has effects on the entire system of deportation, clogging your courts with lawsuits to prevent what appear to be arbitrary deportations. And it is expensive, costing the government, which must pay to hold those it has arrested, and costing the families of those detained since it is often the wage earner who has been arrested—not counting the psychological loss to the family of a spouse and a parent. It rips families apart.[24]

Such examples of raising the bar for the exercise of discretion can be found in every profession. As we saw, in the flu epidemics, it is unfortunately not a rare occurrence for someone with flu-like symptoms to be diagnosed with the flu and sent home, only to die shortly thereafter from a "strep blood infection," for example.[25] Physicians do not order blood tests for every patient, and it is a matter of discretion whether the symptoms a patient has merit further examination or can be assumed to be a mark of what everyone else has in an epidemic.

In some states monthly quotas for traffic tickets appear to be the norm even where prohibited by law. In New York, state troopers are always out toward the end of each month, a sign that they have not issued enough tickets yet for the month. They are also out around the fifteenth of the month, apparently in an attempt to ensure that they do not have too much catching up to do at the end of the month. In such a situation, an officer is obviously more likely to give speeding tickets to those who would, under other circumstances, be given a warning.

§4 Competing Norms

Someone who is empowered by some position or other always operates within some norm about how that power is to be exercised. A police officer in Germany has different criteria for monitoring traffic on the Autobahn than an officer in the United States has for monitoring traffic on the Interstate. Certainly their understanding of what counts as "speeding" is different. Going 90 mph is going to get different reactions on the Interstate than on the Autobahn.

The exercise of power not only differs among members of the same profession in different countries, but may differ among members of the different professions while supposedly working together. Some such differences may lead to ludicrous and dangerous incidents—such as two doctors fighting in an operating room because the surgeon was upset at the anesthetist for asking for tests the surgeon did not agree with. "You stay within your limits," the surgeon said. The surgeon and the anesthetist had different conceptions of what it was appropriate for each to do when they are supposedly working together in an operating room, and the surgeon thought that the anesthetist was trespassing on the surgeon's territory. He thought the norm was that each kept to their own areas of speciality whereas the anesthetist apparently thought he was permitted to help the operation as a whole succeed and to offer advice. The differing norms concerned the roles of the two while working together as a team. To put the conflict somewhat unfairly: keep to your own area or help the team succeed.

Their patient was a pregnant woman whose baby did not survive. It is unclear whether the death was a result of the spat or not, but it is an ethical issue that that question needs to be raised because death can result from such disagreements.[26]

In West Virginia, a police officer responding to a domestic-dispute call found a "visibly distraught" man who pleaded with the officer to shoot him. When the officer ordered the man to show his hands, he "did, revealing a handgun." When he was told to drop it, he responded, "I can't do that. Just shoot me." The officer did not shoot and attempted to de-escalate the situation, but the man, hands at his side, "pleaded repeatedly: 'Just shoot me.'"

He got his wish. Two other police officers arrived, and one, seeing the man waving a gun, shot and killed the man without hesitation. He later accused the first officer of freezing and being a coward, thus putting them in jeopardy. The first officer was fired for "apparent difficulties in critical incident reasoning" as well as not communicating with the other officers.[27]

It is not clear he would have had time to talk to the other officers, and in fact the accusation should have been directed at the dispatcher. The man's wife called to tell the police that her husband had threatened to kill himself with a knife and that when he heard the police were coming, he was getting his gun out of the car so the police would kill him. The dispatcher was also told the gun was unloaded, but failed to communicate any of that information to the officers.

In any event, whatever the details, this case provides a telling example of how competing norms can cause grievous harm. What is at issue is what ought to be the norm when police confront an armed suspect. If the norm is to shoot on sight, then the first officer failed to follow the norm. On that norm, he would indeed be subject to criticism, and the officer who shot the suspect lauded for doing what the first officer ought to have done.

Having a norm that seems to require a forceful response to any such situation will inevitably lead to ethical problems—such as tasering an 87-year-old woman out cutting dandelion greens with a knife. The police report says, "While we were approaching the female she bent down to the ground and cut a weed and stood back up holding the weed in her left hand with the plastic bag." The police confronted her, one pointing a gun at her, and told her to drop her knife. One even illustrated what they wanted her to do by throwing down his knife. She failed to respond.

There were reasons why she did not respond. She has a "poor understanding of English"—as the 911 caller who prompted the police to come had indicated—is hard of hearing, at least slightly demented, and was not doing anything that would explain why anyone would ask her to drop her knife. She must have been very puzzled, as anyone in her situation would be, to be confronted by three police officers and have a gun pointed at her for, apparently, cutting dandelion greens.

As she approached the officers, one officer tasered her, knocking her down. They then "handcuffed her behind her back and detained [her] at a police station on charges of trespassing and obstructing law enforcement officers." She was locked up for two and a half hours. In his response to "criticism of his department's handling of the case," the police chief said, "I am glad I was there and saw it firsthand and understand why it occurred. An 87-year-old woman with a knife still has the ability to hurt an officer"—as though the mere possibility that an 87-year-old woman might attack and hurt someone is sufficient grounds for such a response.

It is a mere possibility because, among other things, no one claims that she threatened the officers or anyone else. Her knife was by her side, and no one has claimed that she raised it in any manner, threatening or not. The 911 caller said that the woman "didn't try to attack anybody or anything." In addition, she is all of five feet tall and "can't get around too well," as the 911 caller reported. It was apparently just enough to justify a forceful response that she had a knife in her hand—a knife that even a casual glance at the dandelion greens in her other hand would explain and the observation of her cutting "weeds" would confirm.

The police chief added that the stun gun "was the lowest use of force we could have used to simply stop that threat at the time"—as though deciding to use "the lowest level of force" rather than shoot her justified their use of force.[28] Such a response can only be thought appropriate within the confines of a norm that makes immediate force the proper response to any situation which someone might deem potentially harmful. "We did not shoot her, after all," only works as an excuse to justify one's actions where shooting immediately is the norm.

But there are competing norms for how officers ought to behave when confronted with a suspect with a gun. In Toronto the norm is to try to de-escalate such situations. If that were the norm in West Virginia, it is the second officer who should be criticized for shooting first and not trying to find out what was going on that would explain the first officer's not shooting the man.

That the norm in Toronto need not lead to violence is illustrated by the police officer in Toronto who refused to shoot the man who "had just plowed into a crowd of pedestrians on a sidewalk at more than 30 mph, killing 10 and wounding 15 more." The man kept raising and lowering his gun, yelling, "Kill me!" Instead of shooting him, the officer walked toward him, gun drawn, and the man surrendered.[29]

There does not seem to be any general criterion by which such competing conceptions can be adjudicated and particularly how they could be adjudicated in the midst of a case. The competing conceptions for how to respond to a suspect who has or is suspected of having a gun cannot be settled without risking either suspects or officers. There is no way the officers could have talked about the competing norms they had and settled on one. The physician and the anesthetist could have talked through whatever problems they came to have if they had realized there was going to be a territorial dispute, but that is not an option in the midst of an operation.

In any event, if we are to come to understand a case fully, we need to be cognizant that differing norms may be in the background, affecting how the power of the participants was exercised. To look to a simpler case, consider a soccer referee at a professional game and one at a game of seven- and eight-year-olds. The context will make all the difference to their calling out a player for roughing it or for being offside. We cannot expect a seven-year-old to have an understanding of what "playing a position" means, let alone their parents yelling, "You're offside!" A referee who fails to take into account the level of maturity of the players has simply failed to tailor the rules and the consequent judgments to the situation at hand. "But you didn't call offside!" on that goal would be appropriate for professionals, but not for young kids still learning how to play.

§5 How to Fail to Exercise Power

The situations we have considered so far involve individuals exercising power, appropriately or inappropriately. But there are a variety of cases in which someone can fail to exercise power, and these raise different kinds of ethical issues than those we have considered so far. Here are four examples, each raising a different kind of ethical issue, but all concerned with how the exercise of power can fail.

(1) Conditional exercise of power—Given the examples we have been using, a reader may get the impression that the exercise of discretion is a simple matter of making a decision. A person exercising power may consider various options and even spend a great deal of time mulling over what choice to make, but, in the end, a choice is made and that is that: the person has exercised power, making a decision that affects whomever it is or whatever it was the person had power over. So the police officer who ticketed my mother-in-law thought a bit about what to charge her for, but once he made a decision and wrote out the ticket, that was that. A physician examines a patient, gets a sense of what might be wrong, and then makes a judgment about how to proceed, orders blood tests, for instance, and is done. But some exercises of discretion are conditioned. They can only be accomplished if series of steps are followed, and the power cannot be said to be exercised until each step is completed and completed properly.

The president of the United States is empowered to remove someone's security clearance, for instance, but the president cannot just say, "I am removing so-and-so's security clearance." The exercise of power can only be accomplished if those facing revocation are provided:

- A "comprehensive and detailed . . . written explanation" of the decision.
- Notice of their right to be represented by a lawyer at their own expense.
- The chance to request "any documents" and reports "upon which a denial or revocation is based."
- A "reasonable opportunity to reply in writing, and request a review" of the decision.
- A right to appeal to a "high level panel" appointed by the head of the relevant agency.
- An opportunity "to appear personally" and present materials before "an adjudicative or other authority."[30]

Civil servants need to sign off on each of these steps, and they are obligated to do so only if, in their judgments, the exercise of power is justified. It is not difficult to imagine a civil servant refusing to approve some step in the process or, for instance, the "head of the relevant agency" delaying the appointment of a "high level panel" until such time as that president no longer is in office.

Exercising power, in short, is not always such a simple act as the example of the police officer and my mother-in-law suggests. It can initiate a process that could "play out for years."[31]

(2) Technicalities—A state legislature passed a law changing the way in which divorces are granted, but the form the new law required was never printed. So no divorces issued after the law was passed were valid because the proper form was not filled out and submitted. Those who were issuing divorce decrees thought the decrees were valid, as did those who sought divorces, but they were not. Those issuing the decrees failed to exercise their power properly because they were using the old and now invalid form. The failure to grant divorce decrees not only meant that the couples who thought they were no longer a couple were still married, but that those who "remarried" became bigamists without realizing it and had bastards if they had children by their new "spouse."

Talk about a legal and ethical mess! Lon Fuller provides the example as a situation where an ex post facto law would make sense,[32] but it also illustrates nicely how those who had the power to grant divorce decrees and those empowered to obtain them were stymied. The right–duty relation does no work here. What went wrong is that they could not exercise their powers, through no fault of their own, and that is why Fuller thinks that in some circumstances an ex post facto law is acceptable. It is not making criminal after the fact something that was not a crime when it was done, but rectifying a problem that left individuals in an illegal—and unethical—situation.

The law is full of such examples. A friend of mine decided to build a garage and, without thinking about it, placed it so only half was on his own property. The rest was on the empty lot next door—which belonged to his neighbor. Neither he nor the neighbor nor the inspector nor the city employee who issued the license realized that my friend could not legally, or ethically, do what he did. The city employee failed to ensure that my friend satisfied the conditions for a proper permit, and so he did not have a proper permit despite the city's apparent approval.

These are examples where something went wrong in the exercise of a power. The professionals in question had the power at issue, and nothing about those liable to such power precluded the professionals exercising their power. But the exercise of any power is conditioned by a variety of circumstances—such as having the proper documents. We are empowered to give someone power of attorney, but only if we do it in the right way with the right forms.

(3) Fakes and mistakes—We have not explored, and will not explore, the conditions required for someone to be empowered. We bypassed that question when we were addressing what empowers persons to be moral agents, and we will bypass it here. The details of a person's becoming empowered vary from profession to profession. We cannot take a person's becoming a police officer as an exemplar of the steps one must follow to become a physician or a lawyer, say. Getting a license to practice law, for

instance, requires a degree from an accredited college or university, recommendations sufficient to get into a licensed law school, several years of study, and then passing the bar in each state in which one is to practice law. There are many possibilities for mistakes and for deception, and cases are constantly arising where someone who has practiced law for years is discovered never to have gone to law school or never to have passed the bar exam, and yet has practiced law—either through deception or, far less likely perhaps, through some misunderstanding about what is required to practice law.

The ethical issue is the same whatever the cause and whatever the profession: individuals offer their "professional services" when they are not in a position to provide them. They may be representing themselves as professionals when they are not, or they may have been professionals but are no longer empowered to offer their services.

Catch Me If You Can tells about how "Frank Abagnale Jr ... successfully forged millions of dollars worth of checks while posing as a Pan Am pilot, a doctor, and legal prosecutor."[33] Abagnale was obviously very good at representing himself as a professional, but no prescriptions he wrote as a physician, for instance, could be valid. Besides lacking the training needed to ensure that those he treated were accurately diagnosed and prescribed the correct medication, he was not empowered to provide prescriptions. Those whom he fooled were empowered to take him on, as they thought, as a physician, but were obviously unsuccessful, whatever they may have thought.

The situation is true for those who have been trained into a profession, but have lost the power to practice. A lawyer in Indiana who had been suspended from practicing law took on eleven new clients while suspended.[34] The clients thought they had hired a lawyer, but failed. A Florida lawyer was permanently disbarred from soliciting and representing clients from other states because she had no license to practice in those states.[35] Those in North and South Carolina who thought they had hired a lawyer failed as well.

Each supposed client thought they had created a duty on the part of the lawyers to represent them, but failed because although they had the power to create a duty, the "lawyers" were not empowered to be lawyers. The clients did not know that and so may have acted on the assumption that they had lawyers, but if they made use of those they thought they hired, nothing their supposed lawyers did that required a lawyer had any legal status. One can just imagine the problems, moral and legal, that would create for someone buying property, or getting a divorce, or making out a will, or needing a defense attorney.

We can, yet again, easily find examples of people pretending to be something they are not, sometimes causing great harm, sometimes just being embarrassed—and arrested. For example, a security guard in Arizona equipped "his black Dodge Charger with police-style emergency lighting and attempt[ed] to pull over [Arizona state] troopers, who were in an unmarked car."[36] When they did not stop, he pulled alongside them and waved them over. They then turned on their lights and pulled him over. He was, shall we say, surprised.

(4) Competence—These examples focus on the professional, but we can also ask whether an individual has the power to create a duty on the part of a professional. At

a minimum, someone must know what they are doing and do it voluntarily, and it is determining whether these conditions hold that physicians often face with elderly patients. They may be on medication that makes them less than fully competent, or they may have dementia, Alzheimer's, or some other mental impairment that incapacitates them. They would not then have the power to hand over their medical care to a physician. The same could be true for those with a bipolar disorder, or schizophrenia, or some other mental issue that makes it unclear that they understand what they are doing or, if they do, are doing it voluntarily.

These sorts of judgments are not easy for physicians to make, and it is easy to go wrong. When our father died, he signed a form saying that he refused extraordinary measures to save his life, but when we children got the death certificate, the physician had written "dementia" as the cause of death. When we asked him why, he explained that he had tried talking to our father, but that he had shown no signs of comprehension. New to the practice where our father went, the physician had apparently failed to read his medical history and so failed to realize he was deaf. He would have responded to a written question, but was going to ignore someone who did not take the time to understand that he was deaf.

We pointed out that the physician had a problem. Either our father was competent to sign the document which authorized the physician not to provide extraordinary measures, or he was not. If he had dementia, he was not, and so the physician, by not providing extraordinary measures, had failed to do what a physician ought to do barring such a document. If he was competent to sign the document, then he was not demented. The physician could not have it both ways. After threat of a lawsuit, the physician changed the death certificate, but the point here is that he had failed to think through what he was doing, or he would have realized that our father could not be both demented and competent. Either our father was empowered to sign off on extraordinary measures, or he was not. Because he was competent and was empowered, he created a liability on the part of the physician not to use extraordinary measures to save his life.

We can easily add case after case where someone thought they were empowered to do something only to discover that they were not because of some condition that was not satisfied. But the point, I think, is made. We need the power–liability relation if we are to understand fully these sorts of examples and their remedies. We will not find the remedies by looking for anyone's rights and duties. We will find them by looking at what empowers those involved—their competence, for instance, or their having satisfied whatever conditions are required for being empowered to do what they are trying to do. We cannot remedy the ethical problem for those who thought they were divorced by appealing to their rights and duties, or the rights and duties of those who thought they were granting divorces. We need to remedy their situation by changing their status, and, as Fuller argues regarding the bigamists, that can only be done in their case by an ex post facto law which says they are divorced despite those who tried to divorce them not having filled out and filed the proper form and having thus failed to exercise their power to divorce them. An ex post facto law retroactively empowers those granting divorces.

§6 How Things Can Go Wrong

Exercising discretion can go wrong in a variety of ways, but the examples we have just seen provide only a small sample. There are many more ways in which the exercise of power can be ineffective. Anyone who has had to go back, over and over, to get paperwork done can appreciate the variety and number of things that can go wrong—the wrong signature, a signature in the wrong place, the wrong date, a coffee-stained paper, the wrong form, and on and on. And that is just the beginnings of a list of what can go wrong when there is a form involved. Problems can arise as well with all the other variables involved. The law is replete with examples of attempts to exercise power that have failed for all sorts of reasons, some more than a little odd and more than a little disconcerting, especially for those involved.

A Romanian returned home in 2018 after being deported from Turkey where he had been since early in the 1990s. He had trouble getting into the country because, as he later discovered, he had been declared dead in 2003. His wife asked for a ruling since she had not heard from him since he left. He had not contacted her because she had been unfaithful, he said, but, in any event, he found that because he was officially dead, he was not eligible for help from social services, could not rent an apartment, or, in fact, do anything that required that he be, well, alive. So he went to court asking it to declare null and void the ruling that he was dead. The court, however, refused, saying that its hands were tied because the statute of limitations prevented it from acting. So he is alive, but, as he put it, "I am officially dead, although I'm alive. I have no income and because I am listed as dead, I can't do anything." He is "banned for life from Turkey, banned from life in Romania," and so he cannot "make a living anywhere."[37]

The court was unable to exercise its power to declare null and void the ruling that he was dead, and because he is officially dead, he is unable to exercise what would be his power as a citizen of Romania to apply for a job or "do anything," as he says. He cannot even appeal his case. The ruling is final, and, besides, as a dead man, he has no standing to appeal.[38] It is now, of course, doubtful if the court should have agreed to hear his case to begin with: how can a dead man have standing to bring a case?[39]

We need not examine other ways in which an exercise of power fails because something has gone wrong that makes the exercise ineffective, and when that occurs, we can have major ethical problems. It is not a minor ethical problem that a man who is alive is officially dead any more than it is a minor ethical problem that individuals who thought they were divorced when they remarried turn out to be bigamists and their children bastards.

A dense book could no doubt also be written about those claiming to be a professional authorized to exercise power, but are not. What are especially problematic, and no doubt raise the most ethical issues, are the cases that arise from those who have worked for years as lawyers in law firms, but falsified their resumes and lack law degrees and a license to practice law.

Here is a typical example. "A former county bar association president in Pennsylvania" was a partner in a law firm and had "forged documents showing that she had attended law school at Duquesne University, passed the bar exam, was licensed to practice law and had paid a required attorney registration fee." The law firm said, "We are undertaking a thorough review of each and every file she may have handled."[40] She was an estate planning lawyer.

Unfortunately, even a thorough review of every file will not resolve the problem her not having a license creates for those whose estates she handled. Other lawyers can vet the relevant documents for legal mistakes, but to the extent that the legal validity of the documents depends upon the lawyer who drafted, signed, and submitted them, those who had their estates planned by this lawyer have both legal and ethical problems— if they are still alive. If they are not, the beneficiaries may now find that they have problems, ethical and legal. They may find that others have quite legitimate claims on what they thought they had inherited. They will then face the legal and ethical issue of whether they should contest such claims or accept that they were the victims, or beneficiaries, of fraud. Again, this is just one of many examples we could find of someone or some entity falsely claiming to be authorized to exercise a power.

11

Rules of Skill

We now know that it may be far more complicated than it may first appear to come to understand and resolve, if possible, ethical problems we have. In constructing arguments that would make sense of what we did or failed to do, we need to determine what kind of ethical problem we are addressing and what kinds of ethical relations are involved. We will find ourselves down a garden path without an end if, for instance, we are facing a conceptually problematic ethical issue and think the issue is factually problematic. We will be at a loss even to understand what the issue is if it involves a power–liability relation and we come at it with only the right–duty relation.

One source of help is to understand and separate out the variety of ways in which ethical considerations enter into our lives and into professions. One source is through the rules of skill we and professionals must learn.

We start learning rules of skill as toddlers as we learn how to talk, how to play with others, how to ride our first bicycle, and on and on. They might seem to have no ethical import, but, as we shall see, they are rich with ethical possibilities. Those are most dramatically obvious in professions.

A special set of skills is an essential feature of a professional. Physicians and surgeons learn how to identify various body parts, but only surgeons need to learn how to extract cancerous tissue, say. Lawyers must learn how to marshal reasons for and against a particular legal claim. Engineers need none of those skills, but within the various engineering disciplines they do need to learn how to brace a building so that it will not succumb to high winds[1] or write software that will not fail at a crucial point of execution.[2] In learning these special skills, professionals are learning rules of skill.

§1 Introduction

These rules tell us how to achieve a particular end: to bake a cake, do such-and-such; to buttress a girder, do so-and-so. They are the tools of the trade, so to speak, for any profession, and they display a wide variety of functions. There are rules that tell us what things are—what symptoms go with which disease, what crosshair signatures are, what shape goes with which organ, and on and on. There are rules that tell us how to do something—how to extract a tooth, how to use a Japanese saw, how to use Matlab, and on and on. There are rules that prescribe the procedures to follow—in writing a valid will or ensuring a fair trial, in minimizing the risks of infection, and on and on.

As we have noted before, we are all familiar with rules. We learn them early on as we learn to count or correct our pronunciation so we can be understood. We know as well what happens when we fail to follow the relevant rules. We open ourselves to criticism and to failure. We learn early on that games must be played in certain ways and not others, for instance, and we learn as well the limits of rules in ensuring that individuals do what they ought to do. Cakes do not always turn out the way they should. Girders are sometimes not properly buttressed. Surgeons amputate the wrong limb. Police officers stop a vehicle merely because the driver is African American.[3]

Rules set norms, and they are no different in that way than, say, the rules of logic. A valid argument form, for instance, gives us a norm for how we ought to reason. When we provide someone with the form for modus ponens—if p, then q and p, therefore q—we are providing them with a sequence of steps that they ought to follow if they are not to risk reasoning from truth to falsity. The same is true for any rule of calculation. That is why tellers at the grocery store cannot just give us any old handful of change. They are constrained by the rules that tell us how we ought to add and subtract. If they fail to give us the correct change, we may properly tell them that they have made a mistake, done something they ought not to do. We are not telling them that they have made a moral mistake—although they may have done that too. We are telling them, effectively, that they are not doing what reason tells all of us we ought to do. When we subtract 76 cents from a dollar, we do not, with good reason, get 21 cents. The norm we have failed to satisfy is one of reason, not morality.

But, as we saw, the norms of a profession carry some ethical weight: a professional ought, ethically, to do such-and-such. A surgeon ought to fix a tear in an artery in such-and-such a way. A failure to do it the way it ought to be done puts the patient at great risk of a deadly heart attack. A lawyer ought to marshal the relevant facts for the closing argument, organize them in an orderly and convincing way, and present them in the proper manner for the case in question. A lawyer is not likely to win a case screaming obscenities during a closing argument, however cogent the argument in which they are set.

Appealing to a norm is not ethically decisive, however. It ultimately says no more than that this is the way others in the profession generally do this. It needs to be backed by reasons, which either will or will not give it ethical weight. As we shall see, some norms have no backing at all. These are what I call floaters, and appealing to them obviously carries no ethical weight.

It is against the background of a profession's rules of skill, however, that we can best come to grips with professional failures. The rules engineers use provide particularly apt examples because we might think, given how oriented to calculations engineering is, that the only rules they might not follow are those involving calculations. But it turns out that there are many more rules engineers use than those requiring a calculator. "Use the same unit of measurement throughout any single project" is a simple rule, but because a subcontractor used imperial units of measurement while NASA used metric units, the Mars Climate Orbiter came into the Martian atmosphere at the wrong angle and burned up.[4] "Take into consideration all the variables" is another rule, somewhat more difficult to follow because it is sometimes not clear what all the variables are. Yet even some obvious variables are sometimes ignored. The Hubble telescope failed to work properly because the engineers forgot to compensate for how zero gravity would affect the curvature of the lens.[5] These sorts of problems ought to resonate for engineers, but all professionals are liable for such professional failures and mistakes related to the rules that mark out their professions.

These rules can be difficult to learn. Yet the rules within a profession can become so natural to its practitioners, so much second nature, that those within the profession may not even realize they are following rules. This sort of problem is commonplace. Ask any group which way to turn a knob to open a door, and many will first raise a hand, turn it the way they would to open a door, and then report the result: "Clockwise!" "To the right!" The habit is so deeply buried that they must replay it to remind themselves of the rule for turning a knob.

§2 A Brief Philosophical Excursion

When we bring such rules to consciousness, if we can, they seem purely practical: if you wish to have so-and-so, then do such-and-such. Some have argued that they have no ethical import at all. One reason is that they tell us how to achieve a determinate end without regard to whether the end is good or bad.

> The prescriptions for the physician thoroughly to cure his man, and for a poisoner reliably to kill him, are of equal worth, in so far as each serves to effect its purpose perfectly.[6]

We can understand why some might claim that rules of skill have no moral import by considering the movie *You Kill Me*. It is about a hit man from Buffalo who fails to kill the man his boss had told him to because, in an alcoholic stupor, he falls asleep while waiting for the man to show up. The movie is a story of double redemption. His boss sends him to California where he joins Alcoholics Anonymous and finally musters courage to tell the others, "I'm an alcoholic, and I kill people." He sobers up, works on his shooting skills, and returns to Buffalo to knock off the man he was supposed to. So he redeems himself as a hit man. Then he returns to California to start a new life, going straight with his new girlfriend.

We ought to have a mixed reaction to the movie. On the one hand, we do not want to applaud hired killers or killers of any sort. This is not an admirable man. But on the other hand, we come to admire his determination to quit alcohol, not an easy commitment for an alcoholic, and we also end up admiring his skills. He is a very good shot and a very efficient killer when he is sober. And, of course, he quits that business and starts a new life—an admirable choice.

But the rules of skill he has honed as a killer cannot be moral rules, some claim, because he is using them for a bad end just as a poisoner would use rules of skill to kill someone. The end of the physician may be a good, but that of the killer is not. So, it is claimed, rules of skill have no moral value.

But it does not follow from some rules of skill being used for immoral ends that all rules of skill lack moral content, and there are at least two problems with that inference. First, we can judge the poisoner and the killer immoral without paying any regard to the rules of skill they are using. It is not the rules of skill for shooting that make the killer morally wrong, but using those skills to shoot someone just as it is not the rules of skill someone must learn to know how to poison someone that are wrong, but using the skills learned in order to poison someone. It is the end that makes the use of rules of skill immoral, not the use itself and certainly not the rules, and we can make a moral judgment about that end without implying any moral judgment about the rules of skill.

Second, those who think rules of skill can have no ethical content seem to think that the *form* of the rule precludes it from ever having ethical weight. Any rule of the form "if you wish to accomplish so-and-so, do such-and-such" lacks moral content, they must be assuming, because some ends that could be accomplished with the rules are immoral. But we can readily sort out which ends are immoral from which are not. A surgeon who cuts out a cancerous tumor is doing good, using rules of skill that could be used to slice through someone's vital organs. An assassin who uses those same rules of skill to cut up someone's heart is not doing good. It is not the form of the rule that matters, that is, but the end for which the rule is used.

All professionals, including assassins, must learn rules of skill, and they are not immune from moral criticism or praise when they use those rules. A physician is to do what can be done to cure a patient—except hang the patient in a smoke house.[7] We have no problem distinguishing what a physician has done in these two different scenarios and no problem calling the one moral and the other not.

So, we should conclude,

- rules of skill articulate norms and, as we have seen, their use, and misuse, can have ethical import. They tell us how we *ought* to achieve a particular end, and
- when the particular end is itself a good, or necessary to achieve that good—the health of patients, the safety of an engineering artifact, the defense of an accused—the norms they articulate have ethical import.

The rules of skill professionals such as engineers and physicians and lawyers must learn to become professionals have some moral standing, their use and misuse leading to moral praise or criticism.[8] But we need to examine some features of rules to put us into a better position to understand how they can carry any ethical weight and thus, as I shall argue, how ethical considerations can enter through them.

§3 The Nature of Rules

When I play *Monopoly*, I throw the dice, pick up my designated piece, my player, that is, and move it along a row of boxes representing properties until I have counted out the number on the dice—neither more nor less. If one die says five and the other three,

I count out eight pieces of property on the board and move my designated player to the eighth piece of property. I make these moves, as mandated by the rules of Monopoly. I am not to subtract three from five to get the two I need to advance to Boardwalk so I can purchase it. The rules preclude any other ordering of these moves and so turn what could be a random set of activities or events into a play in a game—a sequenced order.

We all know how to follow rules. We learn that as children, as I remarked. We played games when we are children, and most of us will remember arguments about the rules, about who was supposed to go first, who did not touch a base before going on, whether you can build on your property in Monopoly if you do not own all the property of the same sort, Boardwalk and Wall Street, say. In such cases, we are arguing about what the rules tell us about the order in which certain events and activities are to occur. You must touch first base before going to second in baseball and softball. That is the rule.

So rules provide a sequenced set of events or activities. They tell us what is to go where in a temporal sequence. That is one feature of rules. But they give coherence as well as order. First, a rule sets the beginning of an activity and an end: I throw the dice first and stop after counting off the correct number of properties. Second, a rule separates out those features of an activity which "belong together by virtue of the rule, and are set off from other activities which may be accidentally associated with it."[9]

A tennis player may blink to clear an eye of dust while preparing to serve, for instance, but blinking is not part of serving. The serve is an activity that begins at some point prior to tossing the ball and ends with the follow through after the racket has hit the ball. Anything occurring before or after is not part of the activity specified by the rule, and we ignore what happens during the toss that lacks standing because it is not marked out as part of what it is to serve. Players in different sports—batters in baseball, for example, and pitchers too—often have little habits that are part of their getting ready. A pitcher may touch his cap. A batter may step up, then back, then up again. None of these little habits are rule-driven. They have no standing as part of the game because nothing in the rules of the game gives them meaning. The rules in fact rule out such little habits as having any meaning in the game.

In addition to providing coherence and order, rules constrain us—to stop at stop signs even when no traffic is about, not to use our hands to hit the ball in soccer, to open a door by following a set of activities. But what constrains us also frees us.

When we teach a child how to open a door, we are liberating the child by showing the thread of effective actions. "Grab the knob, turn it to the right—this way—and then pull. The door will open!" The rule for opening doors describes not only how to open doors, but also how we *ought* to open doors and so both constraints us to a certain coherent sequenced order of steps and frees us from experimentation whenever we go to open a door.

A well-designed stovetop is a wonderful example of how we are both constrained and freed by being constrained. We examined the problems with the error-provocative design of my friend's stovetop, the one where the burners were arranged in a half-circle as though on a clock face at 8, 11, 1, and 4 with the knobs on a smaller half-circle, each knob in front of the burner it was to control. One part of the relatively simple but compound rule created by that design was that if you wish to turn on the burner that is at 11 o'clock, you turn the knob at 11 o'clock. That visual rule, as it were, constrains us, but it also frees us from having to think about which knob controls which burner. The design effectively created a rule we could see just by looking at the placement of the knobs and burners.

For reasons that are difficult to fathom, as we saw, the knobs at 11 and 1 were switched, creating a new rule that ran counter to the visual rule. A cook either had to become habituated to ignoring what appeared obvious by looking or had to think twice before proceeding. That switch forces us to think about what to do because if we do not think about it, we will be led into a mistake by what it appears we ought to do. The switch ensures that even the most intelligent and engaged cook will turn the wrong burner by mistake.

Having to stop and think about how not to turn on the wrong burner is an impediment to a cook busily engaged in cooking. Rules provide an ordered and coherent sequence telling us how to engage in an activity and, in providing a sequenced order, both constrain and free us. They also thereby provide security. If we do what the rule tells us we ought to do, we are as well positioned as we can possibly be to achieve the end the rule is designed to achieve. We are secure, that is, in the knowledge that we have done what we ought to do to achieve the end we are trying to achieve.

We also secure the predictability we need to move about the world and do our business. As easily as we can predict that someone new to my friend's stovetop will turn the wrong burner on or off, we can predict that a player will move a pawn only one square on the chessboard and that we can generally drive to the store without mishap. The rules of chess restrict how the pieces can move, and the rules of the road give us enough regularity in how others drive that going to the store is not risky.

It is the loss of predictability that explains why we can run into problems when we encounter something that does not work as we think we know it ought to work. We know that nuts screw down by being turned clockwise. In some older cars, the lug nuts on the right side are tightened clockwise and so are unfastened by turning them counterclockwise, but the lug nuts on the left side are tightened counterclockwise and so need to be unfastened by turning them clockwise. The lug nuts tend to tighten rather than loosen in driving if fastened in those ways, but it is easy to understand how someone might find it difficult to unfasten the left-handed nuts, the ones that need to be turned clockwise to loosen.

Those differing ways of tightening and loosening lug nuts is likely to cause us problems because we think we know how to proceed. Indeed, we would likely run into problems because those who are used to tightening nuts have come to have a habit of turning them clockwise, a habit that only shows it is inapt when we come to nuts that are tightened counterclockwise. They would be tightening them to the point where they could not be loosened while trying to loosen them.

That is why anyone who encounters a door knob that turns counterclockwise to open is going to make a mistake. We have so trained ourselves into a habit of turning door knobs clockwise to open a door that we are taken aback when what we thought was an unlocked door fails to click open when we turn the knob to the right. Our natural response is not to try alternative ways of opening the door, as though we needed to experiment, but to trust what we think we know. So we assume the door is locked. There is a standard way of turning the knob to open a door, and it is such an embedded standard that it rarely occurs to us that anyone would design a knob that opened differently.

Such standards pervade our lives, both personal and professional. That is why, when a lawyer is asked to defend a physician against a malpractice suit, the lawyer's first question must be, "Did you follow the standard procedure?" The standard procedure is a rule or set of rules honed by a history of use. We have a rule, use it, and discover a problem. So we correct the rule, use it again, find another problem, and correct it again. Eventually we have a rule we can use with the security that comes from knowing it will not have any of the common problems that arise because earlier versions met those problems and the rule was modified to ensure that those problems would not arise.

We have not always had door knobs, for instance. Their present form has a history, and it is that history that has honed the design into the current standard. I live in a house built circa 1830 that has some of its original doors with their original hardware, a latch that one lifts up and pulls to open the door and lets down to close it. The door is opened and closed by putting one's thumb on the latch and a finger underneath. One can easily become habituated to that act, but the latch does get caught on sleeves. So around 1830 or so, someone created hardware with a door knob like those we find today on doors, but with a latch underneath the handle. You are to grab the knob, and in grabbing it you grab the latch as well and open or close the door. That hardware is transitional between the old latches and the newer knobs that we are familiar with. The design changed to make it easier to open and close doors.

The standard procedure is the standard for a reason, that is, and that is one reason we *ought* to use the rule. If the physician answers the lawyer's question by saying, "No. I thought I'd try something different," the lawyer knows that the physician has a problem that will be difficult to finesse in court. It will be the physician at the dock, not the medical profession. The lawyer cannot defend the physician by saying, "This physician did what any physician would, and should, have done. You need to sue the profession, not my client."

We can imagine the lawyer's problem by imagining a child trying to turn a knob counterclockwise and being stymied—or by reminding ourselves of the Larson cartoon of the child trying to enter the School for the Gifted by pushing on a door that is clearly marked "PULL." We want to ask, "You did what?!"

Standards change, obviously, and we do not want to prevent change, but a physician or an engineer adopting a new rule does risk a blot on the profession: "A professional would do that?!" Where to draw a line between a new rule that properly builds on old ones and a new rule that puts a professional and the profession at risk is no doubt a delicate issue, determined in part by the details of particular cases. We want professionals to push the envelope of the rules of skill of their profession. We want innovation and do not want professionals stuck doing what has always been done, but the risk of innovation is that they will not achieve the end they are trying for or will cause unforeseen harms in trying.

In any event, besides providing a sequenced and coherent order to a set of activities, rules set norms for how we ought to engage in those activities, norms sanctioned by the profession. We would admonish those who wrote software however they wished or braced a skyscraper with two by fours. These activities have rules we are to follow, and implicit in these admonitions is the normativity that marks all rules. They tell us what we ought to do, and we open ourselves to criticism if we fail to do what we ought to do. But this fourth feature of rules—a sequenced, coherent, *normative* order—has different aspects we will need to distinguish.

§4 Following the Rules

We need to distinguish several ways in which we can fail to follow a rule:

1. We may use the proper rule, but fail to do all the steps.
2. We may use the proper rule, but fail to do one or more of the steps properly.
3. We may use the proper rule, but do two or more of the steps in the wrong order.
4. We may use the proper rule, but add something that is not one of the steps.
5. We may use the wrong rule.
6. We may fail to use the rule.
7. We may fail to have any rule at all.

In making fudge, for instance, we could just make things up as we go, following no recipe, or somehow use the recipe for chocolate sauce by mistake and wonder why our "fudge" fails to set, or use the correct recipe but put in vanilla at the beginning rather than the end, or put in too little chocolate, or completely forget the chocolate and wonder why our "fudge" fails to turn brown, or cook it too long or too little, and so on and so on.

And, of course, we can fail in any one of these standard ways regarding any rule of skill, and even those possibilities do not cover all the ways in which we can fail. Think of all the ways we can fail in baking—too much flour, too little, too old, the wrong kind, too fine or not fine enough. These ways of failing are standard ways to make a mistake in trying to follow a rule—as the example of following a recipe is meant to illustrate. We can find a multitude of examples of each kind of failure in whatever practice we examine. A casual reading of the sports pages will uncover a variety of ways in which officiating can go wrong, some from judgments about whether and how an infraction occurred, but many from a failure to get a rule right.

Given those general concerns, it will help to concentrate on one particular profession. I will focus on engineering because it is easy to find examples, and if we can find mistakes not involving calculations in a discipline that prides itself on calculating the answers to the problems it faces, and not making value judgments, we have some evidence that we can find them in any profession.

The recall of GM cars over a faulty ignition switch revealed at least two different infractions by the car company. First, it accepted a switch which was admittedly inadequate to do the job because the spring in it was too weak, and then, after changing the switch, the engineer responsible failed to give it a new part number, causing enormous difficulty in trying to track down what was causing the rash of accidents and deaths involving the ignition switch.

The second problem significantly hampered any attempt to find out whether anything was wrong with the switch. As Mary Barra, GM's CEO, said "when asked about the design change without a corresponding change in part number," "it is inconceivable … It is not our process."[10]

The standard process requires a validation sign-off. One was signed on April 26, 2006 authorizing "changes to the switch, including a new spring, designed to increase the force required to move the switch," but "the part number did not change, when redesigned, an issue which GM said hampered its own internal investigation" and "several fields on the document marked as 'required' are left blank or with 'N/A', including purchase order number and 'validation engineer.'"[11] So the switch was changed, but no one could have tracked which cars had the old switch and which had the new one because the part number on the two different switches was the same.

It turns out that you would have to take the switch apart to see whether it is the new version or the old and have at hand both versions for a comparison. If it is the new version, you would see that the "tiny metal plunger in the switch was longer … [and] the switch's spring was more compressed," thus requiring more force "to turn the ignition on and off."[12] It is no wonder that GM was hard-pressed to understand what was going on when it was accused of having a faulty ignition switch in some of its cars.

We do not need to count the number of rules that were not followed, or not followed properly, regarding the switch in switches. It is clear that a crucial rule requiring changing part numbers when changing parts was not followed. The rule is so important that Barra found it "inconceivable" that it was not followed.

The other problem with the switches also involved engineers not following the rules. In this case, they failed to abide by their own criteria for determining whether a part satisfied the specifications. "At the core of the problem is a part in the vehicle's ignition switch that is 1.6 millimeters less 'springy' than it should be. Because this part produces weaker tension, ignition keys in the cars may turn off the engine if shaken just the right way."[13] GM found the problem in 2001 in pre-production tests, and the supplier, Delphi Automotive, told GM in 2002 that the switch did not meet specifications. GM chose to use the switch anyway.[14]

We have, with these examples of how GM engineers failed to follow the rules, two very clear examples of how ethical considerations enter into engineering via rules of skill. In not following the rule requiring a change in a part number when a part is changed, the engineer or engineers responsible made finding the problem extremely difficult and ensured that more people would be killed or hurt than otherwise. And in not following their own specifications for the ignition switch, the engineers caused completely unnecessary harms—including the deaths of many drivers and passengers.[15]

How many? It is difficult to know. GM said that as of spring 2014, the total was twelve or thirteen. But GM only counted those fatalities that occurred because the airbag did not deploy. Only the driver and front-seat passenger were protected by airbags. So when a driver loses control of a car because the ignition turns off and dies with four passengers in the resulting wreck, GM only counts that as two deaths caused by the ignition switch failure, the driver and the front-seat passenger who died because the airbags did not deploy. The other three passengers, who also died, are not counted. GM did announce that "its list includes only those in the front seat of cars whose airbags didn't inflate." The result is that we cannot trust GM's numbers, and determining how many others died as a result of crashes involving ignition switch failures requires a great deal of ongoing research. In any event, those deaths GM did count would not have occurred without the failure to follow well-established rules that it was, well, inconceivable were not followed.

There were other failures in the ignition switch debacle, but these two are enough to illustrate the point: ethical considerations enter engineering by way of the rules of skill engineers must use. The intellectual core of engineering is the solution to design problems. Ethical considerations enter there both because solutions embody values, some of which are ethical, and because once instantiated in an artifact, it will have effects, some good, no doubt, and some bad. In addition, engineers must use rules of skill in solving design problems and executing their design solutions. Ethical considerations enter with those rules as well.

In short, someone cannot be an engineer without solving design problems, cannot solve design problems without using the rules of skill that define the discipline, and cannot convert their solution into an artifact without using rules of skill. Ethical considerations thus permeate engineering, being essential to what it is to be an engineer.

The engineers at GM failed to use the existing rules, 5. in the list above, when they failed to provide a new part number, and though we would need more details to determine what exactly went wrong when they accepted a subpar ignition switch, they clearly failed in some way to follow the rules about what is acceptable and what is not. As I have said, we can readily find examples of other sorts of failures involving rules of skill. It may seem difficult to think of an example of engineers failing to have any rule at all, 6. in the list above, but, in fact, a crucial causal factor in one of our worst environmental disasters was just such a failure.

Determining everything that went wrong in the BP oil spill in the Gulf of Mexico in 2010 and assessing the relative weights of the various causal factors would be a daunting task, but one factor concerns the rule adopted for ensuring that the well was properly closed off so that it could be "temporarily abandoned," as the oil industry says. The "basic sequence" was laid out in an "Ops Note" sent out at 10:43 a.m. on April 20th, the morning the well was being "temporarily abandoned" and the morning of the blowout. The crew responsible for performing the procedure first saw the sequence at a meeting at 11:00 a.m.

We already have two red flags. If this procedure was the standard operating procedure, why would the crew even need to be presented with it—as though it were new? And if it was new, why would they be seeing it for the first time the very day the well was being closed off? It takes time to comprehend and assess any set of rules. So those seeing a set the very day they were to be used means that they had very little time to think about what was being given them or, more important, to be sure that they had the steps of the procedure clearly enough in mind to be able to bring them to mind in case of an emergency.

In any event, here is what they saw:

1. Perform a positive-pressure test to test the integrity of the production casing;
2. Run the drill pipe into the well to 8,367 feet (3,300 feet below the mud line);

3. Displace 3,300 feet of mud in the well with seawater, lifting the mud above the blowout preventer (BOP) and into the riser;

4. Perform a negative-pressure test to assess the integrity of the well and bottom-hole cement job to ensure outside fluids (such as hydrocarbons) are not leaking into the well;

5. Displace the mud in the riser with seawater;

6. Set the surface cement plug at 8,367 feet; and

7. Set the lockdown sleeve.

This rule has seven steps to be performed in sequence. But when we look at its history immediately prior to the blowout, as recounted in the Deep Water report of the National Commission on the BP Deepwater Horizon Spill and Offshore Drilling, we discover at least one reason why the crew needed to see it.

> BP's Macondo team had made numerous changes to the temporary abandonment procedures in the two weeks leading up to the April 20 "Ops Note." For example, in its April 12 drilling plan, BP had planned (1) to set the lockdown sleeve before setting the surface cement plug and (2) to set the surface cement plug in seawater only 6,000 feet below sea level (as opposed to 8,367 feet). The April 12 plan did not include a negative pressure test. On April 14, Morel sent an e-mail entitled 'Forward Ops' setting forth a different procedure, which included a negative-pressure test but would require setting the surface cement plug in mud before displacement of the riser with seawater. On April 16, BP sent an Application for Permit to Modify to MMS describing a temporary abandonment procedure that was different from the procedure in either the April 12 drilling plan, the April 14 e-mail, or the April 20 "Ops Note." There is no evidence that these changes went through any sort of formal risk assessment or management of change process.[16]

We have more red flags. The sequence was different in the April 12th plan, and that plan lacked one step that was in the April 20th plan. The April 14th plan added that step, but changed the sequence. The April 16th plan was different from both former plans and different from the final plan listed above. No wonder the crew needed to see the procedure. There were four different plans floating about, with differing numbers of steps and different sequences of steps—that of the 12th, the 14th, the 16th, and the 20th.

The "basic sequence" lays out a procedure for "temporary abandoning" of a well, for locking it down so it can be left without any fear that the pressure of the oil and gases will blow up the well pipe. That is the end to be achieved. The sequence lays out what we are to do to achieve that end. Do it correctly, we are to assume, and we achieve the end. There may indeed be four or more different ways to achieve the same end, and so all the plans may be proper: each may, if followed correctly, succeed in achieving the end in question.

But things do not appear that way. When changes keep getting made in some recipe, or rule, or procedure, we presume that those proposing the changes are still getting clear on what needs to be done to achieve the end in question. The reason is that we presume reasons for the sequence embodied in a rule. A baserunner is to touch first base before touching second base. A runner who fails to touch first before touching second will be called out. Baseball imposes the rule to ensure that base runners do not cheat by cutting the corners of the diamond and shortening their run. So we would presume that the seven steps in BP's "basic sequence" were each necessary and that the sequence in which they were to be done mattered. Yet the four different sets of basic procedures laid out from April 12th to April 20th certainly make it appear that the particular order of at least some of the steps in the procedure of the 20th did not matter and even that at least one of the procedures, the negative-pressure test, was not really necessary.

The rationale for a rule ought to be understandable to any objective observer, but the changes in "the" procedure from the 12th through the 20th are difficult for an observer to understand. Was a negative-pressure test necessary? If so, why was it left out of the original version? Does it matter which comes first, setting the surface plug or displacing the mud in the riser? The changes in the order of those two steps makes us wonder what the rationale was for ordering the sequence one way rather than another. What was the "correct" rule—if any?

It is not that the engineers failed to follow the proper rule. That was not the problem. The problem was that they failed to have a "basic sequence" in place about how to proceed. It appears, to any objective observer, that they proceeded willy-nilly over several days in designing a "basic sequence." That is a presumption that would need to be proven, but disconcerting in the extreme if true.

Indeed, given the number of changes suggested, we can make no presumption about what rule, if any, the crew followed in trying to lock down the well. Despite the 11:00 a.m. meeting where the latest iteration of the rule was presented, the crew had little time to train themselves to that rule and so had little chance to ensure that every crew member understood how the new iteration differed from the other three—if they were aware of the other versions and were informed of the changes. We cannot presume that every crew member was using the same version of the rule. Even if they had had the same "rule" in front of them as they worked, we cannot know that they did not change the sequence on the job, on the fly, as the disaster unfolded. The obvious inference to draw from all the changes in the rule is that no one had a fix on what would work; so if things began to go awry in following whatever rule was being used, it would not be unreasonable to improvise.

In brief, with no standard basic sequence to which we can appeal, we can have no idea whether the sequence used was proper or improper. It may be that the April 20th version was the correct way to go, or the version of the 16th, or the 14th, or the 12th—or, indeed, none of those at all. It may be, that is, that no rule was followed in temporally abandoning the well. So we cannot know what went wrong because we do not know what rule, if any, was followed and, obviously, cannot know whether a step was missed, taken in the wrong order, or what. The consequence is that we cannot properly prepare ourselves for another temporary abandonment because we do not know what mistakes to avoid.

We have a second problem here as well. Even if a rule was used, it lacked authority for the engineers. We distinguish between rule-directed activities and articulating a rule, and that distinction allows us to make another distinction between rule-directed activities and activities directed at determining the rules themselves. In creating a rule for some end or in ensuring that any changes in an existing rule determinative of an activity will improve the rule, improve, that is, the likelihood of achieving the particular end, some rule or set of rules needs to be followed. Rules of skill come to have an authority for professionals within a profession, that is, only after they have been vetted in some way.

We can appeal to such a rule, what amounts to the standard practice, to justify what we do only because the practice has become standard—the way things ought to be done. This can happen in at least two ways: a rule may either be honed by experience or vetted by somebody authorized to examine and assess a rule and then approve or disapprove it. It can be tested through use, that is, or approved, or, better, both.

We can find a paradigm of how rules are honed by experience by looking at the development of rules in common law. These are created by courts in response to a particular problem—someone apparently trespassing on someone else's property, but claiming that there has been a right of way there for years. A judge or jury decides a case one way, creating a precedent for similar cases, and when new cases arise, a judge or another jury either appeals to the precedent as settling the matter or modifies the precedent to account for changed circumstances. So the old rule is honed, often again and again, and so vetted by the judge or jury in a case, who must hear both sides of a suit and give a judgment with reasons why one side wins the suit and the other loses, and by a long history of acceptance and modification by various judges and juries in various situations. Through its application in a variety of different situations, the rule becomes the standard for how to handle the particular kind of situation to which it applies.

What vets the rule of common law is not just that it solves the problem, but that different objective observers, judges, and juries, that is, have agreed with or only slightly modified the rule in other circumstances. The rule has been tested against the facts by different objective observers. That complex process of vetting gives the rule of common law an authority that a mere suggestion about how to proceed would not and could not have, and it gives the rule an authority that it would not have if it went through four or five changes in little more than a week.

That is why a lawyer for a physician accused of malpractice would be delighted for the physician to have followed standard practice. The development of standards within a profession over time in different situations by different practitioners gives those standards an authority that no un-vetted rule could have. The process ensures, over time, that changes that handle problems are incorporated into the original rule and, in the best of cases, that the ends to be achieved by the rules are more readily achieved.

That process is one way to vet a rule. We can also imagine a body authorized to examine and approve or disapprove rules of skill and proposed changes in them. But, as the Deep Water report indicates, there is no evidence that the "changes [in the rule for temporarily abandoning a well] went through any sort of formal risk assessment or management of change process."[17]

A rule can gain authority only by being honed by experience or by being adopted by an authorized body. There is no other way a rule can become authoritative. It certainly is not sufficient for someone simply to say, "This is how we are going to do it"—no matter where such a person may be in the hierarchy of a corporation or of a profession, no matter what their credentials, no matter what their relation to those to whom they are saying what should be done. Reasons are required to justify a rule, and the reasons need to be accessible to all and must be judged by independent observers to be sufficient to justify the rule.

So if the engineers did use one of the variants of the rule articulated between the 12th and the 20th, that rule had no authority. They cannot claim that they were obligated to do what the rule told them to do. They were not empowered to create a rule or, perhaps better, they were not empowered to create a rule that they had an obligation to follow. They lacked the security that experience with a rule and vetting of a rule give us. They had no idea whether what they did was adequate in those circumstances, let alone the best thing to do, and we can have no idea what they did in the circumstances, or even what they ought to have done, let alone whether what they tried to do was adequate.

Most if not all engineers can readily think of examples where they or some other engineer failed to follow a rule and so created a problem, minor or major. We will look at some other examples later, but the BP and General Motors examples will suffice to make the point about the use of rules having moral significance—in a discipline, engineering, which often seems to pride itself on being purely quantitative.

§5 How Ethics Enters

As we have seen, rules of skill lay down procedures for achieving particular ends: bake a cake by doing this, throw a spiral in a football by doing that. So a failure to follow a rule of skill will prevent our achieving the end or achieving it as fully as we had hoped. For many rules of skill not achieving the end in question raises no ethical issues. Failing to follow all the steps for baking a cake may result in, well, a half-baked cake—not a good culinary end, but of no great ethical concern in most circumstances. But if the end is bad—poisoning a rival, say—a failure of the culprit to follow the proper rules to achieve that end would be occasion for applause, not moral condemnation.

But clearly some failures have consequences that are so harmful that they raise to the level of being morally wrong. The failures in the BP oil spill resulted in eleven deaths and seventeen injured as well as significant damage to the ecosystem and economic damage in the billions to the fishing and tourist industries in the Gulf. We now know that the damage was far greater than previously thought. It had been estimated that "210 million gallons of oil released by the damaged BP Deepwater Horizon Macondo well [had] spread out over the equivalent of 92,500 miles." We now know that the expanse was 30 percent larger and the oil "toxic enough to destroy 50 percent of the marine life it encountered."[18]

When a failure involving a rule of skill results in such harms, we have a moral problem. Leaving out a step in a rule of skill, or taking the steps out of sequence, or failing to follow a rule vetted by past experience and/or approved through a formal process are each morally wrong if, as a result, the proper end is not achieved and significant harm results instead. Engineers, along with all other professionals, have an ethical obligation to use proper rules of skill and to use them properly.

We have examined several kinds of failure here—the failure to have any clear rule, the failure to use an existing rule, and whatever went wrong regarding the rules for vetting parts in choosing the subpar ignition switch part. It does not take imagination to provide examples of the other sorts of failures. We need only examine various engineering failures to see how not having a rule, or not following properly one we do have, has led to significant enough harm to raise to the level of being morally wrong.

Intentions are irrelevant. All that is relevant is whether an engineer used, or failed to use, the proper rule and used it properly. An engineer is not different from anyone else in this regard. If my dentist drills completely through a tooth while daydreaming— "Drill, baby, drill!"—it does not matter whether the act was intentional or not. What matters is that as a professional, my dentist needs to pay attention and not daydream while working. Whatever the intentions of the engineers who approved the epoxy that was used to hold in place the three-ton concrete slabs on the ceiling of the Boston tunnel, they failed to ensure that the slabs would stay in place—despite a warning from a safety officer for the construction company that the slabs were at risk of falling over time.[19] We would also need to query why three-ton slabs that might fall, and would cause serious harm if they did fall, were put on the ceiling in the first place, and why the bolts that were also used to fasten the slabs were stored outside where they rusted before being put in place. In any event, it is not the intentions of the engineers involved that matter, but the failure to do what they ought to have done to achieve the end they were trying to achieve. If we were to sort through the problems with the Big Dig in Boston, we would find, time and again, failures tied to rules of skill.

In examining the rules of skill of engineering, we are defining the role morality of engineering. Among all that someone must master to become a professional within a discipline are rules that are essential to the practice of those within that discipline— both because they sort out disciplines one from another, the rules of skill for lawyers being different from those for surgeons, for instance, and because they tell someone within the discipline how to achieve the ends appropriate to the discipline. Ethics thus enters into the heart of a discipline in two ways.

A person must work within the boundaries set by those rules to work as a professional within that discipline. A general practitioner who decides to amputate a leg had better have a very good reason for not calling on a surgeon. A charge of unprofessional conduct will be difficult to rebut otherwise. A patent lawyer could not be acting as a patent lawyer and amputate a leg any more than a dentist could be acting as a dentist in drawing up a will. Lawyers learn how to make out a will, a seemingly simple matter that unfortunately can go wrong in many ways and requires mastery of a complex set of laws and procedures to get right. Surgeons master a variety of instruments for cutting, and a delicacy and sureness of touch is as crucial a set of skills as a mastery of where to cut and in what order and how deeply. Working outside one's area of professional expertise as though it were in one's area of professional expertise is deceptive and morally wrong. It is also likely to lead to mistakes, of course, but even without the possibility of failure, we are morally wrong to misrepresent ourselves as being professionals of a certain sort when we are not. So electrical engineers, to pick at random a discipline within engineering, should not claim the expertise of mechanical engineers, for instance, but work within the boundaries of the professional expertise they have gained.

In addition to working within the boundaries of our profession, we have a prima facie obligation to follow the rules essential to the profession, as we have seen. The rules articulate how someone within that profession ought to achieve an end in question, and so their use has ethical import. They have ethical import whether they are used properly or not and whether the failure to use them or to use them properly causes harm or not. Someone who uses the proper rules properly should be praised morally just as someone who fails to use them or use them properly is appropriately at blame morally. Ethics thus enters into the heart of every profession—every profession with an ethically admirable end, that is, from curing the sick to defending clients to helping the poor. Rules of skill can have ethical import.

§6 Creating Rules of Skill

We distinguish what we do from how we do it. A soccer player may mistakenly pass a ball to an opposing player, but do so with such a deft touch as to provoke admiration. A surgeon may amputate the wrong leg, but do it well. A dentist may fill the correct molar, but do it so poorly it will not last. We can judge both what we do and how we do it, and the two judgments need not coincide. What is right may be done badly, and what is wrong may be done well. Cicero's last words are said to have been, "There is nothing proper about what you are doing, soldier, but do try to kill me properly."[20]

If we presume a bell curve of professional competence, we can get a sense of what is at issue here. Suppose your primary care physician recommends surgery to save your life. You do not ask, "Can you recommend the worst surgeon you know?" You do not say, "I'll settle for someone mediocre." The same is true for any professional. An engineering firm that advertises that its engineers "are all about average" is not going to get any more customers than one that advertises that its engineers are "pretty much below average." Rather obviously, we prefer the best over the worst. Why is that?

As we saw, rules of skill are conditional. They tell us that if we are to achieve such-and-such, we must do so-and-so. We can easily illustrate why it is important ethically to judge *how* we are to do what we are to do as well as what we do by fastening on engineering again.

Engineers solve design problems, and a design problem calls for the creation of a rule of skill: "This is what you need to do to achieve a solution!" But no design problem determines its solution. No matter how detailed, a statement of the problem to be solved will not necessitate any particular conclusion the way 2+2 necessitates 4. A design solution is a contingent outcome of a design problem, and many solutions are possible for the same problem. Engineers can satisfy all the constraints posed by the problem as well as the constraints of the standing rules and still end up with radically different solutions to a design problem. We humans innovate, and so some solutions are significantly better than others.

That is one way the bell curve of professional competence plays itself out in engineering, with some engineer producing a brilliant solution to a design problem and another a mediocre one. Both solve the problem, we will assume, but the one is significantly better in all the ways that we and engineers measure—easier to use, less expensive to manufacture, longer-lasting, easier to repair, recyclable, and so on. And one value is ethical. Any design solution, once realized in an artifact, will have its causal effects, some beneficial, some not. A solution which causes unnecessary harm raises an ethical red flag. It is significantly worse than a solution which does not cause unnecessary harm. Less than optimal solutions raise ethical questions. They do so in at least three ways.

First, a professional can follow all the rules, and follow them correctly, and still come up with a solution that causes unnecessary harm. An engineer may design a part that could be recyclable in such a way as to make that impossible without, say, a huge expense. A part that could be made of something readily available and not at all harmful to us or the environment may be made with something toxic. Car manufacturers made use of over thirty-six million trunk lights containing mercury prior to 2000, over half of them GM products. The collection and safe disposal of that mercury remains a problem. We presumably do not need to detail the problems having mercury in our environment poses to our health—a presumably unnecessary harm.

Second, professionals have a moral imperative to strive to be the best that they can be. Just as we would find an engineer firm obtuse for advertising that its engineers are all pretty much below average, we would find it obtuse for budding engineers to say, in response to queries about their life's ambitions, "We want to be mediocre." It seems inevitable that varying talents and drives and places of education will produce differing levels of competence and creativity, and we rank those in the professions by how well they do professionally. Some surgeons are better surgeons than others; some engineers are better engineers than others. Yet it is part of the drive of an engineer—one of the animating principles of the profession—to improve things, to ferret out ways to make things work better—more efficiently, simpler, with fewer parts, and so on. Lacking that drive is a character flaw, and that criticism carries moral overtones. The same holds for all professionals. Mediocre professionals are still professionals, but they are tainted by their mediocracy. That taint is ethical when they could do more to cure their patients, defend their clients, or help the poor.

Maternal care is a good example of how health-care professionals have failed to hold themselves to high enough standards to keep the United States from becoming the most dangerous country in the developed world for women giving birth. In 1950 the United States was one of only a few countries where "for the first time in history the maternal mortality rate … [had] been pushed slightly below the apparently irreducible minimum of one maternal death per 1,000 live births." Since then, the maternal mortality rate has soared. "An American woman is three times as likely to die from childbirth as a woman in Canada, and six times as likely as a woman in Scandinavia."[21] Becoming the best requires persistence over time, and the medical profession in the United States failed to keep up the good work that led it to such success in 1950.

Third, each profession serves a social purpose or set of purposes, and the state recognizes, and regulates, a profession to ensure that the purpose or purposes are properly realized, giving those within the profession a monopoly in return. It sets standards for membership in the profession, requires that individuals meet those standards to become a practicing member of the profession, and can, generally, remove professional certification should a member fail in a significant way to meet those standards. Anyone entering into a profession thus comes into a new set of moral relations—to the state and to others in the profession, among others. One obligation members have is to push the envelope of development, strive always to make things better. Someone satisfied with things as they are—"It works. What's the problem?"— is not going to help the profession achieve the goals for which the state gives it a monopoly. That is not just a practical problem for those in the profession who must work with someone who is not concerned to improve matters, but a moral problem as well because that person is a drag on the profession's achieving the purposes for which the state gives it a monopoly.

These are sketches of arguments that would need to be laid out more fully to be fully convincing, but at their core is the view that every professional solves problems—how to write this will, defend this person, operate on that heart. A professional must choose the best solution to the problem at hand, and that solution is itself a rule about how to proceed, creating a precedent and furthering or hindering the profession's raison d'être.

It ought to go without saying that these various rules provide prima facie good reasons for a professional to do things in accordance with the rules. The rules are generally vetted either by experience or by some authorizing organization, but when they are not, or when a novel situation requires a creative solution which defies the conventional response, a professional is obviously obligated not to follow the rules at hand, but to do what is right in that situation.

We find the same issues in our ordinary lives. There are rules about driving that have been authorized by law. It does not take much experience, if any, to realize that we need rules about driving on the same side of the road, stopping at red lights, and so on and so on. It does not take much experience driving to understand why drivers ought not to text while driving. It takes even less to understand why you are not to drive at 81 mph in a 45 mph zone—even to get to your quilting group.

We follow rules at work and at home, and, as with professionals, they provide the coherence and predictability we all need in what can sometimes be our chaotic daily existence. The same sorts of problems that arise for professionals arise for all of us. In putting a ladder in place to clean out the eaves, we should have the feet a foot from the side of the house for every four feet of rise. Going up 20 feet? Make sure the feet are five feet back. That is a rule honed by experience, and we fail to follow it at our peril. Getting an email with a link that purports to be from the Social Security Administration has become a red flag. The operative rule is never to click on a link unless you can be dead sure it will not subject your computer to malware.

The point is that rules of skill are as ubiquitous in our ordinary lives as they are in any professional's life, and, just like professionals, we can create ethical problems by not using them or not using them correctly. One main point of difference is that they are far less likely to make it into written form than the rules of skill professionals must learn, and that itself can create ethical problems.

12

Rules of Skill, Yet Again

We have been looking at the rules of skill individuals learn to become surgeons, lawyers, engineers or any other kind of professional, but have yet to cover all the ways in which ethical issues can arise regarding rules of skill. We have seen how GM engineers failed to follow explicit rules about changing part numbers when replacing part of an ignition switch and how BP engineers failed to have a rule at all when trying to abandon a well temporarily. That spread might seem to cover the possibilities of how professionals can go wrong. Either an existing rule was not followed or there was no existing rule when there should have been.

Would that matters were so simple. We have been looking at cases where the rules seem clear and unambiguous. A kidney is an organ with a certain shape and size juxtaposed within other readily identifiable organs. A surgeon may fail to recognize a kidney, but we would certainly need an explanation for that. For instance, a Florida surgeon removed a perfectly healthy kidney that he mistook for "a gynecologic malignancy, lymphoma and/or other metastatic disease." It was a pelvic kidney, one that fails to "ascend and settle in the flank."[1] So the kidney was not where it would normally be, and that is part of the explanation for the surgeon's misidentification. The surgeon should have done a further check on what the mass was before removing it, but, we might think, nothing is wrong with the rule for identifying a kidney.

That would be too hasty a conclusion. It is possible that the rule does not clearly state that a kidney may be found in other than its usual location. It is possible that it does state that, but that the surgeon did not learn that part of it because it was, say, in the small print. And, obviously, the problem may have arisen because the surgeon misread the rule—or misremembered the relevant details. Or it could even be that the surgeon somehow failed to learn the rule about how to recognize a kidney. There is a lot to learn in becoming a surgeon, and the surgeon may have just missed that one somehow.

We are asking, "What can go wrong regarding the rules professionals learn to become adept in their fields?" The answer, unfortunately, is everything. There are at least five different problems we need to examine to give a sense of what else can go wrong with a rule besides what happened in the sorts of cases we have so far examined:

- Any rule is open to interpretation and misinterpretation.
- Rules are artifacts and may be badly designed.

- Rules may appear so obvious that no one has ever assessed them.
- The meaning of rules is determined by how they are used, and how a rule is used may be quite contrary to what it seems to say.
- Some rules are unwritten, but still guide a professional's practice.

We will be concentrating on problems that arise for professionals, but they can just as easily, perhaps more easily, arise for us in our ordinary lives. Rules regulate our everyday lives—in the sandbox, our homes, schools, businesses, stores, in every social setting. Without rules, implicit if not explicit, we would find ourselves unable to do much at all as we tried to drive to work with no one paying attention to the rules of the road, for instance. So although we will focus on ethical problems that arise for professionals, the lessons, again, apply to all of us in every aspect of our lives.

§1 Rules Do Not Interpret Themselves

Whatever the details, "the very nature and essence of human language, ... renders a total exclusion of every imaginable misapprehension, in most cases, absolutely impossible."[2] We cannot exclude the possibility that even the most carefully crafted rule will be misunderstood in ways we cannot even begin to imagine. It is no more possible to craft a foolproof rule than it is for an engineer to design an artifact immune from misuse by someone. The advantage fools have over the brightest and most knowledgeable is that they can think of ways to see something that are beyond the ken of the brightest and most knowledgeable. The latter cannot imagine that anyone could make "a mistake like that."

Adding qualifying phrases to a rule exacerbates the problem rather than helping since every qualification would require another. If I ask my law clerk, "Can you check this reference for me?," I mean quite a few things besides what I said. I mean that my clerk should look it up in the relevant case book or online, not wander around the office hunting for it—although I did not say that. I mean that my clerk should give me the information after looking it up—although I did not say that. I mean that my clerk should provide me with the information in the usual way, by telling me rather than sending me a letter or a telegram—although I did not say that. We make all sorts of assumptions, that is, whenever we say anything, and we communicate with others when they make at least roughly the same assumptions we do. The difficulty of stating any of the assumptions we make is that they too will only be understood if other assumptions are made. So it is false to believe that "explanation and specification, piled upon explanation, would produce greater and greater clearness" since "in fact they [produce] greater and greater obscurity."[3]

"Stop at the stop sign" might seem a paradigmatic example of a clear rule that cannot be misinterpreted, but there are no doubt many cases where someone failed to understand the point of the sign. A neighbor of mine when I was young, Mrs. Herald, was ticketed for failing to stop at an intersection and, instead, pulling out into traffic because there happened to be a break that allowed her entry without stopping. When she was pulled over and admonished that she should have stopped at the stop sign, she pointed out that she had stopped at the stop sign—which, for unclear reasons, was a good 30 feet or so back from the intersection. She stopped *at* the stop sign, that is, but received a ticket anyway because she failed to understand its point, which was to ensure that drivers stop at the intersection and not drive through it once they reached it—even though they had stopped at the stop sign.

I required in one class that students comment on other students' presentations. Each student chose three names from a hat, and I then made a list:

Ryan—Laura, Lucas, Fahad
Joe—Alex, Fahad, Sean
Pat—Jacob, Laura, Akshit…

One of the students who missed class that day emailed me to ask how to read the list: "Am I to comment on the people to the right of my name, or are they to comment on my presentation?" Because each student in class drew three names to comment on and I then listed after their names the names each had drawn, it had not occurred to me that the list could be read as my student suggested. In other words, I assumed a rule about how to read the list, had not articulated it, and had, as a consequence, left the rule open to an interpretation I had not intended or anticipated.

The context within which I constructed the rule for my students provided an interpretation. Without the context, the absent student could not determine what the rule was. What this tells us is how important it is to understand the context within which a rule functions. We must be making the assumptions others are making if we are to get the rule right, and what that tells us is how important the norms of a profession are—the tacit knowledge practitioners come to have as they learn their rules of skill.

There is the perhaps apocryphal story of someone asking another person in the line for theater tickets when the bus was coming. Upon being informed that the bus stop sign was 10 or so feet away, the person said, "But I can't stand there. The sign says no standing." And I have always wondered how someone like Mrs. Herald would react when first coming up behind a construction truck that says, "Do not follow." "Do I pull over?" "If I stay far enough back, am I following it?" "Do I pull around it?"

Presumably the "Do not follow" sign means that drivers are not to follow the construction trucks into a construction site. Why we would need a sign warning us of that is itself unclear since there is nothing on the truck that can tell us when it is going to enter a construction site. We can only tell that by looking at where the truck is turning, and since a construction site is not likely to be anywhere we would be going, we would not need a sign telling us not to follow in.

In any event, the point I am making is clear enough, I hope. The sign can easily be misunderstood, and we understand it, in part, because taking it as a serious warning never to follow such a truck is so obviously ludicrous. I suspect that no one has ever seen a vehicle pull over so as not to follow a construction truck. We all understand that we are to ignore the warning when we come up behind such a truck on the highway.

One lesson to draw is that rules do not interpret themselves. Adding explanations and specifications to a rule will not help, and there can be no rule about how to interpret a rule that does not raise the same problem in an infinite regress. Are we to have another rule about how to interpret the rule that is about how to interpret the rule that needs to be interpreted? Ludwig Wittgenstein made this point about how a rule, even what seems to be a very explicit one, is open to interpretation. Suppose I say, "2, 4, 6, 8, 10 ... and now you continue." Are you to say "12, 14, 16 ...," taking the rule to be that we are to add 2? But perhaps we are to repeat the sequence in tens: "10, 20, 40, 60, 80, 100?" And then with hundreds? 100, 200, 400, ...? We cannot tell. The point is straightforward. How a rule gets interpreted is not part of the rule.[4] We get a snippet—like the strings of numbers above—or several examples of how someone understands a rule, and we go from there. What comes to be accepted becomes how we understand the rule—at least until someone reads it in a different and more plausible way. We stop at *an* interpretation, that is, one of several possibilities, and we can readily see how we might understand a rule differently and how ethical issues can arise from our taking different interpretations to be the "natural" one for a rule. So if there appears to be an ethical issue, we need to check whether the parties involved are understanding the rule involved in the same way.

We had a nice example of how such problems can arise for professionals when we examined a conceptual misunderstanding where two groups of a team of engineers were upset when they looked at a mock-up of what they had designed. An object was to be embedded in a transparent material, but one part of the team thought the material was "transparent" if you could see the embedded object while the other group thought "transparent" meant not seeing it, but seeing through it as though it were not there. They had agreed on the design solution and thus to a rule or set of rules about how to fabricate the artifact in question, but found themselves at loggerheads because of an ambiguity. The result satisfied one group, but not the other.

Rules are subject to interpretation no matter how clear they may seem to be, and so different professionals may interpret the same rule in different ways. If anyone needs more proof about how elastic a rule can be, just ask parents with children. A parent telling a child, "Your room needs to be cleaned and your clothes put away before you can leave," will quickly discover just how such apparently clear words as "clean" and "put away" can be interpreted in ways the parent would never have imagined. Or consider the young boy who kept holding his breath because he had been told, "Every time you draw a breath, someone in China dies."[5]

Anything and everything can go wrong when we try to communicate, sometimes with disastrous results. A contractor "scribbled down 'an organic kitty litter'" when told to pack barrels of radioactive waste with "inorganic kitty litter." The barrels were stored in caverns carved in salt beds in New Mexico, and a barrel

> burst and spread waste into the cavern. The site was closed for three years, significantly backing up nuclear waste disposal in the United States and costing $500 million to clean.[6]

Just as things can go horribly wrong with communication, anything and everything can go wrong with a rule, creating ethical issues that we would miss if we thought that the only problems are the sorts we examined regarding the BP and GM engineers. Even rules that seem crystal clear are open to interpretation and so open to misinterpretation.

§2 Rules Are Artifacts

When the locking mechanism for our dishwater broke with the door shut, preventing us from opening it, I went online to the manufacturer's website to see if any particular solution was recommended. Their solution was quite simple. You are to pull the dishwasher out from under the counter edge to expose its top. You cannot pull it out until you unscrew the dishwasher from the counter above. The screws are inside the dishwasher. To get to them, you are to open the dishwasher door. Once you open it, you can lean into the dishwasher and unscrew what is holding it to the counter above, pull it out, and get to the locking mechanism to unlock it—so you can open the dishwasher door.

This "solution" garnered a great many comments from dissatisfied customers who had the same problem we had with our dishwasher door, and it is worth repeating the essence of the proposed solution because it is so obviously flawed it is difficult to imagine how anyone could have suggested it.

- What is the problem?
  - The door is locked and cannot be opened because the locking mechanism is broken.
  - The locking mechanism can only be reached to be fixed or replaced if the door is open.
- So how do you open the door?
- The manufacturer recommends the following steps:
  - Open the door to get at the screws holding the dishwasher in place so you can pull out the dishwasher.
  - Once the dishwasher is out, open the door to get to the locking mechanism so you can fix or replace it.

There is presumably a way at getting at the locking mechanism once the top of the dishwasher can be reached. That would seem to be the only reason for pulling the dishwasher out from underneath the counter. So with that in mind, we may understand why we are being told to pull the dishwasher out, and perhaps the convoluted explanation given on the website may have hidden from those who wrote it just how absurd the rule for solving the problem was. They surely could not have thought through the various steps in their recipe to solve the problem to see whether what they recommend could actually be done. Their prescription for what to do would be like telling someone who has locked themselves out of their car with the keys in the ignition, "Well, if you open the door, you can get the keys to unlock the door so you can open it and get your keys." The prescription is not even worth a Monty Python skit.

When I went to the manufacturer's website, I had an end in mind, namely, a clear statement, a rule, that would tell what to do to solve my problems. What I got is a wonderful example of how writing a rule is not an easy matter. As mentioned, writing a foolproof rule is a fool's errand. There are too many ways to go wrong in writing a rule to catalogue all the possible failures and too many different ways of misunderstanding what we might have thought was a clear rule to protect ourselves from misunderstandings.

The problem with "Open the door to unlock the door" is found all too frequently. In the ASME Boiler and Pressure Vessel Code, there is a set of rules about how to create glass-lined vessels. A steel shell is lined with glass powder and put in a furnace. The heat cures the glass. But the new ASME Code requires that after any heat treatment, a vessel must be pressurized to check for leaks. The check must be done before any coating is applied since a coating may obscure a leak.

We obviously have a problem here. You cannot coat a vessel with glass without heating the vessel with glass powder in a furnace. But once a vessel has been heated in a furnace, the Code requires that it be pressurized to see if there are any leaks. But you cannot check for leaks if the vessel has a coating. So it is not possible to check for any leaks after the curing but before any coating is applied.[7] The Code makes it impossible to check for leaks on any glass-lined vessels—as required by the Code—or impossible to make glass-lined vessels.

The rules in the ASME Code and on the website for our dishwasher are badly written, inconsistent, in fact, and are certain to leave anyone trying to follow them stymied. Their inconsistency makes it impossible for anyone to use them, and that is an ethical problem. If our dishwasher is rendered inoperative because the door lock broke, we have lost the money we put into it and the money we will have to put out to get a new one. If the only way to fix the door lock is to open the locked door, then the problem is not with the rule, of course, but with a poorly designed dishwasher. It is an ethical problem that glass-lined vessels cannot be certified as leakproof and that buyers may find themselves with a lemon, as it were. It is an ethical problem for the buyer, of course, and also for the seller who will have to live with the reputation of selling untested vessels.

Unfortunately, inconsistency is only one of the appropriate terms of criticism for rules. Even a consistent set of rules can introduce new problems that are worse than the ones it was supposed to solve. At one time, there was a simple mechanical procedure for setting a clock in a vehicle. There was a control for the hour and one for the minute, and by pushing the control a driver could set the hour and the minute independently. Adjusting for daylight savings time took less than a minute. But engineers at Subaru introduced a new way to set the time, one that required using the vehicle's computer and going through a series of steps to get to the menu for setting the clock and then going through a series of additional steps to set it. I have never succeeded in setting the clock. I find myself at one point in the series of steps where no matter what I do, it seems, I go back to where I started. What was simple was made complex.

I am not the only one exasperated by the change. When I took my Subaru in for a checkup, I asked the manager to make sure the clock got set for daylight savings time. When I went to pick it up, the clock had not been touched. So I asked the manager if he could do it for me. He said, with a rueful grin, "I only have four hours left before going home." I looked startled, and he added, "We only have one mechanic here who is able to set those clocks. I can't do it. Find me the engineer who designed this, and I will provide 20 mechanics to beat him up."

Presumably the software engineer who programmed the onboard computer either thought the steps so obvious and simple that no one could fail to follow them or, less likely, failed to have someone other than a software engineer try them before signing off on the software. This sort of problem is all too common with links in websites where one link leads to another and then to another and then back to the original. I offered to help my frustrated son find the proper state electrical inspector for the house he was building in Colorado. I went online and after getting to the proper webpage, had to click four times to get to a set of options. I clicked the "obvious" one only to be redirected back to where I had started. I clicked four more times to get to the set of options again and clicked on another. Back again. After clicking on all the possible options and being directed back each time, I gave up and tried to call the number on the webpage for the main office—"no longer in service." I suspect this example will resonate with others. The problem is fairly common.

What is wrong? My son and I were following a recipe, as it were, that somehow, after a fair amount of time and energy, took us back to our starting point. It is rather like getting to the end of a race only to discover we have somehow ended up back at the beginning—and must still run the race. Such rules can obviously cause all sorts of problems and some real harms when someone has to contact an electrical inspector within a certain time frame, for instance. The professional who designed the website failed to make it useful and so failed the residents of Colorado, not only frustrating those who tried to contact the state but also preventing them from getting information they needed to move ahead on what they were doing.

The difficulties in designing a rule are all too evident in the law. A case in Maine nicely illustrates the point. Drivers for a dairy company sued for lost wages under a law which "requires time-and-a-half pay for each hour worked after 40 hours." The drivers worked an average of twelve extra hours a week distributing perishable goods. The law carved out a set of exemptions for overtime pay involving, among other things, the "canning, processing, preserving, freezing, drying, marketing, storing, packing for shipment or distribution of" perishable foods. "If there were a comma after 'shipment', it might have been clear that the law exempted the distribution of perishable foods. But the appeals court … sided with the drivers, saying the absence of a comma produced enough uncertainty to rule in their favor. It reversed a lower court decision."

What was at issue is what is called the Oxford comma. That is the final comma in a list of items, and if it is required, we write Peter, Paul, and Mary rather than Peter, Paul and Mary. The Maine Legislative Drafting Manual "specifically instructs lawmakers to not use the Oxford comma," to write "trailers, semitrailers and pole trailers" rather than "trailers, semitrailers, and pole trailers." The legislature did what its style manual said it should do. So the drivers gained and the dairy lost.[8]

We create rules, and when we create them, we are solving design problems. How are we to design a rule that will achieve the end we intend to achieve? Crafting a rule is linguistic engineering, as it were, and although we are generally as successful as engineers in achieving our goals, we can fail in a variety of ways—by fashioning inconsistent rules, for instance, or rules that stymy the best efforts of its users to understand them. No doubt there are rules like engineering artifacts that are error-provocative. Even the brightest, most informed, and motivated person will be led by such artifacts to do exactly the opposite of what they are supposed to do—as with doors with handles that signal they are opened by being pushed when they must be pulled.[9] The point is that we need to take as much care in crafting a rule as engineers must take in solving a design problem. Too many things can go wrong and cause harm if we are not careful. But even great care will not preclude someone from mistaking your meaning—hearing "the girl with colitis goes by" for "the girl with kaleidoscope eyes" of the Beatles song or, as has no doubt happened to many of us, exiting a highway too soon or too late because of misreading a road sign.

§3 Floaters

Some rules are floating conjectures, without the sorts of evidential backing needed to make them reliable. They direct the activities of those within the profession within which they appear and so have effects in the world. But not having been formulated through rigorous experimentation and testing, they may lead professionals astray.

The conjectures are not error-provocative. The brightest, most informed, and motivated professional will not be led to do exactly the opposite of what they are supposed to do by using such conjectures, but if they do not provoke errors, they invoke them. Using an error-invocative rule of skill in any profession is liable, in short, to produce mistakes even among the very best professionals, no matter how skilled and concerned they are to do the best that can be done. Such floaters provide the best examples of why we cannot justify what we do by appealing to norms. The floaters are norms without any backing, and we would, at a minimum, have to provide the backing if we appeal to a norm.

Many rules of road design are floaters, invoking errors because they bear no reliable relation to empirical data on what ought to govern road design, namely, "crash frequency and severity." When civil engineers are making judgments about road design based on the best information available, on estimates that are conservative when required, and on the basis of recommendations from the relevant standards committee, but without crash data and its causes, they are using what Ezra Hauer calls "plausible conjectures."[10] He provides three rather telling examples.

As we know from being on merry-go-rounds as kids, the faster they go, the tighter we need to hold on. What is trying to fling us off is what civil engineers worry will cause vehicles going around a curve to leave the road. So engineers ask, "How curvy should curves be?" The ideal is that they be as safe as straightaways. Engineers have four variables to work with—the friction of tires on the pavement that will help hold a vehicle on track, the banking of the curve, called superelevation, that will help hold a vehicle in, the radius of the curve, and a safe speed for the final result. Setting conservative values for both tire friction and banking, the engineer need only make a simple calculation to determine the safe speed for any radius. If a hill being skirted requires a tight curve, the speed will be lower than it would for a wide curve. There is a simple mathematical formula for that.

Engineers make the plausible conjecture that a design failure occurs when a vehicle moves to the outside of the curve and leaves the road the way a child can be flung off a merry-go-round. The problem is that curves designed using this formula are significantly less safe than straightaways. "Ample data show that on … curves crashes are much more frequent (perhaps by a factor of 3, on the average) than on straight road sections. Also, numerous studies show that the shorter the radius of a curve the higher its crash rate."[11] But the crashes do not occur because the cars are flung off the curve. The "data show that 11%-56% of the vehicles run off on the other side of the road," presumably because drivers overcorrect and lose control when they belatedly realize they are going too fast. In addition, "the speed at which drivers negotiate curves routinely exceeds the design speed."[12] What studies have been done of the relation between curves and crash frequency and severity fail to confirm the plausible conjecture, that is. As it turns out, empirical data shows that flying off the highway on curves is not the main cause of crashes or their severity.

We find the same problem regarding the width of lanes. How wide should they be to minimize crashes and their severity? The plausible conjecture is that "it is the loss of separation between oncoming vehicles that causes crashes." We have, no doubt, all experienced that moment of concern when an approaching vehicle is drifting toward the center line, causing us to move toward the edge of the pavement. It is the narrowing of the separation between us and the oncoming vehicle that is the source of concern, leaving us little margin for error should the oncoming driver drift more. Obviously, it seems, the narrower the lanes, the higher the incidences of concern—and crashes.

But empirical evidence does not confirm what seems obvious—despite its being the standard way to determine road width since the late 1930s and early 1940s. A "large-scale study" in 1953 showed "that 'neither pavement width nor shoulder width nor any combination of them has a determinable effect on the crash rates on two-lane tangents.'" That study was ignored by the committees writing road standards as were other studies, including one in 1954 showing "that for rural two-lane roads, making pavements wider than 22 ft. was at that time detrimental to safety" and another study also showing "an upturn in crash rate after a lane-width of about 11 feet."[13]

We have again a failure to take into account empirical data related to the only variables that really matter, the number and severity of crashes at different widths. What is being measured to determine lane width instead is their relation to "an aspect of driver behavior"— how we feel about the width of the lanes.[14] That variable may be relevant, but the concern we have when an oncoming vehicle seems too close may make us more cautious and so diminish the likelihood of a crash. Without some empirical data that relates our feeling of concern to the number and severity of crashes, that aspect is irrelevant.

The third example concerns how crests in roads block the vision of drivers. If the crest goes up too steeply, a driver may not see over it until on it and so be unable to stop for anything just over the crest—a deer, for instance. The plausible conjecture is that "sight distance limitations are an important cause of crashes on crest curves."[15] The crest should "be sufficiently shallow so that, if there is some object of specified height in the path of the vehicle, it can be seen from far enough for the driver to stop safely."[16] All an engineer needs to do then is to calculate the crest, taking into account "the reaction time, pavement-tire friction, eye height and object height."

There is a formula for that calculation, but, obviously, we need numbers for these variables. The eye height is going to vary as vehicles vary: the higher the vehicle is off the road, the farther a driver can see. A truck driver can see farther than someone driving an Alfa Romeo Spider. That aside, the height of the object in the road is going to make a huge difference to the calculations. A person is taller than a possum. So what are we trying to avoid? Or, better, what should we assume we are trying to avoid?

The original choice was an object 4" high. As those who wrote the original standard put it, "the required length of vertical curve [the crest] is reduced by 40%" by increasing the height from 0" to 4", but choosing any higher number would "not save much in construction cost." They chose 4" "on the basis of what was known, namely the cost of construction."[17] Just how arbitrary that number was is shown by how flexible a variable the height has been. The number is "0" high in Germany, 4" and later 6" in the U.S.A., 8" in Australia and 15" in Canada."[18] Only the first and last choices seem linked to safety. The first allows a driver to see anything in the road, and the last is the presumed height of tail lights. But none of the choices is based on empirical evidence about how often accidents occur because of objects in the road that drivers cannot see, about the height of such objects, or about the severity of the accidents that result.

The addition of this last floater gives us three rules that civil engineers use to construct roads. They float because they bear only an accidental relation, if any, to what ought to guide the engineers in making our roads safe, but roads that satisfy these plausible conjectures are deemed to have met the engineering standards and so are judged "safe."[19]

In each conjecture the end of decreasing the number and severity of accidents has been displaced by a different end: diminishing our concern about having an accident with oncoming traffic, allowing us to see something in the road that we may hit, and keeping us from being flung off the side of the road. These are laudable ends, but they not tied to empirical evidence that shows that they are connected to the end civil engineers ought to be addressing. The floaters each misidentify the problem the civil engineers are supposed to solve in designing roads. The end they all ought to accomplish is the reduction in the number and severity of accidents. That is the test. The floaters were not tested, and using them leads to solutions that can bear only a chance relation to the real problem.

Does using them produce unnecessary harms? Does designing roads to meet these standards produce the best roads, the safest roads, engineers can design? Almost certainly not. As Hauer points out, "it is almost certain that conjectures not supported by evidence will either harm safety or harm other aspects of 'utility'" such as the expenditure of money or time.[20] Civil engineers ought to find such a state of affairs disconcerting indeed, as should the public at large. We are at greater risk of harm than we should be and are yet paying great sums of money for what may be an inferior product.

It is important to note, however, that the floaters are not arbitrary. They are all based on quite plausible assumptions, and that is part of the problem. We would have no trouble identifying floaters if they were completely unhinged from reason and reality, but they are tethered by their plausibility. Who does not remember holding on for dear life on the merry-go-round as it went faster and faster?

We can find such floaters in other professions, floaters that we know cause real harm. Floaters in forensic science have been used to convict innocent people who have then been sentenced to long terms in prison or given the death penalty.

Anyone who reads mysteries or watches crime shows knows that central to a crime's solution is what can be found at the crime scene—"DNA, hair, latent fingerprints, firearms and spent ammunition, toolmarks and bitemarks, shoeprints and tire tracks, and handwriting."[21] Detectives hunt for samples at the scene that can then be compared to samples from a suspect, and they remind everyone not to touch anything at the scene so that when they dust for fingerprints, for instance, their findings will not have been contaminated. They are hunting for fingerprints or hair or something else left by whoever committed the scene crime.

Experts compare the features of what is found at the crime scene with the features of the relevant sample from a suspect, and if there is a match, they have significant evidence that the suspect is the criminal. How significant? That depends upon the validity and reliability of the methods of comparison.

As it turns out, we have a way of determining how accurate the methods of comparison are. Using DNA is not quite the gold standard it is sometimes touted to be. A man who received a bone marrow transplant ended up with the DNA of the donor. He had both his own and his donor's DNA, and, somewhat to his chagrin, we must assume, "all of the DNA in his semen belonged to his donor."[22] We do not have any idea how often that happens, but once is enough to make DNA testing less than the gold standard. In addition, those doing the testing can introduce errors by accidentally touching the artifact being assessed, mistakenly using a contaminated container for the sample or any of a number of other mistakes.[23] But even if a DNA test is not 24 caret gold, it is good enough to provide a basis to assess the validity and reliability of such other comparisons as fingerprints and hair.

As has been shown, feature comparisons are not very reliable at all. As a 2016 Report to the President on forensic science stated,

> Reviews by the National Institute of Justice and others have found that DNA testing during the course of investigations has cleared tens of thousands of suspects and that DNA-based re-examination of past cases has led so far to the exonerations of 342 defendants.[24]

The Innocence Project exonerated more than 350 individuals, and in 45 percent of the cases, those individuals were convicted because of a failure of feature comparisons combined with misleading testimony from experts who ensured juries and judges that they were sure within a "reasonable degree of scientific certainty."[25] That is a phrase that gives great weight to the evidence but has no scientific validity.[26]

The 2016 Report quotes a judge about testimony from an expert that "markings on certain bullets were unique to a gun recovered from a defendant's apartment":

> As matters currently stand, a certainty statement regarding toolmark pattern matching has the same probative value as the vision of a psychic: it reflects nothing

more than the individual's foundationless faith in what he believes to be true. This is not evidence on which we can in good conscience rely, particularly in criminal cases, where we demand proof—real proof—beyond a reasonable doubt, precisely because the stakes are so high.

The Report adds,

> In science, assertions that a metrological method is more accurate than has been empirically demonstrated are rightly regarded as mere speculation, not valid conclusions that merit credence.[27]

The need for evidence and testimony based on evidence is nicely put by US District Judge John Potter, in "an early case on the use of DNA analysis,"[28]:

> Without the probability assessment, the jury does not know what to make of the fact that the patterns match: the jury does not know whether the patterns are as common as pictures with two eyes, or as unique as the Mona Lisa.[29]

So we have floaters in forensic science. Because of them, some individuals were executed. Unlike the "safe" curves on roads, where we do not know what accidents, if any, were caused or avoided by the particular radius and speed chosen, we know that floaters in forensic science can have grievous consequences and that those professionals who testified to their valid application in particular cases were wrong.

We cannot interview the individuals who were wrongly executed, but we can get a sense of how much more damage the use of these floaters has caused by looking at several cases, including the Brandon Mayfield case, which has become a classic example of how misidentification of a sample can mislead investigators, taking them off the scent of the perpetrator, as it were, onto the scent of an innocent person.

In March 11, 2004, ten bombs killed 192 passengers on trains in Madrid and injured more than 1400, according to initial reports.[30] The Spanish authorities found a fingerprint on a bag of detonators and forwarded it to the FBI to see if it could find a match in its database. The FBI's Integrated Automated Fingerprint Identification System (IAFIS) "generated a list of 20 candidate prints."[31] None was a perfect match, but IAFIS also lists close matches,[32] and one belonged to Brandon Mayfield, a lawyer in Oregon. The FBI "immediately opened an intensive investigation of Mayfield, including 24-hour surveillance … and physical searches" of his law office and residence.[33] When news somehow broke that an American was a suspect in the bombing, the FBI detained Mayfield on May 6 because they were "absolutely confident" that Mayfield's fingerprint was on the detonator bags.[34] They kept him in solitary confinement "for up to 22 hours per day."[35]

The fingerprint from Spain was examined by a fingerprint specialist in the FBI who verified it as belonging to Mayfield. That judgment was confirmed by a second FBI fingerprint specialist and by the fingerprint unit chief, all of whom agreed it was Mayfield's. That decision was confirmed by a court-appointed specialist.[36] Four fingerprint experts fingered Mayfield, as it were. The defense attorney's own expert confirmed the judgment of the FBI experts and later said, "No time before in history have there ever been two fingerprints with fifteen minutiae that were not the same person."[37] So there was good reason for the FBI's confidence.

The Spanish authorities identified the person whose fingerprint was on the bag of detonators, and it was not Mayfield. As it turned out, further analysis of the fingerprints showed that Mayfield's was not identical to the one found in Spain, but what is of importance here is that specialists in fingerprint identification judged that it was and that they had absolute confidence in their judgment. The Mayfield case is a dramatic example of why such judgments cannot be relied upon and should not be relied on, especially in criminal cases where the stakes are high. We must have proof beyond a reasonable doubt, and the Mayfield case puts in doubt reliance on fingerprint comparisons.[38]

Another example of a floater in forensic science concerns bite marks. Keith Harward "narrowly escaped the death penalty," but spent thirty-three years in prison after being convicted of rape and murder on the basis of six forensic dentists testifying that the bite marks on the rape victim's legs were his. DNA evidence showed that he was innocent and that a fellow sailor, Jerry Crotty, was responsible. Harward is one of at least twenty-five individuals "to have been wrongfully convicted or indicted based at least in part on bite mark evidence."[39] He is now free, but he says to those who tell him he is a free man, "I will never be free of this ... I spent more than half my life in prison behind the opinions and expert egos of two odontologists."[40]

The 2016 Report to the President pointed out that a "2010 study of experimentally created bitemarks ... found that skin deformation distorts bitemarks so substantially and so variably that current procedures for comparing bitemarks are unable to reliably exclude or include a suspect as a potential biter." In fact, evidence "showed a disturbing lack of consistency in the way that forensic odontologists go about analyzing bitemarks, including even on deciding whether there was sufficient evidence to determine whether a photographed bitemark was a human bitemark."[41] That bite mark evidence still finds its way into court cases is a sad commentary on the failure of our judicial system to come to grips with such forensic floaters.

The comparison of hairs is another floater. Santae Tribble was 17 when he was arrested for murder and convicted based on a comparison of his hair with hair found at the scene of the crime.[42] As he put it, the experts said that the sample "matched my hair in all microscope characteristics." Hilverda was the FBI scientist who said, "There is one chance ... in 10 million that it could [be] someone else's hair." Later analysis showed that of the thirteen hairs in question, nine were from one person, three from different individuals, and one from a dog. None belonged to Tribble.[43]

Tribble spent twenty-six years in jail because of the mistaken judgment that his hair matched the samples found at the crime scene. "Such is the true state of hair microscopy," the lawyer representing Tribble said, that "two FBI-trained analysts, James Hilverda and Harold Deadman, could not even distinguish human hairs from canine hairs." Researchers showed in 1974 that "visual comparisons are so subjective that different analysts can reach different conclusions about the same hair. The FBI acknowledged in 1984 that such analysis cannot positively determine that a hair found at a crime scene belongs to one particular person."[44]

In 2012, the FBI and Department of Justice began a review of over three thousand "criminal cases involving microscopic hair analysis." They found "that FBI examiners had provided scientifically invalid testimony in more than 95 percent of cases where that testimony was used to inculpate a defendant at trial."[45] So nineteen out of every twenty defendants were falsely incriminated by FBI experts. It is difficult to image a less reliable way to determine if someone has committed a crime. Just guessing might be better than a 95 percent failure rate.

The failure of such feature comparisons as hair samples and fingerprints is illustrated by the number of exonerations each year as old cases are reexamined. "More than 150 men and women were exonerated in 2018," having "spent more than 1,600 years in prison" for crimes they did not commit. A main reason is that "experts … have used exaggerated statistical claims to bolster unscientific assertions."[46]

It is no surprise that people can be confident about something or find something plausible or even obvious when the facts do not warrant confidence. We all have beliefs which range from the implausible to certain, and to assess them, we must rely not on how we feel about them but on what the facts support. A feeling that a belief is certain is no guarantee it is true. If we were to construct an argument for the FBI experts' judgment that Tribble's hair was found at the scene of the crime, it would include the following premises regarding the degree of confidence the FBI experts had in their judgment implicating Tribble:

- There is one chance in ten million that the hair is not Tribble's.
- We have only been mistaken nineteen times out of twenty in making such judgments.
- So we experts are absolutely confident the hair is Tribble's.

We have terms of criticism for beliefs, and the one most relevant here concerns the degree of likelihood that the belief is true. We ought to be more or less confident in our beliefs in accordance with the quality of our evidence, and in this case we ought to lack any confidence at all.

A birder trying to identify a particular warbler will follow the usual methodology, making a judgment based on the bird's size, flight pattern, song, and other distinctive characteristics. The birder ought to be more or less confident depending upon how many identifying marks are discernible and how easily they can be discerned. "It's a Palm warbler" is a quite different judgment than "Well, could be a Palm warbler," and they mark how many identifying marks the birder was able to discern and with what degree of certainty. Does the bird have a distinctive yellow eyebrow? A chestnut-colored crown?[47] Catching a glimpse of something chestnut-colored is very different from being able to observe the bird for some period of time.

The methodology for identifying birds is not perfect: experts can use it and still make mistakes. But when used correctly by a competent birder, the success rate is significantly higher than 5 percent. A 95 percent failure rate tells us that the methodology is unreliable and that having a second and third expert check another's judgment using the same methodology will not provide us with any more confidence in the truth of the belief.

If the methodology is faulty, it does not matter how experienced an expert may be, or how many experts chime in. An unreliable methodology will lead to unreliable results. As the President's Report of 2016 put it,

> Without appropriate estimates of accuracy [and error rates], an examiner's statement that two samples are similar—or even indistinguishable—is scientifically meaningless: it has no probative value, and considerable potential for prejudicial impact.[48]

As the Report notes,

> Nothing—not training, personal experience, nor professional practices—can substitute for adequate empirical demonstration of accuracy.[49]

The rules of skill that supposedly gave credence to "expert" testimony are all recipes for mistakes. In comparing Mayfield's fingerprint with the fingerprint from the bag of detonators, FBI fingerprint specialists found ten points of similarity, and the defense's expert found fifteen. "Points" is a technical term here. They occur where individual ridges end or split, and the similarities were "the relative location of the points, the orientation of the ridges coming into the points, and the number of intervening ridges between the points." The Office of Inspector General's Review of the FBI's Handling of the Brandon Mayfield case points out that there is no research on how frequently such similar constellations of points occur in different individuals, but that "anecdotal reports suggest that this degree of similarity ... is an extremely unusual circumstance."[50]

The bottom line, however, is that the experts were relying on a rule of skill that told them that if there are so many points of comparison between two fingerprints, they can have "absolute confidence" that the two were made by the same person.

The other floaters are no better supported. They all depend on rules of skill that tell supposed experts that if they have such-and-such a configuration in two samples—of markings on a bullet, of the impression of teeth marks, of the details of hair—they can be absolutely confident that the samples came from the same firearm, or the same mouth, or the same head of hair. Such confidence is not responsive to reality, but reflects an unwarranted judgment about the reliability of a faulty rule of skill.[51]

It is not just experts who make mistaken judgments about feature similarities. Eyewitness identifications are standard and are remarkably unreliable. A witness or the victim to a mugging gets a glance at someone's face and then identifies the defendant when asked by a prosecutor in the courtroom to point out the person responsible for the crime, but "inaccurate eyewitness identifications ... were introduced as evidence in over 70 percent of the more than 360 cases that the Innocence Project, ... proved were wrongful convictions."[52] Amateurs are no better than experts, that is.

Rules of skill involving feature comparisons float. The only difference between the plausible conjectures we examined in civil engineering and these rules of skill in forensic science is that we know that the latter rules have caused great harm to individuals. What we know from civil engineers using plausible conjectures is that they may not have done the best they can do to make roads safe. What we know from the floaters in forensic science is that some innocent individuals have been executed and that others have been jailed for decades. People have lost their lives and their liberty because supposed experts have relied on unreliable rules of skill, unsupported by the research that ought to have preceded their use in courts of law.

So we have floaters in civil engineering and in forensic science, disciplines so different from one another that we should assume there are floaters we would find elsewhere. These examples ought to make professionals in every profession at least somewhat hesitant about rules they accept as "plausible" or "obvious," and we should follow their lead in our ordinary lives.

§4 Appearance and Reality

Things are not always as they appear. Vagrancy laws were passed to arrest those hanging about with no visible means of support, but for years police arrested prostitutes as vagrants because their means of support were all too visible. The meaning of the law was determined by how it was used. That is the reality.

Oliver Wendell Holmes argued that we cannot tell the meaning of a law by what it seems to say. Instead, he says, "You must look at it as a bad man, who cares only for the material consequences which such knowledge enables him to predict."[53] A lawyer's job, he argues, is thus to predict what will happen to someone who runs afoul of the law, and that is determined by how the police and prosecutors and especially the courts have responded to those who previously ran afoul of the law. "The prophecies of what the courts will do in fact," he says, "and nothing more pretentious, are what I mean by the law."[54] A prostitute might read the vagrancy law and have no idea it puts her at legal risk, but a lawyer could tell her that despite the law's wording, she is liable to be arrested under that law.

Rules are no different. What they may seem to say may have little, if any, predictive value for anyone subject to them. As we saw with the two HIV-positive men who had regularly paid their premiums and had every reason to think they were entitled to what their contract said they were entitled to, something may not mean what it seems to mean.

Any "mismatch between rules as announced and rules as administered" is an ethical issue. Lon Fuller made this point about the law.[55] It is part of what he called the internal morality of the law that there be no "discrepancy between the law as declared and actually administered." The law should not become "a snare" for those who are subject to it, who think they are legally permitted to do one thing, according to what the law or rule says, when they will be charged with breaking the law, according to how it is understood by those administering it.[56] Prostitutes thus had an ethical complaint against those who enforced the laws against vagrancy. They could not know, from a literal reading of that law, that it was interpreted by the police as authorizing arrest.

We will examine in some detail a case at a university that illustrates just how misleading a literal reading of rules can be.[57] Anyone reading the policies and procedures at that university would find both a Staff Performance Improvement policy that appears to have the admirable aim of correcting the behavior of employees before termination becomes necessary as well as a grievance procedure that appears robust, requiring the reasoned judgment of five members of the faculty and staff after hearing the reasons for and against what is at issue. The policy lays out the rules the professionals in the university are to use regarding issues of problematic employee behavior. But a recent case involving a physician employed by the university gives a very different reading to these policies and, unfortunately, raises issues of unprofessional conduct both by those responsible for administering the policy and by other administrative officials.

Getting caught up in the details of this case should not obscure its general point: we cannot trust what a rule seems to say—not only because it may not be interpreted just the way we interpret it, a problem we noted above, but also because the way it is used may bear little resemblance to any reasonable interpretation. The point is generalizable. Holmes was right. Look to how a rule is used to determine what it means.

The physician at the university was employed in the Student Health Center and, as part of her regular practice, provided hormone therapy for transgender students. After she was fired, the students were treated as separate and unequal, a concept whose legal shelf life expired with Brown *v.* Board of Education. Were they really treated equally, even if separately from other students, we would have an ethical problem, but the treatment they now receive is anything but equal. Unlike other students, they must go off campus to clinics with waiting lists of four months at a minimum. At one point they had to carpool 90 miles to the closest treatment center. They had been treated on campus, by that physician, trained to provide hormone therapy, but the university picked them out as a distinct and separate class, not to be treated like "normal" students.

These are students who are going through a lot, emotionally as well as physically, and so are likely to feel different from other students. That feeling is reflected in the extraordinarily high rate of attempted suicide for transgender individuals, 41 percent versus 4.6 percent for the general population.[58] The university reinforced that feeling. It is all the worse that the university went from the high moral ground of treating them like other students to treating them differently in a way that was discriminatory and, the physician argued, medically inappropriate. The university lost the chance for moral praise, earning moral condemnation instead.

The firing is puzzling for a variety of reasons. The physician was fired on May 24, 2017, after being called into the office of the new director—who had taken charge that morning—briefly questioned and then, after several hours, terminated for "continiued [*sic*] violation'" of the Student Health Center's practice that "prohibits prescribing hormone therapy for the purpose of gender transition." A subsequent letter by the director states that the physician was fired for "gross insubordination," and that is reaffirmed in yet another letter by the director's superior in Human Resources (HR), stating that the "termination was not based on your skill as a physician, but rather your intentional decision to not adhere to the directives of the leadership of the Student Health Center."

The physician was taken completely by surprise—and for good reasons. The Staff Performance Improvement policy lays out a three-step procedure for what managers consider problematic behavior. Managers are to give verbal advice first, and if that does not suffice, are to lay out a plan for improving performance that the manager and employee both sign if they agree, and, finally, as a last resort, provide a written warning that termination will follow if the problematic behavior does not cease. All this is to be in writing so that there is no ambiguity regarding what directives were given. If the employee fails to heed the final written warning, the university can show that while it tried to improve the employee's performance, the employee failed to respond to three different attempts to change the unacceptable behavior. So termination can be shown to be justified. This three-step procedure is a paradigmatic example of a rule of skill. It tells us how to achieve the goal of improving an employee's performance.

There are obviously conditions which justify an employee being terminated without recourse to the Staff Performance Improvement policy—stealing university property, threatening members of the university community with a gun or a knife, and so on. These require quick responses to prevent further harm. But we might assume that where such a response is unnecessary, the policy would come into play. We would be wrong. The physician's firing is a case in point.

The physician had no final verbal or written warning or even, she thought, a preliminary warning that her treatment of transgender students was "problematic." The new director immediately jumped to the very last step in the Staff Performance Improvement policy, firing her. The physician must have been further surprised by the reason given for her termination—her "gross insubordination" in continuing to violate the Health Center's practice that "prohibits prescribing hormone therapy for the purpose of gender transition." That reason is puzzling for four different reasons:

1. *There is not and has never been a stated policy prohibiting the prescription of hormone therapy.* As the former interim director wrote in a letter of June 13, 2017, about a meeting in the fall of 2016, "At the time of our discussion, we had no policy or procedure for either initiating or managing a student's hormonal therapy. (At this time, we still do not have any policy or procedures in place for this type of therapy.)"

2. *The university supported the physician's efforts to help transgender students by funding her training.* The former interim director wrote in his letter of June 13 that "adequate training" is essential to be able to offer hormonal therapy. That is presumably why the Student Health Center funded the physician's training at a cost of $7,500 before she started providing hormone therapy in the fall of 2016. If a policy in place prohibited offering hormonal therapy, why would the university pay for her training to provide it?

3. *In the annual performance review a month before her termination, she was rated as successful in complying "with all department and university policies, procedures and standards of conduct."* Hormonal therapy is mentioned—to compliment her on her willingness to undertake new work. If it was the practice of the Health Center to prohibit hormonal therapy, why was the physician praised for her willingness to provide it just a month before being fired for providing it?

4. *Stated policy or not, it was the practice of the Student Health Center to prescribe hormone therapy.* The Center offered "comprehensive primary care" for all students, and comprehensive care includes hormone replacement therapy. Medicare provides it, for instance. Official references by the Student Health Center's Clinical Protocols Policy unanimously supported such treatment in

student health centers, and there is nothing about a prohibition in the staff meeting minutes back through 2015. No clinical provider on staff recalls any verbal or written communication about it. Several made working on the transgender team part of their Plans of Work—which were approved, and all were as surprised as the physician at the Center's having a policy none of them knew about.

It is perhaps no surprise that although the Health Center had advertised itself as offering comprehensive primary care, it changed its website to say it only provides "basic primary care." This was within days of firing the physician. The natural conclusion to draw is that the change was needed because it no longer provided transgender hormone therapy—one more piece of evidence to explain the physician's surprise at being terminated for providing it.

What is also surprising is why the new director did not just inform the physician that she was not to provide hormone therapy in the future. The physician's performance review praises her for complying with directives, and if the new director had read the performance review, she would have known that telling the physician to stop would likely be enough. Indeed, we might think it mere courtesy to request that the physician stop and give her a chance to comply.

But the main ethical problem is that the director enforced a policy ex post facto. There was no policy not to treat transgender students before the director fired her—as the interim director noted and as the physician's coworkers agreed. So the physician was fired for failing to obey a rule that did not exist, or, to put the point more pointedly, the director made it a policy not to provide transgender treatment and fired the physician for having provided it before she made it a policy not to.

The divergence between the apparent admirable aim of the policy and the new director's firing the physician tells us that, despite the policy, an employee may be terminated without prior warning. As with the vagrancy laws, what matters is not what the policy says, but how it is used—or not.

We have several major ethical problems so far:

- The university discriminated against transgender students, piling on students who must already be under a lot of pressure.
- The university applied a rule ex post facto: the physician could not have known she was not following policy.
- The director and her supervisor in HR failed to follow the university's rules, giving them a meaning no rational observer could have imagined.

The most telling example of this failure concerns the requirement in the Staff Performance Improvement policy that an employee be given notification before termination.

It was unclear at the time whether the director and her supervisor just ignored the Staff Performance Improvement policy and were winging it, as it were, or whether they were treating it the way police treated the vagrancy laws—giving it a new meaning by what they did. We shall see that they did try to justify the firing as being in accord with existing policy. So this is a warning to everyone. Pay attention to how a rule is used, not just to what it apparently says ought to be done.

The physician grieved the university, arguing that she had been unfairly treated and wanting to have her termination for "gross insubordination" removed from her record. The grievance policy consists of several steps of mediation and, as a last resort, a quasi-judicial grievance hearing before a body of peers, two chosen by the person who is grieving, two chosen by the person being grieved, and one selected by the four who have been chosen. Each party to the dispute may have an advocate, and, again, we have a paradigmatic example of a rule of skill, a procedure designed to ensure that a fair decision is reached.

The grievance process is run by HR, and it is no small matter that the director who fired the physician was backed in her decision by her supervisor in HR as well as that supervisor's supervisor in HR. So in grieving the university, the physician was grieving supervisors in HR as well as the director of the Center. That is an ethical red flag. We would have no hesitation seeing a conflict of interest if a judge were tried in the judge's own courtroom, presided by the judge who had accused the judge being tried. Having HR in charge of a quasi-judicial procedure while being a party to the grievance is of no less concern. That is not to say that a judge or HR cannot be impartial in such a situation, but it does say that outside observers should be chary of accepting the outcome of such a procedure without ensuring that the procedure was in fact impartial and fair.

The physician grieved on two grounds:

- The termination constitutes discrimination by association because she was terminated for providing services to persons who are transgender. Discrimination on that ground violates both clinical policies and the university's policy against discrimination. In addition, a male physician was also treating transgender students, but was not terminated.
- The Staff Performance Improvement policy should have been used.

The university's policies regarding discrimination seem as admirable as its Staff Performance Improvement policy. The physician's complaints were that she was fired for providing hormone therapy to transgender students, a protected class, and that she and her colleague were both providing hormone therapy to transgender students, but she was fired, and he was not.

The physician had also filed a grievance with the state's Division of Human Rights, and its "investigation revealed that Respondent [the university] has no policy regarding hormone therapy for transgender students and there is no documentation to establish that Complainant was ever told to stop prescribing hormone therapy by a supervisor." The Division determined "that <u>PROBABLE CAUSE</u> exists to believe that the Respondent has engaged in or is engaging in the unlawful discriminatory practice complained of."

So the physician's complaints of discrimination were found sufficiently plausible for the state Division of Human Rights to make a judgment of probable cause and to call for a "public hearing … where there is sworn testimony and the opportunity for cross-examination."[59] The physician would thus seem to have been on solid ground in alleging discrimination.

University policy is that a complaint about discrimination is to trigger an investigation within five business days with an outcome to be determined within sixty days with written notice of the outcome and its rationale given to the person complaining. If dissatisfied, that person can initiate a grievance or appeal. The physician had not heard anything within the specified period of time and plausibly assumed that the issue would be discussed in the university's grievance hearing—if HR set one.

At such grievance hearings, each party provides the Committee with the reasons it has for its position. These hearings are a form of adjudication,

> (1) … a process of decision that grants to the affected party a form of participation that consists in the opportunity to present proofs and reasoned arguments. (2) The litigant must therefore, if his participation is to be meaningful, assert some principle or principles by which his arguments are sound and his proofs relevant. (3) A naked demand is distinguished from a claim of right by the fact that the latter is a demand supported by a principle.[60]

So each party presents their reasons, and those reasons are vetted by being subject to cross-examination by the other party and by members of the Committee. Preparation can be onerous and time-consuming for the parties and their advocates.

HR finally set the date for a hearing and gave the physician and her advocate two weeks notice. They spent the two weeks gathering information and working out their presentation on the complaints of discrimination and of not following the Staff Performance Improvement policy. They had more than a little trouble putting everything together. For instance, HR seemed unable to direct the advocate to the proper policy webpage. But one or two days before the hearing, HR informed the physician that the hearing would only consider the Staff Performance Improvement policy. Whatever the reasons for HR's decision, its timing could not have been worse for the physician and her advocate. It resulted in wasted time and effort and forced them, with little time, to revise their arguments completely.

So in the hearing, the only question considered was whether Staff Performance Improve policy was followed. Its final step is a "written warning … *issued to an employee* when verbal coaching and performance improvement plan processes are not successful, or as a separate corrective action" (my italics). The aim, it should be noted, is still to encourage improvement since the supervisor is to meet "with the employee to deliver and review the warning, convey the seriousness of this action, and answer any questions." The employee's signature is to be secured at the end of the meeting.

The members of the grievance committee, and any objective observer, would be hard-pressed to sort out the variety of reasons given by the director and the two HR representatives for the physician's termination:

- *Her treating students was risky*—Her providing such therapy was an "unacceptable risk to our students." It was, they said, like bringing a knife or a gun to campus and trying to attack someone. In such situations, the Staff Performance Policy need not be followed.

- *She failed to follow protocol*—She provided such therapy when there was no protocol for that "within the student health organization." That is what made her treating students risky.
- *She failed to follow directives*—She failed to follow her supervisor's directives, having been told twice, it was stated by the former director, not to provide hormone therapy treatment.
- *She was provided with a written warning*—She was provided with a written warning in her letter of termination, and so the university policy was followed.
- *Oral communication suffices*—Oral conversations are as good if not better than written statements. There were conversations, and "recollections of oral conversations" suffice to satisfy the university's policy.
- *There were written notes*—Notes were kept of those conversations. So there is something in writing.

Not one of these reasons suffices to satisfy the requirement of providing a written warning to the employee before termination, and some are simply ludicrous.

Oral communications are not equivalent to written documentation, and relying on recollections of them is even less so. Written notes of those conversations would help, perhaps, but none were made available to the physician or the members of the grievance committee, and there would be no guarantee they were not written after the fact. Providing the physician with a written warning in her letter of termination is not a written warning *before* termination: it is part of the termination. So much for the last three reasons.

And the first three? Was her treating students risky? A proper analysis would ask about the risks of stopping treatment without warning. As noted above, some students were left without any recourse except to wait at least four months for an appointment or drive a great distance to obtain treatment. Leaving them without treatment is surely risky for them, and we should weigh the risk to them of not providing versus providing treatment.

Had the physician been asked why she was providing treatment, she would have explained that she was providing it to two students because they were at risk, obtaining drugs from Mexico and treating themselves without any physician supervising. Far from putting students at risk, she was mitigating the risk the transgender students had put themselves in. She was providing the supervision that taking hormone therapy requires.

Was she following protocol? The physician followed the center's protocol of following the national guidelines when there is no center protocol. No one claimed that the physician failed to follow the proper national protocol. In fact, it was specifically claimed that her termination was not based on her skill as a physician, an admission that whatever she was doing was acceptable medical practice.

Did she disobey a directive from her former supervisor? She says she was never told to stop, only that "we'll have to talk about this" and that "for now we're going ahead." From the time her former director says she learned of the physician's treating transgender students—May 6—until she was fired, no one talked to her. The director's immediate HR supervisor said she was "going to need some additional information before we can take a look at it" and also said, "we would need to have a conversation with [the physician] to understand why she was not following the directive her manager had provided her with." But she did not talk with the physician—a professional discourtesy if not a failure to do what she was obligated to do. Had she or either director spoken with her, they would have discovered that she was helping transgender students who had put themselves in a risky position: she was doing exactly what a good physician ought to do.

But all the talking—"conversations"—occurred between the two directors and members of HR and the university's legal department. The physician was not a party to those conversations, was unaware they were occurring and had no idea there was even an issue. Appealing to oral communications *about* the physician is irrelevant to satisfying university policy.

One advantage a written statement has over "recollections" is that it is, well, written: it is a record that others can read without reliance on anyone's memory. And one advantage giving a written statement to an employee about a performance issue and having the employee sign the statement is that we know that the employee knows there is an issue. It is clear that the physician did not understand that she had been told to stop providing hormone therapy. Firing someone for gross insubordination is an awful and dangerous charge to throw at someone, and being grossly insubordinate should not rest on confusion about how to interpret "for now we're going ahead."

The Grievance Committee found that "the Staff Performance Improvement policy was not fairly administered and interpreted by the supervisor" and that the physician "acted in good faith to provide the care she believed she was instructed to provide. Given this, the committee finds no basis for the charge of gross insubordination." The Committee found the firing unfair for two reasons: policy was not followed, and the physician was not grossly insubordinate.

The director thus acted unprofessionally, and the director's supervisor acted unprofessionally in supporting the firing. Unfortunately, rather than censure those responsible, the university president rejected the Committee's finding while claiming to agree with it and so approved their unprofessional behavior:

I have reviewed the report and am in agreement with the Committee that Dr. {X} followed the Staff Performance Improvement Policy; therefore, all actions related to this will matter will stand (email from [President Y], October 19, 2017 at 8:37:50 AM EDT)

We can presume when a university president accepts a Grievance Committee's finding that the reasons for that finding are accepted as well unless the president explicitly adds or rejects some reason, but we are at a loss to know what reasons a president might have for rejecting a finding unless those are stated. Current policy does not require that reasons be given, and the president's one reason for rejecting the Committee's finding and letting "all actions related to this matter ... stand" is at odds with the Committee's finding.

The grievance process is driven by reasons, and the Committee thus gave reasons for its finding. Were it simply to have announced a finding without giving reasons, it would betray the underlying principles of fairness that animate the process. Just so, a president betrays the underlying principles that animate the grievance process in not providing reasons that are responsive to the process. A president ought to be held to the same standard as the Grievance Committee. Otherwise, a president is only saying, "Because I say so," and that is no reason at all. The failure to provide reasons undercuts the point of having a robust grievance process.

We must draw two conclusions from this particular case at the university:

1. An employee may be terminated without warning and so without any chance to explain or to change the supposedly problematic behavior.
2. A quasi-judicial process, driven by reasons, can be ended with a president refusing to accept the finding without giving reasons that are responsive to the process.

Actions have consequences, and the president's rejection of the Grievance Committee's finding has the consequence that the policies regarding employment performance and grievances do not mean what they appear to mean and that any employee of the university should be chary of using its apparently robust grievance process.

What happened to the discrimination complaint? The physician asked about it at a meeting with HR personnel six months after she made it because HR was, out of "courtesy," willing to listen to further information about the alleged discrimination. The physician asked why the complaint was excluded from her grievance hearing. She was told that it "did not qualify" as a ground for grievance "based on the grievance policy itself." When she asked why, she was told that things were "fairly complicated" and that she was there to provide information, not get it. The aim, the HR representative said without a trace of irony, was to complete a "fair, consistent and timely investigation."

The physician then asked, "What more do you need?," after noting that the other physician, a male, did what she did for transgender students and was not fired. Her quite reasonable assumption was that that complaint in itself sufficed to trigger an investigation. She was told, again, "We're not here to give you information."

So the physician was unable to determine what happened to her discrimination complaint. She received no indication that her complaint had triggered an investigation, no written notice of the outcome that was to be determined within sixty days, and so no way to initiate a grievance if she was dissatisfied by the outcome. As far as she can know, her complaint about discrimination disappeared down an administrative rabbit hole.

She did receive a letter, months after her complaint, saying that her initial discrimination complaint "was not and will not be investigated." When she then contacted the Associate Provost of Diversity and Inclusion to exercise her right to appeal, she was told that HR was investigating her complaint and nothing could be done until HR had finished. When she asked about that at a meeting in November, she was told she cannot grieve it because "the grievance is done, and we are not reliving any of the grievance."

The bottom line for her is worth summarizing:

- A jury of her peers found on the basis of evidence both parties provided that she was unfairly dismissed and that she was not grossly insubordinate.
- The university president rejected the finding of the jury of her peers and decided that she was fairly dismissed and had been grossly insubordinate.

- Her discrimination complaint was excluded from her grievance hearing and could not be grieved because she had already had a grievance hearing—from which it was excluded.

The physician found herself in one of Kafka's bureaucratic nightmares.

The administration responded to the problems created by the physician's termination and grievance in a way to ensure the problem would not arise again. Under a new policy, revised immediately after the physician won her grievance, terminated employees can no longer grieve their termination, leaving their supervisors empowered to terminate them without any recourse within the university. What protects employees from such an end? The "robust Staff Performance Improvement policy," to quote an HR representative.

So things are not always as they appear. The gap between how we might naturally understand a rule and what it comes to mean as it is used and enforced can be wide indeed. The university retreated from the high moral ground of having a Performance Improvement policy that aims to improve employees and from having a robust grievance policy that serves to protect employees by a quasi-judicial process. It now has neither, or, perhaps more accurately, it has confusion. Employees are at a loss to know whether the Performance Improvement policy is to be followed, and one has to wonder why anyone would bother using the grievance policy, or why anyone would agree to be an advocate or a member of the Grievance Committee, when the process is onerous and the outcome can by overturned by a president—without giving reasons responsive to the process. The university employees have lost the stability, and thus the predictability, standing rules with a commonly accepted meaning give them.

We should not ignore the red flag we noted: that HR was in charge of ensuring a fair hearing when one of its own was being charged. It would presumably bend over backwards to make sure that the physician and her advocate were treated fairly and that the process itself was fairly administered.

Several aspects of the process put that into question: HR being unable to direct the physician's advocate to the correct website; the last-minute notification of the limited scope of the hearing, making a huge amount of preparation a waste of time; offering and then providing lunch to everyone but the physician and her advocate—pretty petty, and telling; letting the director and her advocate have the room adjacent to the hearing room for their private deliberations and giving the physician and her advocate a room so far away that by the time they got there they had little time to discuss issues the hearing had raised; and, last but not least, failing to respond in a timely manner to the complaint of discrimination.

It is hard to know whether these failures were the result of a pervasive incompetence on the part of HR or purposeful retaliation against the physician for having brought a grievance, but in either case, they serve as a warning for the employees of any organization that those making decisions about the viability of complaints and remedies for behavior are dependent on individuals who have a conflict of interest.

We have examined a great many ethical failures. Individuals failed to do what they ought to do and even failed to do what they said they ought to do. The HR supervisor of the director of the Student Health Center said that she needed to "have a conversation" with the physician so she could understand why the physician was not following her manager's directive. It is not just helpful to hear both sides of the story, but obligatory given the supervisor's position and the harm to the physician and to the students.

That is just one example among many of professionals within the university who failed to do their jobs the way they ought to be done, but those individual failures pale in comparison with two other ethical failures.

First, the university abruptly denied its transgender students the care they had been receiving from the health center's physician, cutting them adrift and letting them find help on their own. This ethical failure was particularly traumatic because the waiting lists for other local providers was long. The university certainly deserves no moral praise for treating its students that way.

Second, the university has another problem that does not bode well for how it will recognize and respond to other issues it will face. As we remarked, a set of rules has its own internal morality, just as Fuller says we find in a legal system, and one of the conditions for its being moral is that there is concurrence between the stated rules and their actual administration. There was no concurrence in this case, a structural failure that precludes its being a moral system.

We have problems when rules are stated but used in ways that belie their clear intent. Such rules are deceptive, giving a sense of what someone ought to expect that belies what will in fact happen. That same sort of problem and others arise when situations are not marked by rules, but by the "customary" ways of handling "such things."

§5 Unwritten Rules

A player on one football team complained that players on the other team broke "an unwritten rule." His team took a knee for their last possession, a signal that they were not going to run a play. The unwritten rule is that the opposing team stands back. There is no sense rushing when the other team is not running a play. But two linesmen on the opposing team rushed and hit him and other players with their knees down, obviously unprepared to fend off 300+ pounds of linesmen hitting them head-on.[61] In Texas, two high school football players tackled a referee, apparently upset about some official calls. There is presumably no rule, and no one thought there was a need for a rule, that football players are not to tackle anyone other than opposing players.[62]

In baseball, it is an unwritten rule that players are to take a strike if the count is "3-0 late in a blowout." A player who swung at such a pitch would have committed no breach of any rule. No umpire would have called anything but a ball or a strike, depending upon where the pitch was relative to the strike zone. But toward the end of "the game, once the lead got to five and therefore out of range of a tying grand slam, it becomes inappropriate to do anything excessive to score runs. Primarily, that means stealing bases and swinging in a 3-0 count."[63]

In tennis, members of the audience are not to distract players. Each game has its own unwritten rules, and it seems that no human activity can function without them. As we saw, we even follow rules when walking on a sidewalk. We avoid bumping into others, we follow those in front of us, and we keep up with those beside us. "These rules of 'attraction' (staying with others ...), 'avoidance' (... while not too close), and 'alignment' (going the same direction and speed as those around you) are sufficient to explain all herd, school, flock, and swarm behavior—not to mention that of big-brained and busy human pedestrians."[64] We follow these without thinking about them, and those who break the unwritten rules by stopping to use their cell phones, for instance, are impediments to the smooth movement of everyone else—and judged accordingly. "There's another tourist" is not a compliment to the miscreant.

These unwritten rules are an essential feature of group behavior and can be found in any organization. I doubt that any professional group has a written policy that women are not to be paid as much as males in the same position or that males are to be preferred over women in promotion considerations. Partners in a law firm may not even realize they are treating women adversely compared to men, but that is one of the problems with unwritten rules. They are the norms that govern professional behavior, and because they are unwritten, the tacit knowledge that people pick up subconsciously in working in a group, they are not noted. We might compare them to the little habitual quirks we all have—how we gesture, how we hold our heads when we listen, or when we talk, how we adjust our eyeglasses by pushing on one side or the other or in the middle. These have become so habitual that we do not even realize we do them, and yet they individuate us. "He's the one who always looks as though he's frowning."

These unwritten rules can create ethical problems. When the engineers at Morton-Thiokol were being overruled by their managers about whether Challenger should be launched, it would never have occurred to any of them to reach out beyond the company to raise an alarm. As Roger Boisjoly pointed out, they were employees who reported to management, and management made the final decisions. It was not for them, he thought, to second-guess what their bosses decided.[65]

13

Professional Character

We spend our lives forming our characters, sometimes self-consciously, sometimes not, and what we make of ourselves or allow others to make of us will create a certain character with all that implies about how we think and act. We may be able to see and understand what others cannot because of our forms of life, but we may end up without the tools others with a different upbringing and, perhaps, more self-awareness can bring to bear on life's problems.

Professionals are no different. The forms of life they come to have as a result of being trained into professions allow them to see and solve problems others cannot, but also can preclude their seeing how others may see them and solve them. Having learned to use a hammer, as the saying goes, they only see nails. If they are not self-aware of how their training has limited them as it has given them knowledge and skills others do not have, they may stumble into ethical problems without realizing it and without the tools to resolve them. We need more than a hammer in our toolboxes.

We are all familiar with the sorts of jokes and cartoons that play off the mindset different professionals come to have—the psychiatrist asking a chicken, "So why did you cross the road?" Or the behaviorist saying to a fellow behaviorist, "You are fine. How am I?" We may ourselves have realized that we were thinking in a certain way that depended on our past training into a profession, but was counterproductive to solving whatever problem we were facing.

I had such an experience right after graduate school when I was in a faculty committee meeting considering whether a student should be expelled from school because he had met the quota of seven failed classes. One of the other faculty made an argument to expel the student, and I, a philosopher, did what any philosopher ought to do, what I was trained to do in graduate school. I took the argument and pinned it to the wall, as it were, criticizing its validity and the truth of several of its premises. I was doing what any nice person would do. I was saving my colleague the embarrassment of a bad argument. This is one of the core skills philosophers learn. But my colleague was not a philosopher and, as you might imagine, was not happy with what he perceived as an attack on him. It was a sign of my naiveté that it had never occurred to me that he might think I was not helping him.

We have explored so far three of the features that mark out professionals from others—their special knowledge, their special skills, and the moral relations they take on. In those explorations, we have discovered that ethical problems are not all of a kind. Some are internal to a profession, some are external. Some are dilemmas, and some are factually or conceptually problematic. We have also seen how we empower professionals and so give them discretion, which may be misused and abused. We have also discovered that although some ethical problems arise because of the actions or inactions of individuals, some arise because of systemic features individuals have little, if any, control over.

We have emphasized that we cannot appeal to norms or codes of ethics to determine what we ought to do in a case, but need to construct arguments for the participants that would make sense of what they did or failed to do. It turns out that some ethical problems arise because of a professional's past training, and that constructing such arguments will depend upon seeing the world the way the professional does. I was thus brought up short when I saw the expression on my colleague's face, having thoroughly failed to foresee how someone other than a philosopher could fail to see that I had just done them a favor.

Being trained into a profession shapes a person's character and, in particular, what kinds of problems they see and how they go about solving them. So a thorough understanding of what a professional does or refrains from doing depends upon more than a passing familiarity with the special knowledge and skills someone learns to become a professional and more than a knowledge of the special moral relations a professional takes on. It also depends upon understanding how those in a profession learn to think like their fellow professionals. A safety engineer who finds a structural defect in a bridge will not have solved the problem by putting up a sign saying, "Dangerous Bridge: Proceed At Your Own Risk." Some official concerned about being sued might do that to warn motorists until the bridge can be repaired, but that engineer would not be thinking like an engineer.

§1 Thinking Like a …

How a professional learns to think in becoming a professional can create ethical problems. We saw an example of that when we examined how, the night before the Challenger launch, Lund at Morton-Thiokol changed his decision procedure when he took off his engineering hat and put on his manager's hat. As an engineer, he was risk-averse, seeing no reason to risk a catastrophic failure when a delay would bring warmer weather, but as a manager, a catastrophic failure was just one risk among many that needed to be weighed against such other risks as his company losing its contract for the booster rockets. Switching hats meant switching the way in which he was thinking about the problem and so switching his decision from no-launch to launch—with the consequences we all know about.

Switching hats was an ethical decision, whether he realized it or not, and in its leading to his using a different decision procedure, it led to a different decision. What this tells us is that different professions, with their different ways of understanding and solving problems, can make different kinds of decisions with different ethical implications.

As David Hume puts it, we are all affected by what he calls moral causes, "all [the] circumstances, which are fitted to work on the mind as motives or reasons, and which render a peculiar set of manners habitual to us." Such causes, he says, fix

> the character of different professions, and alters even that disposition, which the particular members receive from the hand of nature. A *soldier* and a *priest* are different characters, in all nations, and all ages; and this difference is founded on circumstances, whose operation is eternal and unalterable.[1]

A person takes on a form of life, a mindset, as it were, in becoming a professional, with different professionals having at least somewhat different ways of coming to the world, their specialized knowledge and skills allowing them to see and understand what the rest of us are blind to and blinkering them as well by ensuring that the ways of seeing and understanding of other professionals are not natural to them. We want someone trained as an engineer to think and act like an engineer, a surgeon to think and act like a surgeon, an accountant to think and act like an accountant, a scientist to think and act like a scientist.

As one scientist puts it,

> Somewhere in the process of becoming a scientist, a student or someone new to the field often learns to focus only on the metrics of success that the system says matter—testing hypotheses, publishing papers, uncovering one new truth only to pursue another … [Y]ou learn what the system rewards and what it doesn't, that amidst facts and figures, there's no place for emotions.[2]

The forming of a particular form of life continues throughout one's professional career, that is. To be successful, even just to continue practicing as a professional in some field, you need to satisfy "the metrics of success that the system says matter." Physicians who fail too often to diagnose diseases, lawyers who continually lose cases that appear hard to lose, engineers who fail to double check their calculations—these are professionals who are failing to meet the minimal standards of their profession and displaying in various ways a variety of character flaws.

Books on "Thinking like a…" have become a genre of their own. *How Judges Think*,[3] *How Doctors Think*,[4] *Thinking Like a Lawyer*,[5] *Thinking Like an Engineer*,[6] *Thinking Like an Economist*,[7] *Thinking Like a Historian*[8]—the list goes on and on. And there is a long history of essays and books on how it is that those in various professions think.

I will not pretend to have read more than a few of these, but will hazard a guess that all exhibit what I found in those I read. Professionals think just the way all of us do and how I am arguing we should think about ethical problems. They construct arguments, implicitly or explicitly, that are to justify the conclusions they are attempting to prove. The form of their thinking is just the same, that is, as it is for all of us when attempting to prove something—deductive or inductive with premises that they believe true.

There are obvious failures, arguments that are invalid or conclusions not well supported by the empirical data. In that way they are again no different from the rest of us when we try to justify a conclusion. I am putting to one side our predilection for ad hominem "arguments," begging the question, and other fallacies to which we seem all too susceptible. I am referring only to those situations where we reason to a conclusion, and in those situations we reason the way all humans reason.

What is different about how professionals reason is not the form of their arguments, but the differences in their premises. These reflect not just their distinctive form of training, with chemists providing one sort of premise, lawyers another, but are also the result of their selecting premises relevant to the way they see the problems they have been trained to solve or resolve. A geologist is going to think one way about a landscape, a lawyer another. Any arguments we may hear from either are going to reflect their different professional interests, with very different conclusions about, for example, land use and so with very different premises. That they both provide reasons for whatever conclusions they draw may obscure for us the very different ways in which they have come to see the world and so argue for their conclusions.

That we all reason in the same way may also obscure for us how difficult it can be to become a professional. It turns out to be far more complicated, obviously, than just replacing one kind of premise with another.

§2 Building an Engineer

Becoming a professional is a daunting task. Someone who wants to become a lawyer faces three years of intense study on what most of us would consider arcane matters, then studying the laws of the jurisdiction where one wants to practice, passing the bar exam, and then getting a position in some law firm or setting up one's own practice. Or think about someone who wants to become a physician—with all those years of college and medical school, followed by several years of being an intern, often working 12-hour days and being on call when not onsite, and then, finally, becoming a practicing physician.

But just looking ahead to what one must master, the skills and knowledge essential to one's chosen profession, understates just how difficult it can be to become a professional. Once one has achieved that position, one must maintain it, somehow picking up what is new in one's profession—engineers going from slide rules to computers, for instance, biologists going from classifying plants and animals to becoming adept at analyzing DNA, lawyers keeping track of what the legislature has done session by session and what the courts have decided or are likely to decide. Keeping up with one's profession is as daunting a task as becoming a professional.

Yet even that understates the task. Consider what is required to graduate as an engineer. The intellectual core of engineering is the solution to design problems, and engineering design, as defined by Accreditation Board for Engineering and Technology (ABET), is a process of devising a system, component, or process to meet desired needs and specifications within constraints. It is an iterative, creative, decision-making process in which the basic sciences, mathematics, and engineering sciences are applied to convert resources into solutions. Engineering design involves identifying opportunities, developing requirements, performing analysis and synthesis, generating multiple solutions, evaluating solutions against requirements, considering risks, and making trade-offs, for the purpose of obtaining a high-quality solution under the given circumstances. For illustrative purposes only, examples of possible constraints include accessibility, aesthetics, codes, constructability, cost, ergonomics, extensibility, functionality, interoperability, legal considerations, maintainability, manufacturability, marketability, policy, regulations, schedule, standards, sustainability, or usability.[9]

Engineering students must be more than a bit overwhelmed when they first see this definition. They are to find a "high-quality" solution through an "iterative, creative" process using mathematics and the basic and engineering sciences—while ensuring their solution's compatibility with at least nineteen different constraints, from accessibility to usability. They will find it even more disconcerting when they discover that far from there being a single universally accepted set of steps to the process, "a number of approaches have been proposed to organize, guide, and facilitate the design process," including, for example, "Taguchi's theory of robust design, Deming's principles of quality control, [and] Quality Function Deployment." They will be at a loss to know how to choose between these or any other approaches—or how to choose design tools from within the sets available "to obtain input from stakeholders in the design process," "address variability, quality, and uncertainty," and "generate alternatives for designers."[10]

Yet focusing on the ABET definition and design variants obscures what is even more difficult for the students—and for faculty. It would be difficult enough were the students learning something brand new, but they are not. The varieties of decision procedures all provide answers to the following three questions:

1. What is the problem?
2. What solutions are possible?
3. Which is the best one?

Put this way, engineering design problems are no different in kind from any other problem. We have all gone through the process of answering these questions, from figuring out as little kids how to open the cabinet door where the cookies were to resolving, as adults, complications arising from our tax returns. As a result, we carry with us all the bad habits and forms of thought we have picked up along the way: "the more we know how to do something, the harder it is to learn to do it differently."[11]

Faculty are thus rather like an acting instructor teaching actors how to walk in a way consistent with the roles they are to play. The instructor is not teaching them something completely new. They have been walking for a long time. The instructor is teaching them to walk in a different way. Walking appears to be culturally determined as well as very individualistic. We can identify who someone is, with a great deal of accuracy just by seeing the person walk, and we can determine if they are Australian or American by how they walk.[12] So this instructor's students must rid themselves of those deeply engrained habits they have carried with them since childhood, features they have paid no attention to before the instructor points them out as needing change— how they place their feet, space their steps, hold their bodies, move their heads.[13]

Learning something new can be difficult, of course. Think of children facing their first long division problems. But that is much less challenging than replacing something we have long been doing with a new way of doing it. Old habits and forms of thought die hard, but the challenge to students and faculty alike is that students cannot become good engineers without rooting out what they have picked up along the way about solving problems and replacing those habits and forms of thought with a relatively rigorous and measured response to the problems they will meet as engineers.

I speak of forms of thought as well as habits to emphasize that we have habitual responses to the problems we face daily—decision procedures we tend to use. Kahneman gives a delightful example of an investor who invested "some tens of millions of dollars in the stock of Ford Motor Company." Kahneman asked "how he had made that decision," and the investor "replied that he had recently attended an automobile show and had been impressed. 'Boy, do they know how to make a car!'" Kahnman says he was surprised that he had "not considered the one question that an economist would call relevant: Is Ford stock currently underpriced?"[14] If you are going to invest, you really ought to look at how well the company has done and what the experts say its prospects are, but, as Kahneman explains, we naturally tend to make quick decisions that reflect our underlying biases and unvetted beliefs, not ones that require the sort of research and careful thought needed to ensure that the decision is correct. We fool ourselves into thinking we are thinking when we are not.

What is daunting for students and faculty alike is thus that the engineering design process is to replace the very way we think about problems. When my car engine went dead recently, just after I accelerated from a stop light, I steered it to the side of the road. I am not sure I even thought about what to do although, in retrospect, I think I did what I ought to have done. My natural response was to coast out of the way of the traffic that, despite a speed limit of 55 mph, generally goes above 70 mph. Thinking thoroughly about how to respond to a problem is not the optimal choice in such a situation, and, indeed, as Kahneman makes clear, it is not the optimal choice in most situations. It takes time to do the research to understand a problem thoroughly, brainstorm possible solutions, and then make a reasoned choice. Problems in our lives come too quickly for us to do more than respond, and when we do, we are most likely to draw upon the way we have responded to problems since we were little children.

The engineering design process is itself designed, whatever its variants, to slow us down. What we do not want is to present a problem for analysis—my door key not always opening my front door, for instance—and, in asking for how to proceed, have a student yell out, as one of mine did, "Buy a new lock!" If the problem is caused by the catch plate being loose, a new lock is not going to help. We want to be sure we know what the problem is before considering solutions. We want to slow things down so that we can be sure we understand the problem we are to solve, sure we have considered the viable alternative solutions, and sure we have good reasons for solving the problem as we did so others can understand why we did what we did.

In teaching students the engineering design process, faculty are thus teaching them a new way to answer the questions: "What is the problem, the possible solutions, and the best solution?." They are teaching students a certain way of thinking about the world as they pass on their knowledge and teach the rules of skill particular to engineering. Whatever they may think they are doing, they are building character, instilling a set of character traits that are integral to being an engineer.

As the ABET definition makes clear, one feature of that character is a concern that any proposed solution satisfies all the constraints—and more—that ensure a "high-quality solution." Ensuring that all the constraints are satisfied is a time-consuming task, one that itself would ensure a thoughtful and careful response to a design problem. Given how many different kinds of things can go wrong, and do go wrong in design solutions, caution becomes second nature, and engineers become risk-averse.

Being risk-averse can no doubt create problems in some circumstances—as when engineers must take risks to make a damaged bridge road worthy as quickly as possible. But the trait that causes the most ethical issues is the all-too-common assumption that engineering is wholly quantitative. Choosing a girder of a certain design for a bridge is determined by the nature of the problem and by what calculations show, on this view. Ethical considerations have nothing to do with it because they introduce something qualitative about which there are no right answers.[15]

We see this common assumption in the ABET definition. Engineering design is a process "in which the basic sciences, mathematics, and engineering sciences are applied to convert resources into solutions." There are nods to other sources for solutions in, for instance, the appeal to aesthetics as a possible constraint. So unless ABET is assuming as well that all aesthetic considerations are quantifiable, as in the golden ratio, we have a reference to something qualitative. But what is missing is any reference to ethical considerations.

But they permeate the decision process. They arise in engineering's intellectual core, the solution to design problems, and are internal to the profession. Engineers cannot solve design problems without making decisions that reflect ethical considerations. Any design choice, once realized in an artifact, will have effects, some upstream and some downstream. The upstream effects are those that involve obtaining the material needed for the artifact, for instance, and the downstream effects are those that occur once the artifact enters into the causal stream of the world.

At a minimum, engineers should not choose design solutions that produce unnecessary harms when realized in artifacts, and they should test their preferred solution by at least that minimal standard. Making the standard explicit will help ensure that engineers are self-consciously considering whether their design solutions are ethical and, one would hope, help broaden the understanding of what counts in meeting that standard. It is typical for risk assessments to be limited to the risks involved in not completing a project, but a wider consideration would take in the upstream and downstream effects of completing it.[16] We can find plenty of examples where engineers failed the ethical test.

When engineers at GM decided to use mercury in trunk lights, their decision ensured that mercury had to be obtained and that it would present a problem of disposal once the vehicle's life was over. To obtain mercury, cinnabar must be heated, and that releases mercury vapor, potentially poisoning those extracting the mercury. We have known about the damage mercury vapor can do to us for a long time.[17] So engineers cannot blame ignorance for choosing a dangerous substance for the light switches. And downstream—especially when its useful life is over? It must be disposed of safely. It was used in over thirty-six million trunk lights. Before the old GM went bankrupt, a consortium it had joined had collected 6500 pounds of mercury from 2.5 million switches. It does not take a genius in math to realize that recovering all the mercury would present an enormous problem of safe disposal, at great cost—if quantification of harms were required for engineering design choices. We could also no doubt determine, roughly at least, how many individuals died and were poisoned from that mercury and the costs of their treatment and loss.[18]

In any event, whatever decision engineers make when faced with a design problem, their decision is ethical if only because the artifact produced because of that design choice will have its effects, some good, some harmful, all ethically relevant. Engineers cannot help but make such decisions as they go about their central concern, solving design problems, and that is one feature of the design process that ought to be highlighted for students, not buried in an "et cetera" after a list of possible constraints.

My concern is not that engineers make unethical decisions. Few engineers do. We would live in a very different world if they did or if, somehow, engineering faculty were creating evil geniuses focused on causing harm. Obviously, they are not. But those faculty and others who push the false assumption that engineering is purely quantitative are blinding our future engineers to the ethical aspects of engineering practice. The students become risk-averse, but not necessarily to the unnecessary harms their design solutions may cause.

So in addition to the constraints ABET lists in its definition of the design process, we need to add, as a minimum, doing no unnecessary harm. The best solution will be one that meets at least that condition. In our ordinary lives, we presumably do not go out of our way to cause unnecessary harm, but I suspect that few of us self-consciously take that condition into account as we go through our lives. Engineers ought to do that, however, and that illustrates just how difficult it can be to become a professional. We must somehow learn to think differently, replacing our embedded forms of thought formed from our childhood with a new way of thinking and solving problems. Imagine trying to learn to walk in a completely different way—with a different kind of stride, feet splayed in a different way, body held differently—to get a sense of just how difficult it can be to learn how to think in a different way.

§3 Political Scientists

Don E. Fehrenbacher's *The Dred Scott Case: Its Significance in American Law and Politics* won him the Pulitzer Prize in History and for good reason. In its almost six hundred pages, it provides a thorough background for the case, analyzes the arguments given by the Taney court in its 1857 decision in Dred Scott *v.* Sandford, and lays out in great detail the effects of that case.

Dred Scott was a slave who had been taken to free territory and a free state and argued on those grounds that he ought to be free. He was relying on a widely accepted principle that stepping on free soil made a slave free. The Supreme Court disagreed. Figuring out its reasons turns out to be a complicated matter, and Fehrenbacher lays out the complications with great clarity.[19] But the bottom line?

There are two. First, as Fehrenbacher says, "Negroes were not citizens." As a result, Dred Scott had "no right to bring suit in a federal court under the diverse citizenship clause of the Constitution." Second, Dred Scott was a slave. He had lived in the Louisiana Territory and then in Illinois, but neither residence made him free.[20]

Living in Illinois did not make him free because his present status was determined by his state of residence, Missouri. And living in the Louisiana Territory did not make him free either. The Missouri Compromise of 1820 made Missouri and Maine states, but precluded slavery north of the 36°30' parallel. That meant that Dred Scott had lived in free territory. But the Court held that the Compromise was unconstitutional because the Constitution requires that any new state have the same powers as the original thirteen states.

As Chief Justice Marshall put it in McCulloch *v.* Maryland,

> Some State constitutions were formed *before*, some *since* that of the United States. We cannot believe that their relation to each other is in any degree dependent upon this circumstance. Their respective powers must, we think, be precisely the same as if they had been formed at the same time.[21]

In particular, the original states had the power to determine for themselves whether to be slave or free. The Missouri Compromise took that power away from any state formed in the Louisiana Territory and so was unconstitutional.

That is a very truncated version of the court's argument, but it gets to the bottom line: Dred Scott's case should not have been heard by the court because he was not a citizen, being both a Negro and a slave. And the entire Louisiana Territory was now open to slave owners and any who wished to own slaves. They need only vote that any state formed in the territory be a slave state, and that would settle the matter.

The decision was momentous—certainly in regard to the status of any Negro in the United States. Those who had bought their freedom or escaped to the North may have thought themselves citizens, but by this ruling, they were not and could not even leave the United States because, not being citizens, they could not get passports. And it opened the Louisiana Territory to slavery, resulting in slave owners pushing into Kansas, for example, to ensure that it would become a slave state. Some have thought it momentous politically, saying that it " 'helped precipitate' or 'did much to precipitate' or 'helped to bring about' the Civil War."[22]

In answering that question about the political significance of Dred Scott, Fehrenbacher's profession shows through in the very way he frames the question. The "sectional conflict over slavery was already deep-seated and pervasive before 1857," and "what turned a chronic struggle into a secession crisis was the outcome of the presidential election of 1860." So, he says,

> There are two ways in which the Dred Scott decision could have had a critical influence on the election of 1860. One was by contributing significantly to the split in the Democratic party; the other was by contributing significantly to the growth of the Republican party.[23]

Fehrenbacher is a political scientist, and to measure the decision's significance, he turns to what can be measured, the number of votes that are clearly the result of the Dred Scott decision in the elections of 1858 and 1860, in particular. What he found was that the "Dred Scott decision by itself apparently caused no significant number of changes in political allegiance." So, he concludes, it "does not by itself pass the rigorous sine qua non test for an efficacious or sufficient cause." Its only possible political significance is that "the northern reaction to the Lecompton controversy of 1858 [regarding slavery in Kansas] was intensified by the fresh memory of Taney's proslavery ruling in 1857."[24]

In seeing the Dred Scott decision through the eyes of a political scientist, Fehrenbacher has missed what a political theorist might see: the decision ensured a Constitutional crisis regarding that "deep-seated and pervasive" sectional conflict. Fehrenbacher's form of thought prevented him from seeing the case in any other way than by its measurable effects on elections, but before the decision, there was hope that a compromise within the existing constitutional order could at least calm the storm. The decision removed any pretense that there was a constitutionally acceptable way out of the conflict. That consequence was the result of the decision, of a previous court decision and of the ways in which the Constitution and state constitutions empowered officials, preventing them from doing anything to affect the constitutional order or resolve the "pervasive" conflict.

In Prigg *v.* Pennsylvania in 1842, the Supreme Court effectively held that states have no power over the issue of slavery. Pennsylvania had passed a law regulating the recovery of runaway slaves by slave owners and by someone like Prigg, the equivalent of a bounty hunter, hired to bring back a runaway slave. The court held that state legislatures cannot restrict the operation of federal laws even within their own territories and, in particular, cannot enact fugitive slave laws because federal law provided the exclusive remedy for the return of runaway slaves.[25]

Governors had no power regarding the issue of slavery, and, in 1859, the Supreme Court held that state courts had no power either.[26] The president had no power regarding the issue—which is why, when Lincoln issued the Emancipation Proclamation, it covered only those slaves in the Southern states and those only because they were essential to the South's war effort.

The only political actors with any power were thus Congress and the Supreme Court. The Dred Scott decision swept away any pretense that Congress had any power regarding the conflict. Chief Justice Taney's argument was that the United States was founded on two contracts, one between the states and one between the people of the states. The slave-holding states would never have agreed to join the Union if that agreement meant giving up slavery, and individual slave-holders would never have voted in state ratification conventions to join the Union if they had not been assured that a Bill of Rights would be added to ensure that their property—slaves—would not be taken without due process. So slavery was embedded in the constitutive conditions of our having a nation.

That is why Congress could not prohibit slavery or do anything other than regulate it through the Fugitive Slave Law, for instance. And the Court? It had made its position clear in its decision. Those opposed to slavery had a constitutional obligation, found in the very conditions for our having a Union, to uphold slavery.

The only constitutionally available option for those opposed to slavery was to amend the Constitution. But eleven of the thirty-three states at the time were slave states, and since a proposed amendment requires that four fifths of the states ratify it for it to become law, those eleven states would preclude any constitutional settlement of the issue for a very long time to come.

If we look at the situation from the point of view of an abolitionist, we can get a sense of just how politically momentous the decision was. Whether or not it changed any votes, it changed the political landscape so that there was now no doubt that there could not be a constitutional solution to the issue of slavery. John Brown was right: an uncivil war was inevitable because the constitutional order left no civil way of resolving the slavery conflict.

We have here, I think, a good example of how being trained into a profession teaches one to think in certain ways. One "learns to focus only on the metrics of success that the system says matter," and what matters for political scientists is what can be measured. So Fehrenbacher did exactly what his colleagues in political science would no doubt have done. In asking about the decision's political significance, he turned to the only measurable variable. And so he failed to see how the decision decisively undercut any appeal to a constitutional solution.

I do not mean to pick on political scientists, or on Fehrenbacher, but we have a good example, I think, of how one's training into a particular form of thought blinds one to seeing something in a different way. I have not provided here the evidence or arguments that would be necessary to justify my understanding of how the Dred Scott case changed the political landscape, but the position is at least a plausible reading of the decision's effect, and that is all that is necessary.[27] The lesson for professionals is that they need to become, as it were, meta-professionals, thinking about how they have learned, as professionals, to think about the problems their profession is to examine and thus the constrained range of solutions "the system says matter."

§4 Lawyers and Judges

Some professionals work within institutional settings that guarantee they will meet ethical problems. It is not obvious that their professional training prepares them for the inevitable ethical problems they will face in their practice. They ought to be as risk-averse as engineers, but even if they were, the very nature of the system ensures that they will face ethical issues.

One example is the legal system. It may seem surprising, but ethical problems are internal to the legal system. Lawyers, prosecutors, judges, police, anyone authorized to act in a legal capacity within our legal system are going to meet with and sometimes create ethical problems that, being internal, cannot be avoided. It is built into the very nature of a legal system that there will be ethical failures, and those within the law—lawyers, prosecutors, judges, police—need to know how such failures can occur so they can anticipate and prevent them if possible.

I am not referring to the forensic floaters that are supposed to give experts "absolute confidence" in someone's guilt. Anyone within the law who relies on such floaters risks fingering innocent individuals, and for some, hair samples for instance, the chance of getting things right is so low that we can be 95 percent certain we are fingering someone innocent. As we saw, Keith Harward is the man who spent thirty-three years in prison based on "experts" identifying bite marks on the leg of the victim as his, and he said he found it incomprehensible that judges are still allowing bite mark evidence. There is a case in Pennsylvania, he said, and "the judge is going to allow bite mark evidence. How many people have to be wrongly convicted," he asked, "before they realize this stuff is all bogus? It's all made up."[28]

This sort of ethical problem could be removed from the system with a concerted effort to educate judges and police and lawyers about how these floaters in no way provide evidence "beyond a shadow of a doubt" for the guilt, or the innocence, of anyone. It is obviously unconscionable to convict anyone on faulty evidence, and using such floaters is not essential to having a legal system. But we know the answer we will get if we ask the police and prosectors to forego using such floaters. They think it allows police to zero in on the person or persons who committed a crime and makes it easier for prosecutors to convict.

Other ethical problems are so tightly tied to the internal workings of the legal system that they can at best be mitigated, not removed. Trials, for example, are an instance of imperfect procedural justice. We know that what would be just would be finding guilty all and only those who have committed a crime. But "it seems impossible to design the legal rules so that they always lead to the correct result."[29]

Our only recourse is to weigh the procedure one way or the other. We could weigh it to ensure that everyone who has committed a crime is found guilty. The medieval practice of subjecting an accused to an "ordeal," as it was called, involving cold water, boiling water, or hot iron does just that.

> In the ordeal of cold water, the accused was trussed up and cast into a pool to see whether he would sink or float. On the theory that water which had been sanctified by a priest would receive an innocent person but reject the guilty, innocence was proved by sinking—and hopefully a quick retrieval—guilt by floating.[30]

Since breaking the law is a crime against the monarch, and the monarch was taken to be God's representative on earth, we commit a sin in breaking the law. Blessing the water ensures that it will not accept anyone who is guilty: they will float and will thus be proved guilty. If the accused is innocent, the water will accept them: they may well drown, but will thereby be proved innocent. That procedure ensures that everyone who is guilty will be found guilty and spares from such a degrading judgment those who are innocent and so drown.

The preferred option in the American legal system is to force the state to prove guilt beyond a reasonable doubt. That means that some who have committed crimes will not be found guilty. The law will have failed to keep someone capable of committing crimes off the streets and thus put the public at risk, and it will have failed to provide ethical closure for those who suffered because of the crime. But it is also more likely to ensure that those who are innocent are not found guilty.

We know, however, that some innocent individuals will be found guilty. Keith Harward is an example, and hardly a day goes by when there is not another article about another person unfairly convicted. It is the inevitability of that occurring, and of those who have committed crimes not being found guilty, that those in the legal system must recognize and do whatever they can to prevent. Besides judges who fail to keep up with research into forensic science, prosecutors especially need to be on the alert for potential miscarriages.[31]

They have nearly absolute power to determine whether or not to prosecute, and their decisions cannot be reviewed. An example from my own experience will illustrate one way in which the system ensures unethical behavior.

I was at an intersection in Rome, New York, trying to turn left, but traffic was so heavy that it was not until the light had changed that I was able to turn. As I turned, a truck that had stopped suddenly lurched forward and ran into my car. When I got out to check on the driver's condition, I could smell the alcohol on his breath. I said, "Too bad about the accident. I'm glad you're O.K." I got back into my car, waiting for the police to arrive since the whole front side of my car was demolished. A police officer came up, and without asking me anything gave me a ticket, a moving violation for running a red light and causing an accident. I was surprised and asked how he knew I was responsible. "We had a witness." "Who?" "The truck driver." "The guy who ran into me?" "Yes, he said you had apologized for hitting him and was glad he was O.K."

I went to court to contest the ticket, wearing a power suit and being mistaken by the prosecutor and the judge for a lawyer. I explained that I taught ethics and in doing so taught legal ethics. They both explained that they had had legal ethics in law school, and at the end of my explanation of what had happened, I got the following question, "You were driving with a bad muffler, right?" I had no idea where that question came from or where it was going, and I said, surprised, "Yes, after I got hit." "For driving without a muffler, the fine is $75, but we will let that go. You'll still have to pay court costs, however. That's $20."

What happened? I had been charged, and rather than drop the charge, the prosecuting attorney insisted on exchanging it for another, ensuring that he would not lower his conviction rate because of me. Prosecuting attorneys are elected there, it seems, as are judges, and they both wanted to run on a "successful" record. So much for ethical behavior.

Prosecutors can decide whether to charge or not, whether to charge "a suspect with more offenses than is warranted" in order to force a plea bargain, "overstating the strength of the evidence" in plea bargaining, "withholding or delaying the release of exculpatory evidence,"[32] striking potential jurors from a trial on the basis of race,[33] and on and on.

They can refuse to prosecute when a legislature passes a law that they deem unfair or unconstitutional. Concerned about the harms recent state legislation regarding abortion would cause women and physicians, more than forty elected prosecutors urged

> prosecutors to use their discretion and decline to criminalize health-care decisions that have been protected under settled Supreme Court law for nearly 50 years. As the statement notes, "prosecutors must be perceived by their communities as trustworthy, legitimate and fair—values that would be undermined by the enforcement of laws which harm and impose untenable choices on many in the community."[34]

It is thus no surprise to hear a prosecutor "deciding that we have an ethical duty not to prosecute a case because it would be in violation of a constitutional protection afforded to citizens."[35]

Prosecutors are not required to enforce all laws and have a special obligation, as these prosecutors have indicated, not to enforce laws which run counter to settled constitutional doctrine, whatever their personal beliefs may be. But because prosecutors have such discretion they can also do great damage both to individuals wrongly charged and to the sense that the legal system is fair.

A prosecutor in Tennessee has assured those who voted for him that "same-sex partners would not be afforded the protections of domestic violence laws." As "a good Christian man," he does not accept that they can be married. "So I don't prosecute them as domestic." He would apparently not deign to use his discretion to protect Muslims either since, he says, "There are only God given rights protected by the Constitution. If you don't believe in the one true God, there is nothing to protect." So Muslims, he says, have "no constitutional rights."[36]

We might and certainly ought to expect more of judges, who also have a great deal of discretion, but whether out of self-interest or other reasons, hardly a day goes by when we do not hear of a judge sentencing someone to a much longer or shorter term than seems deserved or even putting on probation someone who has committed the most heinous of crimes. There is the 26-year-old school bus driver who raped a 14-year-old who was on his bus route. The judge gave him "10 years probation, and assigned him the lowest level status on New York's sex offender registry."[37] There is the man who kept a teenager "in captivity for more than a year, allegedly forcing her to have sex with him and holding her in a dog cage for so long that she developed back problems." He received a sentence of ten years, but a plea deal gave him "credit for the eight months that he had already served in jail" with probation for the remaining "nine years and four months."[38] There is the Houston case where a physician was convicted of raping a sedated patient. "The crime is punishable by up 20 years in prison." The jury, not the judge, gave him ten years of probation.[39] Or the notorious Brock Turner case where the swimmer was sentenced to "six months in county jail ... and required to register as a sex offender" after "sexually assaulting an unconscious and inebriated female." He would serve only three months, "on the assumption of good behavior." The judge said that "a harsher sentence would 'have a severe impact on him.'"[40]

These are internal problems as the system now exists, and the question is whether we could so change the system, without losing what is of value in it, as to mitigate the harms its current configuration produces.

David Hume argues that in the best of cases, we would have a form of government that so defines the roles of those in it that whatever their character, they are constrained by their roles to act for the public good. As he puts it,

> A republican and free government would be an obvious absurdity, if the particular checks and controuls, provided by the constitution, had really no influence, and made it not the interest, even of bad men, to act for the public good. Such is the intention of these forms of government, and such is their real effect, where they are wisely constituted.[41]

The same is true of our legal system: the best form would ensure that those within it would act out of self-interest for the public good. Ours does not, and that is one reason we get such ethical problems as those we have cataloged and listed for prosecutors and judges. They learn "the metrics of success that the system says matter" and act accordingly.

Hume adds,

> In the smallest court or office, the stated forms and methods, by which business must be conducted, are found to be a considerable check on the natural depravity of mankind. Why should not the case be the same in public affairs?[42]

And why not in the legal system? To change the behavior of those within it, we need to change what features we can to curb self-interest—and "the natural depravity of mankind."

Whatever changes we may make, however, in providing sentencing guidelines, for instance, we will not be able to change the discretion we must give those we empower with upholding the law. With discretion we get judges being too lenient, police too quick to come to judgment, prosecutors shading what they can to get convictions. With discretion, we get bad judgment, even without ill-intent, and that is one way in which ethical issues can arise even if we could change the system to counter self-interest and discourage "the natural depravity of mankind."

Ethical issues also arise because the very nature of law requires that there be rules so that individuals can know what is lawful and what is not. The law cannot consist of one outcome for one case, another for another case that seems the same, and on and on. Without some general understanding of why we have one outcome in a case rather than another, some indication of what features of the case justify one decision rather than another, we cannot make any judgments about what we need to do to be lawful. The law consists, that is, of general rules, and it is the generality of the rules that creates ethical problems.

For one consequence is that we can only achieve the generality needed to guide future behavior by refusing to make an exception in a particular case where an exception may well be warranted. Put bluntly, we may end up treating someone unfairly because the law does not allow us to take into account the extenuating details of the case.

This problem is not unique to the law. It holds for any rule-governed behavior. When we examined the features of rules, we put generality to one side as so obvious that it did not need to be mentioned. But in giving a sequenced, coherent, and normative order to a set of activities, we are setting general rules. So a baseball player who would have touched base but for breaking his leg as he slid in will be called out regardless of whether that is fair or not. The question of fairness will not even be raised. Ditto for a player hitting what would have been a home run except for a fan touching it when reaching out to catch it before it cleared the wall. We may sympathize with the first player and share the second player's anger, but, well, rules are rules.

Judges decide particular cases, but in doing so they create a precedent, an understanding that similar cases will be decided similarly. It may turn out that the long-term consequences of a decision, its precedential power, require a decision like those we just considered in baseball.

Lon Fuller considers how difficult this problem can be for judges as he goes through a series of five hypothetical cases in which judges are "drawing out the necessary, or at least the reasonable, implications of a regime of private property and exchange."

Case No. 1 involves T stealing O's horse and selling it to G. O sues G for the horse and wins. T had no title, and so title was not transferred to G. The point is that "one of the deterrents to thievery is the difficulty of disposing of stolen goods." Holding for G would remove that deterrent.

Case No. 2 involves T buying O's horse with a note T knows is forged. O sues T and wins. "The passage of title was vitiated by the fraud of T."

Case No. 3 is the same except that T then sells the horse to G, who had no reason to know of the fraud. O sues G, but G wins. "It would be an intolerable burden on commerce if purchasers of property were compelled to scrutinize the details of a transaction by which the former owner voluntarily delivered it into the hands of the person now offering it for sale."

Case No. 4 is the same except that G sells the horse to K, who knew of the fraud. O sues, but K wins. If O were to win, anyone in O's position could "destroy the value of the title acquired by G ... Thus the objective of protecting the bona fide purchaser G would be defeated, for his property would become unsalable." The precedent of Case No. 3 requires that result.

And the last case, No. 5? This is like Case No. 4 except that K not only knew of the fraud, but "participated in it." K is now reaping the benefits of his fraudulent behavior, but since G had title and transferred the title to K, does the precedent of Case No. 3 not require that K gets to keep the horse?[43]

We can see the problem for the judge in this last case. It seems wholly unfair that K should be able to keep O's horse, but having gotten it from G, who had title, on what ground is K to be denied the horse? If O recovers the horse because of K's taking part in the fraud, then we have the problem Case No. 3 was meant to solve: no one could ever be sure that they actually owned what they thought they had purchased because somewhere in the past the title may have been fraudulent. But if O loses, then we encourage just the sort of fraud K and T engaged in. All that someone like K and T need to do is to ensure that the property they gained fraudulently passes through some unwitting purchaser, like G, and they then can reap the rewards of their fraud.

So what is a judge to do? Whatever is decided will create problems—for commerce if the judge holds for O and a clear injustice if the judge holds for K. But it is the decision in Case No. 3 that created the conditions for this problem. In holding for the innocent buyer G, the court deprived O of both the horse and the payment for it. That seems more than a little unfair. It was not O's fault that the note was fraudulent, and yet O lost both the horse and the payment for it. Both G and O are innocent of any wrongdoing. It is T who is at fault, but T's wrongdoing does not figure in the decision.

In this series of cases, as Fuller remarks, the judges are pulling out the implications of an economic system that depends upon transfers of property, and they must take into consideration how what they decide will affect the system of transfers. That is why Case No. 3 was decided as it was.

So judges, and lawyers too, work in an institutional setting that guarantees they will meet ethical problems. We could as well have examined other settings. The health-care system provides far too many examples, for instance, but the point here is that professionals need to be aware of the features of the setting they work in—a law firm with its unwritten norms, a legal system with its need for generality, a prosecuting attorney who needs to show a high rate of prosecutions to continue in office. That high rate is what the system rewards, its "metrics of success."

§5 Hidden Hammers

It is a common observation that we tend to make use of what we have at hand. That is why we use wrenches as hammers and screwdrivers as paint scrapers. Abraham Kaplan made this point about scientists:

> It comes as no particular surprise to discover that a scientist formulates problems in a way which requires for their solution just those techniques in which he himself is especially skilled.[44]

Or, as he put it at another point, we tend

> to do the things that we already know how to do. We tend to formulate our problems in such a way as to make it seem that the solutions to those problems demand precisely what we already happen to have at hand.[45]

The tendency is common enough to have a variety of names—Maslow's hammer, the law of the instrument, a Birmingham screwdriver, the latter a gibe at the supposedly "oafish Birmingham worker who would rather hammer in a screw than use the correct tool."[46] It is nicely summed up in the saying, "To a man with a hammer, everything looks like a nail" or, better, "Give a small boy a hammer, and he will find that everything he encounters needs pounding."[47]

This nicely sums up the main thesis of this chapter. We have seen how becoming a professional requires specialized knowledge and a special set of skills. We can now see that it also gives us a distinct way of seeing and thinking about the world.

We saw this with engineering students being trained into a certain form of thinking and of solving problems, ones which require calculations that seem to suffice. They thus are prone, like the GM engineers who chose mercury switches, to miss the ethical issues they also need to address.

We saw how being embedded in an institutional setting can create ethical problems for us, not because of how we are trained into a form of seeing and thinking, but because internal features of the system create ethical problems. We examined how that occurs in the legal system, but we might easily have chosen any other institutional setting. Our healthcare system seems designed to create ethical problems, for instance. Just think of how companies purchase patents for medicine and then raise the prices of the drugs astronomically.

We saw how a professional can formulate a problem in a manner that permits the kind of solution the profession admits—and rewards. Fehrenbacher failed to see how the Dred Scott case fundamentally altered the constitutional terrain and so ensured that there would be no civil resolution of the slavery problem. Because he focused on how the decision changed votes, as a good political scientist should, he failed to see implications for settling the slavery issue without a civil war.

Professionals need to step outside their professions to understand how they have been trained to see and understand the world. It would be putting it mildly to say that such meta-understanding is difficult, but the physicians in Memphis who were examining the embarrassed elderly woman needed just that sort of understanding. They did not realize that they were examining the woman as a case, not as an elderly woman understandably trying to cover herself as she was lying nude in front of them.

They also need to understand how they can become so used to the setting within which they are working that they fail to see how it is affecting them, how they see problems and make decisions, and how it can create ethical issues they may well miss. Wittgenstein put it well:

> The aspects of things that are most important for us are hidden because of their simplicity and familiarity ... The real foundations of his enquiry do not strike a man at all.[48]

And what is true of professionals is obviously true of all of us in our daily lives.

14

Social Responsibilities

We all have responsibilities to those around us and to society at large. We pay school taxes whether we have children in school or not, for instance. We gain by ensuring that future citizens will be literate and so capable of participating in our democracy[1] and by ensuring that those who will care for us in our old age or manage our financial affairs have the basic literacy necessary to obtain the further knowledge and skills they need to become physicians or financial advisors. We are obligated to obey the laws which protect us all and, more generally, not to cause unnecessary harms and to help others when we are in a position to help and have the knowledge and skills necessary.

But some issues cannot be understood, let alone resolved, without the special knowledge and skills that only professionals have. So they have a special obligation to individuals and the public at large regarding those matters they are experts in.

The grounds for this special obligation professionals have are varied, but among them is that society grants professionals a monopoly over the services they are able to provide because of their special knowledge and skills. In addition, citizens gain by having the state certify in some way those professionals whose services they must seek. Citizens gain autonomy because with that information they can make informed choices about whom to see for advice about their financial matters, their health, their legal options, or any other matter for which we have professionals.

§1 Professional Obligations

Every society has some way of caring for its ill and injured. These form a practice, a natural social artifact. Whatever the details of the practice, it is natural because it responds to the inevitable human needs that come when members become ill or injured. The society will respond to those problems in some way, forming a standard way of handling them, a normative practice that tells everyone in the society how to respond to those needs. That is what makes the practice social. The practice is an artifact because, through innumerable acts and omissions, we create the cooperative enterprise that comprises what counts as the health-care system in a society.[2]

Modern health-care systems share one feature, namely, professional healthcare practitioners whose knowledge and skills have prepared them to cure, when possible, and care for the society's ill and injured. They benefit not only individuals, but also society as a whole. A society that permits charlatans to practice medicine, for instance, guarantees that its citizens will not get the health care they need or a health-care system that ensures the health of its citizens.

A depressing example concerns "a region which has a high prevalence of shady medical practices" in south Pakistan where a doctor, "through repeated use of a single contaminated syringe," infected more than 500 people with HIV, including 410 children. As one parent put it, "We are helpless. I have other children and I am afraid they might catch the disease."[3] The parent is right to feel helpless. It is basic to medical practice that needles not be used more than once, and yet that physician was licensed to practice. We do not know why the physician used the same needle repeatedly—ignorant of that basic medical practice, too cheap to purchase more needles, out to infect as many as he could? It does not matter. What matters is that that region of Pakistan has a physician who is licensed but cannot be trusted, and that means those living there do not know what physician can be trusted. No wonder the parent feels helpless.

The example illustrates all too well how a profession is to benefit society as a whole as well as its citizens. If such a physician can be licensed, each citizen now must feel at risk of not getting proper care from physicians there, and the health-care system has lost all claim to benefit the society. It cannot be trusted any more than the physicians within it. To the extent that the health-care system fails to cure the ill and heal the injured, they are harmed, but society is harmed twice over: those who are ill or injured must somehow be cared for, and they themselves cannot well contribute to the society.

A complex modern society would fail miserably in achieving what is essential for the well-being of its citizens, that is, were it not for its professionals. We have seen such failures not only in countries like Pakistan, but in countries that were once relatively well-off, if not wealthy, when war and governmental failures have caused its physicians, lawyers, engineers, and other professionals to leave. In such situations health care is hit-and-miss, if that, and every social good that depends upon other professionals is at risk as well. The legal system cannot function, or function well enough to give citizens confidence that they will be treated justly, if too many of its lawyers and judges have left because of civil strife, for instance. The inevitable failures of its bridges, dams, and other necessities of a complex society cannot be repaired without the professionals who can figure out what went wrong to cause a failure and what needs to be done to make it right again.

A country's professionals provide its social infrastructure. It is the special knowledge and skills of lawyers that give us a functioning legal system. It is the expertise of engineers that gives us the physical infrastructure that makes modern life possible. It is the training and experience of health-care professionals that can give us a world-class health-care system. We can go on and on through all the professions. They are the lifeblood of the various social systems in which they serve.

They are also society's intellectual underpinnings. It is to scientists and engineers and other professionals that we look for the ideas that drive progress and for the expertise that ensures and enhances a society's well-being. They are a public asset, a society's intellectual capital, as it were. They provide the social and intellectual infrastructure that makes life possible for the citizens in any country.

They are the experts, and we look to them for the answers to problems within their areas of expertise. They are the only ones who can provide the answers because they are the only ones with the relevant knowledge and skills. Or, more accurately, others may accurately answer technical questions, but without the background needed to claim professional standing, they will not be taken as seriously as someone with professional standing who we presume knows what they are talking about.

We mark the value professionals have to society as a whole and to those within it by empowering them, and only them, to provide what their special knowledge and skills have trained them for. We exclude others without that background from offering those services. We mark their value, that is, by giving them monopolies. Only a physician can write a prescription that will be accepted by a pharmacist. Only engineers can provide the specifications for a road.

Because professionals are a public asset, they have special obligations to the public. That claim needs more support than I can give it here, but the contours of the argument are pretty straightforward. Becoming a professional depends upon other members of that profession having determined what the necessary knowledge and skills are, upon accrediting agencies and upon institutions of higher education—and thus upon the state, which certifies that the colleges and universities have met the appropriate standards to provide the education needed. A law degree from an unaccredited institution is worth little, if anything. So no one can become a professional without the state's providing and certifying the infrastructure that makes it possible. That would in itself suffice to justify the claim that professionals have special obligations to the public.

It is no small matter that in addition to supplying the means for someone to become a professional, the state gives professionals a monopoly for the services they render, a monopoly justified by their having gained the special knowledge and skills necessary for their professions and a monopoly that makes it impossible for anyone other than a professional to gain the experience needed to use that knowledge and those skills for the good of others.

Perhaps even more to the point, professions exist for moral ends, goals that society has decided can only be achieved by individuals specially educated in how to achieve those goals. It is in the state's interest and the interests of its members that those ends are achieved by professionals, but though many of those goals can be achieved by professionals going about their daily business, physicians seeing patients, lawyers talking with clients, some of those goals can only be achieved by professionals acting outside their usual confines for public purposes. We cannot have fully autonomous citizens unless they are fully informed, but much of the information citizens need is so technical that it needs an expert to decipher. We want a society that works for the benefit of all, but we cannot achieve that without some professionals providing their services pro bono to those who cannot afford the fees usually charged.

For at least these reasons, professionals have a moral obligation to serve and enhance the societal interests in the areas in which they are expert. They serve a variety of those interests in a variety of ways. We will illustrate four—their lending their expertise to investigations that require it; their helping us understand matters of public interest; their speaking out regarding matters in which they are expert where they think others have got things wrong, or where the record needs to be corrected; and their helping other experts in matters that require multiple sources of knowledge and different skills.

§2 Expert Investigations

When we examined the Challenger disaster and the BP blowout in the Gulf of Mexico, we relied heavily on the results of commissions formed to investigate the causes of the failures. Such commissions are standard fare whenever there is a disaster. We need to know what caused it so we can change whatever was at fault to preclude its happening again. Experts are absolutely essential for that job. Only they can determine what happened and why and suggest the changes that need to be made so it will not happen again. Experts are drawn from a variety of disciplines, depending upon the nature of the problem to be investigated.

For instance, NASA experienced two launch failures with its Taurus XL rocket. After the first, in 2009, the company that built the rocket and satellite "redesigned the system for shedding the protective covering." There were three successful launches followed by another failure because "a protective covering on the Taurus XL rocket did not separate as planned," making "the rocket ... too heavy to get the satellite into orbit."[4] The problem was not in the design, however, but in the aluminum used in the protective covering. An Oregon aluminum manufacturer "falsified certifications after altering the results of tensile tests designed to ensure the consistency and reliability of aluminum extruded at the companies' Oregon-based facilities."[5] The aluminum was used "in 'frangible' joints that hold explosive charges in rockets used by NASA and missiles used by the Missile Defense Agency. NASA blames the aluminum parts for two failed rocket launches."[6]

It was an investigation by NASA's Office of Inspector General, the FBI, and the Defense Criminal Investigative Service's (DCIS) Western Field Office that led to the discovery of the tainted test results, an investigation that required professionals in a number of different areas of expertise to work together over an extended period of time. It is an example of experts helping experts in other fields, forming the sort of team that can pool information to make a fully informed judgment about what they are investigating.

We have countless examples of such investigations. Besides the BP oil spill we examined when discussing rules of skill, and the Presidential Commission convened for the Challenger disaster, we standardly have investigations for aircraft disasters. The Boeing 737 MAX disasters are an example of what may well need a special commission to track down the causes and recommend changes.[7] We had an investigation to discover the causes of the walkway collapse in the Kansas City Hyatt,[8] of the bridge collapse in Minneapolis,[9] of the failure of the pedestrian walkway at Florida International University.[10] We find the same sorts of investigations in fields other than engineering when things have gone wrong or defy standard explanations.

The investigations are partly motivated by self-interest. No engineer or physician or any other professional wants to make the mistake that generated a disaster. The aim is to learn from our failures so that we do not repeat them. But service to society is primary. No one should have to fear a catastrophic plane crash because those able to understand and fix the problem are too absorbed in their own work to help us. Expert knowledge itself creates obligations to those who need it.

We need not examine any of these investigations in detail here, having already seen how important these investigative commissions can be in the report of the National Commission on the BP Deepwater Horizon Spill and Offshore Drilling, for instance. The main point is to illustrate a way in which professionals serve society. There are others.

§3 Helping Us Understand

We are all familiar with people meaning something different from what they say. Much of our communication depends upon reading between the lines to catch the real meaning behind what someone appears to say. We learn early on whether a friend who asks, "Do you want some ice cream?," is just asking or hinting. But sometimes an expert is needed to tease out what is between the lines.

A good example is the analysis by an art historian and economist of a speaker's comments on the Holocaust. On Holocaust Remembrance Day, the speaker tweeted "a message honoring 'the 6 million Jewish martyrs of the Holocaust who 3 years after walking beneath the shadow of death, rose up from the ashes to resurrect themselves to reclaim a Jewish future." On first reading, we might applaud the speaker for paying his respects to those who died in the Holocaust, but, as the art historian and economist point out, we need to pay attention to the words he uses:

> The tweet employed the vocabulary ("martyrs") and structure ("resurrection") of Christianity to contain the experience of Jews, making it a message that ... Jews [are] nothing more than instruments in an apocalyptic narrative that seeks the return of Christ. What at first appears to be a well-intentioned, if bungling, message turns out to have an insidious intent: to signal to his base that accommodating gestures made toward Jews are being made in the service of Christian aims.

The view the speaker holds has a long history. Jews are not Christians, and so the historical narrative is that they are inferior "and ought to be treated as such." But they must also be protected since they are the instrument through which Christ will return.

> At the time of the apocalypse, Christ would return to a Jerusalem held by Jews, Jews would convert to Christianity and Christ would then rule all people.

We get a very different understanding of what the speaker was saying when it is subjected to an assessment by those familiar with the history of how Christians have viewed Jews as "inferior but necessary." The speaker's real message, the one between the lines, is directed toward his kind of Christian, not Jews:

> Rather than expressing sympathy about one of the great tragedies of human history, he was exploiting its remembrance to advance his religious views.[11]

The professional analysis is backed with some nice examples from art that illustrate how Christians viewed Jews, but we need not examine those to get the message: the speaker is not really saying what he seems to say.

In speaking out about the speaker's tweet, those who can read between the lines, and published what they read, have changed what we may well have thought when we first read what he wrote. They performed a public service. They did not write for their students or for a scholarly journal, and they did not get paid for their work. They gave freely of their expertise to clarify what perhaps many of us would not have understood from what he said. That is one service professionals ought to provide society, speaking out to clarify and help us understand what may otherwise pass us by because we lack the expertise a professional has.

This is not a minor service. We could scarcely understand much in the world without experts telling us the details we need to comprehend exactly what is going on. It does not take an expert to understand that when someone goes back on their word, again and again, others will not trust the person to keep their word. We thus can understand without an expert's help how the United States's imposing tariffs on Mexico just as the Mexican government embarks on ratifying a new trade agreement between it, Canada, and the United States will make it difficult for the president of Mexico to proceed. But we do need an expert to tell us the various costs the new tariffs will impose. We need someone who knows the details of the trade between the two countries and someone who understands the implications that the loss of stability will have for businesses trying to plan ahead and for governments thinking about making agreements with the United States.

We could give example after example, but the point is made, I should think. We are reliant on professionals to provide us with the explanatory background we need to understand much of what happens in the world. Would we understand the importance of Russia's blocking the Kerch Strait without experts telling us that the Strait provides the only link between the Sea of Azov and the Black Sea and that the bulk of Ukraine's exports move by ship from the sea port of Mariupol and nearby Berdyansk through that strait?[12] Would we understand how it was determined that the painting "Salvator Mundi" was by Leonardo da Vinci? Its recent history would give us no clue. It was auctioned off in 1958 for 45 pounds (about $125 today), purchased fifty years later for $10,000, and then sold for $450,312,500 in November 2017. It took experts to determine its authenticity despite its being mistaken as a copy for years. There is no way anyone else could have known, and we know it is authentic only because the experts tell us so. We can examine their reasons, but it is their assurance, backed by reasons, that is decisive, not any judgment we might make. We owe it to them that we can now admire another da Vinci.

If we are not to rely just on what such professionals say, we must, as we saw, construct an argument that has their judgment as its conclusion and has premises we can plausibly attribute to those who make the judgment that could reasonably explain or justify their judgment. We are then in a position to ask whether the premises are reasonable, whether they in fact support the conclusion, and whether they can explain why those who make it believe it. We can sometimes do this ourselves, but for much of what we read and hear, we need the knowledge and skills of a professional who can understand the argument and assess whether its premises and conclusion are reasonable. Sometimes the professional can make the argument so clear to those who are not professionals that they can understand the argument and assess it without the background knowledge and skills that positioned the professional to clarify the argument.

Those examining the purported da Vinci did just that. One piece of evidence was the discovery, via X-ray, of "a pentimento, a trace of an earlier painting beneath the visible one," in which the right thumb of Jesus was "originally positioned slightly differently. But while working on the piece, da Vinci must have changed his mind and painted over it—the thumb was moved to the position in which it appears today." As one British art critic put it, "If you're making a copy of a picture, there's no way you'd do that."[13] We do not have ready access to the X-ray and so cannot ourselves easily verify the claim, but we can understand why, if true, it makes it highly unlikely that the painting is not a da Vinci. We also know what we would need to verify the claim. We can construct an argument for the claim being made and can understand what the premises mean and what we would need to do to verify them. We are not wholly reliant on an expert.

Sometimes, however, we must just trust the professionals, the arguments depending upon the special knowledge and skills that they have and others do not. Experts can disagree, obviously, and so our trust can be misplaced if we rely on one or two experts about a position for which there is no consensus among the experts. We should obviously hesitate in giving our trust in such a situation. But when the experts have reached a consensus, trust is appropriate, or, to put it another way, someone who is not an expert in an area is not in a position to counter the position of the experts when they have reached a consensus. Disagreement under such conditions is not reasonable.

It is also unreasonable about judgments that wholly depend upon the knowledge and skills of professionals. We are often wholly reliant on experts because we lack the special knowledge and skills that would enable us even to understand the sometimes technical language that marks out a profession. I have written about public policy issues regarding chlorofluorocarbons (CFCs) deleting the ozone layer.[14] But my understanding of chemistry is abysmal, and so when I read the chemical formulae that explain the destruction of the ozone layer, I am at a loss.[15] Ditto for my understanding of any of the subtleties of Einstein's physics, for instance.

I am sure I am not the only one ignorant of such matters. For one thing, professionals tend to develop their own terminology to explain the features they are interested in. So "gigabyte," "flash drive," and "CPU" are foreign to those without even a minimal grasp of computers and how they function, and they are more than likely to misunderstand someone who says, "I've got a bug in my computer." The terminology alone would suffice to explain why we need those who are experts in a field to explain to those of us without the relevant background what is meant. Another problem is that so much of what experts say is based on a long history of development of the discipline that cannot be readily explained to a novice who, without the history, is not likely to grasp the significance of what is being explained even given a translation.

There are limits, that is, to what a professional can do to explain the details within a discipline to those who lack the relevant background. But within the constraints of those limits, professionals serve important moral imperatives in explaining their judgments to those outside their areas of expertise. Rachel Carson's *Silent Spring* was instrumental in changing the public's perception of DDT, for instance. Such individuals are, of course, acting for the good of individuals as well as society as a whole, and some of what they explain helps ensure that we are not harmed by something we cannot understand. Most important, in helping us understand matters of public import, they are helping us be autonomous.

§4 Calling Out Mistakes and Misunderstandings

Experts can certainly disagree with each other. New discoveries make old understandings questionable. Different ways of seeing something can produce thoroughly different judgments. New kinds of instruments provide insights. The history of any discipline is marked by disagreements, and striving to resolve them is what animates discoveries and yet new kinds of instruments and ways of seeing the world.

We owe to Tycho Brahe, for instance, "the design and construction of improved naked-eye instruments and the establishment of new standards of accuracy in astronomical observations," and we owe to Kepler's use of those instruments, the incredibly accurate data Brahe had accumulated, and Kepler's even higher standards of accuracy, the realization that the planets move in ellipses around the sun.[16] Brahe had proposed, in opposition to the Copernican and Ptolemaic systems, that the sun rotated around the earth while the planets rotated around the sun. Kepler could not make the data work for that proposal or for the Copernican or Ptolemaic systems if circular motion were the only permissible motion for heavenly bodies. Settling such disagreements about planetary rotation is how science progresses. We could readily find other examples in science and in other fields.

Indeed, we could readily find very acrimonious disagreements among professionals. We examined two when we saw how historians can disagree about how to tell the truth and how some actuaries are at odds with others on how to calculate retirement benefits.

Even with the acrimony, they presumably see themselves as correcting the errors and misunderstandings of fellow practitioners, all in it together to achieve the same end, however contested. Brahe and Kepler were both after the most accurate description of the orbits of the planets and the nature of the solar system. The historians were all concerned about relating history truthfully, however much they disagreed on how to do that.

These disputes matter to the public, as we saw, since they affect whether we see history as determined by great leaders and whether we can calculate what our retirement income will be. But settling them is unfortunately for those who are in disagreement, not for those most affected by them. Those who are not experts in some field lack the professional standing to have a significant voice in the dispute and are generally "not in a position to evaluate the judgments, advice, and performance of professionals because they lack the expertise professionals profess."[17] It is the experts who have the necessary background to understand the issues and properly adjudicate them.

Access to information on the web has somewhat lessened for us a complete reliance on experts. When a professional tells us something that we want to check, we can sometimes find what other experts say on the matter to determine if the expert's judgment was idiosyncratic or stated the consensus, and if we cannot find what we need online, we can always get a second opinion from another expert. That can never be decisive, but may be weighty enough to allow us to proceed with some confidence on a medical procedure or a lawsuit.

The very best position for us to be in, as noted above, is to understand enough to construct the argument, with plausible premises, that has the expert's judgment as its conclusion. If we are skeptical, it only buttresses our judgment when we find that the expert's opinion was in fact idiosyncratic enough to call forth a public reprimand.

We have an example in the response of over a thousand former Federal prosecutors to the judgment of an attorney general and his deputy that "the evidence developed during the Special Counsel's investigation is not sufficient to establish that the President committed an obstruction-of-justice offense."[18]

The former Federal prosecutors could not have disagreed more with that judgment. They signed an open letter which stated that "the conduct ... described in special counsel Robert Mueller's report would, in the case of any other person, result in multiple felony charges for obstruction of justice."

They went on to say,

> We emphasize that these are not matters of close professional judgment ... [T]o look at these facts and say that a prosecutor could not probably sustain a conviction for obstruction of justice—the standard set out in Principles of Federal Prosecution—runs counter to logic and our experience.[19]

That attorney general and the deputy attorney general took on the roles of prosecuting attorneys in claiming that the evidence in the Mueller Report did not warrant an indictment. The former Federal prosecutors brought a wealth of experience from a variety of backgrounds to their indictment. They "served under both Republican and Democratic administrations at different levels of the federal system: as line attorneys, supervisors, special prosecutors, United States Attorneys, and senior officials at the Department of Justice. The offices in which [they] served were small, medium, and large; urban, suburban, and rural; and located in all parts of our country."[20]

The evidence, they were saying, was not just enough to justify a charge for obstruction of justice, but enough to "sustain a conviction." As they put it in a broadcast,

> We all strongly believe that there is more than enough evidence to indict [the] President ... for multiple felony counts of obstruction of justice ... There's more than enough evidence to convince a jury, beyond a reasonable doubt, that [the] President ... committed the crime of obstruction of justice several times ... This isn't even a close case. If you or I did what [he] did, we'd be facing prison.[21]

We can look to the text itself and do what the art historian did: uncover what it says by reading it carefully and noting the choice of words. We have the advantage of having Mueller's brief statement of its leading points. It is no accident that he said,

When a subject of an investigation obstructs that investigation or lies to investigators, it strikes at the core of their government's effort to find the truth and hold wrongdoers accountable.[22]

The *New York Times* editorial board told us what Mueller was saying:

Translation: Did you notice I said "when" not "if?" Obstruction happened; I'm being coy about who I suspect committed it.[23]

And, of course, if you read the Report, you will find details of ten different instances where justice was obstructed, a majority of them well-supported with sufficient evidence to justify an indictment. After going through them one by one, the Report notes "the … pattern of conduct as a whole":

These actions ranged from efforts to remove the Special Council and to reverse the effect of the Attorney General's recusal; to the attempted use of official power to limit the scope of the investigation; to direct and indirect contacts with witnesses with the potential to influence testimony. Viewing the acts collectively can help illuminate their significance.[24]

As the Report's conclusion makes clear,

if we had confidence after a thorough investigation of the facts that the President clearly did not commit obstruction of justice, we would so state.[25]

They did not.

The former Federal prosecutors performed a public service. They did not just correct an error made by fellow Federal prosecutors. They called them to account: they made an egregious error in judgment that defies logic and the deep and long prosecutorial experience of the former Federal prosecutors. In a matter of such moment, probable crimes by a sitting president, the public deserved to know that that attorney general and his deputy did not speak as one with a host of other experienced Federal prosecutors whose open letter was addressed to the nation's citizens, telling them that matters were not as that attorney general and his deputy claimed they were.

However this dispute may play itself out, and there is much we do not know that may affect any final judgment we make, the former Federal prosecutors have helped us understand that the issues were more problematic than they were represented to be by the attorney general and his deputy.

We can find many an example of one professional calling out another for what appear to be egregious errors in professional judgment. We provided some examples when we looked at what some judges thought were appropriate sentences for crimes that the victims would surely think were far too lenient—like probation for a man who raped a 14-year-old and the same for another man who kept a woman in captivity for over a year, raping her repeatedly and keeping her locked in a dog crate. Such sentences ought to strike us as outrageous. If it turns out to be a commonplace in such cases, we have a very different sort of problem than if such sentences are idiosyncratic.

We cannot know without appealing to professionals, to someone or some group with the time and the resources as well as the special knowledge and skills to scour decisions judges have made in such cases and give us a judgment about their frequency. As I have emphasized, those who are not professionals in a particular field must trust those who are because they lack the necessary background knowledge and skills to assess the professional judgments.[26] However, much we can now check out because we have access to so much information on the web, we are almost never in a position to second-guess a professional's judgment.

Those who are in such a position have an obligation to inform us, and that is what the former prosecutors did for us in calling out that attorney general and his deputy. We can check the text and thus the evidence for ourselves in this matter, but the former prosecutors performed a public service by making it clear to the public that they thought the judgment the attorney general and his deputy made was, at the very least, problematic. Their judgment served as a significant counterweight to the judgment many might have thought privileged because it came from an attorney general and his deputy.

Given the disputes between professionals regarding individual judgments, the trust we put in professionals should not be absolute. We have too many examples of a patient being dissatisfied with a physician's judgment, for example, and pursuing the matter until a proper diagnosis is reached. Professionals may be less than happy to find their judgments met with even modest skepticism, but the reality is that professionals can make mistakes, and a modest skepticism can guard us against one being made regarding us and the general public.

§5 Other Service

There are a variety of other ways in which professionals serve the general public. Lawyers work pro bono, for instance. There are whistleblowers, professionals who see something that is not right and, unable to obtain the changes required, go public with their concerns. Some professions police their own practitioners, sometimes well and sometimes not so well. When they respond appropriately, they save the public from any further damage—although, as we saw, those judged incompetent will often simply find other jobs in other jurisdictions and even get letters of recommendation written to ensure that they leave.

There is a sense of fellowship among professionals, those within different professions as well as those in the same profession, that helps significantly in building the intellectual capital they share and the intellectual infrastructure that is vital to achieving the goals society has decided can only be achieved by those specially educated individuals it designates as professionals. It is the sharing of problems, data, and ideas that allows a professional to do far more than any one professional could possibly do, and it is the consensus that is achieved and discovered by sharing that can both spur public sentiment and inform public policy.

There is now almost unanimous agreement among climate scientists that climate change is real, for instance. It is that consensus that makes it reasonable for us to criticize the judgment of those who claim it is not real. That consensus forces those who doubt to provide some telling fact that would put the agreement in question and so force climate scientists to reevaluate their judgment. Even then, obviously, we would still face the problem that the planet is getting hotter.[27]

We do not, I think, need to detail further examples of how professionals further the common good or additional arguments for why they have a responsibility to further the moral goals that society has recognized need professionals to realize. Society's need for professionals and the good they can provide is well enough illustrated by our calling on engineers, for instance, to investigate what caused a bridge to collapse or an airplane to crash. The aim is to inform us and those who design bridges and build airplanes so that we can avoid such disasters. It is not quite right to say that a failure is the best thing that could happen for an engineer, but engineers learn much from disasters about how to make bridges and airplanes safer,[28] and in fulfilling their social responsibilities through such investigative work, engineers make us safer, achieving one of society's most important moral ends. We can be thankful for how well engineers, and professionals in general, fulfill those responsibilities.

15

Concluding Remarks

We have been engaged in what I might call empirical ethics. It is empirical because I did not begin with an ethical theory and see how a case matched or failed to match the criteria for being ethical laid out by the theory. I rather looked at a case and tried to open it up to see what issues mattered ethically. What did the participants think mattered—if they saw any problems at all? What would an outsider see? As we know, self-interest can get in the way of participants having a good view of what is at issue and how to resolve it, and so we need some check on their understanding to be sure we have properly understood a case.

Two features of this empirical procedure are worth noting. First, I came to the objects of ethical concern laid out in Chapter 1 through an examination of actual cases. What did people criticize ethically? What kinds of issues did they find ethically problematic? It may look as though we started with a theory already in hand, that is, but those objects of ethical concern came through examining cases, those we have considered as well as others.

Second, the procedure we have used to come to judgment requires analyzing ethical problems by constructing arguments for all those involved that make sense of what they did or failed to do. The procedure risks replicating the existing social mores, but has the virtue that its conclusions are always contingent, always open to correction by some new information or new way of understanding what we thought we knew before. As with any empirical endeavor, the procedure is open to correction. We will have an argument that purports to justify a conclusion, and if we discover that its premises are flawed or the entire enterprise misconceived, we have an argument at hand that we can reconsider.

§1 An Open Mind

One impediment to a full understanding of a situation is our first impression, but the procedure we have developed for analyzing and resolving ethical problems puts pressure on any initial response we might have to a problem. As is often remarked, it is difficult to get first impressions out of our minds, and we need to since, as Bharara remarks, "First beliefs are sticky":

> People tend to tune out facts that conflict with their original thesis ..., downplay contrary evidence or, even worse, may not even recognize new facts as undercutting their first belief.[1]

But in requiring that we make sense of how others see the situation by constructing arguments that make sense of what they see, we are being forced out of our own point of view and so out of our first impression of how to understand a case. We can tune in facts that conflict with, and perhaps explain, our original sticky first impression by seeing what others involved in the situation found sticky. We are forced, as it were, to become open-minded even about a case in which we have a significant stake, and being open-minded "means proceeding without a theory. You develop a thesis from the facts, not vice versa."[2]

We proceeded by looking at how others saw the case involving the two men with HIV who were denied their health-care benefits by their companies. Our first reaction was to think that the men had been treated very unfairly, having paid their health-care premiums the entire time they were employed and then being denied the benefits they thought they knew they had. But once we looked at the situation from the point of view of the managers responsible for distributing benefits, we came away with a dilemma, with two competing imperatives, helping the men or helping the other employees. We did not settle the matter since we did not delve deeply enough into the case to see if there were other alternatives available, but we did discover another object of ethical concern—structural features that cause ethical problems for individuals.

That said, we may not have succeeded in analyzing successfully all the cases we examined. There is too much free play between being completely objective and our seeing things from other points of view for us to be completely sure we have not just replicated our own biases from the point of view of others. But the procedure we have developed provides a remedy for that.

If an analysis seems off in some way, start over, looking at the facts and constructing the relevant arguments for those involved. Any discrepancy between the original reading and your new reading will be obvious. It will lie in the premises of the arguments, and you can now focus on whether the original reading or the new one is correct by assessing the competing premises. You may simply replicate your biases, of course, but the remedy for that is to ask someone else to examine the case using the procedure and to do so without first looking at any other analysis.

We do for ethical problems what we do with any problem. We first figure out what seems wrong, work out the possible solutions, and then pick the best one. If that solution does not fix things, then we look again at what seemed wrong to see if we fastened on the correct issue or look again at the solution we chose to see if an alternative might be better. And if we fail yet again, we ask someone else to look at it to see if another point of view will surface the problem.

Again, there is nothing esoteric about any of this. Just as we find ourselves hearing ethical judgments on the playground that are just like the ones we hear in the office or at home or in public, we find ourselves with ethical problems amenable to solutions just like the ones we have at home and elsewhere.

"Why does the storm door lock not always lock the door?" It could be that I fail to pull it completely shut before moving the switch for the lock. It could be that something internal to the lock sometimes does not click into place. It could be that the latch does not catch properly even when the door is pulled completely shut. We work with the possible sources of the problem and eventually come up with an answer by going through all the ways in which failure can occur. Again, if we are unable to get it right, we ask someone else to have a go at it. Ethical problems are no different. Just as we presume that the storm door lock can be made to lock, we are to presume that any ethical problem can be resolved. It may take someone who is an expert in a profession to understand the ins and outs of an ethical issue within a profession, but, again, the procedure we use is the same there.

When we are involved in a contentious ethical issue, we can easily get stuck and want to throw up our hands and say, "We just disagree"—as though there were no objective way to resolve ethical problems. But we ought to presume that however difficult an ethical problem may seem, we can settle it somehow and settle it ethically. We may run into a conceptually problematic situation, but calling out a problem as conceptually problematic is a last resort, only to be used when all else has failed and other observers have weighed in and been unable to help untangle the problem.

That said, we have uncovered a way of recognizing an ethical problem. We are to look for unnecessary harms. We found them in every case we examined:

- the unnecessary harm engineers may have subjected women to in picking the median for men as the sweet spot for being safe with airbags, leaving the majority of women drivers at much greater risk than men,
- the unnecessary harm the physician in Memphis caused the family of the woman who was brain dead,
- the unnecessary harm actuaries cause individuals and institutions and corporations by calculating future pensions at an unreasonably high interest rate, making those results public, and keeping private the actual value.

The list could go on, but the point is made.

In each case we found unnecessary harms, and in each case our ethical judgment was backed by ethical principle. We blamed the actuaries for failing to provide individuals and institutions the information they needed to make informed decisions, denying them their autonomy—an unnecessary harm. There is no good reason not to have a realistic projection of interest rates. We have a history of rates to appeal to, and though a projection based on past rates may be mistaken, it will at least be objective, founded on facts, not on speculation. We blamed the engineers for treating women unfairly, denying them the same measure of safety they provided men—causing them unnecessary harm. The engineers had no evidence that the sweet spot for being cradled by an airbag was the 50th percentile for men—and the 95th percentile for women. By focusing on unnecessary harms, we were able to recognize ethical problems, recognize them as kinds of problems, and appealed to ethical principles to justify the ethical judgments we made.

The aim has been to approach ethical problems with an open mind, lay out the facts and see where they lead. As we worked through the cases, we would have uncovered the five objects of ethical concern with which we began—character, knowledge, intentions, actions or inactions, and consequences. Although I put them up front, to give us some clue about what we were hunting for, they came to light as ethically important in examining cases and no doubt properly belong at the end. In any event, their origin ensures, as best we can, that we do not approach cases with a thesis already in hand. We can instead focus on the problematic situation itself and then let the facts speak for themselves.

They will come to light as we look at a situation from the points of view of all those involved in it and then develop arguments for them that would make sense of what they did or failed to do. As we build the arguments, we will discover what premises each is relying on for their understanding of the situation and its resolution, and discovering those premises will reveal what those involved in the situation think are the relevant facts. We will then be in a position to see whether we have all the facts needed, whether some are missing some facts, or whether everyone is missing something crucial.

§2 What is Missing

I have throughout relied on our common understanding of what constitutes a harm, not having defined it except through the many examples provided. I cannot imagine that anyone, on looking back, was brought up short, thinking, "That's a harm?!" A harm is the loss of something of value, and in each case we found such losses. We might misplace a watch or lose a finger, forget an important meeting or have an accident. The range of what we value is large and varied, and so the harms that can come from a loss are themselves varied and of greater and lesser import. A watch can be replaced, a finger not so easily.

I do not think we have missed anything of value in not defining harm as we proceeded, but we have left undiscussed an ethical problem we may face. What are we to do when we must weigh one harm against another, the loss of one thing of value versus the loss of another? In no doubt the majority of cases, that does not require much thought, but in some it may. Unfortunately, there is no formula for how to proceed in such cases, and a quick summary of our options is as likely to mislead as to clarify. So I will put this problem aside. We must rely on our common understanding of the different values we give to various things, recognizing that disagreements are to be settled just as ethical disputes are to be settled. Every party to a disagreement needs to provide a reasoned argument, and each can then compare the arguments and assess the premises, working their way to a common understanding when that is possible.

We have another shortcoming as well. I have mentioned only once the need for empathy and sympathy, for the emotional capacity, that is, to see a problem from another's point of view. Being able to sympathize with a child whom everyone ignores and teases requires a capacity for understanding what it must be like to be treated poorly. It is a capacity some certainly seem to lack, but I have assumed it in requiring that we resolve ethical cases by providing arguments for each party's point of view since getting into position to understand another's point of view itself requires at least a modicum of sympathy. We must try, as best we can, to get out of our point of view into that of another, and seeing a problem as another sees requires letting go of our emotional response and sympathizing with that of another.

A full accounting of the role emotions and passions play in our ethical lives requires far more than the nod I have just given to its importance, but the scope of the subject would take us far afield from the threads we have been following here.

§3 Professions

Two threads have been running through this work—one about how to understand and resolve ethical problems and the other about the nature of professions. We have the latter because cases in professional ethics are rich in problems and complexities that make them ideal for developing and illustrating the first thread. In examining such cases, we have learned much about the nature of professions, but though the cases generally involve ethical issues that arise for professionals, much of what we have examined is relevant to those who are not professionals. We all face factually problematic and conceptually problematic cases as well as dilemmas, for instance. We are all moral agents, empowered to create moral relations, among other things. Much of what we have learned is true of any moral life, that is, not just a professional's moral life. Yet what I have provided has some features that need to be noted if we are to take in its full scope.

First, the cases are illustrative. They are meant to provide paradigmatic samples, where possible. We have obviously not examined all the sorts of cases that can arise in any one profession. The operating assumptions are that the sorts of problems that arise regarding rules of skill, for instance, arise for all professionals, not just the ones we happened to examine, and that the particular issues we fastened on are again illustrative, a sample of the kinds of issues that can arise regarding rules of skill. Rather obviously, we all use rules of skill, and so the illustrative cases could just as well have been drawn from our ordinary lives. It was, as I indicated, the richness of cases in the professions that make them prime candidates to illustrate how ethical problems arise.

Second, what I have provided is limited by my ignorance of what it is like to be a chemist, or a geologist, or a dentist, or most other kinds of professionals. I lack the special training that creates such professional forms of life as those of a lawyer, a physician, or an engineer, to name just a few that I know something about. The lesson here is that professionals must examine their own forms of life, come to understand how those forms both privilege them by teaching them to see and understand what others cannot while yet constraining them by how they come to see and understand. Only by examining their own forms of life can they understand how the sorts of cases we have examined will appear to them within their professions.

Third, as we know, it is difficult to get out of ourselves, as it were, to see anything amiss in what we do, and if professionals are not taught that what they are doing can be ethically problematic, if that is not part of the training that results in their thinking like an engineer, or a lawyer, or physician, or scientist, we are inculcating habits of thought that, if we are successful, so permeate the way they view the world and see problems that it is exceedingly difficult for them to see any ethical problems in what they do.

As we saw, one large study of what working engineers thought were the major ethical problems they faced gave case after case of external ethical issues. No one gave a case of any ethical problem they had as an engineer. It was as though they were saying, "If you just leave me alone and let me do my work, I will not have any ethical problems at all."[3] That, we know, is false. Ethical decisions permeate professional practice, from deciding what to study as a scientist to how to treat one's patients and colleagues.

Fourth, I have concentrated generally upon examples of professionals causing unnecessary harm, an ethical fault that we all ought to avoid. I have thus perhaps given a misleading impression that our only moral concern ought to be that we not cause unnecessary harms, and we obviously live far richer moral lives than that would suggest and have concerns as well about furthering individual autonomy, benefitting other individuals as well as society at large, and doing all this in a just manner. By concentrating upon examples of unnecessary harms, I have shown how ethical considerations permeate professional practices, but have put aside such tough questions as how we are to choose between alternative ways of doing good, for instance, or how much harm is permissible when it is necessary. We all have to wrestle with these and similar questions when we try to justify what we are doing or not doing with arguments that reflect the complexities that can arise in our lives, professional and otherwise.

Fifth, I assumed as we worked through cases that we should draw our understanding of what is morally important from our actual practice in making moral judgments. We did not approach the cases with any thesis in hand, but let the cases speak for themselves. One test for our analyses of the cases in professional ethics we examined is to find a parallel case in our ordinary lives and see if we are to respond to the problem in the same way we judged a professional should.

Another case that came out of my stay as a medical fellow in Memphis illustrates that point well. A physician was examining a patient for the first time. She had a large lump in her abdomen, and the physician asked why she had not come in earlier. She said, "I'm afraid it's cancer. My sister died of cancer. Please don't tell me it's cancer." He felt the lump and, ignoring her, turned to me and, within her hearing, said, "It's certainly cancer."

I suppose we could say that the physician did not tell her she had cancer. He told me instead—in a situation where she could overhear it. We have no trouble, I should hope, judging him callous in that case any more than we would think it callous for someone, at a party perhaps, to say to a friend, within the hearing distance of an acquaintance in a troubled marriage, "She doesn't know it yet, but he's filing for divorce and seeking custody of the kids."

When we make ethical judgments of professionals, we are doing no more than applying the same principles to the same sorts of features we apply to those who are not professionals. A professional and a friend may have the same character deficiency, and we would criticize them in the same way. Just as professionals can fail to use rules of skill properly, drivers can fail to follow the rules of the road. Neither the form of the criticism nor the object is different.

Notes

Acknowledgments

1. Roger Boisjoly, David Hoeker, Stefan Young, and Wade Robison, "Representation and Misrepresentation: Tufte and the Morton Thiokol Engineers on the Challenger," *Science and Engineering Ethics*, 2002, vol. 8, no. 1, pp. 1–24.

1 Objects of Ethical Concern

1. Insurance Institute for Highway Safety, Fatality Facts 2018, Trends; available online at https://www.iihs.org/topics/fatality-statistics/detail/gender; accessed April 14, 2020.
2. Wade Robison, *Ethics Within Engineering: An Introduction* (New York: Bloomsbury, 2016), pp. 159–64.
3. David Hume, *An Enquiry concerning Human Understanding*, ed. Tom Beauchamp (Oxford: Oxford University Press, 1999), part 4, paragraph 6; see also part 5, paragraph 3.
4. Neil A. Lewis, "A Friendship, a Washington Bank and a Trail of Money Leading to B.C.C.I.; Clifford and Altman, Mentor and Protege, At Center of Inquiry," *New York Times*, September 3, 1991.
5. Marjorie Williams, "Clark Clifford: The Rise of a Reputation," *Washington Post*, May 8, 1991.
6. Queen *v.* M'Naghten, 8 Eng. Reg. 718 (1843).
7. For an extended discussion of this issue, see Robison, *Ethics Within Engineering*, pp. 102–3.
8. Jack Nicas, James Glanz, and David Gelles, "In Test of Boeing Jet, Pilots Had 40 Seconds to Fix Error," *New York Times*, March 25, 2019.

2 Making Ethical Judgments

1. H. L. A. Hart, *The Concept of Law*, 2nd edition (Oxford: Oxford University Press, 1997), pp. 56–7.
2. Victoria Gill, "Chimpanzee Language: Communication Gestures Translated," *BBC News*, July 4, 2014; available online at https://www.bbc.com/news/science-environment-28023630; accessed January 9, 2020.
3. Isaac Asimov, *Foundation*, revised edition (New York: Bantam Spectra Books, 1991), part IV: The Traders, section 1.
4. Daniel Kahneman, *Thinking, Fast and Slow* (New York: Farrar, Straus and Giroux, 2011), p. 22.
5. Ibid., p. 11.

6. Ibid., p. 35.
7. Ibid., pp. 13–14.
8. Johannes Müller, et al., "A New Approach to the Temporal Significance of House Orientations in European Early Neolithic Settlements," *PLOS ONE*, January 10, 2020; available online at https://journals.plos.org/plosone/; accessed January 11, 2020.
9. Joanna Brooks, "New Voices: To the Left—Pseudoneglect," *The Psychologist*, July 2014, vol. 27, pp. 518–59; available online at https://thepsychologist.bps.org.uk/volume-27/edition-7/new-voices-left-pseudoneglect; accessed January 11, 2020.

3 Professions

1. Linda Greenhouse, "Inmate Whose Lawyer Slept Gets a New Trial," *New York Times*, June 4, 2002.
2. Chad Terhune, "The $200 Billion Perils of Unnecessary Medical Tests," *Kaiser Health News*, May 24, 2017; available online at https://www.pbs.org/newshour/health/200-billion-perils-unnecessary-medical-tests; accessed February 25, 2020.
3. Mike Baker, "Pets Are Just 'Property', So Owners Can't Do Much When Vets Harm Them," *New York Times,* February 4, 2020.
4. "Notes of Debates in the Federal Convention of 1787," reported by James Madison, ed. Adrienne Koch (Athens: Ohio University Press, 1966), pp. 245, 265, 267, 288, and 552.
5. One source for a different understanding is a letter from Gouverneur Morris to Henry W. Livingston in 1803 in which Morris says that Congress cannot "admit, as a new State, territory, which did not belong to the United States when the Constitution was made." He adds, "I always thought that, when we should acquire Canada and Louisiana it would be proper to govern them as provinces, and allow them no voice in our councils" and that he tried to say that when authoring article IV, section 3, clause 2 about the power of Congress to make "all Needful Rules and Regulations" regarding territory belonging to the United States. Available online at https://www.consource.org/document/gouverneur-morris-to-henry-w-livingston-1803-12-4/; accessed March 1, 2020.
6. For a sustained examination of the problems associated with describing the nature of a profession, see the introduction in chapter 2, "Professions and Professionalization," in Joan C. Callahan (ed.), *Ethical Issues in Professional Life* (Oxford: Oxford University Press, 1988), pp. 26–48. Included there are Michael D. Bayles, *"The Professions" from Professional Ethics* (Belmont, CA: Wadsworth, 1981); Everett C. Hughes, "Professions," *Daedelus*, vol. 92 (Fall 1963), pp. 655–68; Bernard Barber, "Professions and Emerging Professions," *Daedelus*, vol. 92 (Fall 1963), pp. 669–88; and John C. Merrill, 'The Professionalization of Journalism,' in *The Imperative of Freedom: A Philosophy of Journalistic Autonomy* (New York: Hastings House, 1974), 133–42. An extended bibliography, somewhat dated but very thorough, is on pp. 468ff.
7. Richard Rayner, "Channelling Ike," *New Yorker*, April 26, 2010; available online at http://www.newyorker.com/magazine/2010/04/26/channelling-ike; accessed March 22, 2015.
8. Ibid. See also Paul Harris, "Band of Brothers Author Accused of Fabrication for Eisenhower Biography," *The Guardian*, April 24, 2010; available online at http://www.theguardian.com/world/2010/apr/25/stephen-ambrose-eisenhower-biography-scandal; accessed March 22, 2015.

9. Rayner, "Channelling Ike."

10. Doris Kearns Goodwin, *No Ordinary Time* (New York: Touchstone Press, 1994), pp. 509–10.

11. Gordon S. Wood, "History as Fiction," in *The Purpose of the Past* (New York: Penguin Books, 2008), p. 109. Wood cites the historian Richard D. Brown as pointing this out.

12. Ibid., p. 106.

13. Ibid., pp. 107–8.

14. Statement on Standards of Professional Conduct (updated 2019), American Historical Association; available online at https://www.historians.org/jobs-and-professional-development/statements-standards-and-guidelines-of-the-discipline/statement-on-standards-of-professional-conduct; accessed February 14, 2019.

15. The American Bar Association's criteria for accreditation is a lengthy document. See https://www.americanbar.org/groups/legal_education/accreditation/; accessed January 31, 2020.

16. See the American Bar Association's information on Bar Admissions at https://www.americanbar.org/groups/legal_education/resources/bar_admissions/; accessed January 31, 2020.

17. "What is a PE?," National Society of Professional Engineers; available online at https://www.nspe.org/resources/licensure/what-pe; accessed January 31, 2020.

18. Wade Robison, *Decisions in Doubt: The Environment and Public Policy* (Hanover: University Press of New England, 1994), chapter 2, pp. 14–34.

19. This principle obviously has to be qualified in a variety of ways. Not every individual has a right to make choices. A toddler is not old enough. Senility can prevent someone's understanding of the options available. I will not pursue this issue here. It is clear enough for the work I require of it.

20. Ron Lieber, "Fiduciary Rule Is Now in Question. What's Next for Investors," *New York Times*, February 3, 2017; John C. Bogle, "Putting Clients Second," *New York Times*, February 9, 2017.

21. Arthur E. Hertzler, *The Horse and Buggy Doctor*, reprint of the 1938 edition (Lincoln: University of Nebraska Press, 1970), p. 47.

22. Tanya Basu, "Timeline: A History of GM's Ignition Switch Defect," NPR, March 31, 2014.

23. Hiroko Tabuchi and Danielle Ivory, "Takata's Faulty Airbags Still Exact Toll as Recalls Lag," *New York Times*, January 30, 2016.

24. Tom Beauchamp, "The Principle of Beneficence in Applied Ethics," *Stanford Encyclopedia of Philosophy*; available online at https://plato.stanford.edu/entries/principle-beneficence/; accessed February 24, 2019.

25. See Tom Beauchamp, "The Principles Approach," Hastings Center Report 23.S9 (1993) and "Principlism and its Alleged Competitors," Journal of the Kennedy Institute of Ethics 5 (1995), pp. 181–98.

26. Adam Smith, *An Inquiry into the Nature and Causes of the Wealth of Nations*, eds. R. H. Campbell, A. S. Skinner, and W. B. Todd (Indianapolis: Liberty Classics, 1981), vol. I, book IV, chapter II, p. 453.

27. 2018 Steel Price Forecast; available online at https://gensteel.com/building-faqs/steel-building-prices/forecast; accessed February 8, 2019.

28. Seth Kugel, "NEIGHBORHOOD REPORT: WASHINGTON HEIGHTS; Midwives Fear for Their Role in Hospital Deliveries," *New York Times*, June 14, 2003.

29. Elisabeth Rosenthal, "American Way of Birth, Costliest in the World," *New York Times*, June 30, 2013.

30. Ibid.

31. Marian F. MacDorman, Eugene Declercq, Howard Cabral, and Christine Morton, "Is the United States Maternal Mortality Rate Increasing? Disentangling Trends from Measurement Issues," Obstetrics & Gynecology, September 2016, vol. 128, no. 3, pp. 447–55; summary available online at https://www.ncbi.nlm.nih.gov/pmc/articles/PMC5001799/; accessed February 9, 2018.

32. Available online at https://data.worldbank.org/indicator/SP.DYN.IMRT.IN; accessed February 9, 2018.

33. Wade Robison, "Monopoly with Sick Moral Strangers," in *Reading Engelhardt: Essays on the Thought of H. Tristram Engelhardt, Jr.*, eds. Brendon Minogue, Gabriel Palmer-Fernandez, and James E. Reagan (Dordrecht: Kluwer Academic, 1997), pp. 95–112.

34. Rachel Martin and Geoff Edgars, "Lawsuit Against Boston Symphony Orchestra Exposes Extensive Gender Pay Gap," NPR, morning edition, December 22, 2018; available online at https://www.npr.org/2018/12/11/675505122/lawsuit-against-boston-symphony-orchestra-exposes-extensive-gender-pay-gap; accessed February 24, 2019.

35. John Rawls, *A Theory of Justice* (Oxford: Oxford University Press, 1999), pp. 85–6.

36. 40th Statewide Investigating Grand Jury REPORT I Interim—Redacted, p. 4; available online at http://media-downloads.pacourts.us/InterimRedactedReportandResponses.pdf?cb=42148; accessed February 28, 2019.

37. "Church Allowed Abuse by Priest for Years," *Boston Globe*, January 6, 2006; available online at https://www.bostonglobe.com/news/special-reports/2002/01/06/church-allowed-abuse-priest-for-years/cSHfGkTIrAT25qKGvBuDNM/story.html; accessed March 2, 2019. See also "Geoghan Preferred Preying on Poorer Children," *Boston Globe*, January 7, 2006; available online at https://www.bostonglobe.com/news/special-reports/2002/01/07/geoghan-preferred-preying-poorer-children/69DE1kOuETjphwmIBcgzCM/story.html; accessed March 1, 2019. Also see Candy Woodall, "Catholic Church Still Breaking Its Own Laws, 16 Years after Priest Abuse Scandal Exposed," *York Daily Record*, December 13, 2018; available online at https://www.ydr.com/story/news/2018/12/13/pa-priest-abuse-catholic-church-breaking-rules-set-after-boston-child-sexual-assault-transparency/2295523002/; accessed March 16, 2019.

38. Marci A. Hamilton, "Self-Policing of Criminal Behavior Will Never Work," CNN, March 11, 2004; available online at http://www.cnn.com/2004/LAW/03/11/hamilton.church/index.html; accessed March 16, 2019.

39. Beth LeBlanc, "Nessel to Catholic Dioceses: 'Stop Self-Policing Clergy Abuse Reports,'" *Detroit News*, February 21, 2019; available online at https://www.detroitnews.com/story/news/religion/2019/02/21/nessel-catholic-dioceses-stop-self-policing-clergy-abuse-reports/2938345002/; accessed March 16, 2019.

40. William Neuman, "They Were Accused of Sexual Harassment, but the City Hid It From Future Employers," *New York Times*, March 19, 2019; available online at https://www.nytimes.com/2019/03/19/nyregion/sexual-harassment-neutral-reference.html; accessed March 21, 2019.

41. Deanna Paul, "These Journalists Have a List of Criminal Cops. California is Trying to Keep It Secret," *Washington Post*, March 2, 2019.

42. John Fauber and Matt Wynn, "Bad Docs Give Up Licenses, But Not Medical Practices—More than 250 give up licenses in one state, but still practice in another," *Milwaukee Journal Sentinel* and *USA Today Network*, November 30, 2018; available

online at https://www.medpagetoday.com/special-reports/states-of-disgrace/76584; accessed March 1, 2019.

43. Steven M. Levin and John J. Perconti, "Bad Doctors Can Skip the State to Practice Elsewhere," Illinois Medical Malpractice Blog, December 10, 2018; available online at https://medicalmalpractice.levinperconti.com/bad-doctors-can-skip-the-state-to-practice-elsewhere/; accessed March 1, 2019.

44. Fauber and Wynn, "Bad Docs Give Up Licenses."

45. Uri Dub, "How to Write a Recommendation Letter That You Don't Really Mean"; available online at http://commonplacebook.com/jokes/funny-lists/write-a-recommendation-letter-you-dont-mean/; accessed March 1, 2019.

46. "Not long ago, a female senior executive we know was sitting at a board meeting next to several more junior male colleagues when the board chairman asked her to fetch him a soda." Adam Grant and Cheryl Sandberg, "Madam C.E.O., Get Me a Coffee," *New York Times*, February 6, 2015.

47. Ian Haney López, *Dog Whistle Politics: How Coded Racial Appeals Have Reinvented Racism & Wrecked the Middle Class* (Oxford: Oxford University Press, 2014), pp. 181–9.

4 Norms and Professional Codes of Ethics

1. See the Illinois Institute of Technology's collection of codes of ethics at https://ethics.iit.edu/ecodes/#main-content; accessed August 10, 2020.

2. Matthew L. Wald, "Faulty Design Led to Minnesota Bridge Collapse, Inquiry Finds," *New York Times*, January 15, 2008.

3. Joe Morgenstern, "The Fifty-Nine-Story Crisis," *New Yorker*, May 29, 1995, pp 45–53.

4. John Kultgen, "Evaluating Codes of Professional Ethics," in *Profits and Professions: Essays in Business and Professional Ethics*, ed. Wade Robison, Michael S. Pritchard, and Joseph Ellin (Clifton, NJ: Humana Press, 1983), pp. 225–73. See also John Kultgen, "The Ideological Use of Professional Codes," in *Ethical Issues in Professional Life*, pp. 411–21.

5. Dorothy Emmet, *Rules, Roles, and Relations* (Boston: Beacon Press, 1966), p. 40. The remark that one ought to help one's mother is Emmet's example.

6. Paul Krugman, "Trump and His Team of Morons," *New York Times*, January 14, 2019.

7. Doha Madani and Associated Press, "California Man Learns He's Dying via 'Robot' that Video Conferenced His Doctor," NBC News, March 8, 2019; available online at https://www.nbcnews.com/news/us-news/california-man-learns-he-s-dying-robot-video-conferenced-his-n981106; accessed March 10, 2019.

8. "Man Told He's Going to Die by Doctor on Video-Link Robot," *BBC News*, March 9, 2019; available online at https://www.bbc.com/news/world-us-canada-47510038; accessed March 10, 2019.

9. Dakin Andone and Artemis Moshtaghian, "A Doctor in California Appeared via Video Link to Tell a Patient He Was Going to Die. The Man's Family Is Upset," CNN, March 11, 2019; available online at https://www.cnn.com/2019/03/10/health/patient-dies-robot-doctor/index.html; accessed March 11, 2019.

10. Ken White, "With Trump Over Mueller?," *New York Times*, November 28, 2018.

11. Robert S. Mueller, III, Report on The Investigation of Russian Interference in The 2016 Presidential Election, US Department of Justice, Washington, DC, March 2019, vol. II, pp. 127 and 121, respectively.
12. Ken White, "Why Did Manafort Cooperate with Trump Over Mueller?," *New York Times*, November 28, 2018.
13. For a thorough examination of the problem, see Lawrence J. White, *The S & L Debacle* (New York: Oxford University Press, 1991).
14. Joshua Mills, "Accounting Settlement in Australia," *New York Times*, January 26, 1994.
15. Code of Professional Conduct of the American Institute of Certified Public Accountants, ET section 51, article II, section .01; available online at https://www. aicpa.org/Research/Standards/CodeofConduct/DownloadableDocuments/2010June 1CodeofProfessionalConduct.pdf; accessed September 24, 2016. Similar statements appear in other versions of the codes of ethics for accountants.
16. For a more thorough examination of this tension, see Bruce Oliver and Wade Robison, "Moral Issues in Accounting," *Professional Ethics*, vol. 4, no. 2, pp. 3–11.
17. Mary Williams Marsh, "A Sour Surprise for Public Pensions: Two Sets of Books," *New York Times*, September 17, 2016; available online at http://www.nytimes. com/2016/09/18/business/dealbook/a-sour-surprise-for-public-pensions-two-sets-of-books.html; accessed September 18, 2016.
18. Ibid.
19. Steve Malanga, "Covering Up the Pension Crisis," *Wall Street Journal*, August 25, 2016; available online at http://www.wsj.com/articles/covering-up-the-pension-crisis-1472164758; accessed September 25, 2016.
20. Ibid.
21. Ibid.
22. Barry E. Burr, "Actuarial Leaders Disband Task Force, Object to Paper on Public Plan Liabilities," Pensions and Investments, August 3, 2016; available online at http://www. pionline.com/article/20160803/ONLINE/160809964/actuarial-leaders-disband-task-force-object-to-paper-on-public-plan-liabilities; accessed September 25, 2016.
23. Malanga, "Covering Up the Pension Crisis."
24. Mary Williams Walsh, "Dallas Stares Down a Texas-Size Threat of Bankruptcy," *New York Times*, November 20, 2016; available online at https://www.nytimes. com/2016/11/21/business/dealbook/dallas-pension-debt-threat-of-bankruptcy.html?r ref=collection%2Fbyline%2Fmary-williams-walsh&action=click&contentCollection= undefined&region=stream&module=stream_unit&version=latest&contentPlacement =2&pgtype=collection; accessed November 20, 2016.
25. Thucydides, *The Peloponnesian War*, trans. Thomas Hobbes and David Grene (Chicago: University of Chicago Press, 1989), p. 14.
26. Pierre Bayle, "Scepticism," in *An Historical and Critical Dictionary, Selected and Abridged from the Great Work*, vol. III (London: Hunt & Clark, 1826), p. 214.
27. David Hume, *Essays: Moral, Political, and Literary*, ed. Eugene F. Miller, Revised Edition (Indianapolis: Liberty Classics, 1987), p. 422.
28. Shelby Foote, "The Great American Butchery," *New York Review of Books*, March 6, 1975.
29. Michael D. Hattem, "Where Have You Gone, Gordon Wood?," The Juno: A Group Blog on Early American History, January 21, 2013; available online at https:// earlyamericanists.com/2013/01/21/where-have-you-gone-gordon-wood/; accessed October 2, 2016.

30. Gordon Wood, "Star-Spangled History," *New York Review of Books*, August 12, 1982.

31. Jackson Lears, John Patrick Diggins, and Cushing Strout, reply by Gordon S. Wood, "Writing History: An Exchange," in response to "Star-Spangled History," *New York Review of Books*, December 16, 1982.

32. Jane Coaston, "Trump, Andrew Jackson and Ourselves," *New York Times*, May 2, 2017; available online at https://www.nytimes.com/2017/05/02/opinion/trump-andrew-jackson-and-ourselves.html; accessed May 5, 2017.

33. Quoted by Gordon Wood, "The March of Folly: From Troy to Vietnam," *New York Review of Books*, March 29, 1984.

34. Eric Foner, "Is This History Necessary," *New York Review of Books*, April 20, 1972.

35. William P. Taylor, "Repossessing America," *New York Review of Books*, October 13, 1983.

36. Gordon S. Wood, "History as Fiction," in *The Purpose of the Past* (New York: Penguin Books, 2009), p. 109. Wood cites the historian Richard D. Brown as pointing this out.

37. "43rd President is 'Gut Player' Who Eschews Personal Change," NBC News, August 28, 2004; available online at http://www.nbcnews.com/id/5762240/ns/politics/t/rd-president-gut-playerwho-eschews-personal-change/#.WU_QscaZN3k; accessed June 25, 2017.

5 Virgin Eyes: Seeing from Other Points of View

1. I owe the phrase "virgin eyes" to Raquel Delevi. She used it while discussing her presentation at a conference of the Society for Ethics Across the Curriculum and in connection with coming to a foreign country where everything seems fresh and different. Once we have been in that country for a while, we lose our virginity, as it were.

2. Gareth Davies and Paddy Dinham, "Yob Who Kicked Woman Down a Flight of Stairs at Berlin Subway Station Has Fled to His Native Bulgaria, Say German Media," *Daily Mail*, December 14, 2016; available online at http://www.dailymail.co.uk/news/article-4033278/Yob-kicked-woman-flight-stairs-Berlin-subway-station-fled-native-Bulgaria-say-German-media.html; accessed February 9, 2017.

3. Michelle Hunter, "Watch Gretna Police Officer Kick Handcuffed Suspect; Officer Fired, Arrested," *Times-Picayune*, September 16, 2016; available online at http://www.nola.com/crime/index.ssf/2016/09/robert_wallow_gretna_police_ki.html; accessed February 9, 2017.

4. I was with this group as an outside observer while on my medical humanities fellowship.

5. Nate Silver, *The Signal and the Noise* (New York: Penguin Press, 2012), pp. 31, 196. See the Report of the Financial Crisis Inquiry Commission, pp. xxiii–xxiv and chapter 5, esp. pp. 78–9; available online at http://fcic.law.stanford.edu/report; accessed February 25, 2019.

6. Milt Freudenheim, "Employers Winning Wide Leeway to Cut Medical Insurance Benefits," *New York Times*, March 29, 1992.

7. See https://polimak.com/en/urun/loading-spouts/; accessed July 22, 2019.

6 Understanding Cases

1. David Hume, *A Treatise of Human Nature*, ed. David Fate Norton and Mary J. Norton (Oxford: Oxford University Press, 2000), p. 6.

2. Frans de Waal, *Are We Smart Enough to Know How Smart Animals Are?* (New York: Norton, 2016), p. 61.

3. See Nicholas Wade, "When England Split From Europe, in a Big Way," *New York Times*, April 4, 2017.

4. Glenn Hodges, "Formed by Megafloods, This Place Fooled Scientists for Decades," National Geographic, March 11, 2017.

5. This information was displayed on Wunderground, the weather website, on March 14, 2017. Wunderground does not keep its daily postings, but anyone familiar with the site can find similar language in other daily postings.

6. Bill Chappell, "Maryam Mirzakhani, Prize-Winning Mathematician, Dies At 40," NPR News, July 15, 2017; available online at http://www.npr.org/sections/thetwo-way/2017/07/15/537419982/maryam-mirzakhani-prize-winning-mathemetician-dies-at-40; accessed July 20, 2017.

7. Boston Globe, cited by Tufte: see https://www.edwardtufte.com/tufte/books_vdqi; accessed March 11, 2017. See Anna Codrea-Rado, "Show, Don't Tell," *Columbia Journalism Review*, August 15, 2012; available online at http://archives.cjr.org/data_points/spreadsheets_sankey.php; accessed May 5, 2017.

8. Edward Tufte, *Visual Explanations: Images and Quantities, Evidence and Narrative* (Cheshire, Connecticut: Graphics Press, 1997).

9. Ibid., p. 30.

10. Ibid., p. 31.

11. Robison, Boisjoly, Hoeker, and Young, "Representation and Misrepresentation," p. 64.

12. Tufte, *Visual Explanations*, p. 23.

13. Ibid.

14. Ibid., p. 30.

15. Ibid., p. 20.

16. Computer Literacy Bookshops Interviews with Edward R. Tufte (1994 and 1997); available online at https://kkh.ltrr.arizona.edu/kkh/dendro/PDFs.Tufte/Edward%20R.%20Tufte%20--%20CLB%20Interview%201994-1997.pdf; accessed January 18, 2021.

17. Tufte, *Visual Explanations*, p. 23.

18. Roger Boisjoly, "Ethical Decisions—Morton Thiokol and the Space Shuttle Challenger Disaster," ASME Proceedings. December 13–18, 1987.

19. Aristotle, *Nicomachean Ethics*, trans. W. D. Ross (Kitchener: Batoche Books, 1999), book II, chapter 6, p. 27.

20. Howard Burkes, "30 Years After Explosion, Challenger Engineer Still Blames Himself," NPR News, January 28, 2016; available online at http://www.npr.org/sections/thetwo-way/2016/01/28/464744781/30-years-after-disaster-challenger-engineer-still-blames-himself; accessed March 14, 2017.

21. Adam Liptak, "Did the Supreme Court Base a Ruling on a Myth?," *New York Times*, March 6, 2017.

22. Will Oremus, "Fox News Claims Solar Won't Work in America Because It's Not Sunny Like Germany," Slate, February 7, 2013; available online at www.slate.com/blogs/future_tense/2013/02/07/fox_news_expert_on_solar_energy_germany_gets_a_lot_more_sun_than_we_do_video.html; accessed July 23, 2019.

23. Ibid.

7 Kinds of Ethical Problems

1. https://en.oxforddictionaries.com/definition/ethical_dilemma; accessed August 17, 2017. See also http://examples.yourdictionary.com/ethical-dilemma-examples. html; accessed July 9, 2017. See also Terrance McConnell, "Moral Dilemmas," *Stanford Encyclopedia of Philosophy*, https://plato.stanford.edu/entries/moral-dilemmas/#ConMorDil; accessed August 17, 2017.

2. Marwa Eltagouri, "12-Year-Old Was Told She Had the Flu. The Misdiagnosis May Have Caused Her Death," *Washington Post*, January 10, 2018.

3. Jackie Salo, "Mom Misdiagnosed with Flu Battles Dangerous Flesh-Eating Virus," *New York Post*, January 22, 2018.

4. Linda Greenhouse, "Inmate Whose Lawyer Slept Gets a New Trial," *New York Times*, June 4, 2002.

5. Henry Petroski, *To Engineer Is Human: The Role of Failure in Successful Design* (New York: Vantage Books, 1992), p. 87; Matthys Levy and Mario Salvadori, *Why Buildings Fall Down: How Structures Fail* (New York: W. W. Norton, 1994), pp. 221–30.

6. Pam Belluck, "Woman Killed as Slab Falls from Big Dig Tunnel," *New York Times*, July 11, 2006; available online at http://www.nytimes.com/2006/07/11/us/11cnd-boston. html?mcubz=1; accessed August 18, 2017.

7. Ashley Southall, "Police Officer Who Manhandled Tennis Star James Blake Avoids Trial," *New York Times*, May 14, 2017; available online at https://www.nytimes. com/2017/05/14/nyregion/james-blake-arrest-officer-no-trial.html?mcubz=1; accessed August 17, 2017.

8. This is a case I witnessed while I was on my medical humanities fellowship at the University of Tennessee.

9. As in Michael D. Bayles, *Professional Ethics* (Belmont, California: Wadsworth Press, 1988).

10. Sir Arthur Conan Doyle, 'The Silver Blaze,' The Memoirs of Sherlock Holmes; available online at https://sherlock-holm.es/stories/pdf/a4/1-sided/mems.pdf; accessed January 6, 2018, p. 11.

11. Linda Reeser and Wade Robison, *Ethical Decision-making in Social Work* (Needham Heights, MA: Allyn & Bacon, 2000), pp. 200–3.

12. Flint Water, "Advisory Task Force Final Report," March 21, 2016; available online at https://www.michigan.gov/documents/snyder/FWATF_FINAL_REPORT_21March2016_517805_7.pdf; accessed January 6, 2018.

13. Anna Maria Berry-Jester, "What Went Wrong in Flint," FiveThirtyEight, January 26, 2016; available online at https://fivethirtyeight.com/features/what-went-wrong-in-flint-water-crisis-michigan/; accessed January 16, 2018.

14. Robison, *Decisions in Doubt*, pp. 114–17.

15. Aaron Sidder, "Remember the Ozone Hole? Now There's Proof It's Healing," National Geographic, June 30, 2016; available online at https://news.nationalgeographic. com/2016/06/antarctic-ozone-hole-healing-fingerprints/; accessed January 8, 2018. But see Ethan Siegel, "Sorry, Earth, The Ozone Layer Isn't Healing Itself After All," *Forbes*, February 6, 2018 and Chris Mooney, "It Looked as If Earth's Ozone Layer Was Healing Nicely—until Now," *Washington Post*, February 6, 2018.

16. Monica Davey and Richard Pérez-Peña, "Flint Water Crisis Yields First Criminal Charges," *New York Times*, April 29, 2016.

17. Josh Keller and Derek Watkins, "How Officials Distorted Flint's Water Testing," *New York Times*, July 29, 2016.

18. Berry-Jester, "What Went Wrong in Flint."

19. Gardiner Harris, "Doctor Admits Pain Studies Were Frauds, Hospital Says," *New York Times*, March 11, 2009.

20. Silver, *The Signal and the Noise*, pp. 29, 26, 176–7.

21. Kahneman, *Thinking, Fast and Slow*, pp. 13, 50–1.

22. Natalie Angier, "Many Animals Can Count, Some Better Than You," *New York Times*, February 5, 2018.

23. Daniel Kahneman and Amos Tversky, "Intuitive Predictions: Biases and Corrective Procedures," Cybernetics Technology Office, Defense Advanced Research Projects Agency, Office of Naval Research, Engineering Psychology Programs (December 19, 1977), p. ii.

24. "The Scorpion and the Frog" at http://allaboutfrogs.org/stories/scorpion.html; accessed February 15, 2017.

25. See the discussion at Reddit Real Estate; available online at https://www.reddit.com/r/RealEstate/comments/2mcmhh/failure_to_disclose_lien_advice_needed/; accessed February 16, 2017.

26. Katie Thomas, "J.&J. To Pay $2.2 Billion in Risperdal Settlement," *New York Times*, November 4, 2013.

27. Deborah Tannen, *That's Not What I Meant* (New York: Ballantine Books, 1992), pp. 19–25.

28. W. B. Gallie, "Essentially Contested Concepts," in *Philosophy and The Historical Understanding*, 2nd edition (New York: Schocken Books, 1968), p. 158.

29. Michael Lewis, *The Big Short* (New York: W. W. Norton, 2010), p. 12.

30. Carol Gentry, "Surgeon Removes Kidney by Mistake," Health News/Florida, June 10, 2009; available online at https://health.wusf.usf.edu/hnf-stories/2009-06-09/surgeon-removes-kidney-by-mistake; accessed February 13, 2017.

31. Ibid., p. 130.

32. Hearing before the Committee on Oversight and Government Reform, House of Representatives, One Hundred Tenth Congress, second session—OCTOBER 22, 2008—Serial no. 110–55.

33. Testimony of Raymond W. McDaniel, chairman and chief executive officer, Moody's Corporation, before the United States House of Representatives Committee on Oversight and Government Reform, October 22, 2008. Section 1.a. of that testimony is entitled "Credit Ratings Are Opinions about Future Outcomes" and says, among other things, "The heart of our service is expressing opinions on the relative credit risk of long-term, fixed-income debt instruments"; available online at https://oversight.house.gov/sites/democrats.oversight.house.gov/files/documents/20081022125014.pdf; accessed July 31, 2019.

34. *Inside Job*, directed by Charles Ferguon, from 56:00 to 57:02. See also Gretchen Morgenson, "Credit Rating Agency Heads Grilled by Lawmakers," *New York Times*, October 22, 2008.

8 Internal and External Moral Problems

1. Alexandra Horowitz, "Walk Like a Fish," *New York Times*, December 15, 2012.

2. Wood, "Star-Spangled History."

3. Barry Meier, "Defect in Heart Devices Exposes a History of Problems," *New York Times*, October 20, 2005.

4. Ricky Champagne, "Baby Decapitated Due to Doctor's Actions," BBC news, June 4, 2018; available online at https://www.bbc.com/news/uk-scotland-tayside-central-44357023; accessed May 19, 2019.

5. Sherry F. Colb, "Do Defendants Have the Right to Make Bad Decisions?," *Verdict*, February 12, 2018.

6. Vivian Wang, "ABC Suspends Reporter Brian Ross Over Erroneous Report About Trump," *New York Times*, December 2, 2017.

7. See e.g., Carl Kandutsch, "#95. Carl Kandutsch Writes on Terms of Criticism for Contemporary Painting: A Note on David Salle on Laura Owens," June 7, 2017; available online at https://abcrit.org/category/carl-kandutsch/; accessed June 25, 2019.

8. Gil Duran, "Trump Has Turned Words into Weapons. And He's Winning the Linguistic War," *The Guardian*, June 13, 2018.

9. Michael Pritchard, "Cases for Teaching Engineering Ethics"; available online at http://www.onlineethics.org/Resources/csaindex.aspx.

10. Charles Ornstein, Lena Groeger, Mike Tigas, and Ryann Grochowski Jones, "Dollars for Docs," ProPublica, December 13, 2016.

11. Wayne Drash, Sergio Hernandez, and Aaron Kessler, "Medicare Spent $2 Billion for One Drug as the Manufacturer Paid Doctors Millions," CNN, June 29, 2018.

12. Ron Fonger, "Former Water Plant Operator Says Flint Rushed to Use Flawed Treatment Plant," Michigan Live, February 22, 2018.

13. Monica Davey and Richard Pérez-Peña, "Flint Water Crisis Yields First Criminal Charges."

14. "All Things Considered," NPR News, November 18, 1998.

15. Gustav Niebuhr, "Bishops Take Bolder Stand in Battle against Abortion," *New York Times*, November 19, 1998.

16. Erin B. Logan, "Walgreen Pharmacist Denies Woman Miscarriage Medicine Because It Goes against His Ethics," *Washington Post*, June 25, 2018.

17. Kat Chow, "Walgreens Pharmacist Refuses to Provide Drug for Ariz. Woman with Unviable Pregnancy," NPR News, June 25, 2018.

18. For a detailed analysis of the Challenger disaster see Robison, Boisjoly, Hoeker, and Young, "Representation and Misrepresentation" and Wade Robison, *Ethics Within Engineering*, chapter 8, section 6.

19. Diane Vaughan, *The Challenger Launch Decision: Risky Technology, Culture, and Deviance at NASA* (Chicago: University of Chicago Press, 1997), p. 317.

20. Ibid., p. 318.

21. Michael Davis, *Thinking Like an Engineer: Studies in the Ethics of a Profession* (New York: Oxford University Press, 1998), p. 67.

9 Fundamental Moral Relations

1. Wesley Hohfeld, *Fundamental Legal Relations* (New Haven, Connecticut: Yale University Press, 1964), p. 28.

2. Ibid., p. 53.

3. Ibid., p. 52.

4. Jacinda Townsend, "How the Green Book Helped African-American Tourists Navigate a Segregated Nation," *Smithsonian Magazine*, April 2016; available online at https://www.smithsonianmag.com/smithsonian-institution/

history-green-book-african-american-travelers-180958506/#TsTdhcOcwJ0zLW17.99; accessed February 8, 2018. See also Kaitlyn Greenidge, "A Black Motorists' Guide to Jim Crow America, Newly Relevant," *New York Times*, October 18, 2018 and Meredith Mendelsohn, "How an Artist Learned About Freedom From 'The Negro Motorist Green Book,'" *New York Times*, January 19, 2018.

5. Hart, *The Concept of Law*, pp. 27–33, 79–80.
6. John Stuart Mill, *Utilitarianism* ed. George Sher (Indianapolis: Hackett Publishing Company, 1979), pp. 30–3, 47.
7. Chris Perez, "White Man Calls Police on Black Family at Neighborhood Pool," *New York Post*, July 5, 2018.
8. Cleve R. Woodson, Jr., "A Black Yale Student Fell Asleep in Her Dorm's Common Room. A White Student Called Police," *Washington Post*, May 11, 2018.
9. Ibid.

10 Discretion

1. Susannah Cullinane and Amanda Jackson, "A Man Harasses a Woman for Wearing a Puerto Rico Shirt, Saying It's 'un-American,'" CNN, July 11, 2018.
2. Phil Helsel, "Man Seen in Video Harassing Woman in Puerto Rico Shirt Charged with Hate Crime," NBC News, July 12, 2018.
3. Christopher Mele, "Video Shows Orlando Police Pulling Over Florida State Attorney," New York Times, July 13, 2017. See also Amy B. Wang, "Video Shows Police Trying to Explain Why They Pulled Over a Florida State Attorney," *Washington Post*, July 13, 2017.
4. Willie David, "State Attorney Aramis Ayala Racially Profiled By Orlando Police?" Florida National News, July 6, 2017; available online at http://floridanationalnews.com/blog/video-state-attorney-aramis-ayala-racially-profiled-by-orlando-police/; accessed January 30, 2018.
5. For some other issues the stop raised, see ibid.
6. Farnoush Amiri, Ethan Sacks, and Kerry Sanders, "Georgia Officers on Leave after Coin-Toss Used before Decision to Make Arrest," NBC News, July 13, 2018.
7. Aristotle, *Nicomachean Ethics*, trans. W. D. Ross, p. 27.
8. Cleve R. Wootson Jr., "'You're Going to Jail': Officer Fired for Abuse of Power after Pulling over Daughter's Boyfriend," *Washington Post*, June 24, 2018.
9. Peter Losin, "Aristotle's Doctrine of the Mean," *History of Philosophy Quarterly*, 1987, vol. 4, no. 3, pp. 329–41.
10. Lawrence H. Summers, "Trump's Budget Is Simply Ludicrous," *Washington Post*, May 23, 2017.
11. Rick Rojas, "How a Judge's Nomination Turned Ugly in Connecticut," *New York Times*, March 21, 2018.
12. "Burger King: No Shoes Rule Taken Too Far When Mom with Barefoot Baby Asked to Leave," Fox News, August 6, 2009. I owe this example to Dan Wueste.
13. Derek Hawkins, "How an Arizona Couple's Innocent Bath Time Photos of Their Kids Set Off a 10-Year Legal Saga," *Washington Post*, January 24, 2018.
14. Amy B. Wang and Maria Sacchetti, "A Chemistry Professor Got His Kids Ready for School. Then ICE Arrested Him on His Front Lawn," *Washington Post*, February 4, 2018.

15. Derek Hawkins, "A Michigan Father, Too Old for DACA, Is Deported after Three Decades in the U.S.," *Washington Post*, January 16, 2018.
16. Samantha Schmidt, "ICE Detains a Polish Doctor and Green-Card Holder Who Has Lived in the U.S. for Nearly 40 Years," *Washington Post*, January 22, 2018.
17. Editorial Board, "Unshackled by the Trump Administration, Deportation Agents Discount Basic Decency," *Washington Post*, January 28, 2018.
18. Hawkins, "A Michigan Father, Too Old for DACA."
19. Nick Miroff and Maria Sacchetti, "Trump Takes 'Shackles' Off ICE, Which Is Slapping Them on Immigrants Who Thought They Were Safe," *Washington Post*, February 11, 2018.
20. Ibid.
21. Samantha Schmidt, "An Immigrant Called 911 to Report a Crime. Police Took Him to ICE in Handcuffs," *Washington Post*, February 14, 2018.
22. Samantha Schmidt, "Video Shows Border Patrol Officers Asking Greyhound Passengers for IDs, Taking Woman into Custody," *Washington Post*, January 23, 2018.
23. Miroff and Sacchetti, "Trump Takes 'Shackles' Off ICE."
24. Jonathan Blitzer, "Donald Trump's ICE Is Tearing Families Apart," *New Yorker*, February 13, 2018.
25. Marwa Eltagouri, "12-Year-Old Was Told She Had the Flu."
26. Rakesh Goswami and Dinesh Bothra, "Doctors Fight in Operation Theatre in Jodhpur Hospital, Woman Loses Newborn," *Hindustan Times*, August 31, 2017.
27. Amy B. Wang and Kristine Phillips, " 'Just Shoot Me', an Armed Man Told a Cop. The Officer Didn't—and Was Fired, His Lawsuit Claimed," *Washington Post*, February 12, 2018.
28. Christine Hauser, "Georgia Police Dept. Defends Use of Taser on 87-Year-Old Woman," *New York Times*, August 17, 2018.
29. Amanda Erickson, "How Do You Capture a Mass-Killer Suspect Without Firing a Shot? Ask Toronto Police," *Washington Post*, April 24, 2018.
30. Fred Barbash, " 'Revoking' a Security Clearance Is Not as Simple as Trump Made It Sound. Battles Could Play Out for Years, Lawyers Say," *Washington Post*, August 20, 2018.
31. Ibid.
32. Lon Fuller, *The Morality of Law*, revised edition (New Haven: Yale University Press, 1964), pp. 53–4.
33. http://www.imdb.com/title/tt0264464/; accessed February 12, 2018.
34. In the Matter of Rodney P. Sniadecki, Indiana Supreme Court, No. 71S00-0811-DI-608 (April 1, 2010).
35. Joseph A. Corsmeier, Lawyer Ethics Alert Blog, The Florida Bar *v.* Alma C. Defillo, Case No. SC15-593 (August 28, 2015); available online at https://jcorsmeier.wordpress.com/2015/10/19/florida-lawyer-permanently-disbarred-for-inter-alia-soliciting-and-making-misrepresentations-on-website-and-representing-clients-in-other-states/; accessed February 11, 2018.
36. BrieAnna J. Frank, "Arizona Man Impersonating Officer Arrested After Attempting to Pull Over Troopers," *USA Today*, July 15, 2018.
37. Colin Dwyer, "Man Says He's Not Dead. Court Doesn't Buy It," NPR News, March 16, 2018.
38. "Romanian Court Rejects Man's Claim That He's Alive," *New York Times*, March 16, 2018.

39. As odd as the Romanian's case may be, it is not unique. A French woman was declared dead in 2017 and is now in a fight for her life, as it were. Elaine Ganley, "Woman Ruled Dead in 2017 Fights to be Declared Alive," Associated Press, January 18, 2021; available online at https://apnews.com/article/woman-declared-dead-2017-is-alive-2256556e1c682d8ca561cc14b58b0228; accessed January 23, 2021.
40. Martha Neil, "Convicted of UPL, Former Bar President with No Law Degree 'Provided a Good Service', Her Lawyer Says," *ABA Journal*, March 25, 2016.

11 Rules of Skill

1. Morgenstern, "The Fifty-Nine-Story Crisis."
2. "Pilot's Wrong Keystroke Led to Crash, Airline Says," *New York Times*, August 24, 1996, p. 9; Stephen Manes, "When Trust in 'Data' Is Misplaced," *New York Times*, September 17, 1996, p. C9.
3. Wang, "Video Shows Police Trying to Explain Why They Pulled Over a Florida State Attorney."
4. Mars Climate Orbiter Mishap Investigation Board Phase I Report, 6; available online at ftp://ftp.hq.nasa.gov/pub/pao/reports/1999/MCO_report.pdf; accessed: January 7, 2014.
5. "Hubble's Painful Birth," BBC News, February 10, 2000.
6. Immanuel Kant, *Groundwork for the Metaphysics of Morals*, revised edition, trans. and ed. Mary Gregor and Jens Timmerman (Cambridge: Cambridge University Press, 2012), p. 29.
7. Wallace Matson, *The Existence of God* (Ithaca, NY: Cornell University Press, 1965), p. 85.
8. Kant's ethical theory does not allow rules of skill moral standing, but we see here one theoretical advantage of doing ethics from within a profession: we uncover moral truths that a theoretical approach would preclude us from seeing. If we were to look for ethical problems through Kantian lens, we would never see rules of skill or the ethical problems that can arise from using them.
9. Robert Paul Wolff, *Kant's Theory of Mental Activity* (Cambridge: Harvard University Press, 1963), p. 123.
10. Paul Lienert and Marilyn Thomson, "GM Didn't Fix Deadly Ignition Switch Because It Would Have Cost $1 Per Car," *Reuters*, April 2, 2014.
11. Ibid.
12. Bill Vlasic, "An Engineer's Eureka Moment with a G.M. Flaw," *New York Times*, March 28, 2014.
13. Basu, "Timeline: A History of GM's Ignition Switch Defect."
14. Anton R. Valukas, "Report to Board of Directors of General Motors Company Regarding Ignition Switch Recalls," May 28, 2014, esp. pp. 25ff.; available online at https://s3.amazonaws.com/s3.documentcloud.org/documents/1183508/g-m-internal-investigation-report.pdf; accessed January 10, 2014. See also Bill Vlasic, "G.M. Inquiry Cites Years of Neglect Over Defect," *New York Times*, June 5, 2014.
15. Jennifer Liberto, "Two Died in 2006 Cobalt Crash. But GM Counts Only One," CNN Money, May 28, 2014; available online at http://money.cnn.com/2014/05/28/news/companies/gm-recall-death/index.html; accessed: January 10, 2015. See also David Undercoffler, "As Many as 303 Deaths Linked to Faulty Ignition Switches in Recalled GM Cars," *Los Angeles Times*, March 13, 2014.

16. "Deep Water: The Gulf Oil Disaster and the Future of Offshore Drilling," Washington, DC: National Commission on the BP Deepwater Horizon Spill and Offshore Drilling, 2011, p. 104.

17. Ibid.

18. Darryl Fears, "The Toxic Reach of Deepwater Horizon's Oil Spill Was Much Larger—and Deadlier—than Previous Estimates, a New Study Says," *Washington Post,* February 12, 2020.

19. K. Zezima, "Boston Papers Say Memos Question Tunnel Safety," *New York Times,* July 27, 2006.

20. This story may well be apocryphal. It is repeated as gospel whenever anyone writes of Cicero's death, but I have not found a reliable citation. In any event, the distinction Cicero is said to have made is exactly the distinction between what we do and how we do it.

21. Renee Montagne, "To Keep Women from Dying in Childbirth, Look to California," NPR News, July 29, 2018.

12 Rules of Skill, Yet Again

1. Crystal Bonvillian, "Lawsuit: Florida Surgeon Removed Woman's Kidney by Mistake during Back Surgery," AJC: Atlanta News Now, November 8, 2018; available online at https://www.ajc.com/news/national/lawsuit-florida-surgeon-removed-woman-kidney-mistake-during-back-surgery/RmZMDhFeIaoRdfQ0Q6vQVI/; accessed March 4, 2019.

2. Francis Lieber, *Legal and Political Hermeneutics* (New York: Legal Classics Library, 1994), p. 27; a reprint of the original, published in Boston by Charles C. Little and James Brown, 1834.

3. Ibid., p. 28. As an example of the assumptions any statement makes, Lieber has a mistress saying to a domestic, "fetch some soupmeat." I have replaced the housekeeper with a lawyer.

4. Ludwig Wittgenstein, *Philosophical Investigations* (Oxford: Blackwell, 2001), originally published in 1953, §§185–243.

5. Emmet, *Rules, Roles, and Relations*, p. 139, fn. 1.

6. Michael Lewis, *The Fifth Risk* (New York: W. W. Norton, 2018), p. 55.

7. I owe this example to Matthew Zielinski, one of my engineering students in a course in professional ethics at the Rochester Institute of Technology.

8. Daniel Victor, "Lack of Oxford Comma Could Cost Maine Company Millions in Overtime Dispute," *New York Times,* March 16, 2017; available online at https://www.nytimes.com/2017/03/16/us/oxford-comma-lawsuit.html; accessed March 16, 2019. See also Daniel Victor, "Oxford Comma Dispute Is Settled as Maine Drivers get $5 Million," *New York Times,* February 9, 2018; available online at https://www.nytimes.com/2018/02/09/us/oxford-comma-maine.html; accessed March 16, 2019. See also Kenneth A. Adams, "Bamboozled by a Comma: The Second Circuit's Misdiagnosis of Ambiguity in American International Group, Inc. v. Bank of America Corp.," *Scribes Journal of Legal Writing,* 2014; available online at http://www.adamsdrafting.com/wp/wp-content/uploads/2013/10/Adams-Bamboozled-Forthcoming-10.7.13.pdf.; accessed March 16, 2019.

9. Robison, *Ethics Within Engineering,* pp. 22–8.

10. Ezra Hauer, "Safety in Geometric Design Standards I: Three Anecdotes," in *Proceedings, 2nd International Symposium on Highway Geometric Design*, ed. R. Krammes and W. Brilon (Cologne: Forschungsgesellschaft fur Strassen- und Verkehrswesen (FGSV), 2000–6), p. 12.

11. Ibid., p. 19.

12. Ibid., pp. 19–20.

13. Ibid., p. 18.

14. Ibid., p. 15.

15. Ibid., p. 12.

16. Ibid., p. 11.

17. Ibid., p. 12.

18. Ibid., p. 13.

19. Ezra Hauer, "Safety in Geometric Design Standards II: Rift, Roots and Reform," in *Proceedings, 2nd International Symposium on Highway Geometric Design*, ed. R. Krammes and W. Brilon (Cologne: Forschungsgesellschaft fur Strassen- und Verkehrswesen (FGSV), 2000–6), pp. 24–34.

20. From an email from Hauer to me, April 11, 2019.

21. Report to the President, Forensic Science in Criminal Courts: Ensuring Scientific Validity in Feature-Comparison Methods, Executive Office of the President, President's Council of Advisors on Science and Technology, September 2016, p. 1; available online at https://obamawhitehouse.archives.gov/sites/default/files/microsites/ostp/PCAST/pcast_forensic_science_report_final.pdf; accessed April 1, 2019.

22. Heather Murphy, "When a DNA Test Says You're a Younger Man, Who Lives 5,000 Miles Away," *New York Times*, December 7, 2019.

23. Sharon Otterman, "She Was Fired After Raising Questions About a DNA Test. Now She's Getting $1 Million," *New York Times*, April 23, 2019.

24. Report to the President, p. 3.

25. The Innocence Project, Misapplication of Forensic Science; available online at https://www.innocenceproject.org/causes/misapplication-forensic-science/; accessed April 1, 2019.

26. Ibid., pp. 19, 30.

27. Ibid., p. 54.

28. Report to the President, p. 54.

29. Ibid.

30. Elaine Sciolino, "BOMBINGS IN MADRID: THE ATTACK: 10 Bombs Shatter Trains in Madrid, Killing 192," *New York Times*, March 12, 2004.

31. A Review of the FBI's Handling of the Brandon Mayfield Case, Office of Inspector General, Oversight and Review Division, January 2006, p. 1; available online at https://oig.justice.gov/sites/default/files/legacy/special/s0601/PDF_list.htm; accessed January 19, 2021.

32. Ibid., p. 7.

33. Ibid., p. 2.

34. Ibid., p. 10.

35. Ibid., p. 20.

36. Ibid., pp. 1–2.

37. Preet Bharara, *Doing Justice* (New York: Vintage Books, 2020), p. 44. The FBI report refers to ten points of comparison. The defense's expert found fifteen, it appears. In either case, we have an unlikely coincidence.

38. For a careful analysis of the Mayfield case, see Bharara, *Doing Justice*, pp. 35–46.

39. The Innocence Project, "Keith Allen Harward"; available online at https://www. innocenceproject.org/cases/keith-allen-harward/; accessed April 4, 2019.

40. John Oliver, "Forensic Science: Last Week Tonight," October 1, 2017. From 13:21 to 14:40 in the video; available online at https://www.youtube.com/ watch?v=ScmJvmzDcG0; accessed April 4, 2019.

41. Report to the President, pp. 28–9.

42. Spencer S. Hsu, "Santae Tribble's 1980 Murder Conviction Overturned by D.C. Judge," *Washington Post*, May 16, 2012.

43. Oliver, "Forensic Science: Last Week Tonight," from 2:40 to 4:30 in the video.

44. Spencer S. Hsu, "Convicted Defendants Left Uninformed of Forensic Flaws Found by Justice Dept.," *Washington Post*, April 16, 2012.

45. Report to the President, pp. 3, 30.

46. Heather Murphy, "A Leading Cause for Wrongful Convictions: Experts Overstating Forensic Results," *New York Times*, April 20, 2019.

47. David Allen Sibley, *The Sibley Guide to Birds* (New York: Alfred A. Knopf, 2000), p. 441.

48. Report to the President, p. 6.

49. Ibid., p. 46.

50. "A Review of the FBI's Handling of the Brandon Mayfield Case," pp. 6–7.

51. For a thorough examination of these issues, see Strengthening Forensic Science in the United States: A Path Forward, National Research Council of the National Academies (Washington, DC: National Academies Press, 2009); available online at http://www. nap.edu/catalog/12589.html; accessed April 1, 2019.

52. Jed S. Rakoff, "Our Lying Eyes," *New York Review of Books*, April 18, 2019.

53. Oliver Wendell Holmes Jr., "The Path of the Law," *10 Harvard Law Review*, 1897, vol. 457, p. 459.

54. Ibid., p. 461, fn. 2.

55. Cass R. Sunstein and Adrian Vermeule, "The Very Structure of Modern Government Is Under Legal Assault," *Washington Post*, September 15, 2020.

56. Lon Fuller, *The Morality of the Law*, pp. 81 and 83, respectively.

57. As with all the cases we have examined, this is a real case. I was a consultant and so am intimately familiar with its details, but to ensure that no further harm comes to the physician, I will keep her name and the name of the university private.

58. Ann P. Hass, Philip L. Rodgers, and Jody L. Herman, "Suicide Attempts among Transgender and Gender Non-Conforming Adults," American Foundation for Suicide Prevention, the Williams Institute, January 2014; available online at https:// williamsinstitute.law.ucla.edu/wp-content/uploads/AFSP-Williams-Suicide-Report-Final.pdf; accessed May 8, 2019.

59. The quoted passages are from the Division's "Determination After Investigation," and to protect the physician, I am not providing either the state or the case number. I hesitate not to provide a complete citation and ask for the reader's trust, but hope that since the Division's determination only confirms what we know on other grounds, a complete citation is not considered absolutely essential.

60. Lon Fuller, "The Forms and Limits of Adjudication," *Harvard Law Review*, 1978, vol. 92, no. 2, p. 369.

61. I recall reading about this incident, but cannot now track down the reference. Undercutting the unwritten rules is, however, a common enough occurrence that we could supply any of a number of other examples—e.g., having someone from the back of a plane push to the front rather than wait for others to disembark.

62. "2 Texas high school football players who tackled ref suspended," CBS News, September 7, 2015; available online at https://www.cbsnews.com/news/2-texas-high-school-football-players-who-tackled-ref-suspended/; accessed March 17, 2019,

63. Adam Kilgore, "Baseball's Unwritten Rules May Be Softening, but They Haven't Gone Away," *Washington Post*, August 22, 2020.

64. Horowitz, "Walk Like a Fish."

65. I worked with Roger Boisjoly on a paper we jointly authored with two of my students, and this was said in response to questions the students had about why the engineers did not do anything about what they thought was a mistaken decision.

13 Professional Character

1. Hume, *Essays: Moral, Political, and Literary*, p. 198.

2. Lauren E. Oakes, *In Search of the Canary Tree* (New York: Basic Books, 2018), pp. 117–18.

3. Richard Posner, *How Judges Think* (Cambridge, MA: Harvard University Press, 2008).

4. Jerome Groopman, *How Doctors Think* (Boston: Houghton Mifflin, 2008).

5. Frederick Schauer, *Thinking Like a Lawyer: A New Introduction to Legal Reasoning* (Cambridge, MA: Harvard University Press, 2009).

6. Elizabeth A. Stephan, David R. Bowman, William J. Park, Benjamin L. Sill, and Matthew W. Ohland, *Thinking Like an Engineer: An Active Learning Approach*, 4th edition (New York: Pearson, 2017).

7. Randell Barlett, *Thinking like an Economist: A Guide to Rational Decision Making* (London: Teaching Company, 2010).

8. Nikki Mandell and Bobbie Malone, *Thinking Like a Historian: Rethinking History Instruction* (Madison: Wisconsin Historical Society, 2008).

9. ABET, Introduction, Definitions; available online at https://www.abet.org/accreditation/accreditation-criteria/criteria-for-accrediting-engineering-programs-2020-2021/; accessed January 23, 2021.

10. Theoretical Foundations for Decision Making in Engineer Design (Washington, DC: National Academies Press, 2001); available online at https://www.nap.edu/read/10566/chapter/3; accessed June 7, 2019.

11. Abraham Kaplan, *The Conduct of Inquiry: Methodology for Behavioral Science* (Scranton, PA: Chandler, 1964), p. 29.

12. Leo Benedictus, "The Movements That Betray Who We Are," BBC Future, September 13, 2020; available online at https://www.bbc.com/future/article/20200911-the-hidden-accents-that-betray-who-you-are; accessed September 14, 2020.

13. Woody Hockswender, "Fast-Track Tool: A Walk with Style," *New York Times*, February 1, 1989; available online at https://www.nytimes.com/1989/02/01/garden/fast-track-tool-a-walk-with-style.html?searchResultPosition=17; accessed May 2, 2019. See also Stuart Miller, "Teaching the Art of a Silent Walk," *New York Times*, January 5, 2003; available online at https://www.nytimes.com/2003/01/05/nyregion/teaching-the-art-of-a-silent-walk.html?searchResultPosition=4&login=email&auth=login-email; accessed May 2, 2019.

14. Kahneman, *Thinking, Fast and Slow*, p. 12.

15. Robison, *Ethics Within Engineering*, chapter 9.

16. Elizabeth DeBarto and Wade L. Robison, "Risk Management and Ethics in Capstone Design," American Society for Engineering Education, Salt Lake City, Utah, June 24–7, 2018.

17. Alfred Stock, "The Dangerousness of Mercury Vapor," Kaiser-Wilhelm-Institut fuer Chemie (Eingeg. February 9, 1926); available online at https://web.stanford.edu/~bcalhoun/AStock.htm; accessed April 30, 2019.

18. Robison, *Ethics Within Engineering*, p. 176.

19. Don E. Fehrenbacher, *The Dred Scott Case: Its Significance in American Law and Politics* (New York: Oxford University Press, 1978), pp. 322–414.

20. Ibid., pp. 330 and 323, respectively.

21. M'Culloch *v.* State of Maryland, 17 U.S. (4 Wheat.) 316 (1819), p. 410; available online at http://cdn.loc.gov/service/ll/usrep/usrep017/usrep017316/usrep017316.pdf; accessed May 5, 2019.

22. Fehrenbacher, *The Dred Scott Case*, p. 562.

23. Ibid., pp. 562–3.

24. Ibid., p. 567.

25. Ableman *v.* Booth, 62 U.S. 506 (1859); available online at https://www.law.cornell.edu/supremecourt/text/62/506; accessed July 28, 2019.

26. Prigg *v.* Pennsylvania, 41 U.S. 539 (1842); available online at https://supreme.justia.com/cases/federal/us/41/539/; accessed July 28, 2019.

27. My very different reading may be found in "Constitutional Argument and Contract Theory," in Praktische Vernunft und Theorien der Gerechtigkeit, Vol. II, special edition of *Archives for Philosophy of Law and Social Philosophy*, 1992, pp. 185–94 and "Hard Cases and Natural Law," in *Law, Justice and Culture*, ed. André Jean Arnaud and Peter Toller (Stuttgart: Franz Steiner Verlag, 1998), pp. 49–55.

28. Hearing of the National Commission on Forensic Science, 2017. The relevant part of the hearing is available online at https://www.youtube.com/watch?v=ScmJvmzDcG0, at 13:23; accessed May 5, 2019.

29. Rawls, *A Theory of Justice*, p. 85.

30. Leonard W. Levy, *Origins of the Fifth Amendment: The Right Against Self-incrimination* (Oxford: Oxford University Press, 1968), p. 6.

31. For an excellent discussion of some of the major ethical issues involved in prosecutorial discretion, see Bharara, *Doing Justice*, pp. 217–18.

32. "An Epidemic of Prosecutorial Misconduct," Center of Prosecutor Integrity, White Paper, December 2013; available online at http://www.prosecutorintegrity.org/wp-content/uploads/EpidemicofProsecutorMisconduct.pdf; accessed May 8, 2019.

33. Gilad Edelman, "Why Is It So Easy for Prosecutors to Strike Black Jurors?," *New Yorker*, June 5, 2015.

34. Miriam Aroni Krinsky, "We Are Prosecutors. We Will Use Our Discretion on New Antiabortion Laws," *Washington Post*, June 7, 2019.

35. Isaac Stanley-Becker, "'A Responsibility to Say No': Prosecutors Vow Not to Bring Charges Under Severe Abortion Laws," *Washington Post*, May 21, 2019.

36. Deanna Paul, "This 'Good Christian' Prosecutor Is Overlooking Domestic Violence Charges for Same-Sex Couples," *Washington Post*, June 5, 2019.

37. Kyle Swenson, "A School Bus Driver Raped a 14-Year-Old. He Won't Spend a Day in Prison," *Washington Post*, April 30, 2019.

38. Antonia Noori Farzan, "A Teen Girl Was Coerced into Sex and Held in a Dog Cage. Her Captor Will Serve No Prison Time," *Washington Post*, May 2, 2019.

39. Kristine Phillips, "A Jury Convicted a Doctor of Raping a Patient at a Hospital—and Sentenced Him to Probation," *Washington Post*, August 19, 2018.
40. Nick Martin, "Former Stanford Swimmer Gets Six Months in Jail for Sexual Assault of Unconscious Woman," *Washington Post*, June 3, 2016,
41. Hume, *Essays: Moral, Political, and Literary*, pp. 15–16.
42. Ibid., p. 24.
43. Fuller, "The Forms and Limits of Adjudication," pp. 376–7.
44. Kaplan, *The Conduct of Inquiry*, p. 28.
45. Abraham Kaplan, "The Age of the Symbol—A Philosophy of Library Education," *Library Quarterly* (October 1964), vol. 34, no. 4, p. 303.
46. Oxford Reference, online at https://www.oxfordreference.com/view/10.1093/acref/9780199829941.001.0001/acref-9780199829941-e-3614; accessed May 10, 2019.
47. Kaplan, *The Conduct of Inquiry*, p. 28.
48. Ludwig Wittgenstein, *Philosophical Investigations*, §129.

14 Social Responsibilities

1. Alexis de Tocqueville, *Democracy in America*. ed. J. P. Meyer and Max Lerner (New York: Harper & Row, 1966), pp. 38–9, 59.
2. Robison, *Decisions in Doubt*, chapter 2.
3. Adam Withnall, "'Rogue Doctor' Gives Hundreds of People HIV with Contaminated Needle," Independent, May 16, 2019; available online at https://www.independent.co.uk/news/world/asia/pakistan-hiv-aids-doctor-larkana-rato-dero-sindh-a8916591.html; accessed May 28, 2019.
4. "Launch Fails to Get NASA Satellite into Orbit," *Washington Post*, March 4, 2011.
5. "Aluminum Extrusion Manufacturer Agrees to Pay Over $46 Million for Defrauding Customers, Including the United States, in Connection with Test Result Falsification Scheme," Justice News, Office of Public Affairs, Department of Justice, April 23, 2019; available online at https://www.justice.gov/opa/pr/aluminum-extrusion-manufacturer-agrees-pay-over-46-million-defrauding-customers-including; accessed May 12, 2019.
6. Rachel Weiner, "NASA Subcontractor to Pay $46 Million Fine over Aluminum NASA Cited in Rocket Failures," *Washington Post*, April 23, 2019.
7. See e.g., Jack Nicas, Natalie Kitroeff, David Gelles, and James Glanz, "Boeing Built Deadly Assumptions Into 737 Max, Blind to a Late Design Change," *New York Times*, June 1, 2019.
8. See e.g., "The Hyatt Regency Walkway Collapse," American Society of Civil Engineers, January 1, 2007; available online at https://www.asce.org/question-of-ethics-articles/jan-2007/; accessed June 3, 2019.
9. Matthew L. Wald, "Faulty Design Led to Minnesota Bridge Collapse, Inquiry Finds," *New York Times*, January 15, 2008.
10. See e.g., Francisco Alvarado, Susan Svriuga, Falz Siddiqui, and Aaron C. Davis, "Death Toll Rises to Six after New Pedestrian Bridge Collapses Near Miami, Crushing Cars Underneath," *Washington Post*, March 16, 2018.
11. Sonja Drimmer and Casey Quinn, "The Apocalyptic Vision behind Mike Pence's Holocaust Comments," *Washington Post*, February 1, 2018.

12. Anton Trolanovski, "How the World's Shallowest Sea Became the Latest Flash Point between Russia and Ukraine," *Washington Post*, November 27, 2018.

13. Travis M. Andrews and Fred Barbash, "Long-Lost da Vinci Painting Fetches $450.3 Million, an Auction Record for Art," *Washington Post*, November 16, 2017.

14. Robison, *Decisions in Doubt*, pp. 111–12.

15. E.g., $Cl + O3 ------> ClO + O2$ and $ClO + O ------> Cl + O$, "Depletion of the Ozone Layer," Chemistry LubreTexts, May 10, 2019; avaialable online at https://chem.libretexts.org/Bookshelves/Physical_and_Theoretical_Chemistry_Textbook_Maps/Supplemental_Modules_(Physical_and_Theoretical_Chemistry)/Kinetics/Case_Studies%3A_Kinetics/Depletion_of_the_Ozone_Layer; accessed June 1, 2019.

16. I. Bernard Cohen, *The Birth of a New Physics, Revised and Updated* (New York: W. W. Norton, 1985), pp. 55–6 and 134–7, respectively.

17. Daniel E. Wueste, *Professional Ethics and Social Responsibility* (Lanham, MD: Rowman & Littlefield, 1994), p. 7.

18. Dana Farrington, "READ: Attorney General Barr's Letter on Mueller Report," NPR News , March 22, 2019; available online at https://www.npr.org/2019/03/22/706016316/read-attorney-general-barrs-letter-on-mueller-report; accessed May 30, 2019.

19. Statement by Former Federal Prosecutors, Medium, May 6, 2019; available online at https://medium.com/@dojalumni/statement-by-former-federal-prosecutors-8ab7691c2aa1; accessed May 29, 2019.

20. Ibid.

21. Protect Democracy; available online at https://twitter.com/protctdemocracy/status/1134089330576777216?s=12; accessed May 31, 2019.

22. "Full Transcript of Mueller's Statement on Russia Investigation," *New York Times*, May 29, 2019; available online at https://www.nytimes.com/2019/05/29/us/politics/mueller-transcript.html; accessed May 30, 2019.

23. Editorial Board, "Decoding Robert Mueller In short: No exoneration. (And please don't make me testify!)," *New York Times*, May 29, 2019.

24. Mueller Report, Vol. II, Section L.2.a., p. 157.

25. Mueller Report, Vol. II, p. 2.

26. Hartwick, "Towards an Ethics of Expertise," in Wueste, esp. pp. 84–9.

27. Wade Robison, "Global Warming and Decisions in Doubt," *Teaching Ethics*, Spring 2014, vol. 14, no. 2, pp. 35–52.

28. William J. Broad, "Taking Lessons from What Went Wrong," *New York Times*, July 19, 2010. See also Henry Petroski, *Success Through Failure*, reprint edition (Princeton: Princeton University Press, 2018).

15 Concluding Remarks

1. Bharara, *Doing Justice*, p. 6.

2. Ibid., p. 5.

3. Pritchard, "Cases for Teaching Engineering Ethics"; available online at http://www.onlineethics.org/Resources/csaindex.aspx.

Index